The American Dream

American Political Thought

Wilson Carey McWilliams and Lance Banning
Founding Editors

The American Dream
In History, Politics, and Fiction

Cal Jillson

University Press of Kansas

© 2016 by the University Press of Kansas

All rights reserved

Published by the University Press of Kansas (Lawrence, Kansas 66045), which was organized by the Kansas Board of Regents and is operated and funded by Emporia State University, Fort Hays State University, Kansas State University, Pittsburg State University, the University of Kansas, and Wichita State University

Library of Congress Cataloging-in-Publication Data

Names: Jillson, Calvin C., 1949– author.
Title: The American dream : in history, politics, and fiction / Calvin C. Jillson.
Description: Lawrence : University Press of Kansas, 2016. | Series: American political thought | Includes bibliographical references and index.
Identifiers: LCCN 2016026154
ISBN 9780700623099 (hardback)
ISBN 9780700623105 (paperback)
ISBN 9780700623112 (ebook)
Subjects: LCSH: American Dream. | American Dream in literature. | Social mobility—United States—History. | Social mobility in literature. | BISAC: HISTORY / United States / General. | LITERARY CRITICISM / American / General. | POLITICAL SCIENCE / Political Ideologies / Democracy.
Classification: LCC HN57 .J55 2016 | DDC 305.5/130973—dc23
LC record available at https://lccn.loc.gov/2016026154.

British Library Cataloguing-in-Publication Data is available.

Printed in the United States of America

10 9 8 7 6 5 4 3 2 1

The paper used in this publication is recycled and contains 30 percent postconsumer waste. It is acid free and meets the minimum requirements of the American National Standard for Permanence of Paper for Printed Library Materials Z39.48-1992.

TO MY PARENTS
It helped to see character modeled.

Contents

Preface

Our business is not to lay aside the dream, but to make it plausible. We have to aim at visions of the possible by subjecting fancy to criticism.
—Walter Lippmann, *Drift and Mastery*, 1914

"The American Dream" has long been one of the most evocative phrases in our national lexicon. Americans know instinctively what it means: a fair chance to succeed in open competition with others for the good things of life. The grand promise of the American Dream has always been that those willing to learn, work, save, persevere, and play by the rules will have a better chance to grow and prosper in America than anywhere else on earth. Still, as Walter Lippmann said more than a century ago (and as quoted in the epigraph to this preface), the dream needs regularly to be reexamined, criticized, and even challenged, to ensure that it still marks the way to a future that serves the real needs and interests of our nation and its people. *The American Dream: In History, Politics, and Fiction* brings two rich dialogues, one among the proponents of the dream and the other among its critics, into conversation.

Political leaders, and social and economic elites more generally, all and always praise the American Dream. Benjamin Franklin, Thomas Jefferson, Abraham Lincoln, Andrew Carnegie, Theodore Roosevelt, Franklin Delano Roosevelt, John F. Kennedy, Lyndon Johnson, Ronald Reagan, Barack Obama, and many others have lauded the singular promise of American life. Most Americans, both leaders and citizens, share the conviction that the American story has been remarkable, even exceptional: a bountiful continent settled over the course of a century and a half, winning freedom, and rising to economic primacy in its first independent century and to cultural and military dominance in its second. The American Dream, the right to rise unfettered, urged wave after wave of immigrants and each new generation of Americans to the effort, innovation, and entrepreneurship that cumulated over time to national wealth and power. Leaders know that citizens will applaud praise of the American Dream, so they regularly offer it in the hope of basking in that applause themselves.

Nonetheless, there has always been a Greek chorus[1] of skepticism toward, even outright rejection of, the American Dream. Our most prominent novelists—Nathaniel Hawthorne, Herman Melville, Mark Twain, Theodore Dreiser, Sinclair Lewis, William Faulkner, John Steinbeck, John Updike, Toni Morrison, and Philip Roth, among many others—have warned of the dangerous implausibility of the American Dream. The great characters of our national fiction, including Hester Prynne, Captain Ahab, Huckleberry Finn, George Babbitt, Bigger Thomas, Seymour "the Swede" Levov, and Miles Roby, remind us that victories and defeats, dreams and nightmares, all are common to the human experience. Politicians declare that America offers opportunity to all who will prepare well, work hard, save, and invest, but novelists warn, in Kurt Vonnegut's memorable phrase, that most people are "the listless playthings of enormous forces."[2]

Political leaders, especially in great national campaigns and while in office, make stirring speeches intended to pluck at our collective heartstrings. They recall our national triumphs, and they promise that America's best days lie ahead. They work to craft majority support by promising that they, through their policies and programs, will advance (if they are in office) or restore (if they are out of office) the American Dream. For example, Americans were stirred by Franklin Roosevelt's sixth Fireside Chat, delivered in the depths of the Great Depression, in which he promised that the nation under his New Deal program was moving "to greater security for the average man than he had ever known before in the history of America." We know why he said it, and we even believe his words had a settling effect on a frightened and doubtful public. But novels offer a different pattern of communication, not famous and powerful speakers addressing anonymous and passive listeners, but ordinary people conversing among themselves. Novels allow us to listen to people talking about their lives, opportunities, choices, limits, dashed hopes, and fears. Readers of John Steinbeck's *Grapes of Wrath*, with tears in their eyes, experienced the anguish of the Joad family as it slowly came apart under the pressure of the very depression that Roosevelt was struggling to combat. Understanding the American Dream requires listening both to Franklin Roosevelt and to John Steinbeck's remarkable Joad family.

This book weighs the assurances of our political, social, and economic elites against the warnings of our literary elite about the role and place, the benefits and the costs, of the American Dream. It presents the history of the American Dream as an ongoing debate between our political and literary traditions. I demonstrate that a distinctive ideal, "the American Dream," took shape very early in our national experience, defined the nation throughout its growth and development, but has always been challenged, even rejected, in our most celebrated literature.

Fiction holds up a mirror to the American Dream, and the images we see reflected there are often bruised, battered, and broken by forces broader, deeper, and more fundamental than most people can manage. Fiction reminds us that life has always been challenging, often harsh, and frequently overwhelming. Lawrence Buell, a professor of literature at Harvard and the author of *The Dream of the Great American Novel* (2014), described our most prominent fiction as "a custodian and carrier of the collective conscience and national self-criticism . . . disputing conventional valuations of success, satirizing the self-made man myth as chimerical or deformative, and casting themselves more as cautionary tales of failure or overreach than as tales of triumph."[3]

Readers might take just a moment to think about their own favorites among great American novels: how many, if any, featured heroes who rose from obscurity to prominence, from poverty to wealth, by dint of their own virtues well and steadily applied? For many, Horatio Alger Jr. and his stream of late nineteenth-century rags-to-riches novels will come to mind, and they have won a place in our national consciousness, but few read them today and no one considers them great American novels. Alger's books belong on a lower shelf with the self-help books of Norman Vincent Peale and Tony Robbins. Until recently, Harper Lee's *To Kill A Mockingbird* (1960) would have come to many minds, with the noble Atticus Finch standing for justice and the rule of law against a community opposed to either for blacks. But we now know that *Go Set a Watchman* (2015) was the book that Lee wrote and intended to write before being redirected by her agent toward the more positive and comfortable *Mockingbird*. In *Watchman* Atticus is a far less noble figure, defending not justice but community standards, the right of the majority culture to be tragically wrong until their own base instincts grudgingly evolved. Our great novels frequently challenge and seldom reinforce our national myths—that is their great value.

My intent in *The American Dream* has been to juxtapose the commitment of our comfortable classes to the American Dream with the cautionary lessons that our most prominent novelists teach about life among the vulnerable. Classic American novels, from Nathaniel Hawthorne's *Scarlet Letter* and Harriet Beecher Stowe's *Uncle Tom's Cabin* to Richard Russo's *Empire Falls* and Jonathan Franzen's *Freedom*, simply have not shown the American Dream, of preparation, hard work, and frugality leading to increasing security, as available throughout the society. Overwhelmingly, they have told not stories of smooth accomplishment by deserving protagonists, not even stories of challenges overcome, but mostly stories of challenges too great to surmount, challenges that grind down, cripple, and eventually crush. Most often, perhaps even always, the message has been that the American Dream was illusory, beyond reach, a nightmare.

Fiction has effectively challenged the broadest claims of the American Dream—that America offers the unfettered right to rise to all of its citizens willing to work and compete—but it has had little to put in its place. Fiction has reminded us that playing by society's rules is no guarantee of success, that life is hard and failure is common, but it has offered no alternative path to security and success. Azar Nafisi, author of *The Republic of Imagination* (2014), criticized politicians for praising American freedom as the right to compete for power and wealth. She argued that novelists better understood that "the freedom that so many fictional characters lay claim to is . . . a freedom to turn their back on society and what is expected of them and to forge their own lonely path."[4] Unfortunately, the idea that fictional characters like Hawkeye, Ahab, Huckleberry Finn, Elmer Gantry, or "Rabbit" Angstrom should be our models makes no more sense than that the robber barons of the late nineteenth century or the hedge-fund billionaires of the early twenty-first century should be our exemplars. The problem, obviously, is that the vast majority of Americans live their lives between the freedom of the open road and the freedom of the Madison Avenue penthouse. What the American Dream has to say to real Americans has always been and is still in dispute.

Though the American Dream so cherished by our political and economic elites encourages complaisance and the critique made in our best fiction offers few plausible alternatives, we are fortunate that modern social science is of more service. Social scientists see the American Dream as a structural, even foundational, element of our individual and social identity. Nonetheless, they worry that an ominous gap has opened between the promise of the American Dream and the reality of too many American lives. An avalanche of recent analysis showing increasing inequality and decreasing mobility demonstrates that many Americans, of all races, ethnicities, and genders, are simply not in the competition for America's top spots—or even for modest security and comfort. Political scientist Robert D. Putnam, author of *Our Kids: The American Dream in Crisis* (2015), and sociologist Mark Robert Rank and his colleagues, authors of *Chasing the American Dream* (2014), point to structural inequalities that increasingly perpetuate themselves. Both Putnam and Rank use data analysis and interviews to highlight the dramatic differences in opportunity available to today's privileged youth and to those who come from less privileged backgrounds. Rank quoted an interviewee named Chris, who said, "You know partly it's just history. . . . Opportunity leads to opportunity, and lack of opportunity leads to lack of opportunity. . . . People don't recognize how hard it is if you're born with . . . headwind, how hard it is to move up compared to someone who's got a tailwind just helping them along."[5] So we say again, as Lippmann said a century ago, "Our business is not to lay aside the dream, but to make it plausible." More pointedly, while we celebrate that the dream remains plausible for those fortunate enough to have "a tailwind just helping them along," national attention must turn to making the dream plausible for those who struggle against the headwinds of modern life.

The basic structure of *The American Dream* is broadly historical, describing both the evolution of the American Dream and the fictive challenges to it from first settlement to the early twenty-first century. Chapter 1 describes the American Creed and the American Dream and the shaping role that these seminal ideas and ideals have played in American history. Chapters 2 through 8 divide American history into familiar periods and trace both the evolving content of the American Dream and the classic challenges to it in our national fiction. In each chapter I ask how the American Dream was articulated, how it was voiced, and what promises it held out to the doers, the strivers, and the achievers of that era. In each chapter I also ask how fiction described the reality and plausibility of the American Dream. What forces did our greatest storytellers—Hawthorne and Melville; Stowe and Twain; Dreiser and Sinclair; Morrison, Updike, and Roth; Russo and Franzen—believe kept the dream beyond the reach of many, perhaps even most,

Americans? Those forces include human weakness and fallibility, but also what Ralph Waldo Emerson called "the lords of life"—the fury of nature; poverty and need; sex, gender, and race; religion and culture; violence and war—those natural and social forces against which individuals struggle and frequently fail.

Chapter 9 opens by asking how the American public feels about its dream today. Extensive polling over the last half century shows that majorities still cling to the idea of the dream, the idea that hard work is the best path to success and prosperity, but they also show that confidence has begun to erode, particularly among parents about the prospects of their children. We also ask how the average working- or middle-class citizen stands in regard to the American Dream today and more particularly how those formerly excluded, women and minorities, stand in regard to the dream. Every reader will be aware that concern is rife today that rising inequality and falling mobility threaten the dream for many. Some contend that opportunity is so constrained in modern America that the dream is slipping away for all but a privileged few.

American mythology, whether in the Declaration of Independence's stirring assertion that "all men are created equal" or in the American Dream's promise that "all" who work hard and play by the rules will have the chance to prosper, has always been couched in general, even universal, terms. Our politicians and social elites have always assured common citizens that the national promises are made to all. Perhaps the greatest service that our novelists have performed—from the beginning and to this day—has been to show us that it has never been so. Great themes, broad, deep, and continuous themes, in our literature highlight the narrow choices and bleak prospects facing the poor, minorities (especially blacks), and women. These Americans, two-thirds of our citizens, when they were considered citizens, often cried but rarely dreamed. The fact that they cry less today is progress, but there are miles left to go.

The health of the American Dream has always been defined by the interaction between individual preparation and effort and the structure of social and economic opportunity. Individuals must prepare themselves well and work hard when they get the opportunity, but only well-designed law and policy can ensure that social and economic opportunities are available for Americans to compete over. Government creates, maintains, and updates the legal and political structures that define opportunity and how it is pursued within American society. The triumph and the tragedy of American history has been that for nearly 400 years the nation's dream has drawn it forward to a fuller and fairer future than it has ever quite been able to realize. America has entered a new century, as it has entered other new centuries, challenged to make the dream real in every American life.

Acknowledgments

Many people, over many years, in ways large and small, have contributed to the evolution of this book. The matchmaker that brought me together with the idea for a book about the American Dream was Fred Woodward, then the director of the University Press of Kansas. In the fall of 1997, I told Fred that my next book would treat one of the key ideas of American life—liberty, equality, opportunity, responsibility, or some such—but that I had not settled on a topic. Fred said, How about the American Dream?, and we were off to the races. *Pursuing the American Dream* appeared in 2004, but the ensuing years proved difficult for the nation and its dream, and I revised my thinking. The University Press of Kansas, now in the capable persons of Director Chuck Myers and editor Larisa Martin, has continued to support my thinking and writing. The result, *The American Dream*, is a broader, and in some ways bleaker, reading of what the dream has meant and means in American life. To gauge that meaning, we must listen as closely to the doubters as we have always listened to the dreamers.

Many thoughtful people, led by my wife, Jane, have read drafts, listened to musings, and responded to queries along the way. I am grateful to all of them, especially Phil Abbott, Lawrence Buell, Joe Cooper, Cecil Eubanks, Ruth Grant, Ezra Greenspan, Jennifer Hochschild, Jim Hollifield, Mike Lienesch, Jeff Stonecash, Guillermo Velasco, and Steve Weisenburger, for helpful comments and astute guidance. As always, librarians, curators, and other angels of the world of letters deserve special praise. I am exceedingly grateful for the support of Southern Methodist University's Political Science Department, the John Tower Center for Political Studies, and the Southern Methodist University libraries.

As always, perfection eludes, and the faults that remain are mine.

1 | The Ambiguity of the Dream in American History

The new world . . . once pandered in whispers to the last and greatest of all human dreams; for a transitory enchanted moment man must have held his breath in the presence of this continent . . . face to face for the last time in history with something commensurate to his capacity for wonder.
—F. Scott Fitzgerald, *The Great Gatsby*

No phrase captures the distinctive character and promise of American life better than "the American Dream." As Bill Clinton said in his 1997 State of the Union address, "America is far more than a place. It is an idea." And as Barack Obama said in a 2007 campaign address entitled "The American Dream," "Americans share a faith in simple dreams . . . American dreams." Throughout our national history, and even earlier as we shall see, our leaders have lauded the broad promise of American life, what we have come to call "the American Dream," but dreams have to be embodied in the lives of real people before they have substance and weight. Our dilemma is that while our American hearts swell to the idea of the American Dream, we know it was denied to many Americans for most of the nation's history. So how are we to think about ourselves and our history: with undiluted pride, with deep shame and remorse, or with some complicated and evolving mix of pride, shame, and hope?

Fortunately, hope is justified, because a society born in hierarchy and exclusion has become dramatically more free and inclusive. As Barack Obama said in the heat of the 2008 presidential campaign when he was called upon to disclaim the incendiary racial comments of his pastor, the Reverend Jeremiah Wright, "America can change. That is the true genius of this nation. What we have already achieved gives us hope—the audacity of hope—for what we can and must achieve tomorrow."[1] That America has changed over the course of its history, all agree; but what were the forces of exclusion that historically barred some from full access to the American Dream, and what were the alternative forces of inclusion that promoted, sometimes haltingly and often only partially, equality and opportunity for the formerly excluded? And, because we know that the inclusion of some has been only partial, what remains to be done? To answer these questions we must first unpack two related ideas: the American Creed and the American Dream.

The American Creed

Louis Hartz, one of the leading American historians of the mid-twentieth century, described colonial America as a "fragment" society.[2] Hartz meant that the Englishmen and women who immigrated to America in the seventeenth century did not represent the full range of English, let alone European, political, social, and religious opinion. The fragment of English society that fled the tensions and conflicts of the Old World to seek a better life in the New World was composed mostly of middling men, small landowners, artisans, and tradesmen. In the political battles of the 1620s, these men placed their hopes with the reformers in Parliament and in the Church of England. When King Charles I and Archbishop William Laud began to resist reform with force in the 1630s, John Winthrop, John Cotton, and more than 20,000 of their followers removed to North America.

The liberal fragment of English thought that wave after wave of settlers carried to the New World drew heavily but selectively upon the Old World. First, the seventeenth-century Protestantism that the Puritans and Quakers shared, even when leavened by the Anglicans in Virginia, the Catholics in Maryland, and the thin smattering of Jews and others throughout, stressed covenanted communities, Christian millennialism, and a consuming sense of God's immediate presence in the world. Second, the early eighteenth-century focus on Enlightenment ideals highlighted the individualism latent in Protestantism while bringing increased attention to natural rights, popular sovereignty, and limited government. And finally, throughout the colonial period, most Americans maintained a deep reverence for English political and legal traditions. For example, the English common law tradition lay behind American reverence for such ideals as a government of laws, not men; law and order; and the rule of law.

Colonial Americans drew on this cultural and intellectual heritage to create communities that then developed and evolved in interaction with the continent itself. By the late eighteenth century, America's self-image, its political creed, was set. Thomas Jefferson, Benjamin Franklin, John Adams, and their revolutionary colleagues in the Congress of 1776 grounded the new nation's independence on the declaration "that all Men are created equal, that they are endowed by their Creator with certain unalienable Rights, that among these are Life, Liberty, and the Pursuit of Happiness." The luminous phrases of the Declaration of Independence put liberty, equality, and opportunity at the core of the American Creed. While Jefferson and the Founding generation knew that they were articulating an aspiration rather than a current truth, that aspiration has been resonant and powerful throughout U.S. history.

Nor is the importance of the Declaration to the American Creed simply American mythology. A long line of foreign observers have pointed to the Declaration as the wellspring of American values. The British sage G. K. Chesterton, in his 1922 classic *What I Saw in America*, declared, "America is the only nation in the world that is founded on a creed. That creed is set forth with . . . theological lucidity in the Declaration of Independence."[3] Another prominent foreign observer, the Swedish sociologist Gunnar Myrdal, writing during World War II, declared that the American Creed was grounded on "the essential dignity of the individual human being, of the fundamental equality of all men, and of certain inalienable rights to freedom, justice, and a fair opportunity."[4]

Moreover, contemporary analysts still point to the same familiar ideas and concepts as being fundamental to the American Creed. Samuel Huntington concluded his study of the American Creed by declaring that "the same core values appear in virtually all analyses: liberty, equality, individualism, democracy, and the rule of law under a constitution."[5] Seymour Martin Lipset concluded that "the American Creed can be described in five terms: liberty, egalitarianism, individualism, populism, and laissez-faire."[6] Both Huntington and Lipset highlighted liberty, equality, and individualism. These are the Jeffersonian core of the American Creed. Finally, Lipset's inclusion of laissez-faire (by which he means a dedication to capitalism, markets, and competition) and Huntington's of rule of law under a constitution draw attention to our base commitments to democracy, limited government, and free markets. Hence, a general description of the fundamental values of the

American Creed would include liberty, equality, individualism, populism, laissez-faire, and the rule of law under a constitution.

Yet even as we proudly describe the American Creed, we know that these ideals have never been fully embodied in our public life. Consider three of the authors and books referred to in the paragraphs immediately above. Myrdal's famous book *An American Dilemma: The Negro Problem and Modern Democracy* is a landmark study of the continuing presence of racism in a society that boasts of its commitment to liberty, equality, and opportunity. Huntington's study of the American Creed is entitled *American Politics: The Promise of Disharmony*, and Lipset's study is entitled *American Exceptionalism: A Double-Edged Sword*. All three titles exude ambivalence about the state of our national life. The source of this ambivalence is not hard to find. America has never fully lived up to its creed.

One of the most insightful analyses of the conflicting strains of thought and action in American life is Rogers M. Smith's *Civic Ideals* (1997). Smith described the American civic culture as made up of "multiple traditions," including the liberal individualist tradition that Hartz highlighted, the hierarchical tradition of civic republicanism that scholars identify with Bernard Bailyn and Gordon Wood, and an exclusivist (nativist, racist) tradition that he calls "ascriptive Americanism." In Smith's description of American history, the hierarchical influences of republicanism and the exclusivist strains of nativism and racism are woven throughout American culture, thought, and action, are always present, and often triumph.[7] Moreover, as we shall see immediately below, they explain why the American Dream was denied to many, including women, minorities, and poor white men, for much of American history.

The American Dream

At the dawning of the eighteenth century, decades before American independence, Virginia planter Robert Beverly (1673–1722), building on William Penn's description of America as "a good poor man's country," described America as "the best poor man's Country in the World." Benjamin Franklin made a similar point in assuring immigrants that though many arrive in America as poor "servants or Journeymen, . . . if they are sober, industrious, and frugal, they soon become Masters, establish themselves in Business, marry, raise families, and become respectable Citizens."[8] Penn, Beverly, and Franklin were at the head of a long line of commentators who have seen America as holding out a distinctive promise of opportunity to citizens and immigrants alike. Throughout the nineteenth century, Franklin was the most widely cited exemplar of opportunity and success in the society. One nineteenth-century orator lauded Franklin as "a man who rose from nothing, who owed nothing to parentage or patronage, who enjoyed no advantages of early education, which are not open,—a hundredfold open,—to yourselves, . . . but who lived to stand before Kings, and died to leave a name which the world will never forget."[9] By the end of the century, Emma Lazarus's famous lines "Give me your tired, your poor, your huddled masses yearning to breathe free. . . . Send these, the homeless, tempest-tost, to me" adorned the new Statue of Liberty. America's reputation for openness to the dreams and aspirations of common men made it the destination for many in Europe and, later, elsewhere.

While the idea of a distinctive American Dream has been central to our national history, the phrase itself did not come into common use until the twentieth century. Still, both J. Hector St. John de Crevecoeur, the author of *Letters from an American Farmer* (1782), and Henry Adams, the grandson and great-grandson of presidents, in his magisterial *History of the United States during the Administration of Thomas Jefferson* (1889), described the powerful American ethos of freedom and opportunity as a "dream."[10] The young Walter Lippmann used the phrase "the American dream" in *Drift and Mastery* (1914) to condemn the Jeffersonian localism of the nineteenth century and to call for a new "dream" worthy of the new century.[11] James Truslow Adams's classic *Epic of America* (2001) popularized "the *American dream*, that dream of a land in which life should be better and richer and fuller for every man, with opportunity for each according to his ability or achievement."[12] While the exact phrase "the American Dream" may have been popularized by Adams, the idea, the insight, and the feeling have been present from first settlement.

Moreover, contemporary analysts describe the American Dream in terms almost identical to those used by Franklin, Lazarus, and Adams. Harvard political scientist Jennifer Hochschild's prominent book *Facing Up to the American Dream* (1995) declared, "The American Dream . . . promises that everyone, regardless of ascription or background, may reasonably seek success through action and traits under their own control."[13] John Schwarz wrote that the promise of the American Dream is that "everyone who steadfastly practices certain practical virtues will find a place at the table. . . . These virtues—self-control, discipline, effort, perseverance, and responsibility—stand at the core of our . . . idea of good character. . . . The notion that people do have a capacity to control their own destinies is an enormously strong, almost insistent feature of our American culture."[14]

The American Dream is the promise that the country holds out to the rising generation and to immigrants that hard work and fair play will almost certainly lead to success. All who are willing to strive, to learn, to work hard, to save and invest will have every chance to succeed and to enjoy the fruits of their success in safety, security, and good order. Education (physical and intellectual skills), good character (honesty, cleanliness, sobriety, religiosity), hard work (frugality, saving, investing), and a little luck form a broad pathway to the American Dream. Some start life with more wealth, more prominence, and more influence, but the opportunity to rise in society is promised to everyone—and not just to rise but, if the breaks go right, to have a shot at the top. If Abraham Lincoln and Barack Obama could become president and if Andrew Carnegie and Bill Gates could become the richest men of their times, then others can reasonably seek to rise as well.

So that is the dream—a shimmering vision of a fruitful country open to all who come, learn, work, save, invest, and play by the rules. The reality, as we all know, has had darker dimensions. The continent's original inhabitants were slowly but inexorably dispossessed by a rising tide of alien settlement. Of the new arrivals, not all came in any meaningful sense: some were brought, held, and used. Others were barred. Only America's most fortunate sons and few if any of her daughters were allowed, at least initially, to compete for her accolades and prizes. What influences and forces limited the application of the dream to some Americans while barring others?

Patterns of Exclusion

The American Dream has always been more open to some than to others, more open to wealthy white men than to women or people of color. In fact, Howard University's Jane Flax argued that "the normative American citizen has always been a white man and, though others have won rights, he remains so."[15] Moreover, when immigrants, minorities, and women did achieve new rights, those rights usually amounted to the right to compete against well-entrenched white men in a matrix of established law and policy that they had developed to protect their current interests and future prospects. Hochschild reminded us that throughout American history, "the emotional potency of the American Dream has made the people who *were* able to identify with it the norm for everyone else. . . . Those who do not fit the model disappear from the collective self-portrait."[16]

Others might have a place in society, but it was a limited and subordinate place. Race, gender, wealth, ethnicity, and religion have all been used to exclude persons and groups from the community of American citizens.[17] The treatment of blacks has been the most glaring deviation from the American Creed. The Virginia House of Burgesses formalized chattel slavery in 1661, Maryland followed in 1663, and over the remainder of the century, the "peculiar institution" spread throughout the South. The Constitution recognized slavery, without ever mentioning the word, in its provisions on continued importation, representation, and taxation and in subsequent legal guarantees concerning the return of fugitive slaves. Even though the slave trade formally ended in 1808, slavery continued to expand right up to the outbreak of the Civil War. Moreover, throughout the nineteenth century, even after the end of slavery, most blacks continued to live in the agricultural South, and most were tied to the land almost as effectively by the sharecropping and crop-lien systems as they had been by slavery. Early in the twentieth century, the black social scientist and social activist W. E. B. Du Bois declared that the movement to erase the "color line" from American society would be the defining struggle of the new century. As America entered the final decade of the twentieth century, the legal scholar Derrick Bell declared, "Racism is permanent."[18]

Women's struggle for equality in America, while less overt and less obviously intense than the struggle of blacks, has in its own way been just as difficult. Women were held in subjection at least partially by religious and cultural assumptions in which they shared. The Christian teaching that wives were to love, honor, and obey their husbands was powerfully reinforced by the common law principle of "coverture." Coverture held that a woman was subsumed, or covered, by the legal personality of her father until marriage and of her husband after marriage. With limited exceptions prior to 1850, a woman's property went to her husband at marriage, as did any wages or income she might earn after marriage. She could not sue in court in her own name, serve on juries, vote, or otherwise assume a posture of equality in the public sphere. Divorce was rare, but when it did occur, property and children remained with the husband. Not until the middle of the twentieth century did growing movements for racial and gender equality gain traction in America.

Despite the presence of inequality and discrimination, the dream made America a magnet for immigrants. Throughout the colonial and early national periods, most Americans saw immigrants as important to settlement, defense, and economic development. But when too many immigrants arrived too quickly, concern grew that the fundamental nature of the country might be submerged in a sea of unacculturated newcomers. Major nativist reactions against immigrants erupted in the mid-1790s with Federalist concerns over Irish and French radicals and again when Irish Catholic immigration picked up substantially in the 1840s. An upsurge in immigration and a change in the sources of immigration heightened nativist concern between 1880 and 1920. About 25 million immigrants came to the United States, including 4 million Italians, mostly Catholic, and 4 million eastern European Jews, mostly from Russia, Germany, and the Austro-Hungarian Empire. These new immigrants aroused widespread suspicion, and a wave of discrimination ensued that lasted through World War II. Immigration remains a prominent national issue today.

Finally, the relationship between Native Americans and later settlers remains a deeply tragic story. From the first appearance of Europeans in the Americas at the end of the fifteenth century to the last Indian wars of the late nineteenth century, the population of Native American peoples declined, because of war and disease, from perhaps 10 million to a mere quarter of a million. From the earliest days, colonial and later state and federal government policy was to remove Native Americans from the advancing line of white settlement. By the closing decades of the nineteenth century, Native Americans had been subdued and restricted to reservations. Throughout the twentieth century, with brief interludes in the Franklin Roosevelt and Lyndon Johnson administrations, national policy was to wean Indians from federal protection and support and to immerse them in the mainstream society and economy. As the twenty-first century dawned, Indian reservations still existed, and despite the glitz of the occasional casino, they were among the bleakest and most impoverished places in America.

The Special Power of Fiction

Scholars and general readers know that blacks, women, immigrants, and others long had only limited access to the American Dream. But knowing and feeling this history are two different things. While any description of discrimination is sobering, one rarely feels a lump in the throat or a tear in the eye with social science and historical research. Not so with the two novels we turn to now: Harriet Beecher Stowe's *Uncle Tom's Cabin; or, Life among the Lowly* (1852) and Henry Adams's *Democracy: An American Novel* (1880). Fiction has an emotional depth and range that nonfiction simply cannot plumb.

Harriet Beecher Stowe (1811–1896) was the seventh of thirteen children borne by two wives to the prominent New England minister Lyman Beecher. Though Stowe had been a writer for two decades, passage of the Fugitive Slave Act of 1850 moved her to address slavery directly for the first time. She initially envisioned a modest project, "some sketches" of slavery as she had seen it during her travels in the upper South, but her deepening emotional involvement in the subject motivated a broader treatment. *Uncle Tom's Cabin* was serialized in the antislavery weekly the *National Era* from June 1851 to April 1852. The book appeared in March 1852. The serial was widely read, but the book was a phenomenon, selling 3,000 copies on the first day, 10,000 in the first two weeks, and more than 300,000 in the first year. *Uncle Tom's Cabin* was the second-best-selling book of the nineteenth century, after only the Bible, and the most impactful novel in American history.

Uncle Tom's Cabin reflected Stowe's intensely personal, deeply emotional, evangelical conviction that slavery was simply inhumane and had to be not just opposed but exposed. The novel's emotional power came from its unblinking focus on the absolute control that slave owners, even the best of them, like Arthur Shelby and Augustine St. Clair, let alone the worst of them, like the loathsome Simon Legree, had over their human property, selling husbands away from wives and children away from mothers. Deepening the northern white revulsion against slavery's destruction of families was the unremitting focus on the rampant intergenerational sexual violence of slavery. Several of the leading slave characters in the novel are described as being of mixed race: mulatto (half white/half black), quadroon (three-quarters white/one-quarter black), and octoroon (seven-eighths white/one-eighth black), with quadroons and octoroons regularly being described as white enough to pass. Critically, both northern and southern audiences knew quite well that a quadroon child meant two successive generations of white owners had raped their female slaves and an octoroon child meant that three successive generations had done so. Mixed-race slaves declared that sexual exploitation was pervasive in slavery.

There were many notable characters in *Uncle Tom's Cabin*, including Tom (the title character), Eva, Topsy, Cassy, and Simon Legree. But the novel began and ended with a slave family, George Harris, his wife Eliza, and their son Harry. Their travails showed the radical sense in which the American Dream and the pursuit of happiness remained their goals even as they were denied them in America. Eliza was the young, beautiful, quadroon or octoroon slave companion and servant of Emily Shelby, wife of Kentucky plantation owner Arthur Shelby. Mrs. Shelby acquired Eliza young, raised and educated her, and treated her well, allowing and respecting her marriage to George Harris, an intelligent and inventive mulatto slave from a neighboring plantation. George and Eliza were as happy as slaves could be, well treated, married, and the parents of a young son. This happy tableau was soon shattered by two undeflectable blows. George's owner hired him out to a bagging factory where he thrived and where his talents were appreciated. George's evident pride and pleasure in his accomplishments at the factory aggravated his owner, who, to teach him his proper place, took him out of the factory and put him to mindless manual labor. George's manly pride was hurt, and he declared to Eliza his plan to escape to Canada, saying in slavery, "What's the use of our trying to do anything, trying to know anything, trying to be anything? What's the use of living? I wish I was dead."[19] George declared that the American Dream's promise that those who learned well and worked hard would have a good chance to succeed simply did not apply to slaves. Eliza reminded George of his duties as a slave and a Christian, but soon Eliza's world was even more deeply shaken when she discovered that her seemingly good but indebted master had agreed to sell her young son Harry to a slave trader. Eliza took Harry and ran too.

One of the great scenes in American literature is Eliza's flight, Harry in her arms, from slave Kentucky across the Ohio River to the free state of Ohio. Pursued by slave catchers and their dogs, Eliza and Harry reached the river in winter. The river was jammed with floating ice, and no boat was available, so, dogs baying at her rear, Eliza swept up Harry and crossed the river on foot, leaping from ice floe to ice floe, until she collapsed on the Ohio shore. A Good Samaritan took Eliza and Harry to Old Cudjoe, the free black servant of a prominent local family, John and Mary Bird. Senator John Bird was an Ohio legislator who supported the Fugitive Slave Act as an unfortunate but necessary compromise in a nation divided by slavery. Bird explained to his skeptical wife that peace and order required that southern interests be respected. Mary, a good Christian woman, wife, and mother, was unwilling to believe that the Bible's injunction to help those in need could be overridden by man's compromising laws. As their desultory, fairly abstract, argument went on, Cudjoe beckoned Mrs. Bird to the kitchen, and Mary then called the senator. In the kitchen was "a young and slender woman, with garments torn and frozen, with one shoe gone, and the stocking torn away from the cut and bleeding foot."[20] Political abstractions evaporated in the moment, and within hours Cudjoe and the senator were spiriting Eliza and Harry away in the dead of night to a safe connection to the Underground Railroad and the route to Canada and freedom.

Before the conductors on the Underground Railroad could reunite George, Eliza, and Harry, George, literate and light-skinned enough to be staying at an inn posing as a businessman, encountered Mr. Wilson, his former boss at the factory. Wilson advised George to go back to his master and admonished him for breaking the law, saying, "Why, to see you, as it were, setting yourself in opposition to the laws of your country," to which George replied, "'*My* country,' . . . with a strong and bitter emphasis; 'what country have I.'" Later in the exchange, George was even more vehement, saying, "Sir, I haven't any country. . . . But I'm going to have one. I don't want anything of *your* country, except to be let alone, to go peaceably out of it; and when I get to Canada, where the laws will own me and protect me, *that* shall be my country, and its laws I will obey."[21] Once George, Eliza, and Harry were reunited, Eliza echoed George's rejection of America, saying, "O, Lord, have mercy! . . . let us get out of this country together, that is all we ask." When the slave catchers finally overtook them, George again declared that the country and its laws had no meaning for him: "We don't own your laws; we don't own your country; we stand here as free, under God's sky, as you are; and, by the great God that made us, we'll fight for our liberty till we die." Later, with Canada just a day away, freedom just a day away, George whispered to Eliza, "Oh, tell me! can this great mercy be for us? Will these years and years of misery come to an end?—shall we be free!"[22]

White Americans in the North were horrified by the intimations of pervasive sexual violence in slavery, but they were also troubled by the rejection of the nation and its laws by those who were denied its freedom. The novel closed with George, Eliza, and Harry having left Canada for Europe, where George was educated in France, looking forward to a life of accomplishment—but not in America. In a letter to a friend, George declared, "I may be excused for saying, I have no wish to pass for an American. . . . The desire and yearning of my soul is for an African *nationality*."[23] Stowe has been criticized for having George Harris and his family choose Africa over America, suggesting that she was unable to envision a biracial America.[24] On the other hand, Stowe made entirely believable George and Eliza's rejection of America as incapable of providing a home for black people, even accomplished black people such as they had become. Why would they not simply say Hell no to a country that refused to foster their dreams?

No one doubts that nineteenth-century American blacks, both before and after slavery, faced exceedingly narrow options. In fact, George and Eliza saw no path at all in America to fulfilling their dreams of peace, security, and respect. Similarly, nineteenth-century novels are full of stories about poor white girls, city girls like Stephen Crane's Maggie and small-town girls like Theodore Dreiser's Carrie, struggling against long odds merely to survive. But Madeleine Lee, Mrs. Lightfoot Lee, the central figure in Henry Adams's *Democracy: An American Novel* (1880), was distinctive. Young, beautiful, intelligent and well educated, wealthy and connected, Madeleine Lee emerged from the devastation of the death of her husband and son in search of meaning in her life. Surely society had ways to use her time and talents that would distract her from her loss and leave her accomplished and fulfilled—useful.

Henry Brooks Adams (1838–1918) was a leading figure in the Washington power circles of the second half of the nineteenth century. A scholar and author, a sometime Harvard professor of medieval history, he was deeply concerned about the rise of corporate power and political corruption in post–Civil War America in the period frequently referred to as the age of the robber barons. Adams's authorship of *Democracy*, with its slashing picture of political corruption in Washington, was not revealed during his lifetime, though guessing who might have written it was a Washington parlor game for decades.

Madeleine Lee was as personally, socially, and financially secure as a woman could be, but all was not well. After the death of her husband and son, she was bereft, without direction or purpose. She first sought refuge in the world of New York philanthropy. When this proved unful-filling, Madeleine moved with her younger sister, Sybil, to Washington, where she was well-known and well connected. Her cousin was married to a U.S. senator, and the Lee family ancestral home had been, before the war, just across the river. Madeleine's desire to be involved, to be useful, to make a contribution, was soon discovered to mask a deeper desire. "What she wished to see, she thought, was the clash of interests, the interests of . . . a whole continent, centering at Washington; . . . the tremendous forces of government, and the machinery of society, at work. What she wanted, was POWER."[25] But there were two problems. One was that while she flattered herself that she wished to do good, post–Civil War politics was rife with corruption. The other, just as challenging, was that she was a woman. How would a woman get power, and if she got it, what would she do with it, and what would it cost her to wield it?

As Madeleine moved in Washington society, she quickly came into contact with a Republican senator from Illinois, Silas P. Ratcliffe, "the Prairie Giant." The widowed Ratcliffe was a leading figure in the Senate and a leading candidate for the presidency. Ratcliffe, a master politician, sensed Madeleine's ambition and played on it. Ratcliffe flattered Madeleine that she could reach her goal through him, in partnership with him, as his wife. She had youth, beauty, status, and wealth; he had power. Ratcliffe took Madeleine to the mountaintop and offered her all that she saw below, saying, "You are kind, thoughtful, conscientious, high-minded, cultivated, fitted better than any woman I ever saw, for public duties. Your place is there. You belong among those who exercise an influence beyond their time. I only ask you to take the place that is yours."[26]

Madeleine was at sea, stranded between the emptiness of all the good things that she had—the money, home, furnishings, fine intelligent friends, and travel—and the power beyond her grasp. Adams wrote, "She had only asked whether any life was worth living for a woman who had neither husband nor children. Was the family all that life had to offer? could she find no interest outside the household? And so, led by this will-of-the-wisp, she had, with her eyes open, walked into the quagmire of politics."[27] Ratcliffe had, of course, beckoned her forward, but he had not been entirely dishonest. When Madeleine asked him about corruption in politics, he plausibly explained that "great results can only be accomplished by great parties," so sometimes power had to be secured through darker arts. "If virtue won't answer our purpose, we must use vice, or our opponents will put us out of office. . . . To act with entire honesty and self-respect, one should always live in a pure atmosphere, and the atmosphere of politics is impure."[28]

The Prairie Giant, the man of influence and power, had made his best case, Madeleine had nearly succumbed, but finally, with the help of Sybil and others, the scales fell from her eyes. Evidence was brought to hand that Ratcliffe had accepted a bribe, not to buttress his party against its enemies but to enrich himself. Madeleine was both relieved, as the fever for power had been broken, and devastated by the realization that there was no useful place for her in the world. "Life was emptier than ever now that this dream was over. Yet the worst was not in that disappointment, but in the . . . keen mortification of reflecting how easily she had been led by mere vanity into imagining that she could be of use in the world."[29] How could she—outside the roles of wife and mother—as a woman, be of real use?

Adams's words, put in Madeleine's mouth, are powerful indeed. What was the American Dream for nineteenth-century women? Was there a dream, outside marriage and family, for women rich or poor? Adams said not. Even a woman as prominent, wealthy, and secure as Madeleine Lee had no path of her own to walk in the world. Madeleine's disappointment was cushioned by her wealth; the money clearly had uses, but it just as clearly had limitations. *Democracy* concluded with Madeleine again plagued by ennui, saying, "Sybil, dearest, will you go abroad with me again? . . . I want to go to Egypt, . . . democracy has shaken my nerves to pieces."[30]

Processes Leading to Inclusion

Exclusion has been a persistent and destructive fact of American social life, but it has not been a permanent and unchanging fact. Over time, the right to dream the American Dream has been opened, at least formally, to new and increasingly diverse groups. Critically, the core ideas of the American Creed—liberty, equality, opportunity—were always available to be claimed by the excluded. Not every claim was honored or even acknowledged immediately; resistance was continuous and often tenacious, but the claimants had Jefferson's words and America's best sense of itself on their side.

Vernon Parrington, a prominent historian of the early twentieth century, explained the power of the American Creed as an inclusionary vehicle. He wrote, "The humanitarian idealism of the Declaration has always echoed as a battle cry in the hearts of those who dream of an America dedicated to democratic ends. It cannot be long ignored or repudiated, for . . . it is constantly breaking out in fresh revolt."[31] To the Declaration of Independence and the U.S. Constitution and Bill of Rights, later generations of Americans added the Gettysburg Address, the Pledge of Allegiance, and the "I Have a Dream" speech of Martin Luther King Jr. These sacred texts evoke the central tenets of the American Dream in each new generation. Poor white men, women, and minorities achieved rights incrementally and over time as they doggedly pressed for the right to share in the promise of the American Dream. Paul Berman makes the critically important point that all these movements were long-term "campaigns to lead one sector of society after another upward from the gloom of bottom-place standing in the social hierarchy into the glorious mediocrity of the American middle."[32]

The long and winding spiral staircase that leads to "the glorious mediocrity of the American middle" is well-worn because, as Pauline Maier has observed, "the ultimate authority of the Declaration," and of the American Creed and American Dream more generally, "rests, as it always has, . . . in the hearts and minds of the people, and its meaning changes as new groups and new causes claim its mantle, constantly, reopening the issue of what the nation's 'founding principles' demand."[33] But hearts and minds do not change mysteriously; there are no showers of moral clarity that leave them pure and new. Usually society must evolve and change in ways that draw old ideas, or at least their existing institutional embodiments, into question. Nobel Prize–winning economist Robert William Fogel has described this process, arguing, "There has been a recurring lag between the vast technological transformations and the human adjustments to these transformations. It is this lag that has provoked the crises that periodically usher in profound reconsiderations of ethical values, that produce new agendas for . . . social reform, and that give rise to political movements that champion the new agendas."[34] Socioeconomic change can so reconstitute society that its political structures no longer seem to promote the fundamental principles of equity and justice that Americans believe is their birthright.

Key dynamics creating change within American society have included democratization, westward expansion, the rise of markets, urbanization, industrialization, education, and the transition from physical to mental labor. These have steadily carried yesterday's others closer to the center of American life. Great differences in status, wealth, and opportunity still remain, and some of them are growing, but over time new groups of contestants entered the great game, learned its rules, and began to take home at least some of the prizes. The easy availability of land, the presence of a whole continent to conquer and tame, created a powerful and enduring sense that America was the land of opportunity. Hector St. John de Crevecoeur, Alexis de Tocqueville, Frederick Jackson Turner, and many others have been eloquent on these points.

How, then, has American society and the opportunities that it provided to citizens, whether the "normative" white male or those once marginalized and excluded, evolved and changed over four centuries? This book tells that story by looking closely at both the claims our politicians and their elite allies make for American exceptionalism and widespread opportunity and the doubts and reservations expressed by our greatest novelists and storytellers.

2 | The Promise and Peril of Life in the New World

We shall be as a city upon a hill. The eyes of all people are upon us. So that if we shall deal falsely with our God in this work . . . we shall be made a story and a by-word through the world . . . till we be consumed out of the good land whither we are going.
—John Winthrop, 1630

The American Dream includes images both of the nation within the world and of the individual within the nation. The vision of America's place in the world that still defines the American Dream has deep roots in John Winthrop's promise to the Puritan faithful that they would be as "a city upon a hill." Winthrop reminded his brethren that their reason for leaving England to settle in the howling wilderness that was then North America was to build a society that the world could emulate. Later generations of Americans have been just as certain that the world would do well to follow their example. Hence, presidents from Washington to Lincoln to Reagan to Obama and beyond have reminded Americans of their role in the world by employing the image of the United States as, in Ronald Reagan's often-used formulation, "a shining city on a hill."

Although we still hold John Winthrop's elevated view of America, we do not recognize his Americans. Winthrop's vision had little room for the individual and less for individualism, choice, and diversity. But to be fair, Winthrop led English Puritans, not Americans, and their dream was to construct a holy commonwealth, to raise up a New Israel within a New Eden on Massachusetts Bay. In this holy commonwealth, the saints, excluding others by force if necessary, would form covenanted communities to live in harmony with God and nature. John Winthrop and his fellows had a dream, but it was not yet an American dream, certainly not "the American Dream." Outside the vision of early New England held by the Puritan fathers stood not only those of other races and religions but also their own wives and daughters. Two prominent women of early

New England—one historical, Anne Hutchinson, and one fictional, Hester Prynne—highlight the constrained roles and narrow choices faced by their gender. Hester Prynne is the pivotal figure in Nathaniel Hawthorne's classic *The Scarlet Letter* (1850).

The image now central to the American Dream, the individual as an independent, hardworking entrepreneur, did not come to North America with the earliest settlers. Rather, it emerged over the course of the seventeenth century in an ongoing confrontation between the early moralist visions of leaders like Winthrop, John Cotton, and William Penn, and the fruitful and robust vastness of the continent itself. Over the course of the eighteenth century the American Dream assumed its familiar shape. In fact, one might almost say that it took a human form in the person of Benjamin Franklin (1706–1790). Franklin was the central figure of the American eighteenth century. He was a printer, an investor, a politician, a scientist, a diplomat, and a philanthropist.[1] Both as author and as exemplar, he consciously molded and shaped the broad outlines of the American Dream.

As population expanded and pushed back from the coast, and as civilization and its laws took hold, some of the earliest residents—including fiction's most famous woodsman, Natty Bumppo, or "Hawkeye"—decried and resisted the loss of freedom. Natty Bumppo became the classic model for the man alone, without family, community, or external constraint. As the English literary critic D. H. Lawrence wrote of Natty, "You have there the myth of . . . the integral soul. . . . A man who turns his back on white society. A man who keeps his moral integrity hard and intact. An isolate, almost selfless, stoic, enduring man . . . but who is pure white."[2] America's first great novelist, James Fenimore Cooper, followed Natty Bumppo from early manhood through old age in the five-volume Leatherstocking series. In this chapter, we consider the social and cultural presumptions on display in Cooper's most famous novel, *The Last of the Mohicans* (1826), and in *The Pathfinder* (1840) and *The Deerslayer* (1841).

European Dreams in the New World

The first settlers in North America came either to achieve quick wealth or to live in ways not permitted them at home. Those who came as adventurers in search of quick wealth were almost invariably disappointed.

But those who came as covenanted communities, sharing a vision of social and religious life, usually survived, then thrived, and ultimately laid the foundation upon which later generations built. These covenanted communities shared an understanding of God and his word that told them how society should be organized politically and economically to support true religion best.

Social conflicts in England and in Europe more generally pushed wave after wave of immigrants to American shores. Among those conflicts, none was more fundamental than the religious upheaval of the Protestant Reformation. Much of Europe was involved in intermittent religious warfare from the early sixteenth century through most of the seventeenth century. Reform currents in England were diverted when Henry VIII (reigned 1509–1547) rejected Catholicism without fully embracing Protestantism. Henry declared the Catholic Church in England to be independent of Rome, renamed it the Church of England, and declared himself to be the Defender of the Faith. Having established his royal control over the church, Henry saw little need to tinker with church vestments, liturgy, or doctrine.

Puritans were English Protestants who thought that the Church of England needed to be thoroughly reformed and purified. Low-church Anglicans (as members of the Church of England were called) agreed with the Puritans that the hierarchy and Latin liturgy of the Church of England should be reformed; high-church Anglicans cherished the traditional liturgy as a bulwark of social stability. Catholics awaited the return of the true faith. The seventeenth-century civil wars that wracked England pitted a rising Puritan middle class against the traditional Anglican elites and their Catholic allies. Once Charles I (reigned 1625–1649) suspended the Puritan-dominated Parliament in 1629 and instructed Archbishop William Laud to suppress Puritan dissenters within the Anglican Church, many despaired of political revolution and church reform in England. During the 1630s and '40s Puritan leaders organized an exodus of 21,000 faithful out of England to New England, where they vowed to build a "holy commonwealth" that could serve as an example and an encouragement until their coreligionists across Europe could transform and purify their own societies.

John Winthrop, the first governor of the Massachusetts Bay Colony, reminded his colleagues that they had bound themselves formally to God for performance of this critical task and that they would be judged on their faithfulness. "Thus stands the cause between God and us," Winthrop dramatically warned his Puritan brethren aboard the *Arabella*, "we are entered into a Covenant with him for this work. . . . If we shall neglect the . . . ends we have propounded, . . . the Lord will surely . . . be revenged of such a perjured people and make us know the price of the breach of such a Covenant."[3] Fortunately, what the covenant required of the faithful was quite clear. John Cotton, the Massachusetts Bay Colony's most prominent minister, explained that "the word, and scriptures of God do contain . . . not only of theology, but also of other sacred sciences, (as he calleth them) . . . which he maketh ethics, economics, politics, church-government, prophecy, academy . . . for the right ordering of a man's family, yea, of the commonwealth too, so far as both of them are subordinate to spiritual ends."[4]

Puritans believed that God ordered the world to its right end and that the role and place of every person was set by God from the beginning of time. Though humanity could know God's intention only vaguely, a person's every effort was to be expended in understanding it better. Each person could best serve God by hard work in the social and economic role to which he or she was called. The prominent social scientist Zachary Karabell wrote, "The idea was simple: if the Puritans worked on their own purification and sanctification, then God would grant them peace, security, and material bounty. . . . While the point of this life was to prepare for the next, material prosperity was seen as God's gift in return for fulfilling the covenant with Him."[5] Failure and poverty suggested the absence of God's favor, usually as a punishment for sloth and ignorance. Hence, Puritans valued hard work but not individualism. They worked to serve God, their communities, and their families, not, at least not overtly, to serve their own desires, needs, and interests.[6]

The Quaker settlements in Pennsylvania were just as God-centered as the earlier Puritan settlements in New England. The Quaker movement that arose in England in the middle of the seventeenth century was a utopian variant of the dominant Puritanism of the age. Quakers eschewed a formal ministry out of reverence for the inner light that illuminated the heart and soul of every man and woman. No church hierarchy, as in the Catholic tradition, or covenanted congregation, as in the Puritan tradition, could interpret the scriptures, ordain a liturgy, or intercede with God for the individual Christian. Yet since God was eternally one, the inner light kindled in each soul was expected to yield the same broad counsel to every Friend, as Quakers called the members of their community.

Like the Puritans, the Quakers who followed William Penn to Pennsylvania in the early 1680s believed that religion should give form and direction to politics and economics so that life in this world might be a well-marked path to salvation in the next. Quaker theology attended principally to the New Testament and within the New Testament to the Sermon on the Mount. The Sermon on the Mount presented to Quakers a mandatory ethic of peace, love, and charity. Following this ethic constituted walking with Christ and living in the inner light of the Holy Spirit. Frederick Tolles, the leading historian of colonial Pennsylvania, described a shared confidence between the Quaker and God: "If one kept one's inner eye single to the Lord and labored diligently in one's calling, one could expect that God would show His favor by adding His blessing in the form of material prosperity."[7] The religious fervor that Puritans and Quakers brought to work in the world produced security and even prosperity for most of them.

Massachusetts and Pennsylvania were settled by families and sometimes whole communities that shared religious goals and were willing to sacrifice greatly to achieve them. Puritans and Quakers dreamed of peaceful, prosperous communities in which they might tend their souls and walk humbly with their God. But England was home to other men as well, noble men, men who contested for the royal favor and sought to expand the monarch's and their own lands and riches. These men followed an ethic most baldly stated by the poet and essayist Ben Jonson (1573–1637): "Get place and wealth—if possible with grace. . . . If not, by any means get wealth and place." While Massachusetts and Pennsylvania warned such men away, Virginia offered them an open field upon which to pursue their dreams of wealth and glory.

Virginia was born in a rush of adventurers out to make a quick fortune by discovering gold or an easy passage to the Indies. Historian T. H. Breen wrote, "By all accounts, early Virginians were ambitious, self-confident men. . . . They were extraordinarily individualistic, fiercely competitive, and highly materialistic. . . . Establishing economic privatism as the colony's central value, the Virginia Company of London spawned an aberrant society, a sub-culture . . . based upon the expectation of almost unlimited personal gain." Even after the gold fever subsided and the search for commercially viable crops began, Virginians kept their individual interests in clear view. The discovery that tobacco grew well and enjoyed a steady demand in Europe set off an intense scramble for prime land along the Potomac, York, and James rivers.

Virginians wanted the freedom to contest for wealth and status and to enjoy what they won. Individualism, competition, and luck played distinctive roles in the Virginians' view of the world. "In public these men determined social standing not by a man's religiosity or philosophic knowledge but by his visible estate—his lands, slaves, buildings, even by the quality of his garments." While Puritans and Quakers fought hard to limit drinking, gambling, laxity, and public display, Virginia gentlemen reveled in them all. Hence, unlike the Puritans and Quakers, "seventeenth-century Virginians never succeeded in forming a coherent society. . . . Voluntaristic associations remained weak; education lagged, churches stagnated, and towns never developed."[8]

These descriptions in the modern historical literature of godly Puritans and Quakers and freebooting Virginians may seem unfair to the Virginians and their southern brothers; but the origins of these descriptions are old and illustrious. Alexis de Tocqueville's *Democracy in America* (1835) has long been judged the most incisive account of the early United States ever written. Tocqueville famously opened chapter 2, "Origin of the Anglo-Americans," with a description of the different and conflicting social origins and patterns of development of New England and the South. On Tocqueville's reading, New England was the positive model for future development, while the South was a deeply flawed alternative model that would have to be overcome, even in blood.

Recall the title of Tocqueville's book, *Democracy in America*, and then ponder his description of the motivation and character of those who settled New England:

> The settlers who established themselves on the shores of New England . . . presented the singular phenomenon of a society containing . . . neither rich nor poor. . . . The immigrants of New England brought with them the best elements of order and morality; they landed on the desert coast accompanied by their wives and children. But what especially distinguished them . . . was a purely intellectual craving . . . [for] the triumph of an idea. . . . Puritanism was not merely a religious doctrine, but corresponded in many points with the most absolute democratic and republican theories.

Now ponder Tocqueville's description of the motivation and character of those who settled Virginia and the South.

> The men sent to Virginia were seekers of gold, adventurers without resources and without character, whose turbulent and restless spirit endangered the

infant colony and rendered its progress uncertain. . . . No lofty views, no spiritual conception, presided over the foundation of these new settlements. The colony was scarcely established when slavery was introduced; this was the capital fact which was to exercise an immense influence on the character, the laws, and the whole future of the South.[9]

The covenanted communities of New England believed that social order required the support of institutions, law, and policy to survive and thrive in a dangerous world. Even before the Puritans stepped ashore at Massachusetts Bay, Governor Winthrop was careful to stress that the covenant they had entered into with God was to establish "a due form of Government both civil and ecclesiastical." The Puritan's "due form of Government" was to be a "holy Commonwealth," a true Bible polity, where piety lived under the protection of a strong and watchful secular authority. Winthrop reminded his fellow voyagers that the magistrates, called to their offices by God through the suffrage of the people, were responsible for maintaining the covenant and implementing the mandates that flowed from it. The people's responsibility, once they had chosen good men to be magistrates, was to honor and obey them. Winthrop explained that "when the people have chosen men to be their rulers, and to make their laws, and bound themselves by oath to submit thereto, . . . the people . . . are to be subject." Further, Winthrop contended, to resist or disobey laws "savors of resisting an ordinance of God."

The Puritans who founded Massachusetts thought that the Bible described the due form of church and state and traced out the separate but closely related and mutually supportive responsibilities of each. John Cotton explained that "God's institutions (such as the government of church and of commonwealth be) may be close and compact, and co-ordinate one to another, and yet not confounded."[10] The church held the keys to salvation and eternal life, but because God's kingdom was not of this world, church discipline extended only to expulsion. The state, on the other hand, could draw upon force, even deadly force, to maintain good order in the community. To the Puritan mind, it was not mixing church and state to recognize that one of the state's key responsibilities was to enforce the laws of God. As Perry Miller observed more than sixty years ago, "The unity of religion and politics was so axiomatic that very few men would even have grasped the idea that church and state could be distinct."[11]

The Quakers, like the Puritans, viewed government as hierarchical, general, and intrusive. William Penn reminded his fellow Quakers of the appropriate relationship between magistrates and subjects in the preface to his famous *Frame of Government of Pennsylvania* (1682). Penn wrote, "This the Apostle teaches . . . 'Let every soul be subject to the higher powers; for there is no power but of God. The powers that be are ordained of God: whosoever therefore resisteth the power, resisteth the ordinance of God.'" Proprietor Penn also agreed with Governor Winthrop and Reverend Cotton that the separate provinces of church and state were closely related and even intertwined. Again in the preface to the *Frame*, Penn wrote, "Government seems to me a part of religion itself, . . . sacred in its institution and end. For, if it does not directly remove the cause, it crushes the effects of evil, and is as such (though a lower, yet) an emanation of the same Divine Power, . . . the difference lying here, that the one is more free and mental, the other more corporal and compulsive in its operations."[12]

The Puritan and Quaker sense that government, working closely with the church, was an institution authorized by God to combat evil and do good in the world held weaker sway in Virginia. As Breen noted, the intensely competitive individualism that characterized Virginia society throughout the seventeenth century "poisoned political institutions. Few colonists seem to have believed that local rulers would on their own initiative work for the public good. Instead, they assumed that persons in authority used their offices for personal gain. . . . In fact, Virginia planters seem to have regarded government orders as a threat to their independence, almost as a personal affront."[13] As the British colonies in North America grew and prospered, both the tight communalism of Boston and Philadelphia and the unconstrained individualism of the Virginia tidewater would leave their marks, but each would be shaped and molded by new immigrants, future generations, and the call of the continent itself.

Anne Hutchinson, Hester Prynne, and *The Scarlet Letter*

Most of the early colonists brought from Europe the conviction that hierarchy was the best guarantee of social order. It seemed clear to them that nature and nature's God authorized exclusions and preferences based on religion, class, race, ethnicity, or gender. Hence, throughout the colonial period, American society was shot through with myriad forms of subordination and dependency that most of the population, even many of the excluded, thought natural.

Religion, law, and circumstance all made clear to women that they were subordinate to and dependent upon men—their fathers before marriage and husbands after. The theologian John Calvin (1509–1564), fountainhead of English Protestantism, said, "Let the woman be satisfied with her state of subjection, and not take it amiss that she is made inferior to the more distinguished sex." The great English Puritan poet John Milton (1608–1674), in his classic *Paradise Lost*, defined gender relations in the famous epigram "He for God only, she for God in him."[14] Not surprisingly, Cotton taught that God thought it "good for the Wife to acknowledge all power and authority to the Husband, and for the Husband to acknowledge honor to the Wife."[15] Most women, in deference to these and so many other authorities, gave the obedience expected and hoped that honor would be their reward.

A husband's honor might bring love and safety to a woman in her normal social roles, but what she was owed in her civil role was somewhat less. The English common law principle of coverture made daughters and wives the wards of their fathers and husbands. Married women, *femmes covertes*, were subsumed within the legal personality of their husband; they could not vote, represent themselves in court, claim property, sue for divorce, or claim children if their husband sued for divorce. Although unmarried adult women, *femmes soles*, did have an independent legal position in society, their economic circumstances were often dire indeed.[16]

Provisions of the *Massachusetts Body of Liberties*, adopted in 1641, reflected the role of women in colonial society. Adult men were free to buy and sell property, but "any Conveyance or Alienation of land or other estate what so ever, made by any woman that is married, any child under age, idiot or distracted person, shall be good if it is passed and ratified by the consent of a general Court." Men could buy and sell property as they saw fit; married women, children, and idiots needed the permission of the General Court. Nonetheless, other provisions allowed women to appeal to the General Court if their husbands did not provide for them in their wills or sought to administer "bodily correction or stripes" with unseemly enthusiasm.

Anne Hutchinson discovered what happened to women who defied male authority in the public sphere. She challenged the political and religious authorities of Massachusetts Bay Colony, charging that they valued a covenant of works over a covenant of pure grace. As her strong personality and natural charisma drew a following, the authorities responded with a withering attack designed to intimidate and silence her. When she was called before the General Count to hear the magistrate's admonitions, Winthrop called her a most "disorderly woman" and declared, "We do not mean to discourse with those of your sex." The Reverend Hugh Peter warned Hutchinson, "[You have] stepped out of your place, you have rather been a Husband than a Wife and a preacher than a Hearer; and a Magistrate than a Subject."[17] All of this, they were clear, was unbecoming to and unacceptable in a woman. When she persisted, she was exiled by the government in 1637 and excommunicated by the church the next year. Outside the protection of society, her husband dead, Anne and six of her children were massacred by Indians in 1643.

Like Anne Hutchinson, Hester Prynne, the tragic but noble heroine of Nathaniel Hawthorne's *Scarlet Letter*, was an independent-minded woman. She was born in England and was married young to an older wealthy scholar, with a deformity of the back, named Prynne. Hester was sent ahead to Boston with the understanding that Prynne would follow, but he never arrived and was assumed lost at sea. Alone, Hester fell in love with a young minister, a frail, sensitive, English-trained scholar named Arthur Dimmesdale. Hester was "of an impulsive and passionate nature" and Dimmesdale was decidedly not, but a single forest liaison left Hester pregnant.[18] As her pregnancy proceeded and she gave birth to a daughter, Pearl, she was subject to the full weight of community disapprobation and punishment. She was tried, jailed, sentenced to public humiliation on a scaffold on the town common, and required to wear a scarlet *A*, for "adultery," on her bosom for the rest of her life. Strangely, as Hester stood on the scaffold and surveyed those gathered to witness her ignominy, her eyes landed on a bedraggled figure on the fringe of the crowd. Her husband, Prynne, was not lost but rather had been a captive of the Indians for a year and was now ransomed. Prynne urged Hester to name her lover, and when she refused, he swore her not to divulge his identity either. Prynne, under the name Roger Chillingworth, remained in Boston to uncover Hester's lover. So began a tale of agency and freedom versus custom and law, in which Hester, like Anne Hutchinson and Madeleine Lee, found that there was no role for an independent woman, a free woman, to play in the world.

Nathaniel Hawthorne (1804–1864) was born into a Salem, Massachusetts, family with roots in the Puritan exodus to New England in the 1630s. The role of his great-grandfather, John Hathorne, in the infamous Salem witch trials of 1692–1693 spurred Hawthorne to add a *w* to the traditional spelling of the family name to separate himself from that dark history. Nathaniel Hawthorne read deeply in the early Puritan writings, including those of John Winthrop, John Cotton, and Cotton and Increase Mather, to map the currents and eddies of Puritan thought. Hawthorne focused not on the light cast by the city on a hill but on the narrow intolerance that was just as revelatory of the Puritan mind and soul. Hawthorne's Gothic romances, most famously *The Scarlet Letter* but also *The House of the Seven Gables* (1851), laid bare the impact of history, culture, and social mores on individual horizons, options, and choices. *The Scarlet Letter*, set in the new Puritan town of Boston in the 1640s, highlighted the power of social structures—authority, laws, norms—to crush those who challenged them. Although Hawthorne was at times ambivalent about the social claims of authority over individual freedom and choice, in the end he accepted the limits that communities placed on individuals because he mistrusted man's, and in this case, woman's, darker drives and motivations.[19]

Modern readers warm easily to Hester Prynne because she made her own choices, followed her own counsel and her own heart, and stood her ground against public condemnation. Hawthorne made Hester an attractive figure, but one who in the end paid a heavy price for her independence. Cast off by her community, alone and unmoored, Hester thought beyond community norms, but Dimmesdale could not follow her.[20] In isolation and despair, "the same dark question often arose into her mind, with reference to the whole race of womanhood. Was existence worth accepting, even to the happiest among them?" She answered no, not on current terms, and not on any terms likely to be forthcoming in the foreseeable future. A world comfortable for women would require that "the whole system of society . . . be torn down, and built up anew. Then, the very nature of the opposite sex, or its long hereditary habit, which has become like nature, . . . [would need] to be essentially modified." Even more important, "Woman cannot take advantage of these preliminary reforms, until she herself shall have undergone a still mightier change; in which, perhaps, the ethereal essence, wherein she has her truest life, will be found to have evaporated."[21] Whereas the Puritan fathers believed that liberty included obeying good laws, Hester Prynne dreamed of overthrowing the law, the magistrates, and the social order they served. But these were just fevered dreams; Pearl was real, and Dimmesdale, though weak, was real too. Perhaps she could still build a life around them.

Seven years after Pearl's birth, Hester contrived to meet Dimmesdale again in the woods. She surprised the minister beside a forest path as he returned to Boston from a nearby Indian village, told him who Chillingworth really was, and discussed with him how to escape the old man's wrath. Hester bent every effort to lift Dimmesdale up, share her energy with him, and show him the path to freedom, but he was dead weight. She asked, "'Doth the universe lie within the compass of yonder town ...? Whither leads yonder forest-track? Backward to the settlement thou sayest! Yes; but onward, too! ... deeper, into the wilderness.... There thou art free!' ... 'It cannot be!' answered the minister, listening as if he were called upon to realize a dream. 'I am powerless to go.'" Hester tried one more time, saying, "Leave this wreck and ruin here ...! Meddle no more with it! Begin all anew! Hath thou exhausted possibility in the failure of this one trial? Not so! The future is yet full of trial and success. There is happiness to be enjoyed! There is good to be done! ... Do any thing save lie down and die!"[22]

A plan to flee to Europe, weakly agreed to by Dimmesdale, was to be executed soon after he gave a long-scheduled and prominent Election Day sermon. Dimmesdale's sermon, delivered before the newly elected magistrates, fellow ministers, and the public, was an absolute triumph: "He stood, at this moment, on the very proudest eminence of superiority, to which the gifts of intellect, rich lore, prevailing eloquence, and a reputation of whitest sanctity, could exalt a clergyman in New England's earliest days." Spent by the effort of the sermon, before the assembled political and ministerial elite of the city, Dimmesdale chose his final course. "He turned towards the scaffold, and stretched forth his arms. 'Hester,' said he, 'come hither! Come my little Pearl! ... Come, Hester, come! Support me up yonder scaffold. ... Is not this better,' mumbled he, 'than what we dreamed of in the forest? ... ' 'I know not! I know not!' she hurriedly replied."[23] The minister confessed his own sin, greater than Hester's because unacknowledged for so long, and died. Rather than the individuality that Hester chose or the freedom that they had "dreamed of in the forest," Dimmesdale chose the tradition that he had violated, that had weighed him down, drained the life from him, and ultimately killed him, but in which he believed unreservedly.

Hester's husband, Prynne (known in Boston as Roger Chillingworth), Dimmesdale, and the Puritan tradition all believed that a wrong step, once taken, led to inevitable loss and destruction. Chillingworth warned Hester, "By thy first step awry, thou didst plant the germ of evil; but, since that moment, it has all been a dark necessity." Dimmesdale's last words, as he lay dying on the scaffold, were "I fear! I fear! It may be, that, when we forgot our God,—when we violated our reverence each for the other's soul,—it was thenceforth vain to hope that we could meet hereafter, in an everlasting and pure union."[24] Hester believed in decision, choice, and agency, even in second chances and a fresh start, but her time and place did not.

When Chillingworth died, less than a year after Dimmesdale, it was found that he had left a substantial inheritance of property in England and America to Pearl. Hester and Pearl left Boston for Europe, where Pearl grew to womanhood and married well, though the details were left obscure. With Pearl settled, Hester returned to America, in fact, to Boston and her old cottage at the boundary of the town, the woods, and the sea. She restored the scarlet *A* to her bosom and lived out a calm life at the margins of her society, rejected though acknowledged with something akin to awe by her fellow citizens. Through the years, Hester became a refuge and a resource to people who "besought her counsel, as one who had herself gone through a mighty trouble. Women, more especially,—in the continually recurring trials of wounded, wasted, wronged, misplaced, or erring and sinful passion, . . . came to Hester's cottage, demanding why they were so wretched, and what the remedy!"

Hester counseled with and advised her battered and broken sisters as best she could, but her own life and history spoke volumes about the limited choices available to them. But she also told them of her deep conviction, once almost rejected in favor of suicide, that "at some brighter period, when the world should have grown ripe for it, in Heaven's own time, a new truth would be revealed, in order to establish the whole relation between man and woman on a surer ground of mutual happiness. Earlier in life, Hester had vainly imagined that she herself might be the destined prophetess," but like Madeline Lee, she discovered that the role of independent woman simply did not exist in her time.[25] Great novelists, and Nathaniel Hawthorne surely was one, not only illuminate the time in which their novels are set but also smuggle into those times ideas that belong to the future. The future that Hester—or was it Hawthorne?—imagined for American women emerged slowly and still only partially.

The Slow Dawning of American Individualism

The promise that America held out to its early settlers was both singular and multidimensional. Its core was always the chance to live well. Its elements were always the chance to live rightly and to prosper. To live rightly, at least for seventeenth-century Englishmen, was almost always to live rightly in the eyes of a Protestant God by praising his name, expanding his kingdom, and praying for signs of his grace in one's life. To live well required good land and hard work. The earliest settlers believed that God had created a particularly rich and receptive land for them. At the height of the Great Migration of Puritans out of England, the poet Thomas Tillam saluted his new country: "Hayle holy-land, wherein our holy lord hath planted his most true and holy word. . . . Methinks I hear the Lamb of God thus speak. Come my dear little flock, who for my sake have left your Country, dearest friends, and goods, and hazarded your lives o'er the raging floods, possess this Country."[26] Tillam's poem was one of the first classic calls to Europe's oppressed to find peace and security in America.

The Puritan city on a hill was not a collection of isolated individuals; it was the Lord's "dear little flock," a community with interests and goals to foster and defend.[27] The Quakers, like the Puritans, assumed from the beginning that they would only realize their fondest dreams if they stuck together, advising, counseling, and correcting one another where necessary.[28] At least initially, the Puritan and Quaker visions of America had little to do with the individualism, freedom, and entrepreneurship that ultimately became so central to the American Dream.

Yet while Puritans and Quakers were keenly aware of the priority of their religious lives over their secular lives, many came in the hope of doing better in the world than was possible at home. Political and religious elites worked hard to maintain the primacy of religion, but common people could not help but see the continent stretching to the horizon. In 1685 the Pennsylvania immigrant Thomas Ellis wrote to George Fox, the leading Quaker in England, in the still quavering voice of the European peasant, uncertain of his right to reach out and partake of the bounty before him, saying, "I wish that those that have estates of their own and to leave fullness to their posterity, may not be offended at the Lord's opening a door of mercy to thousands in England . . . and other nations who had no estates either for themselves or children."[29] Many walked, hesitantly at first but then with an increasing sense of right, through the "door of mercy" that God had opened for the poor in America.

Material success eroded the social and religious expectations carried to America by the early settlers, especially the tight communalism of the Puritans and Quakers. Alan K. Simpson's memorable description of the ebbing of Puritan religious enthusiasm still resonates: "Everywhere the taut springs relax, the mass rebels, and compromises eat away at a distinction on which the whole system is based. The history of the New England Way is the history of a losing struggle to preserve the intensity of the experience of the saint and his authority over society."[30] The struggle was lost, somewhat incongruously, because, as Perry Miller explained, "pious industry wrecked the city on a hill. . . . The more everybody labored, the more society was transformed. The more diligently the people applied themselves, . . . the more they produced a decay of religion and a corruption of morals."[31]

Frederick Tolles told a very similar story about the Quakers. He asked, "What happened to a religious group . . . with a pronounced mystical and perfectionist outlook in the presence of material prosperity, social prestige, and political power?"[32] He answered that Quaker society gave way to a broadly entrepreneurial culture because "there was a conflict implicit in the Quaker ethic. . . . On the one hand, Friends were encouraged to be industrious in their callings by the promise that God would add his blessing in the form of prosperity; on the other hand, they were warned against allowing the fruits of their honest labors to accumulate lest they be tempted into luxury and pride."[33]

Before long, the social hierarchy that Puritans and Quakers thought necessary to assure order and stability was compromised because wealth often seemed to flow toward new men rather than toward the traditional elite. Each year new men arrived, others served out their indentures or took up their first small plots of land, and still others increased their holdings and began to rise in society. The Puritan and Quaker elites could not miss the success of ordinary men in wrestling the necessities and even the comforts of life from the wilderness. America offered special opportunity to the man who earned bread by the sweat of his brow.[34]

As the eighteenth century dawned, traditional leaders sought to defend the importance of religious life even as they acknowledged and made room for the secular concerns with equality and opportunity rising in society. *Advice of William Penn to His Children Relating to Their Civil and Religious Conduct* was the Quaker patriarch's justly famous injunction to his children to tend first the inner plantation of the heart and soul in the humble presumption that worldly security would follow. Penn's advice was contained in three letters. The first letter enjoined his children to a lifelong immersion in their faith. A grounding in faith and a focus on family and the Quaker meeting would keep one steady in the light of the Lord. The second letter was admonitory, dwelling mostly on what and whom to avoid in life (basically, the snares and distractions of the world). The third and most famous letter, written around 1699 but published posthumously in 1726, was organized in twelve numbered sections. Each presented, explained, and grounded in scripture a virtue that Penn admonished his children to attend to: "(1) Be humble. . . . (2) From humility springs meekness. . . . (3) Patience is an effect of a meek spirit and flows from it. . . . (4) Show mercy when ever it is in your power. . . . (5) Charity is a near neighbor to Mercy. . . . (6) Liberality or Bounty is a noble quality in man. . . . (7) Justice or Righteousness, is another attribute of God. . . . (8) Integrity is a great and commendable virtue. . . . (9) Gratitude or Thankfulness, is another virtue of great luster. . . . (10) Diligence is another virtue. . . . (11) Frugality is a virtue too. . . . (12) Temperance I must earnestly recommend to you."[35]

Good Quakers, like good Puritans, living humbly and working diligently in their callings, almost inevitably accumulated wealth. Penn described explicitly and in some detail the kinds of virtues he believed made for success in the world. In the third letter Penn praised diligence and frugality at length. "Diligence," he said, "is a discrete and understanding application of one's self to business; . . . it loses no time, it conquers difficulties, recovers disappointments, . . . it is the way to wealth. . . . Frugality is a virtue too, and not of little use in Life, the better way to be rich, for it has less toil and temptation, . . . for this way of getting is more in your own power, and less subject to hazard."[36] Working, saving, and investing led to prosperity and enhanced one's role in the community because thriving was taken to be a visible sign that one was living in the light of the Lord's grace.

The formidable Cotton Mather (1663–1728), son of Increase Mather and Maria Cotton, grandson of John Cotton, was the leading minister and intellectual of his New England generation. A social and religious conservative, he was also a scientific progressive, famously supporting inoculation against smallpox and other diseases when many still thought that was madness. Mather's *Bonifacius: An Essay . . . to Do Good* (1710) was addressed to men, especially prominent men, both as an injunction to good and an instruction in how to do good in one's soul, family, and community. Mather encouraged men to start each day with the question, "What *Good* may I do?" and to return to this question throughout the day. But Mather's was a world in which divine judgment was real and immediate, so men were expected to lean into their good works. He instructed his reader, "Suppose thy Last Hour come; . . . What wouldest thou wish to have done, more than thou hast already done, for thine own Soul, for thy Family, and for the People of God."[37]

Mather's *Essay . . . to Do Good* advised men on how to discipline and improve not just themselves but also their wives, children, servants, slaves, friends, neighbors, and broader community. He advised that men be gentle, if possible, but intrusive and insistent enough to have the desired effect. More positively, Mather reminded his readers that "what is done for *Schools*, and for *Colleges*, and for *Hospitals*, is done for the *General Good*."[38] Penn's injunction to inculcate personal virtues and Mather's to build public institutions to support and advance the public good became the core of Benjamin Franklin's personal and social ethics and actions.

No man more clearly embodied America rising than Benjamin Franklin. Franklin's life, as well as his ideas and writings, came to define the American Dream. Franklin was born in Boston on January 17, 1706, to Josiah and Abiah Franklin. Josiah's first wife Anne bore him seven children, and Abiah gave him ten more. Benjamin was the tenth son and third youngest of seventeen children. Josiah, a dyer by trade in England, became a soap and candle maker in Boston. Though he was a solid and respectable member of the community and of Boston's South Church, his work kept him too busy to participate actively in town affairs, and he was too poor to educate his children beyond the basics of reading, writing, and arithmetic.

Ben, initially seen by his father as a "tithe" to the church, being the tenth son, was enrolled in one year of grammar school at age eight. A precocious reader, he did well and was promoted midyear. However, when the grammar school proved too expensive, Ben was given one more year of common school, focusing on writing and arithmetic, before attention was turned to finding him a trade. His interest in reading and obvious disinterest in the candle shop led his father to apprentice him at the age of twelve to his older brother James, a printer. The print shop fed Ben's interest in reading, writing, editing, and persuasive argument. As he matured physically and intellectually, tensions arose between Ben and James, his brother, nine years his senior, and his master.

A few months after his seventeenth birthday, in one of the most richly symbolic events in American history, Benjamin Franklin fled the personal, political, and religious constraints of Puritan Boston for New York and then Philadelphia. Franklin left in a hurry, traveling light, with little money, but packed in his intellectual baggage were the lessons of Mather's *Bonifacius: An Essay . . . to Do Good.* In his own *Autobiography,* Franklin later reported that he read *An Essay . . . to Do Good* as an eleven-year-old, and Penn's letters to his children were published in Philadelphia just three years after Franklin arrived.[39] Both shaped him directly. As we shall see, Franklin adopted and practiced Penn's personal virtues and Mather's broad injunction to public service but rejected the hierarchical, elitist, and intrusive aspects of Mather's social ethic.[40]

One of the key lessons taught in Franklin's *Autobiography* was the value of education. Franklin explained that he worked hard to perfect a limited formal education. For example, as soon as he reached Philadelphia in 1723 and settled into a printer's job, he organized a club "among the young people of the town, that were lovers of reading." When somewhat better established, Franklin gathered his most "ingenious acquaintances into a club of mutual improvement, which we called the JUNTO; The rules . . . required that every member . . . once in three months produce and read an essay of his own writing, on any subject he pleased. Our debates were . . . conducted in the sincere spirit of inquiry after truth."[41] Franklin saw writing, like carpentry, as a skill that one had to practice to improve.

Franklin worked just as hard on his personal habits and character as on his intellectual skills. Franklin's remarkable dedication to self-improvement was reflected in a *"plan . . .* for regulating my future conduct in life" that he devised at eighteen and pursued the rest of his life. Franklin developed what today we would call a day planner, in which each day was divided into about eight hours of work, three of reading and study, and an evening dedicated to thought, preparation, conversation, and diversion. Like Mather, Franklin advised that each day begin with the question, "What good shall I do this day?" and end with the question, "What good have I done to-day?"[42]

More famously, Franklin concluded that though scholars and sages seemed to define the virtues differently, a review of their work suggested that thirteen virtues were most important. These virtues, reflecting lists by Mather, Penn, and many others, were temperance, silence, order, resolution, frugality, industry, sincerity, justice, moderation, cleanliness, tranquility, chastity, and humility. Franklin planned to make these virtues, as much as possible, a permanent and habitual part of his character and conduct. First, Franklin tried for a full week to do nothing that was intemperate. Then, while trying to remain temperate, he moved on to "silence" and tried to speak only "what may benefit others or yourself; avoid trifling conversation." Then, trying to hold to temperance and silence, he dedicated a week to "order" and so on through all thirteen virtues before beginning the cycle again.[43] Even though Franklin had something of a sense of humor about all of this, he believed that there was an "art of virtue" that one had to study and practice just like any other art or skill.

Franklin cast his program for self-improvement into a social philosophy and elaborated it for public edification in "The Way to Wealth" (1758).[44] Franklin chose his title from *Advice of William Penn to His Children,* wherein the Quaker patriarch advised his children that diligence and frugality point "the way to wealth." In Franklin's clever hands, "The Way to Wealth" became a long parable featuring a character called Father Abraham. Father Abraham was a wise old man who came upon a group of his fellow citizens complaining about the difficulty of their lives. The old man reminded his listeners that the road to success was well marked and that "God helps them that help themselves." How men could help themselves rise in the world was the focus of "The Way to Wealth."

The value and importance of education, preparation, hard work, frugality, and perseverance were central to the teaching that Franklin communicated through Father Abraham and through many editions of his famous *Poor Richard's Almanac.* In general, Franklin advised, "Early to Bed, early to rise, makes a Man healthy, wealthy, and wise." Concerning preparation, he advised, "He that hath a Trade hath an Estate," and "Keep thy Shop, and thy shop will keep thee." Concerning hard work, he enjoined, "Industry need not wish," and "Sloth makes all Things difficult; but industry all easy." Frugality was crucial to Franklin's counsel. He said, "Beware of little Expenses; a small Leak will sink a great Ship," and "If you would be wealthy, think of Saving as well as Getting." And in regard to perseverance, Franklin reminded his readers that "Little Strokes fell great Oaks," and "Diligence is the Mother of Good luck."

Franklin concluded his parable, most of which was unremittingly practical, with an injunction that is oftentimes overlooked but that was central to his vision of social responsibility. After all the advice about hard work, frugality, and perseverance as the keys to getting on in the world, Franklin advised men not to "depend too much upon your own Industry, and Frugality, and Prudence, though excellent Things, for they all be blasted without the Blessing of Heaven . . . and be not uncharitable to those that at present seem to want it, but comfort and help them." Franklin's own life was evidence of how seriously he took the counsel to serve God by serving one's fellow men.

Following Mather's injunction, Franklin became the moving force behind a remarkable number of public projects in Philadelphia. He initiated a fire company, a hospital, a philosophical society, and what would become the University of Pennsylvania. He gained international fame as the inventor of the Franklin stove, refusing a patent that was offered, and of the lightning rod to draw lightning away from homes and other buildings. Franklin focused on civic activities and practical workaday inventions because he believed that "human felicity is produced not so much by great pieces of good fortune that seldom happen, as by little advantages that occur every day."[45] Franklin taught personal virtues, but men were to use them in the service of the community.

Franklin's specifically religious views highlight the difference between the Puritan and Quaker foundings and the more secular concerns of the eighteenth century. In his eminently practical way, Franklin undertook to distill the fundamental tenets of every major religion while avoiding particular doctrinal points to which some might object. Franklin concluded that six tenets might form the religious core of an "Art of Virtue":

> That there is one God, who made all things.
> That He governs the world by His providence.
> That He ought to be worshipped by adoration, prayer, and thanksgiving.
> But that the most acceptable service of God is doing good to man.
> That the soul is immortal.
> And that God will certainly reward virtue and punish vice, either here or hereafter.[46]

Benjamin Franklin taught that self-control and self-improvement led to sufficiency, security, and respect. Franklin and his surrogate voices, Poor Richard and Father Abraham, recommended and even celebrated a characteristically bourgeois set of virtues that were both practical and democratic. Anyone could adopt them, practice them, benefit by them, and improve his or her lot in life. And many did. Poor Richard and Father Abraham, taken up in McGuffey's Readers, were taught and recited as the nation's common wisdom throughout the nineteenth and into the twentieth centuries. They were and are the moral core of the American Dream: education, work, thrift, dedication, and a dash of good fortune will put an honest man in a position to thrive and prosper.

The Decline of Hierarchy and the Democratization of Opportunity

The twin pillars of English hierarchy, the monarchy and the Anglican Church, were shaken but not topped in the 1680s. New England's stubborn support for Parliament in its struggle with the king was rewarded when the English civil wars culminated in the fall of Stuart absolutism and the rise of parliamentary supremacy. They thrilled to John Locke's *Two Treatises of Government* (1689), which found the natural and secular origins of government in the consent of free men. Arguments for equality, individual rights, and popular sovereignty were in the air, and Americans breathed them in and felt empowered and energized by them.

Freemen debated important issues and learned that difference, even conflict, need not threaten the peace and good order of a community. Men began to think about the origins, purposes, and conduct of government in new ways. Three changes were most profound. First, the origins of government came to be seen as secular and rational rather than religious. Second, the purposes of government came to be seen as peace and order, as the protection of life, liberty, and property, rather than as an all-encompassing effort to re-create Eden. And third, with the origins and purposes of government lowered and limited, public officials came to be seen as accountable to the people rather than to God.

Religion remained powerful in the eighteenth century, but the covenanted community that the Puritans had so cherished gave way to a more individualistic focus when a major evangelical revival inundated the English-speaking world in the late 1730s and the 1740s. In America, Jonathan Edwards, the leading New England minister of the mid-eighteenth century, blurred the distinction between saints and sinners by declaring that though salvation was by the grace of God alone, it could occur in an instant in anyone of any age. It was never too late. A bad beginning did not preclude a glorious end for anyone whose heart had truly changed. The so-called New Light message of the First

Great Awakening was a rousing, often boisterous, emotional appeal that promised a spiritual rebirth to all who would accept Jesus as their Savior. Religious conviction became more a matter for the individual heart, and the public sphere became the forum for addressing social and political issues.

Increasingly, men began to see how liberty could still mean abiding by law, especially while the scope of government was closely defined and clearly limited. Law-abidingness within the legitimate scope of government, leaving judgment and discretion to guide where law did not determine, left new room for opportunity, competition, and choice. In 1764 James Otis explained, "The *end* of government being the *good* of mankind, points out its great duties. It is above all things to provide for the security, the quiet, and happy enjoyment of life, liberty, and property."[47] Here was a vision of secular life in which a distinctively American Dream might arise and thrive. Before long, it did.

Moreover, during the eighteenth century, the frontier line pushed back from the coast, and the western counties of Massachusetts, New York, Pennsylvania, and Virginia filled. The westering spirit that Frederick Jackson Turner and so many others credit with nurturing the love of liberty, individualism, and opportunity in America became more insistent. Land of one's own, to support one's family and pass on to one's children, was the proximate goal of most free immigrants. As James Truslow Adams wrote, "It was this 'land in the woods' as a possibility for almost every inhabitant of America that was to prove one of the most powerful of the forces which worked toward a democracy of feeling and outlook, toward the shaping of our American dream."[48] Opportunity also beckoned in America's cities and towns. Rapid economic and demographic growth transformed the colonies from the fairly static, inward-looking, traditional village cultures of the seventeenth century to the more dynamic, expansive, and entrepreneurial cultures evident on the eve of the Revolution.

In a secularized version of Winthrop's "city on a hill," Jonathan Mayhew captured this confident sense of America's future when, in 1759, he predicted "mighty cities rising on every hill and by the side of every commodious port . . . happy fields and villages . . . through a vastly extended territory."[49] As the revolution approached, nearly two-thirds of white men worked on land that they owned or were buying, and their families, at least the most fortunate of them, enjoyed increasing economic security and comfort. Although hierarchy had eased for white men, and although their wives and children enjoyed some of the resultant benefits, hierarchies of class, race, and gender remained strong. Moreover, as the settlement line pushed steadily westward, the region's first settlers, the explorers, hunters, and trappers of the virgin forests, decried intrusions on their freedom and set their steps toward new frontiers.

Woodsmen, Women, and Race in the Leatherstocking Tales

The first great American novelist was James Fenimore Cooper (1789–1851). Cooper was born in Burlington, New Jersey, but was taken by his parents, William and Elizabeth Cooper, at the age of one to central New York State. William Cooper founded the frontier village of Cooperstown and became wealthy in land speculation and development. At twenty, James Fenimore Cooper married Susan Augusta DeLancey of the very prominent New York DeLancey family. Cooper inherited wealth at his father's death in 1813, and the success of his earliest novels, *Precaution* (1820) and *The Spy* (1821), allowed him to move to New York City and pursue writing full-time.

James Fenimore Cooper wrote more than thirty novels, but his fame rests on the five-volume Leatherstocking series and its hero Natty Bumppo, also called Hawkeye, Pathfinder, Deerslayer, and similar sobriquets. Here we focus on three of the Leatherstocking Tales, especially *The Last of the Mohicans,* the most famous, as well as *The Pathfinder* and *The Deerslayer.* All three focus on the majestic beauty and the ever-present dangers of the untamed forests of upstate New York in the middle of the eighteenth century and on the cultural presumptions of Cooper and his literary creations. A social and political conservative by upbringing and marriage, Cooper was eager to reinforce his era's assumptions about race, class, and gender.[50]

The Last of the Mohicans depicted Natty Bumppo (also known as Hawkeye) and his good Indian companions Chingachgook and Chingachgook's son Uncas battling hostile Indians as they escorted two young women, Alice and Cora Munro, and Alice's intended, Major Duncan Heyward, to their father, Colonel Munro, in command at Fort William Henry. Hawkeye was the archetypal "man alone," admirable in many ways, the consummate scout, woodsman, and Indian fighter. Hawkeye was unwaveringly honest, forthright, and dependable. When he said he would do something, such as bring the daughters through the forest to the fort, only death could stop him. On the other hand, Natty Bumppo was narrow, limited, and partial in any broad or humane view. He was also defiantly illiterate throughout his life. In *Mohicans* he ended a discussion in which an itinerant minister had cited "holy books" as the source of his views on predestination by responding, "Book! . . . do you take me for a whimpering boy . . . ? Book! What have such as I, who am a warrior of the wilderness . . . to do with books?" In *Deerslayer* he expressed some ambivalence about being unable to read or write but concluded, "I'm a hunter—and . . . no missionary; and, therefore, books and papers are of no account with such as I."[51]

Beneath the surface of these forest adventure tales are remarkable discussions of human nature, culture, race, class, and gender. These discussions jump out at the modern reader but would have seemed obvious descriptions of social norms, expectations, and roles in the period between the novel's setting in the mid-eighteenth century and their publication in second quarter of the nineteenth century. Cooper's view of human nature, which he put into the mouths of white and red characters alike in *Mohicans*, was that though God gave all men a broad but thin human nature capable of humane instincts, a thick overlay of racial culture defined and shaped most behavior. An early exchange between Heyward, Alice, and Cora made this point. Alice was so impressed by the proud, almost regal, bearing of their Indian guides, especially Uncas, that she expressed confidence in their character and fidelity. Heyward tempered her confidence, saying, "But let us not practise a deception upon ourselves, by expecting any other exhibition of what we esteem virtue than according to the fashion of a savage. As bright examples of great qualities are but too uncommon among Christians, so are they singular and solitary with the Indians; though, for the honor of our common nature, neither are incapable of producing them." Especially in warfare, white and Indian culture defined different behavior as virtuous. Hawkeye said in regard to Uncas's taking an enemy scalp, "'Twould have been a cruel and an unhuman act for a whiteskin; but 'tis the gift and natur' of an Indian." Elsewhere, when Hawkeye had the renegade Magua in his power and was urged to kill him immediately, he declined, saying, "The gifts of my color forbid it."[52]

A long and explicit discussion of race occurred between Hawkeye and Henry "Hurry Harry" March in *The Deerslayer*. Harry March expressed the widely shared view of the day, saying, "This is what I call reason. Here's three colours on 'arth,—white, black, and red. White is the highest colour, and therefore the best man; black comes next, and is put to live in the neighbourhood of the white man, as tolerable, and fit to be made use of; and red comes last, which shows that those that made 'em never expected an Indian to be accounted as more than half-human." Hawkeye, Deerslayer in this tale, patiently responded, "God made all three alike, Hurry." Hurry sputtered, "Alike! Do you call a nigger like a white man, or me like an Indian?" Later in the same conversation, Deerslayer again said, "[I] look upon the red man to be quite as human as we are ourselves, Hurry," to which Hurry responded, "That's downright missionary. . . . Now, skin makes the man. This is reason; else how are people to judge each other."[53]

While Deerslayer did not share Harry March's particular brand of racism, he was deeply and proudly racist in his own way. First-time readers of *The Last of the Mohicans* often puzzle over Hawkeye's frequent reference to being "a man without a cross." Slowly it becomes clear to most that he was not referring to religion or to irreligion but to his pure white blood to explain who he was and how he must act. Listen to Hawkeye: "I am genuine white"; "I, who am a white man without a cross . . . "; "As for me, who am of the whole blood of the whites . . . "; "though I am a man who has the full blood of the whites . . . "; "there is no cross in my veins"; "descent from men who knew no cross of blood." Finally, in *Deerslayer*, Hawkeye says, "White I was born, and white I will die; clinging to colour to the last."[54]

The discussion of virtue and race in *The Last of the Mohicans* is particularly poignant in regard to the sisters Alice and Cora Munro. Both are described as cultured, pampered, and beautiful young women. The initial descriptions are telling: Alice, the younger sister, had a "dazzling complexion, fair golden hair, and bright blue eyes." Alice was developed as Cooper's classic female character, open, expectant, even entitled, but in continuous need of care, protection, and saving. Cora, on the other hand, was described as a darker beauty: "The tresses of this lady were shining and black, like the plumage of the raven. . . . And yet there was neither coarseness nor want of shadowing in a countenance that was exquisitely regular and dignified, and surpassingly beautiful."[55] Alice was soft and dependent; Cora was fearless and resolute. When danger threatened, Alice cowered and collapsed; Cora comforted her sister and aided in addressing the danger.

Alice, Heyward's intended from the beginning of the story, was the less interesting and less developed of the sisters. As the story proceeded, it was "the dark-eyed Cora" to whom both the valiant Uncas and the renegade Magua were drawn. As Magua and his warriors were about to capture Heyward and the sisters, conversation turned to consequences. When Cora observed, "The worst to us can be but death," Duncan warned ominously, "There are evils worse than death." Once the capture was effected and they were in Magua's hands, he offered to allow "the light eyes" to return to her father if the "dark-haired woman" would stay with him as a wife. Cora put aside the proposal, asking what pleasure he could take in a wife that did not love him. Magua's answer came in a cold, wordless, stare: "The Indian . . . bent his fierce looks on the countenance of Cora, in such wavering glances, that her eyes sank with shame, under an impression that, for the first time, they had encountered an expression that no chaste female might endure." When Cora reported the offer to Alice and Duncan, saying, "He would have me," Alice responded, "Cora! Cora! . . . Name not the horrid alternative again; the thought itself is worse than a thousand deaths."[56]

Hawkeye, Chingachgook, and Uncas freed the captives and brought them safely to the fort. Soon after the daughters were reunited with their father, Heyward informed Colonel Munro that he wished the hand of one of his daughters in marriage. Munro assumed that he wanted the older, more mature, more grounded Cora. When Heyward spoke for Alice instead, Munro erupted in anger, thinking that Cora had been spurned unfairly. When he recovered, he explained his emotional defense of Cora. As a young man, he had joined the king's service and had been posted to the West Indies, where he met and married the daughter of a wealthy plantation owner. The planter's wife "was the daughter of a gentleman of those isles, by a lady whose misfortune it was, if you will," said Munro proudly, "to be descended, remotely, from that unfortunate class who are so basely enslaved." Cora, then, was "remotely" of mixed blood, black blood, and Munro's emotion flowed from his fear that Heyward, "born at the south," might have rejected Cora as being "of a race inferior to [his] own." Duncan denied the prejudice, pleading a simple love for Alice, but was "at the same time conscious of such a feeling, and that as deeply rooted as if it had been ingrafted in his nature."[57] Munro's second wife, from his Scottish homeland, was Alice's mother.

Cora's foreboding sense of the import of her mixed blood was revealed in an extended exchange with the venerable Indian sachem and wise man Tamenund. The sisters again captive, and Cora again sought by Magua as a wife, Tamenund had the power to say yea or nay. Cora pled for Alice rather than for herself, saying, "Like thee and thine, venerable chief, . . . the curse of my ancestors has fallen heavily on their child. But yonder is one who has never known the weight of Heaven's displeasure until now." Tamenund, unaware of Cora's mixed blood, still took her point, saying, "I know that the pale-faces are a proud and hungry race. I know that they claim . . . that the meanest of their color is better than the sachems of the redman. . . . [They would never] take a woman to their wigwams whose blood was not the color of snow."[58] Tragically, Cora knew this too. Soon, Cora was dead, killed by Magua when he could not "have" her, but Duncan and Alice survived and were married.

The "curse" that fell on the "dark-eyed Cora" was mixed blood, "remote" as it was and as little evident as it was on her beautiful countenance. As we shall see, "dark" women often meet an unfortunate fate, but Cora was the first example in American fiction of the "tragic mulatto." Mixed blood, even when not evident, was a curse both because it might be found out and because it might evidence itself in the next generation. Cora knew she carried a "curse" because the assumptions about nature, culture, and race, about the superiority of whites and the inferiority of all others, were all around her. This theme of mixed blood, black blood, especially when not evident to the eye, has been continuous in American fiction: in Harriet Beecher Stowe, as we have seen, but also in Mark Twain, William Faulkner, Philip Roth, and others.

Pathfinder and *Deerslayer* also are tales of the frontier forest, tales of fighting marauding Indians, saving damsels, and upholding nature, culture, and right. Much more than *Mohicans*, both *Pathfinder* and *Deerslayer* deal with class, ambition, accumulation, and, most particularly, gender. In *Pathfinder*, Hawkeye again escorted a young woman, Mabel Dunham, through hostile Indian territory to the fort where her father, Sergeant Thomas Dunham, was stationed. The sergeant, a longtime friend and intimate of Pathfinder, had, unbeknownst to Mabel, promised her to Pathfinder should he, after becoming acquainted with her, so wish. Both the sergeant and Pathfinder assumed that Mabel would happily acquiesce in her father's selection of his trusted friend as her mate. As Pathfinder got to know Mabel, he began to doubt whether he was worthy of her and whether she would be satisfied with a rude guide and hunter for a husband. Complicating the issue was the presence of another young man, Jasper Western. Jasper was somewhat younger than

Pathfinder and was deferential to him throughout, even in regard to Mabel, but he was more natural, more social—more civilized—in his instincts and expectations.

In *Pathfinder*, the scout actively contemplated marriage, a home, property, and their attendant responsibilities, but he was always doubtful, fearing the loss of his freedom. As Pathfinder tried to get to know Mabel, he observed, "I'm sometimes afear'd it isn't wholesome for one who is much occupied in a very manly calling, like that of a guide, or a scout, or a soldier even, to form friendships for women—young women in particular—as they seem to me to . . . turn the feelings away from their gifts and nat'ral occupations." Not aware that marriage was on Pathfinder's mind, Mabel responded, "I believe you are happier when alone, Pathfinder, than when mingling with your fellow creatures. . . . To me, it seems, you only want a home to return to, from your wanderings, to render your life completely happy. Were I a man, it would be my delight to roam through these forests at will." Mabel was being honest and candid: Pathfinder's boundless freedom was attractive, though unavailable, to her, so when he again said he "might be happier" with a wife, she responded incredulously, "Happier!—In what way, Pathfinder?—In this pure air, with these cool and shaded forests to wander through, . . . men ought to be nothing less than as perfectly happy, as their infirmities will allow."

As the idea slowly took shape in Mabel's mind that Pathfinder was proposing marriage to her and that this was also her father's wish, she was, at least momentarily, horrified. She blurted out, "While I esteem, respect—nay reverence you, . . . it is impossible that I should ever become your wife." Pathfinder was immediately undone, laboring, his breathing constricted. To lessen the impact, Mabel said, "What I wish you to understand is, that it is not likely that you and I should ever think of each other, as man and wife ought to think of each other." Pathfinder beat a disorderly retreat, gasping, "I do not—I shall never think in that way, again, Mabel—. . . . No—no—I shall never think of you, or any one else, again, in that way." Mabel tried again to explain: "Pathfinder—dear Pathfinder—understand me—. . . . A match like that would be unwise—unnatural, perhaps." Pathfinder gasped, "Yes, unnat'ral—agin natur' . . . ," and tears flowed down his face.[59]

Despite the stunning destruction of Pathfinder's half-formed hopes, they arose again near the novel's close. But Jasper Western also averred his love for Mabel, and Pathfinder, always mystified by women, love, and emotion, stepped back. Mabel chose the younger man, but also the civil, commercial, enterprising man. Mabel had had aspirations from the beginning, but she had no means to fulfill them except through a fortunate marriage. She knew that her class status as a sergeant's daughter compromised her marriage opportunities and said to Jasper, "I am in an awkward position, for while I am not good enough to be the wife of one of the gentlemen of the garrison, I think, even you will admit, Jasper, I am too good to be the wife of one of the common soldiers." Jasper thrilled her by assuring that "all do not remain in the stations in which they were born, Mabel, some rise above them, and some fall below them."

Pathfinder, on the other hand, had no sense that his hunter's life could be improved, except, briefly, when he imagined a cabin and a wife to return to from his hunts. Late in the novel, Cooper wrote, "The desire of rising above his present situation, never disturbed the tranquillity of Pathfinder, nor had he ever known an ambitious thought, . . . until he became acquainted with Mabel." Pathfinder himself testified, "I trouble myself but little with dollars, . . . I once hunted for two summers, . . . and I collected so much peltry that I found my right feelings giving way to a craving after property, and if I have consarn in marrying Mabel, it is that I may get to love such things too well, in order to make her comfortable."[60]

As a woman, Mabel had no course in life that she could chart on her own. All she could do is make a smart choice in marriage, and that choice was only tenuously hers. But make a smart choice she did: Jasper. Jasper and Mabel rose in life; Jasper became a successful New York City merchant and they had a family; Pathfinder returned to the woods. These options—Natty, the man alone, boundlessly free in the trackless woods, or Jasper, the man embedded in his family, business, and community—remain in our literature to this day. Jasper was the honorable man, but Natty was the legend. Nonetheless, there was no question that Mabel chose well. She was fortunate, but not all women were. The search for a mate, a marriage partner, was fraught with limitations— by considerations of class and cultural norms and, on the frontier, by a shocking dearth of options. A wrong step, even the intimation of a misstep, brought tragedy to many women, including Judith Hutter in *Deerslayer*.

The events in *Deerslayer* occur over just five days in the early 1740s, again in New York's Lake Champlain region. The novel opened as

Deerslayer and another woodsman, Henry "Hurry Harry" March, push through the woods to an idyllic location called Lake Glimmerglass. Deerslayer was on his way to meet Chingachgook and Harry was to visit Thomas Hutter and his two daughters, especially the strikingly beautiful Judith, who lived on the isolated lake. Thomas Hutter, with a vague criminal and piratical past, was on the lake because it was beyond the reach of law and authority. Hutter had acted as an adequate but somewhat distant father and protector to Judith and her attractive but mentally limited sister, Hetty, in the wake of their mother's death. Their mother had been a young woman of quality and position swept away by a dashing young gentleman of quality but no character; with her virtue compromised, she plummeted to such a level, in her own and society's estimation, that Hutter was the only one who would have her. Like Hester Prynne, the girls' mother loved too early, compromised her only asset, and was left a social outcast.

Although on the surface *Deerslayer* appears, again, to be a story about the forest and the men it shaped, especially the young Deerslayer, the novel's moral center was Judith Hutter, the isolated beauty on the lake. In the opening pages of the novel, before reaching the lake, "Hurry" Harry appeared as a bear of a man in his midtwenties, tall, thick, and strong, strikingly handsome, with a blond beard, but thoughtless, emotional, and blustery. He was strongly drawn to Judith, but he had reservations. Hurry told Deerslayer that because of her rare beauty and the dearth of women on the frontier, "Judith has had *men* among her suitors, ever since she was fifteen, which is now near five years." Officers from the forts in the region come to the lake to fish and hunt, and, March said, "then the creatur' seems beside herself! You can see it in the manner in which she wears her finery, and the airs she gives herself with the gallants." Deerslayer responded that such behavior was "unseemly in a poor man's darter, . . . the officers are all gentry, and can only look on such as Judith with evil intentions." He advised Harry "to think no more" of Judith, "but turn any mind altogether to the forest; that will never deceive you, being ordered and ruled by a hand that never wavers."[61]

Soon after Deerslayer and Judith actually met, she responded to his openness and honesty by confirming that her feminine defenses had been tested from an early age, saying, "You are the first man I ever met who did not seem to wish to flatter—to wish my ruin—to be an enemy in disguise." Deerslayer found "Judith . . . scarcely forward in her manner, though there was sometimes a freedom in her glances, that it required all the aid of her exceeding beauty to prevent from awakening suspicions unfavourable to her discretion, if not to her morals." Freedom for Deerslayer, Harry, and other men was an uninhibited choice; for Judith freedom suggested a dangerous approach to a moral precipice. Later in the book, Cooper wrote of Judith, "Hitherto she had been compelled to stand on the defensive in her intercourse with men—with what success was best known to herself." Elsewhere, Cooper suggested that Judith had lost her struggle, describing her as a "beautiful but misguided girl" with "a heart as treacherous, as uncertain, and as impetuous in its feelings, as that of the spoiled and flattered beauty."[62]

But Judith's options were few; the gentlemen officers had trifled with her, Harry was crudely eager but had reservations, and Deerslayer was admirable in many ways but deeply puzzling to her. She declared to him, "This is a terrible life for women, . . . I should be a thousand times happier to live nearer to civilised beings—where there are farms, and churches, and houses built, as it might be, by Christian hands; and where my sleep at night would be sweet and tranquil." Judith's vision, women's vision, of farms and churches and security in the night was lost on Pathfinder. So his response when a despairing Judith offered herself to him—promising to burn her finery and, once they were formally married, to live with him where he would—comes as no surprise. Deerslayer deflected the proposal, and Judith, with neither recourse nor pride left, asked Deerslayer whether anything Henry March said of her might have influenced his feelings. Deerslayer did not answer with words, but "Judith read his answer in his countenance; and with a heart nearly broken by the consciousness of undeserving, she sighed to him an adieu."[63]

Several critical themes run throughout the Leatherstocking series. One of the requirements of male independence was that females be kept at a distance. For Hawkeye, women hold no interest, physical or cultural, whatsoever. Hawkeye found women profoundly mysterious. To the extent that he grasped what they were thinking, what attracted and motivated them, he rejected and even feared it. With Mabel, he wavered, almost imagining a cabin to return to, but Mabel knew better. Anticipating a rough frontier cabin and a husband gone for extended periods, she very sensibly chose Jasper. Judith, also doubtful but too despairing to quibble, offered to give him everything on his own terms, and he rejected her in favor of the forest.

Themes of class were ever present in Cooper's novels, and class boundaries, though not impermeable, were positive and meaningful for him. A woman seeking to rise above her class was particularly problematic. But racial boundaries were even more powerful for Cooper, and though in the Leatherstocking books they are also not impermeable, the novels suggest that Cooper thought they should be. Hawkeye was ever adamant about racial purity and quite clear that race mixing was declension and would have harsh consequences. All white women in Cooper, even Cora, were convinced that sex with Indians must be worse than death. In fact, both Cora's father, who had married a woman of mixed race, and Cora knew that knowledge of black blood would lead immediately to social exclusion and, given the weight of fate, much worse.

Conclusion

Seventeenth-century Puritans and Quakers immigrated to America as families and congregations intent on founding godly communities. They were convinced that the social, political, economic, and religious design for Christian communities was revealed in the Bible. The resulting communities were intensively governed by magistrates and ministers who shared authority and were convinced that individual missteps would bring communal punishment. Nonetheless, Tocqueville and much modern scholarship have found in these tightly bound and insular communities the seeds of American individualism, freedom, and democracy.

However, these seeds did not sprout immediately. Nathaniel Hawthorne's classic *The Scarlet Letter* recounted the one-sided battle between Boston, led by a unified, confident, and empowered religious and political elite, and Hester Prynne. Hawthorne made Hester a compelling character, imaginative, strong, and independent, and made her lover, the Reverend Arthur Dimmesdale, timid, weak, and dependent. Yet Hawthorne, and ultimately Hester too, agreed that the community norms and rules that Dimmesdale clung to so desperately were civilization's limits on individual desire. Hester and Dimmesdale had sinned, and Hester acknowledged it. When she died, many years after Dimmesdale, she arranged for there to be a single headstone for them both, but for the graves to be separated by a respectful space, "as if the dust of these two sleepers had no right to mingle."[64]

As the colonial population grew, settlements spread along the coasts and into the backcountry, social and religious diversity increased, community bonds loosened, and individual rights and opportunities assumed a higher priority. John Locke's political theory of natural rights and Jonathan Edwards's religious doctrine that repentance and salvation were possible at any place in life opened the way to the secular concerns of Benjamin Franklin and his time. Franklin's eighteenth-century America grew more open, egalitarian, competitive, and entrepreneurial. Nonetheless, hierarchy and restraint in custom and law still tightly bound the indentured, women, and minorities. Most blacks were slaves, but the foreboding that surrounded the admirable Cora in *The Last of the Mohicans*, due to a remote tincture of black blood on her mother's side, speaks loudly.

The growth of population, the spread of cities and towns, and the diversification of local and colonial economies, experienced as progress by most, was experienced as the loss of freedom by a few. James Fenimore Cooper's classic frontiersman, Natty Bumppo or Hawkeye, the archetypal "man alone," prided himself on being "pure white," but, as D. H. Lawrence noted, he turned his back on white society and all that it meant. Hawkeye rejected family, community, property, law, and even literacy to live alone in the trackless forest with only nature and nature's God to guide him. Hawkeye thought only once, with Mabel Dunham in *Pathfinder*, of marriage, family, home, and property, but Mabel rejected him in favor of Jasper Western, the literate, social, and commercial man who gave her love, respect, family, and security. Jasper and Mabel moved, grew, and thrived, but Hawkeye returned to the forest and never again thought of a home and family. *Pathfinder* concludes with a striking image: Mabel, escorted by her sons, returned to the frontier, about twenty years after having chosen Jasper over Hawkeye. On a visit to the Mohawk, Mabel "observed a man, in a singular guise, watching her, in the distance." He did not approach, but when she inquired about him she was told that "he was the most renowned hunter of that portion of the State— . . . a being of great purity of character, and of as marked peculiarities, . . . by the name of the Leatherstocking."[65] In the years that Mabel had been gone, Hawkeye had not changed a wit; he remained a woodsman, a hunter, an "isolate," a man alone. Cooper wrote that seeing Hawkeye, even in the distance, made Mabel melancholy, but one can also imagine a wry smile playing across her lips—she had chosen well.

3 | The Founders' Dream and Its Limits

Welcome to my shores, distressed European; . . . If thou wilt work, I have bread for thee; if thou wilt be honest, sober, and industrious, I have greater rewards to confer on thee—ease and independence.
—J. Hector St. John de Crevecoeur, *Letters from an American Farmer*

All the pieces of the American Dream were in place by the 1780s. Benjamin Franklin, both in his own remarkable life and in the pages of *Poor Richard's Almanac*, had been defining the core of the dream for decades: prepare, work, save, invest, catch a break, and success will be yours. J. Hector St. John de Crevecoeur promised that the American Dream also belonged to immigrants: if they would come, learn, work, and save, they too could prosper as they never could in Europe. But precisely how government should be designed and administered to promote freedom, prosperity, and security remained uncertain. In the standard telling, two elite visions predominated; one was the liberal, egalitarian, agrarian vision of Thomas Jefferson, and the other was the individualistic, competitive, commercial vision of Alexander Hamilton. But novelists highlight the irrelevance of both visions to the excluded majority of Americans. Jefferson's bucolic vision masked the growing horror of slavery, and Hamilton's developmental state sorted losers from winners without compunction or pity.

The Jeffersonian vision was a calm, almost sedate, promise of equality, sufficiency, and security for propertied whites. It was a rural vision of slow but steady accumulation, natural growth, and competition restrained by community. The big gain was unlikely, but the steady application of effort could lead to larger and more secure holdings over a lifetime. The Hamiltonian vision was more aggressively entrepreneurial; it envisioned a rising commercial and manufacturing economy guided by an elite endowed with talent, wisdom, and wealth. In the new nation's first half century, though the Hamiltonian vision predominated for a time, the Jeffersonian vision effectively shaped the new nation because it comported so well with the hopes and aspirations of the white westering agricultural multitudes.

Still, most Americans remained outside the civic ken of the Founding generation. The declaration that "all men are created equal" left ample room to acknowledge the hierarchies that white elites thought so clearly intended by God and nature. At most, theirs was the fairly narrow sense that all adult, white, male property owners were citizens and therefore had some place in the governing class. Several important novels ushered the excluded many onto center stage in ways that the elites rarely did. Jefferson's agricultural utopian vision was challenged directly in two novels that dealt with slavery and the threat of slave revolts. *Clotel; or, The President's Daughter* (1853), by William Wells Brown, one of the nation's first black novelists, challenged Jefferson directly and personally. *Benito Cereno* (1856), by Herman Melville, laid bare the psychological damage slavery caused both blacks and whites. Two more novels from James Fenimore Cooper's Leatherstocking series, *The Pioneers* (1823) and *The Prairie* (1827), and Melville's *Billy Budd* (1891), all set in the two decades on either side of 1800, highlight the struggle to find a balance between individual freedom and social order, between liberty and the rule of law, in the new nation.

The Promise and Meaning of American Independence

Among American elites, independence gave new momentum to intellectual forces that had been on the rise in Europe and America for more than a century. Sir Isaac Newton (1642–1727), father of modern empirical and experimental science, sought to explain the natural world as the interplay of physical forces, gravity being the most prominent, acting according to universal laws of motion. Newton demonstrated that the balance, symmetry, and harmony of the universe, variously described as "celestial mechanics" or the "harmony of the spheres," operated according to natural, and therefore discoverable, general laws. The educated persons who accepted that the heavens were held together by gravity, rather than hung in place for all eternity by the hand of God, thought of their world differently than did the masses.

The search for balance and harmony spread beyond the natural sciences. Within the social sciences, students of human motivation adhered to a perspective called faculty psychology. Faculty psychology highlighted three human faculties: reason, passions, and interests. Each had a legitimate and even critical role to play in human life, but the relationships between and among them varied. In some people they were in harmonious balance, while in others they were in perpetual conflict. In the ideal interaction of the human faculties, found in the fairly small group of men Jefferson referred to as the natural aristoi, or natural aristocracy, reason would direct the proper, healthy, and measured pursuit of the passions and interests. Unfortunately, for most men most of the time and for virtually all women, children, and nonwhites, passions and interests overwhelmed reason.

The best minds of the eighteenth century thought that the uniformity of human nature described by faculty psychology made history a storehouse of empirical data, of natural experiments, showing what worked and what did not work in human social organization. If human nature was uniform and unchanging, like the matter in Newton's universe, then well-built institutions, like well-built machines, might order the world to the benefit of man. John Adams wrote, "The systems of legislators are experiments made on human life, and manners, society and government. Zoroaster, Confucius, Mithras, Odin, Mohamet, Lycurgus, Solon, Romulus, and a thousand others may be compared to philosophers making experiments on the elements."[1] Similarly, as General George Washington resigned his military commission to return to civilian life in June 1783, he observed, "The treasures of knowledge, acquired by the labors of Philosophers, Sages, and legislators, through a long succession of years, are laid open for our use, and . . . may be happily applied in the Establishment of our forms of Government. . . . At this auspicious period, the United States came into existence as a Nation, and if their Citizens should not be completely free and happy, the fault will be entirely their own."[2]

Clearly, the Founding generation's leading men believed that many pieces of a new and potentially transformative order were present, but no one claimed to know exactly how all the pieces fit together to assure peace and prosperity. Monarchy was discredited, democracy was still thought dangerously unstable, and between them lay a disconcertingly broad spectrum of political regimes called republics. John Adams reflected the sense of many that republicanism provided a direction in which to search, but not a destination. Adams observed, "There is no good government but what is republican. . . . Of republics there is an inexhaustible variety, because the possible combinations of the powers of society are capable of innumerable variations."[3]

What the Founders were looking for was what Aristotle had called a "polity," a balanced government in which the disparate interests of the few rich and the many poor were carefully balanced to produce security and prosperity. However, scholars and theorists had long taught that governments in which the many poor played a prominent role had to be small so that the people could come together to discuss issues, vote, and work their will. Larger, wealthier, more powerful republics tended to be governed by elites. The most authoritative presentation of this view came from the French scholar Charles Secondat (1689–1755), the Baron de Montesquieu, in *The Spirit of the Laws* (1748). Still, new insights were working their way into the public consciousness.

David Hume (1711–1776), a British historian and political economist, offered a dramatic new perspective on the relationship between state size and regime type. In a beautifully titled essay, "Idea of a Perfect Commonwealth" (1741), Hume rejected "the common opinion that no large state . . . could ever be modelled into a commonwealth." In fact, he declared, quite the opposite was true: "In a large government, which is modelled with masterly skill, there is compass and room enough to refine the democracy, from the lower people who may be admitted into the first elections . . . , to the higher magistrates who direct all the movements. At the same time, the parts are so distant and remote that it is very difficult, either by intrigue, prejudice, or passion, to hurry them into any measures against the public interest."[4] On their reading of Newton, Montesquieu, and Hume, the Founders came to believe that a constitution "modelled with masterly skill" might "check interest with interest, class with class, faction with faction, and one branch of government with another in a harmonious system of mutual frustration."[5]

Elites of the revolutionary generation were convinced that America had been set aside by God for a special experiment in human freedom. Yet virtually no one in that generation believed that those benefits were intended for any but the new nation's propertied white inhabitants. Yale University president Ezra Stiles declared in 1783 that the new nation, which he called "GOD's American Israel," had combined faith, freedom, and opportunity to create "a most amazing spirit" among the people. "Never before," he declared, "has the experiment been so effectually tried, of every man's reaping the fruits of his labour, and feeling his share in the aggregate system of power."[6] Benjamin Rush, Philadelphia's leading physician, also saw the hand of God in America's peculiar success. Rush declared, also in 1783, "America seems destined by heaven to exhibit to the world the perfection which the mind of man is capable of receiving from the combined operation of liberty, learning, and the gospel upon it."[7] Finally, Noah Webster highlighted the difference between America and Europe in a 1798 Fourth of July oration. Webster declared, "America alone seems to be reserved by Heaven as the sequestered region, where religion, virtue and the arts may find a peaceful retirement from the tempests which agitate Europe. If, in the old world, men are . . . perpetually shedding each other's blood, . . . we have the more reason to cling to the constitution, the laws, to the civil and religious institutions of the country."[8]

Thomas Jefferson: The Heights and Depths of a Founding Vision

The most intriguing, because the most complex and ambiguous, figure of the Founding generation was Thomas Jefferson (1743–1826). His intellectual and literary abilities made him the author of independence, and his private life made him a man of his times and his region and an exemplar of white privilege. Jefferson's place in the American pantheon, which we will treat first, derived from his distinctly positive and uplifting view of human nature. Richard Hofstadter, no idealist himself, wrote, "Through all Jefferson's work there runs like a fresh underground stream the deep conviction that all will turn out well, that life will somehow assert itself."[9] Joseph J. Ellis has written that "the most visionary version of the American Dream" derived from Thomas Jefferson.[10] Jefferson himself simply said, "I am among those who think well of the human character generally."[11] Jefferson's hope for and trust in the future became a steady breeze beneath the wings of the American Dream. The fact that he spoke in broad terms, and often in universal terms, allowed generations of Americans to ignore that he was speaking only to whites.

Jefferson's vision for America was encapsulated in the Declaration of Independence. While the Declaration was the work of a committee, further amended on the floor of the Congress, Jefferson's vision of an egalitarian individualism lived out in the context of peace and plenty shone through.[12] Jefferson put human rights, the rights of individuals to security, respect, and self-development, at the core of the American promise. The justly famous second paragraph of the Declaration reads, "We hold these truths to be self-evident, that all men are created equal, that they are endowed by their Creator with certain unalienable Rights, that among these are Life, Liberty, and the pursuit of Happiness.—That to secure these rights, Governments are instituted among Men, deriving their just powers from the consent of the governed,—That whenever any Form of Government becomes destructive of these ends, it is the Right of the People to alter or to abolish it, and to institute new Government, laying its foundation on such principles and organizing its powers in such form, as to them shall seem most likely to effect their Safety and Happiness."

The opening sentence of that paragraph made several points that became foundational to the American Dream and to our national sense of self. First, it defined as "self-evident"—that is, beyond demonstration and dispute—"certain unalienable Rights," among which are "Life, Liberty, and the pursuit of Happiness." The idea of self-evidence is a wonderful way of saying that despite all the visible evidence of difference and inequality, a free society must see men as fundamentally equal. These words have proven to be so alluringly open that each succeeding generation has more broadly understood the "all Men" who are "created equal" and "endowed" with the "unalienable Rights" of "Life, Liberty, and the pursuit of Happiness." Moreover, the simple phrase "among these" suggests that there may be additional self-evident and unalienable rights.

Second, John Locke's identification of life, liberty, and property as fundamental rights was significantly softened, broadened, and enriched by Jefferson's substitution of "pursuit of Happiness" for "property." Life and liberty remain as important for Jefferson as for Locke, and there is no doubt that Jefferson valued property, but "pursuit of Happiness" was forward looking, egalitarian, and aspirational, whereas "property" was conservative, defensive, and exclusionary. The Founding generation believed that property supported security, independence, and autonomy, but Jefferson's "pursuit of Happiness" suggested a goal well beyond security, a goal that we might call human fulfillment and thriving.

Third, widespread happiness or fulfillment was made a defining purpose of government. The second paragraph of the Declaration mentioned happiness twice, once in the list with life and liberty and once later in the paragraph. The second reference to happiness came as Jefferson explained that people had a right to change a government that did not suit their needs, laying the foundation of a new government "on such principles and organizing its powers in such form, as to them shall seem most likely to effect their Safety and Happiness." "Effect" means "realize," so that seldom-noted phrase meant that people empowered government in the expectation that it would help them realize or achieve security and happiness.[13] Jefferson defined the goals of American public life—the promise of life, liberty, and the pursuit of happiness—in positive and expansive language that has thrilled and challenged every subsequent generation of Americans.

Jefferson believed that society and government should act to maximize individual liberty and then help people take advantage of the opportunities available to them. His broadest insight was that freedom and education made democracy possible. To Jefferson and the Founding generation, freedom for white men meant individual autonomy and independence. In a nation of small villages and farms, independence meant access to land and the means to work it. Jefferson famously thought that the agrarian life encouraged and sustained personal virtue. In *Notes on the State of Virginia* he wrote, "Those who labour in the earth are the chosen people of God, if ever he had a chosen people, whose breasts he has made his peculiar deposit for substantial and genuine virtue."[14] Jefferson believed that the new nation's social health and character depended upon the widespread pursuit of agriculture. In 1787 he wrote, "I think our governments will remain virtuous for many centuries; as long as they remain chiefly agricultural; and this will be as long as there shall be vacant lands in any part of America."[15]

Jefferson's closest political associate, and in some sense his own more practical self, was fellow Virginia planter James Madison (1751–1836). Madison followed Jefferson's lead, but frequently he also moderated Jefferson's more abstract instincts. Madison was known as the Father of the Constitution for the key role he played in initiating and bringing to fruition the Constitutional Convention of 1787. The opening paragraph of the Constitution restated the Declaration's goals of ordered liberty based on popular sovereignty, declaring, "WE THE PEOPLE of the United States, in Order to form a more perfect Union, establish Justice, insure domestic Tranquility, provide for the common defence, promote the general Welfare, and secure the Blessings of Liberty to ourselves and our Posterity, do ordain and establish this Constitution for the United States of America."

The Founders believed that a wisely contrived constitution might divert human ambition toward the public interest and the common good. Following David Hume, James Madison argued that thoughtfully "contriving the interior structure of the government" would make men and institutions check and balance each other. Madison explained in *The Federalist Papers*, "Ambition must be made to counteract ambition. The interest of the man must be connected with the constitutional rights of the place." He promised that "this policy of supplying, by opposite and rival interests, the defect of better motives" would provide good government even if good men did not always rule.[16]

Madison saw that the American commitment to written constitutions allowed well-defined executive, legislative, and judicial powers to be placed in separate hands. Beneath the broad separation of powers might be constructed an intricate machinery of checks and balances that would permit self-interested officeholders to employ and protect their powers and responsibilities over time. Indirect and mediated elections of presidents and senators, for differing terms, by differing constituencies, were designed to "extract from the mass of society the purest and noblest characters; such as will at once feel most strongly the proper motives to pursue the end of their appointment, and be most capable to devise the proper means of attaining it."[17]

The Constitution defined the powers of government and sought to protect against their ill-use by a complex system of separation of powers and checks and balances, but the debate over ratification made clear that many Americans worried that their rights and liberties were vulnerable. Even Jefferson, on diplomatic service in France when the Constitution was drafted, wrote to Madison expressing concern about the absence of a bill of rights. Madison began to worry that a cloud of doubt would hang over the Constitution if more protections for individual rights were not added. He ushered the first ten amendments to the Constitution, which have come to be known as the Bill of Rights, through Congress and the ratification process. The Bill of Rights, broadly conceived, accomplished two things. First, it defined a preserve of personal autonomy, choice, and expression into which government power should not intrude. The First Amendment offered the expansive assurance that "Congress shall make no law respecting an establishment of religion, or prohibiting the free exercise thereof; or abridging the freedom of speech, or of the press; or the right of the people peaceably to assemble, and to petition the government for a redress of grievances."

Second, the Bill of Rights defined how persons would be subject to the power of government. Isolated individuals, especially common people, must quake before the concentrated power of a national government unless that government is required to proceed slowly, carefully, and according to well-known rules and procedures. Hence, the Bill of Rights confirmed the rights to a speedy trial before an impartial jury, to confront witnesses, and to have the aid of counsel (Amendment 6). The Bill of Rights protected citizens against unreasonable searches and seizures (Amendment 4), double jeopardy and self-incrimination (Amendment 5), and excessive bail or cruel and unusual punishments (Amendment 8). The Ninth Amendment, like the Declaration of Independence, suggested that citizens as human beings had more rights than those specifically listed in the Constitution and its amendments. The Declaration said that "among" the unalienable rights that the Creator gave men were life, liberty, and the prospect of happiness. The Ninth Amendment said, "The enumeration in the Constitution, of certain rights, shall not be construed to deny or disparage others retained by the people." These reassuring commitments encouraged citizens to give the new Constitution a chance. Just as Madison had hoped, support for the Constitution increased to near unanimity within a few years.[18]

J. Hector St. John de Crevecoeur (1735–1813) assured European immigrants that the American promise belonged to them too. Crevecoeur was born in the Normandy region of France, came to America about 1760, and after serving France in the Great Lakes area and the Ohio Valley, settled on a comfortable farm in Orange County, New York. His *Letters from an American Farmer* (first published in London in 1782, with the first American edition published in Philadelphia in 1793) provided the first full articulation of the American Dream from the immigrant perspective. Crevecoeur was concerned both to praise America to potential immigrants and to assure native-born Americans that it was reasonable to welcome strangers to the new nation. Some Americans were concerned that immigrants carried monarchical and aristocratic ideas and attitudes that might pollute republican America. Crevecoeur argued that immigrants came not to re-create their European past but to find their American future. He asked, "What attachment can a poor European emigrant have for a country where he had nothing? . . . Can a wretch who wanders about, who works and starves, . . . call England or any other kingdom his country? A country that had no bread for him, whose fields procured him no harvest, . . . who owned not a single foot of the extensive surface of this planet? No!"

Rather, Crevecoeur assured his native-born countrymen that in choosing America, the immigrant becomes an American: "His country is now that which gives him land, bread, protection, and consequence." Crevecoeur drove home his point by asking a justly famous question: "What then is the American, this new man?" And he answered, "He is an American, who, leaving behind him all his ancient prejudices and manners, receives new ones from the new mode of life he has embraced, the new government he obeys, and the new rank he holds."[19] In America, Crevecoeur reminded his readers, "the bright idea of property, of exclusive right, of independence . . . [and] precious soil . . . constitute the riches of the freeholder." Opportunity encouraged the freeholder's hopes and molded his behavior. All Americans, old and new, were "animated with the spirit of an industry which is unfettered and unrestrained, because each person works for himself."[20]

Like Franklin, Crevecoeur reminded his readers that opportunity had to be grasped and that not everyone would thrive, even in America. Crevecoeur explained, "It is not every emigrant who succeeds; no, it is only the sober, the honest, and industrious. . . . If he is a good man, he forms schemes of future prosperity . . . ; he thinks of future modes of conduct, feels an ardor to labour he never felt before." Crevecoeur hastened to add, "I do not mean that everyone who comes will grow rich in a little time; no, but he may procure an easy, decent maintenance, by his industry."[21] Crevecoeur was so dead-on about the sense and feel of the American Dream that he described the immigrant's opportunity to work, save, and invest in his own land as "a dream." Crevecoeur highlighted the Germans as particularly effective in studying and pursuing the opportunities available in America. He said, of an immigrant's owning "absolute property of two hundred acres of land," that it was "an epocha in this man's life! He is become a freeholder from perhaps a German Boor—he is now an American," adding that these Germans, "by dint of sobriety, rigid parsimony, and the most persevering industry, . . . commonly succeed. Their astonishment . . . is very great—it is to them a dream."[22]

Crevecoeur recommended that those who would be Americans listen closely to their new nation's promise lest they miss its conditionality:

After a foreigner from any part of Europe is arrived, and become a citizen; let him devoutly listen to the voice of our great parent, which says to him, "Welcome to my shores, distressed European; bless the hour in which thou

didst see my verdant fields, my fair navigable rivers, and my green mountains!—If thou wilt work, I have bread for thee; if thou wilt be honest, sober,
and industrious, I have greater rewards to confer on thee—ease and independence. . . . Go thou and work and till; thou shalt prosper, provided thou
be just, grateful, and industrious."[23]

Despite Crevecoeur's assurance to European immigrants that they
would find a place in America, many Americans, then as now, were skeptical of immigrants. Nonetheless, as Crevecoeur suggested, white male
immigrants and their families usually blended into the new society with
time and good effort.

Gender, Race, and the Corruption of the Founding Vision

The Founders' survey of history showed that no republic in the ancient
or modern world had ever been equally free to all. Defining freedom
and equality in terms of economic independence, in terms of the possession of sufficient property to attest an ongoing stake in the community,
drew a bright line between citizens and mere inhabitants. The vast majority of white, male Americans of the revolutionary generation thought
that members of dependent classes lacked property because they lacked
the requisite characteristics and virtues to compete successfully for it.
They thought that women, children, slaves, idiots, and propertyless
white men all lacked the capacity for independent judgment and rational planning that led to property, autonomy, and security. Hence, half a
million slaves, virtually all women, and many poor and dependent white
men were outside the "imagined community" of American citizens at
the Founding.

Women and blacks were thought to differ from white men in natural capacity, though in different ways and to different degrees. While
men were equipped for the public marketplace and forum, the natural
talents and instincts of women fitted them for domestic life. The most
famous exchange of the Founding period over the relations between
the sexes occurred between John and Abigail Adams in the spring of
1776. John had been in Congress off and on for almost two years, the
British had occupied Boston and now held New York City, and Abigail
had been managing the family's affairs in Boston and Braintree, Massachusetts. Abigail Adams, it must be said, was intelligent, articulate, and

engaged well beyond the expectations of her time. She began her letter of March 31, 1776, by scolding John for not sending more political news and saying, "I long to hear that you have declared an independency." Abigail then went on to remind her congressman husband to "Remember the Ladies" when it came time to write "a new Code of Laws." She asked John to see that America's lawmakers

> be more generous and favorable . . . than your ancestors. Do not put such unlimited power into the hands of the husbands. Remember, all Men would be tyrants if they could . . . but such of you as wish to be happy willingly give up the harsh title of Master for the more tender and endearing one of Friend. Why then, not put it out of the power of the vicious and Lawless to use us with cruelty . . . ? Regard us then as Beings placed by providence under your protection and in imitation of the Supreme Being make use of that power only for our happiness.

Abigail's letter is a wonderful mix of the assertiveness of an intelligent woman, the plaintiveness of one who knows that the operative cultural assumptions are not on her side, and resort to arguments from utilitarianism and traditional religion for whatever they might be worth.

John's reply of April 14, 1776, is the classic evasion of justice by power. Rather than confront Abigail on the merits of her argument, he sought refuge in levity, saying, "As to your extraordinary Code of Laws, I cannot but laugh. . . . We have only the Name of Masters, and (to) give up this . . . would completely subject Us to the Despotism of the Petticoat." Only in a separate letter of May 26, 1776, to John Sullivan, did John Adams adopt the standard defense for the legal subjection of women to men: The common sense of the matter was that women's "delicacy renders them unfit for practice and experience in the great businesses of life, and the hardy enterprises of war, as well as the arduous care of the state. Besides, their attention is so much engaged with the necessary nurture of their children, that nature has made them fittest for domestic care."[24]

A stronger challenge to traditional male attitudes toward women came from Judith Sargent Murray in a 1790 essay, "On the Equality of the Sexes." Murray adopted the dominant social-science theory of the day, faculty psychology, to question the basis of male superiority. Murray argued that although women were thought to have weaker powers of reason and stronger emotions than men, these were a function of nurture, education, and clearly communicated social expectations rather than permanent differences of nature. Murray asked, "Is it upon mature consideration we adopt the idea, that nature is thus partial in her distributions? Is it indeed a fact, that she has yielded to one half of the human species so unquestionable a mental superiority?" She answered no, saying that women were equal in reason, imagination, and memory and would be equal in wisdom and judgment if appropriately trained and educated: "We can only reason from what we know, and if opportunity of acquiring knowledge has been denied us, the inferiority of our sex cannot fairly be deduced from thence." Boys are "taught to aspire" while girls are "confined and limited." The "*apparent* superiority" of men comes from the better education of boys. "Yes, ye lordly, ye haughty sex, our souls are by nature *equal* to yours."[25]

While Abigail Adams might chide her husband, saying, "Remember, all Men would be tyrants if they could . . . but such of you as wish to be happy willingly give up the harsh title of Master for the more tender and endearing one of Friend," she was speaking of and for free white women. Similarly, when Murray called for better education for women, she also had only white women clearly in mind. Though white women were not the equals of their fathers and husbands, they shared many of their privileges; they lived in their homes, ate at their tables, wore clothes of similar quality, and sat with them in their pews at church. Not so slave women. White men, married and not, could tyrannize over slave women at will. They were masters in every sense of the word, and both they and the women they owned knew it.

It is just here that we find the dramatic contradiction that lay at the core of Thomas Jefferson. Jefferson married and deeply loved Martha Wayles Jefferson, the only daughter of John and Martha Eppes Wayles. When Martha Eppes married John Wayles she brought with her a slave named Susanna and Susanna's eleven-year-old mulatto daughter, Betty Hemings. After Martha and two subsequent white wives died, John Wayles took Betty Hemings as his concubine, and she bore him six quadroon children over twelve years. These children, including the youngest, Sally Hemings, were half siblings to his white child, Martha Wayles, later Jefferson's wife. Betty Hemings and her children became part of the Jefferson household upon John Wayles's death. Martha Jefferson died September 6, 1782, at age thirty-three. Her husband, Thomas Jefferson, was thirty-nine and her half sister Sally was nine. As Sally matured, perhaps resembling her half sister, Jefferson's beloved Martha, he took her as a mistress and had six octoroon children with her, four of whom lived to adulthood. DNA evidence that Jefferson fathered children with Sally Hemings is incontrovertible, though scholars and the public still struggle to imagine what kind of relationship this might have been.

Jefferson supporters—and who is not a Jefferson supporter at some level?—dismissed and decried evidence of the Jefferson-Hemings liaison for more than two centuries. What went virtually unnoticed for most of that time was that one of the first major novels by an American black, the escaped former slave William Wells Brown, explored the dynamics of such master/slave relationships and of the antebellum southern society in which they flourished. Just as important was the extent to which Brown's novel undercut the Enlightenment claims of the Founding elite. Faculty psychology argued that in some men, educated elite men like Thomas Jefferson, reason might guide and control the passions and interests that ran riot in most men and women. This charming possibility melted in the bubbling cauldron of interest and passion that was slavery. As Abigail Adams said, "All Men would be tyrants if they could," and many could be and were.

William Wells Brown's *Clotel; or, The President's Daughter* was set in the half century between 1790 and 1840. It is a novel about the emotional riot and violence of slavery, about the market for light-skinned slave women, and about the cultural milieu that spawned and supported them. *Clotel* depicted in starkest terms a point made by the author and social critic James Baldwin. "It must be remembered," Baldwin wrote, "that the oppressed and the oppressor are bound together within the same society; they accept the same criteria, they share the same beliefs, they both alike depend on the same reality. . . . It is the peculiar triumph of society . . . that it is able to convince those people to whom it has given inferior status of the reality of this decree."[26] Baldwin's point, which he made initially about Harriet Beecher Stowe's *Uncle Tom's Cabin*, published the year before *Clotel*, informs the latter just as deeply.

The premise of *Clotel* is that Currer, the mother of Clotel and Althesa, "in her younger days . . . had been the housekeeper of a young slaveholder; . . . Thomas Jefferson, by whom she had two daughters. Jefferson being called to Washington . . . Currer was left behind." Currer was later sold to a Mr. John Graves, who permitted her to hire her own time as a laundress, paying him a fee and using the rest of her earnings to raise her daughters. Remarkably, or not, given the options available, Currer raised her daughters to appeal to white men who might patronize and protect them from worse—for the standard price. Brown wrote that Currer had brought up Clotel, sixteen at the time the novel begins, and Althesa, then fourteen, "to attract attention, and especially at balls and parties. . . . Nearly all the negro parties in the cities and towns of the Southern States are made up of quadroon and mulatto girls, and white men. . . . It was at one of these parties that Horatio Green, the son of a wealthy gentleman of Richmond, was first introduced to Clotel."[27]

Currer was thrilled by the attention that Green showed to Clotel and facilitated the courtship in her home. Green was an honest, well-intentioned young man of twenty-two but, as it turned out, weak and entitled. He promised to buy Clotel and make her mistress of her own home. Currer envisioned her daughter emancipated and established in white society. Despite these plans, John Graves's unexpected death brought Currer and her daughters to the auction block. Currer, then forty, and Althesa were sold to a slave trader from New Orleans. Clotel created a particular stir at auction; Brown wrote, "The appearance of Clotel on the auction block created a deep sensation amongst the crowd. There she stood, with a complexion as white as most of those who were waiting with a wish to become her purchasers; . . . The auctioneer commenced by saying, that 'Miss Clotel has been reserved for the last, because she was the most valuable. How much gentlemen? Real Albino, fit for a fancy girl for anyone.'"[28] Clotel was purchased for $1,500, but to her great relief, her new owner was Horatio Green.

Green settled Clotel in an attractive cottage just outside of Richmond. Clotel required a marriage, and Horatio gladly complied, though both knew that the law neither recognized nor sanctioned it. A child, Mary, her complexion even whiter than her mother's, came soon, and Clotel's life was secure until Horatio's social, economic, and political goals began to demand more of his time and attention. His social position and political aspirations required a white wife, so he married Gertrude, the daughter of a prominent family. Horatio still wanted Clotel, continued to maintain her and Mary in the cottage, and begged Clotel to understand the difficulties of his situation. She declined to answer his pleas. Green deteriorated, his political aspirations dashed; he began to drink; and Gertrude, now aware of Clotel and Mary, took control. Clotel was sold to a slave trader, who sold her to a merchant, Mr. James French of Vicksburg, Mississippi. Gertrude took Mary into her own home so that she could treat the young child harshly under Horatio's nose.

Clotel was to be a servant to Mr. French's wife, but Mrs. French was immediately suspicious. Brown explained, "Every married woman in the far South looks upon her husband as unfaithful, and rejects every quadroon servant as a rival. Clotel had been with her new mistress but a few days, when she was ordered to cut off her long hair."[29] Mr. French soon decided to sell Clotel to relieve the tension in his home. Clotel's next master was kind and generous, showering her with presents, in the clear hope of winning her gratitude and then her favors. She protested that she was married back in Virginia and resolved to escape.[30] With the help of a fellow slave, William, Clotel escaped and headed back to Richmond in search of Mary.

Meanwhile, Althesa, Clotel's younger sister, had found great happiness. She was initially purchased by James Crawford, a Vermonter living in New Orleans. Althesa was soon noticed by and later courted by and married by the Crawford's friend, another Vermonter, the physician Henry Morton. Morton purchased Althesa from the Crawfords, but he treated the beautiful, young, apparently white fifteen-year-old as in every way his wife. Henry Morton and Althesa lived happily and equally together and had two young daughters, again, both white to all appearances. The girls were raised in privilege and educated in New England, but soon after they returned to New Orleans their parents were swept away by yellow fever. James Morton of Vermont, Henry's brother, arrived in New Orleans to settle Henry's estate and take the girls home with him. Henry Morton, apparently prosperous, had in fact been deeply in debt. In settling the estate, it was found that Althesa, though bought and married by Henry, remained legally a slave, and as a result, so were her daughters. Both appeared to be young white girls, but they were slaves who could be used at will and were sold at auction "after a fierce contest between the bidders," one to an old gentleman, the other to a "dashing young man, who had just come into the possession of a large fortune." Ellen, the older daughter, who was bought by the old gentleman, "he said, for a housekeeper," soon found that she had been bought for other purposes. "The morning after her arrival, she was found dead in her chamber, a corpse." Jane, bought by the dashing young man, "needed no one to tell her of her impending doom."[31] Jane's rescue was attempted by a young protégé of her father, but he was shot dead by her master. Soon Jane too was dead of a broken heart.

Clotel's end was soon in coming. Back in Richmond to find Mary, Clotel was discovered, arrested, and imprisoned. She was transferred from Richmond to the "negro pens" in the District of Columbia to await a vessel to New Orleans. The evening before she was again to be shipped south, just as the prison was being closed for the night, Clotel broke for freedom. She ran for the "Long Bridge" over the Potomac hoping to make the Arlington woods beyond. She reached the bridge with her pursuers well behind, "but God by his Providence had otherwise determined." On the Virginia side, three men blocked her way, and with her pursuers closing in, her stark choice was slavery or death. She chose death: "Far below rolled the deep foamy waters of the Potomac. . . . With a single bound, she vaulted over the railings of the bridge, and sunk forever beneath the waves of the river! Thus died Clotel, the daughter of Thomas Jefferson, a president of the United States."[32]

A second novel, Herman Melville's *Benito Cereno*, explored other dimensions of the violence that permeated slavery. Melville, like Hawthorne, thought that there were devils in the world and that they were too numerous and powerful, and often hidden until too late, for men to overcome. In *Benito Cereno*, Melville showed how good men could be completely misled, even wholly mystified, by the evil scheming of others. In 1799, Captain Amasa Delano of Duxbury, Massachusetts, was in command of the *Bachelor's Delight*, a sealer and general trading ship, then in the port of St. Maria, Chile. Captain Delano was a man of "singularly undistrustful good nature," open, joyful, charitable, always ready to help, and slow to attribute "malign evil to man." As a result, when a strange ship, obviously battered and struggling, limped into port, Delano offered food, water, and other aid.

The crippled ship was commanded by a Spanish-Peruvian, Don Benito Cereno, weakened by his ordeal, barely coherent at times, but steadied and served by "the negro Babo." Babo was a slave, but was seemingly dedicated to Don Benito's comfort and welfare. The often-dazed and sometimes mute Don Benito was gently advised and assisted by Babo in conversation with Delano about the history, trials, and needs of their ship. Watching Babo serve Don Benito in his morning toilet, shaving, clipping, combing, and dressing him, Delano observed complacently, "There is something in the negro which, in a peculiar way, fits him for evocations around one's person. Most negroes are natural valets. . . . When to this is added the docility arising from the unaspiring contentment of a limited mind," one has the natural body servant. Melville noted that "like most men of good, blithe heart, Captain Delano took to negroes, not philanthropically, but genially, just as other men to Newfoundland dogs."[33] The condescending racism of New England saw blacks not as devils but as children.

In addition to being quite taken with the faithful Babo, Delano admired the mulatto steward, Francisco. Francisco was a highly trained personal servant, steward to his owner, elaborately polite and fastidious in his service. Delano was fascinated that "the mulatto was hybrid, his physiognomy was European—classically so." As Francisco led them to a well-prepared lunch, Delano whispered to Don Benito, "I am glad to see this usher-of-the-golden-rod of yours; the sight refutes an ugly remark once made to me by a Barbadoes planter; that when a mulatto has a regular European face, look out for him; he is a devil."[34]

Soon, Delano's blindly accepting sense of the stricken ship's history was destroyed, but even then it took a long time for reality to penetrate his thick racial assumptions. As Delano was leaving to return to his own ship, Don Benito tumbled from the deck into his boat and three white sailors leaped into the sea and swam madly for the boat, while the black sailors on deck went into an uproar. Delano assumed that Don Benito and his men were attempting to take him hostage as part of a plan to seize his ship. In fact, Don Benito and the fleeing white sailors were the last survivors of a slave revolt at sea, masterminded by Babo and brutally carried out by Francisco and others. In the revolt, Don Benito's close friend and the owner of the slaves, Don Alexandro Aranda, had been murdered; the flesh had been stripped from his bones, and his skeleton had been fastened to the ship's figurehead with the inscription "Follow Your Leader." Those white crew members not slain outright had been tossed into the sea to drown. Babo kept Don Benito alive, though under his total control, in case whites, such as the affable Delano, needed to be misled. Delano did not see Babo's command of Don Benito because his racial assumptions did not permit it; he thought "The whites, . . . by nature, were the shrewder race" and that the blacks "were too stupid" to carry a plot against their betters.[35]

Don Benito, more familiar than Delano with black slaves, held harsher views toward them. Hence, the revolt, the gruesome murder of his friend and crew, and his total domination for months by Babo destroyed his body, mind, and soul. Even after he was freed and Babo had been tried, found guilty, and executed, Don Benito remained mired in deep depression. In the closing paragraphs of the novel, the two captains explored the events that had befallen Don Benito and his response to them. Don Benito bemoaned how little men know of each other, saying to Delano, "So far may even the best man err, in judging the conduct of one with the recesses of whose condition he is not acquainted.

But you were . . . in time undeceived. Would that, in both respects, it was so ever, and with all men." But Don Benito knew that it was not so; men were easily and frequently deceived, and too often the deception was not discovered, evil men prevailed, and good men suffered, sometimes horribly.

Delano thought that Don Benito's dismay was no longer warranted. He urged the don to remember that he was free and that his tribulations were over, and to feel the sun and the gentle trade winds on his face. The world had moved on, turned over a new leaf, and Don Benito should as well. He responded, disconsolately, that the world was not human and had no memory. Delano asked, "You are saved; what has cast such a shadow upon you?" Don Benito answered with two words, "The negro," and went silent.[36] Within three months, Don Benito Cereno, ship's captain, was dead of grief. Today, we might say that Cereno suffered from posttraumatic stress disorder (PTSD) or that he had been tortured. In fact, he had been used as a cat's-paw, terrorized, emasculated, even raped, psychologically if not physically, by those in the world he least respected. For white slave masters, being dominated by blacks was so devastating that death was welcome for the end it brought to humiliation and sadness.

Alexander Hamilton: POWER and Authority in Government

The Jeffersonian or southern vision of the American future, focused on agriculture, states' rights, and a limited federal government, was polluted by slavery. Government's power and authority were modest, but government licensed authoritarian powers to its plantation elite. The Hamiltonian or northern vision assumed that a more powerful national government would promote finance, trade, and manufactures. The northern vision permitted but did not depend upon slavery; its flaws were embedded in a competitive individualism that pressed heavily on the poor, women, and even children. As Bernard Weisberger observed, "Hamilton saw society as a theater of perpetual conflict rather than cooperation for security."[37] A light touch from government would be more likely to produce chaos than order. Public order, whether in the marketplace or in the public square, had to be created, enforced, and protected.

Hamilton began from a skeptical view of human nature and concluded that an authoritative and powerful national government was required to secure and maintain peace and prosperity. Hamilton warned his fellow delegates to the Constitutional Convention that "mankind in general . . . are vicious—their passions may be operated upon. . . . One great error is that we suppose mankind more honest than they are. Our prevailing passions are ambition and interest, . . . these ever induce us to action."[38] Hence, Hamilton refused to idolize or flatter the people. He observed, "The voice of the people has been said to be the voice of God; and however generally this maxim has been quoted and belicved, it is not true in fact. The people are turbulent and changing; they seldom judge or determine right."[39]

Nonetheless, like others of his generation, Hamilton believed that well-built institutions could secure and defend social, political, and economic order. Madison followed this insight to his historic place as father of the Constitution. Hamilton could as justly be called the father of the American economy. Hamilton envisioned a national economy designed, organized, and regulated by government to foster competitive development of the new nation's human and natural resources. Hamilton believed that Britain's rise to European and then global supremacy began with the founding of the Bank of England in 1694. The bank both fueled the Industrial Revolution in England during the middle decades of the eighteenth century and provided a source of credit for the government. Hamilton advocated a Bank of the United States to facilitate commercial and manufacturing activity, to provide a source of public credit to the government, and to manage the currency and credit of the private economy. He also sought to define and control the postwar public debt, whether owed by the national government or by the state governments, to create a consolidated national debt. The revenue required to fund the debt would come principally from tariffs on imported goods. This tariff wall would also serve to protect nascent American manufactures from foreign competition until they could get established.

When President Washington organized his first administration, he made Jefferson secretary of state and Hamilton secretary of the treasury. Congress asked the treasury secretary how an efficient national economy might be organized, and he answered over the course of nearly two years in three brilliant state papers. The first dealt with the means of establishing the nation's currency and credit markets, the second dealt with the need for a banking system, and the third discussed how to stimulate manufacturing in the new economy. These three reports to the Congress provide the foundation for Hamilton's lasting reputation as the father of the American economy. As Weisberger wrote, "Hamilton already had an uncanny anticipation of a national economy in which encouragement to the investing classes, a numerical minority, would generate productivity that would enhance everyone's well-being—but it necessarily meant allowing room at the top for fortunes to be made by the few."[40]

Hamilton's great insight was that funding the debt at par, meaning at the face value of the notes rather than at the deeply discounted rates at which they had recently traded, would create pools of active capital in a nation that had little. Rather than wait for capital to accumulate slowly over time, Hamilton proposed using the debt as a substitute for capital and currency. He noted, "In countries in which the national debt is properly funded, and an object of established confidence, it answers most of the purposes of money."[41] With the English model in mind, Hamilton proposed to reconfigure the debt as interest-bearing bonds that might be held for the interest payments like modern treasury bonds or traded in the marketplace like modern currency.

The English model also envisioned a national bank. Stable and well-managed banks, Hamilton argued, "increase the active capital of a country . . . and [keep] the money itself in a state of incessant activity." Moreover, "banks in good credit can circulate a far greater sum than the actual quantum of their capital in Gold & Silver . . . at the proportions of two and three to one." Hence, Hamilton assured the Congress, "by contributing to enlarge the mass of industrious and commercial enterprise, banks become nurseries of national wealth."[42] Hamilton's goal was to raise the discounted value of the debt by promising secure government funding, thereby creating new wealth and new mobile capital, and then leveraging the economic impact of the new capital by a factor of two or three through the creation of a national bank.

Finally, Hamilton believed that government, especially the government of a developing nation, could and should nurture, encourage, and direct economic development. Manufacturing stood in particular need of protection and support. Hence, Hamilton favored the aggressive use of tariffs and bounties to protect and foster the rise of manufactures in America. Hamilton noted in the "Report on Manufactures" that "minds of the strongest and most active powers" thrive in a diverse economy. "When all the different kinds of industry obtain in a community, each individual can find his proper element, and can call into activity the whole vigour of his nature."[43]

Nonetheless, Hamilton elsewhere made clear that market incentives to good and wise conduct might sometimes be insufficient. Then the appropriate source of constraint on the human passions and interests, in Hamilton's view, was government and law forcefully applied. Hamilton believed, "Government supposes controul. It is the POWER by which individuals in society are kept from doing injury to each other and are bro't to co-operate to a common end."[44] Hamilton was convinced that people only had meaningful rights under a strong government. If government was weak or if its legitimacy was questioned, then people's rights were at risk. Hence, Hamilton believed that "the rights of government are as essential to be defended as the rights of individuals. The security of the one is inseparable from that of the other."[45] Jefferson liked a little rebellion now and then. Hamilton definitely did not.

Some of Hamilton's strongest statements on the nature and authority of government came in 1794 during the Whiskey Rebellion. In 1791, on Hamilton's recommendation, Congress had passed a tax on domestically distilled spirits. The tax sparked rebellion in newly settled western Pennsylvania and threatened to spread. The whiskey rebels took up arms and attacked the fortified home of a federal tax collector. Hamilton declared it "*inherent* in the very *definition* of government . . . that every power vested in a government is in its nature *sovereign*, and includes, by the *force* of [that] *term*, a right to employ all the *means* requisite."[46] Hamilton urged Washington to raise a federal army to put down the rebels. Instead, Washington called the militia of five states into federal service, personally leading a force of 13,000 men into the backcountry. Hamilton and Virginia governor Henry Lee were Washington's immediate subordinates. Resistance collapsed, Washington pardoned most of the rebels, and federal authority was upheld. Hamilton was not entirely satisfied. When President Washington withdrew, leaving Hamilton and Lee in charge of the mop-up, Hamilton had 100 rebel leaders locked up, intending to make a more striking example of them, but Washington again stayed his hand. In Hamilton's view, power not used cannot awe and eventually will atrophy. He meant that power should be well and publicly exercised.

Balancing Freedom and Order in the New Nation

Washington and Hamilton knew that the government could not allow its laws to be challenged directly. They also knew that life in the backcountry, life at and beyond the settlement line, was harsh and dangerous. At the administration's request, Congress had placed a tax on whiskey, the backcountry had resisted, and Washington led a show of force to maintain the new government's authority. Nonetheless, the whiskey tax remained hard to collect, many frontiersmen ignored it without resorting to violence, and the tax was rescinded in 1801 as one of the first acts of the Jefferson administration. How and how vigorously to enforce law on the frontier remained a concern of government and a theme of novels throughout the nineteenth century.

During the colonial and early national periods, settlers poured over the mountains, first into western New York, western Pennsylvania, and the Carolina backcountry and then into the territories of Kentucky and Tennessee. Once the Constitution was in place, the new federal government had to define in law and policy how and on what terms it would make land available to settlers. Land in the woods represented independence and opportunity for most Americans. Nonetheless, influence by speculators and the government's need for revenue led in 1785 and again in the famous Northwest Ordinance of 1787 to the adoption of a policy that required the public domain to be surveyed and divided into townships of six square miles each. Each township was then divided into sections of 640 acres, or one square mile, and sold at public auction for not less than one dollar per acre. Congress knew that the large plot size of 640 acres meant that most sales would be made to wealthy speculators and land companies. The hope was that the initial purchasers would repackage their large tracts into smaller units, provide credit, and sell them to individual farmers, thus saving the government the administrative burden of overseeing small sales and time payments.

The federal government controlled the unsettled lands in the West, and the state governments controlled the unsettled lands within their boundaries. New York, Pennsylvania, Virginia, the Carolinas, and Georgia all contained extensive unsettled lands, and just as the federal government sold the lands in the West, states sold their unsettled lands to investors who in turn sold off parts of their larger holdings to settlers. James Fenimore Cooper's father, William Cooper, was one such investor in New York State. The first book of the Leatherstocking series, *The*

Pioneers, was a fictionalized retelling of William Cooper's founding of Cooperstown, New York, in the mid-1780s. Cooperstown was a frontier outpost, located in Otsego County, near the source of the Susquehanna River, in west-central New York. The story was set in 1793, about seven years after William Cooper bought the land and three years after he moved his family, including one-year-old James Fenimore, to the raw frontier town.

In *The Pioneers*, the founding family's name was changed from Cooper to Temple and the town's name to Templeton. Cooper's role as founder and principal landowner was filled by Judge Marmaduke Temple. The judge owned a track of 100,000 acres (156.25 square miles, or an area of about 12 miles by 13 miles), his grand but rough home dominated the forty buildings that made up Templeton, and he sold homestead plots to settlers and rented to others. Judge Temple was one of the leading men in central New York, a member of the state legislature, and an entrepreneur determined to bring order and development to this still only partially settled portion of the state. As the town's leading figure and judge, he decided disputes, formally and informally, and funded the construction of local churches, schools, and public buildings. His leadership was personalistic, and hierarchy was still an underlying assumption of his time, but he was fair and generous and understood himself to be building toward regular political and legal institutions. Among the longtime inhabitants of the region were Natty Bumppo and Chingachgook, now called Indian John, both in their early seventies. Natty had long been the best hunter and woodsman in the region, honest and direct, but sullen and resentful of the changes occurring around him. Indian John had adopted some of the white man's ways, including a vague Christianity that still found room for the Great Spirit, and a taste for liquor. He was sad, tired, and broken.

The Pioneers presented a fascinating picture of the clash between freedom and order, liberty and the rule of law, the frontier and the village life that pursued it and pushed it onward. The story opened when Judge Temple and his daughter, Elizabeth, about eighteen and just returned to Templeton from four years at school in New York City, encountered Natty and his young associate Oliver Edwards. Natty and Edwards were pursuing a deer. The judge, hearing a commotion in the woods, exited his carriage with his gun, and they all fired at the deer. A friendly squabble ensued over whose shot actually killed the deer, but an underlying tension was evident. The judge, a good and good-humored man but used to the deference that his wealth and status commanded, claimed that it might have been his shot that felled the deer. Natty and Edwards also claimed the deer, with Natty saying, "although I am a poor man, . . . I don't love to give up my lawful dues in a free country. Though, for the matter of that, might often makes right here, . . . for what I can see." Natty had acted according to his own good and sound judgment all his life, and now he felt hemmed in. The reason was soon clear: "An air of sullen dissatisfaction pervaded the manner of the hunter. . . . 'Ah! The game is becoming hard to find indeed, Judge, with your clearings and betterments,' said the old hunter with a kind of compelled resignation." Natty's "sullen dissatisfaction" and "compelled resignation" reflected his knowledge that his world was receding and the judge's was coming on fast. This banter ended abruptly with the discovery that one of the judge's shots had wounded young Edwards, though not dangerously.

The judge's response to wounding Edwards was rich with the privilege of position and power. He promised Edwards medical care in his own home until he recovered and the privilege of hunting on his land in perpetuity. The judge majestically declared, "I here give thee a right to shoot deer, or bears, or anything thou pleaseth in my woods, forever. Leatherstocking is the only other man that I have granted the same privilege to, and the time is coming when it will be of value." Natty listened to the judge's generous offer to Edwards, which was accompanied by a $100 banknote to buy the dead deer (vastly beyond its real value). Perhaps encouraged by being mentioned in the judge's soliloquy, he responded, "There's them living who say that Nathaniel Bumppo's right to shoot on these hills is of older date than Marmaduke Temple's right to forbid him."[47] Temple, of course, had not forbidden Natty to hunt on his land; in fact, he had specifically and generally authorized him to, but that nettled Natty. Natty was arguing a prior claim, a public and general natural right to hunt on open land. The judge was arguing an owner's private right to allow or to exclude others as he saw fit; he had allowed Natty and now Edwards, but he was declaring his sovereign legal right to exclude others, and that brought a scowl to the old hunter's face.

After Edwards had been stitched up and had left the judge's house, the judge's estate manager and cousin, Richard Jones, argued that the judge had been too lenient with both Natty and Edwards. Jones demanded, "Well, 'duke, . . . do you not own the mountains as well as the valleys? Are not the woods your own? What right has this chap, or the Leatherstocking, to shoot in your woods without your permission?"

Later, the judge replied, "he has a kind of natural right to gain a livelihood in these mountains."[48] Temple understood and respected the fact that Natty had a claim to use the woods as he had for so long, but he understood better than Natty did that the day when elite discretion could decide such issues was ending. The judge, in his capacity as a state legislator, had supported passage of hunting and land-use laws that prohibited killing deer during the breeding season. The judge explained to Natty that these laws "were loudly called for, by judicious men." The judge's "judicious men" were, undoubtedly, propertied men wishing to hold their property more securely, more exclusively, but to Natty they were the men who put might over right. Natty appealed to usage, saying, "You may make your laws, Judge. . . . Game is game, and he who finds may kill; that has been the law in these mountains for forty years." The judge responded with reference to legal rights and court enforcement: "I hope to live to see the day when a man's rights in his game shall be as much respected as his title to his farm." Natty would have none of it, declaring, "Your titles and your farms are all new together, . . . it's the farmers that makes the game scarce, and not the hunters."[49] Marmaduke Temple knew and Natty Bumppo feared that the days in which farmers and their property rights would hold sway over untrammeled hunters in the open woods were imminent.

Those days arrived with force when Natty and Indian John, despite Edwards's warning them against it, killed a deer in clear violation of the new laws. Elizabeth and the judge sought to manage the situation on Natty's behalf; the law would have to be acknowledged, but it was expected that an admission of wrongdoing and a modest fine might set things right. Natty, however, was unrepentant, and when officials arrived at his cabin to investigate, he held them off with a rifle and forced them to retreat. In the eyes of Temple and most of the townspeople, Natty's resort to his rifle changed the situation entirely. As a local lawyer observed, "Assaulting a magistrate in the execution of his duty and menacing a constable with firearms . . . is a pretty serious affair, and is punishable with both fine and imprisonment." The judge himself, beseeched for leniency by Edwards, countered, "Would any society be tolerable, young man, where the ministers of justice are to be opposed by men armed with rifles? Is it for this that I have tamed the wilderness?" Natty, of course, would have scorned the idea that Marmaduke Temple had tamed the wilderness, but the judge was right in a sense. He had brought the law, and he meant to enforce it, even over his own preferences, saying, "I must be governed by the law. . . . My private feelings must not enter into— . . . "[50]

Natty was arrested, tried, and sentenced to one hour in the public stocks, a month in jail, and a fine of $100. The stocks, like the scaffold on which Hester Prynne was displayed, were a device for public humiliation, which affected the old hunter deeply. And he did not have the $100 to pay the fine or the means to earn that sum while in jail. He escaped, intending to earn $100 by trapping so he could pay his fine, but he was sidetracked by a forest fire that threatened Elizabeth and Oliver Edwards and that Indian John let himself succumb to in order to end a life of which he had grown tired. Natty's heroics earned him a pardon, but his days in the clutches of law and civilization were over. Despite the objections of Elizabeth and Oliver, who were about to be married and who hoped to make his old age comfortable, Natty determined to go once again into the woods. He explained, "I'm weary of living in clearings and where the hammer is sounding in my ears from sunrise to sundown. . . . I crave to go into the woods ag'in, I do." In the final sentence of *The Pioneers,* Cooper explained that Natty "[had] gone far towards the setting sun—the foremost in that band of pioneers who are opening the way for the march of the nation across the continent."[51] Before the year 1793 was out, Natty Bumppo was into the Ohio Territory, and the new century found him in the shadow of the Rockies.

The most distinctive, even unusual, of Cooper's Leatherstocking series was the third, *The Prairie.* Natty, now called the Old Trapper, in his early eighties, still lean, capable, and wise but slower, was in the Far West, probably what is now western Nebraska or Wyoming. The novel is set in 1805, just two years after Jefferson purchased the territory from Napoleon, when the Indian tribes were at their full strength. The only whites in the area, besides the Old Trapper, were army explorers, including the Lewis and Clark Expedition, and four wagons containing the family and goods of Ishmael Bush. The Bush clan was made up of Ishmael, about fifty; his wife, Esther; several adult sons and a brood of younger siblings; Esther's brother; and Ellen, a cousin. The Bushes, save for Ellen, were rough and uncivilized, the detritus pushed on by the advance of civilization. Though very different men, both the Old Trapper and Ishmael Bush rankled under the law and civilization, and they moved west as soon as the leading edge of civilization reached them.

Ishmael and the Old Trapper met soon after Indians had stolen Bush's livestock. Initially, Ishmael suspected that the trapper might be in league with the Indians, so they shared background stories to get to know each other and settle doubts. Ishmael explained that he and his family had come west to escape the bonds of civilization: "I found the law sitting too tight upon me, and am not over fond of neighbors who can't settle a dispute without troubling a justice and twelve men." Much later in the tale, the Old Trapper offered similar reservations about the law and the justice of the settlements, explaining what had happened to him a decade earlier in Templeton: "Ay, court-houses. . . . I was carried into one of the lawless holes myself once, and it was all about a thing of no more value than the skin of a deer. The Lord forgive them! . . . And yet it was a solemn sight to see an aged man, who had always lived in the air, laid neck and heels by the law, and held up as a spectacle for the women and boys of a wasteful settlement to point their fingers at!"[52]

While the Old Trapper's experience of the settlements and their laws was still raw, he had learned over his long life that they had value for some. Undoubtedly thinking far back to his own experience with Mabel Dunham, who had chosen Jasper Western over him, he asked Ellen, "Did you not know that when you crossed the big river you left a friend behind you that is always bound to look to the young and feeble like yourself?" She asked, "Of whom do you speak?" The trapper responded, "The law—'tis bad to have it, but I sometimes think it is worse to be entirely without it. . . . Yes—yes, the law is needed when such as have not the gifts of strength and wisdom are to be taken care of." Later he advised Paul Hover, who was tracking the Bush family to recover Ellen, to think of her needs, telling him, "It has become your duty to consider her, as well as yourself, in setting forth in life. You are a little given to skirting the settlements; but to my poor judgment, the girl would be more like a flourishing flower in the sun of a clearing, than in the winds of a prairie. Therefore, . . . turn your mind on the ways of the inner country."[53] If the Old Trapper had heeded his own advice, his life might have been quite different. As it was, Natty Bumppo died, facing west and with the setting sun on his face, full of years and satisfied, at the end of *The Prairie*.

Natty Bumppo knew that law was necessary, but he also knew that it was not always just. Herman Melville, perhaps the greatest American novelist of the nineteenth century, also explored the necessity and the shortcomings of law. For Melville, going to sea meant renouncing individual freedom, choice, and volition for obedience to authority. In both *Billy Budd* and *Moby Dick*, the individual stripped of choice, discretion, and agency was more radically subject to fate than he otherwise would be. A bad captain, like Ahab, monomaniacal, driven, and obsessed, exercised undisputed sway, even as fellow officers and subordinates smelled doom. Even a good captain, as the Honorable Edward Fairfax Vere surely was in *Billy Budd*, may be subject to forces and fates that he cannot control. Good men, upholding rules in which they believe, sometimes knowingly do wrong in a particular case—as in Billy's case.

Billy Budd was a young English sailor, twenty-one years old, in the summer of 1797. Inbound to England on the merchantman *Rights of Man*, the ship was hailed and boarded by officers of HMS *Indomitable*. The *Indomitable* had put to sea shorthanded and had boarded the *Rights of Man* to exercise the king's right to impress seamen as needed for naval duty. The *Indomitable* took only one seaman, the *Rights of Man*'s best, Billy Budd. Billy was a striking figure, admired and beloved by officers and men on the *Rights of Man* and soon, though not universally, on the *Indomitable*. Billy was "happily endowed with the gaiety of high health, youth, and a free heart." He was handsome, pure, and honest; he "was a foundling," an orphan, but "no ignoble one. Noble descent was as evident in him as in a blood horse." But as pure, honest, and beautiful as Billy was, he had flaws that would prove his undoing. They were not the normal flaws of low-born sailors, drinking, gambling, whoring—rather, Billy was passive and trusting. Melville wrote, "He was, without knowing it, practically a fatalist."[54] He floated along, doing what was asked of him, even to the point of "[making] no demur" when he was removed from the *Rights of Man* to the *Indomitable*. Moreover, Billy, although alert and intelligent, was "a sort of upright barbarian," illiterate but pure of heart, with a singular natural flaw: "Under sudden provocation of strong heart-feeling his voice . . . was apt to develop . . . a stutter or even worse."[55]

Billy's open and trusting nature made him easy prey for John Claggart, the ship's master-at-arms, and his tools. Claggart "looked like a man of high quality, social and moral," but in fact, he was what we might today call a sociopath. Melville explained, drawing on Plato's description of "natural depravity," that for some men, like Claggart, "though the man's even temper and discreet bearing would seem to intimate a mind peculiarly subject to the law of reason, not the less in heart he would seem to riot in complete exemption from that law, having apparently little to do with reason further than . . . the accomplishment of an aim which in wantonness of atrocity would seem to partake of the insane."[56] The presence of natural depravity made the world a particularly random and dangerous place; how does one plan and prepare, and why should one work hard, save, and invest, if depravity lurks? Melville asked, "What can more partake of the mysterious than an antipathy spontaneous and profound such as is evoked in certain exceptional mortals by the mere aspect of some other mortal, however harmless he may be, if not called forth by this very harmlessness itself?"[57]

The inevitable conflict between Claggart and Billy was produced by Claggart's scheme to have Billy accused and convicted of treason. One of Claggart's associates surreptitiously approached Billy to say that there was a gang of impressed seamen on board and urged Billy to join them; for what purpose was not said because Billy denounced and threatened the emissary before he could finish. Thinking the exchange dealt with, Billy said nothing and later was accused by Claggart of conspiracy. Billy and Claggart were brought before Captain Vere, where the accusations were declared to Billy's face. Billy, caught unaware, was so emotionally overwrought that his occasional stutter was aggravated to total, protracted, speechlessness. Billy stood mute, his outrage growing, until, unable to speak, he lashed out at his accuser, striking and killing him with a single blow. Vere, suspicious from the beginning of Claggart's charges, knowing Billy and thinking well of him, was amazed at Billy's natural but barbaric response to his inability to defend himself verbally against the unjust charges. Vere was a good and fair man, an intellectual and a gentleman, and loved Billy as so many others did, but he stood as captain of a naval ship at sea in time of war. As the blow was struck, "'Fated boy,' breathed Captain Vere in tone so low as to be almost a whisper, 'what have you done!'" Soon thereafter, the captain exclaimed, "Struck dead by an angel of God! Yet the angel must hang!"[58]

When Claggart fell, both Billy and Vere knew what had to happen thereafter. Billy and "every sailor, too, is accustomed to obey orders without debating them; his life afloat is externally ruled for him." Vere reasoned that "irrespective of the provocation to the blow, a martial court must needs in the present case confine its attention to the blow's consequence. . . . The prisoner's deed—with that alone we have to do."[59] When Billy testified that he had eaten the king's bread and been loyal to him, despite Claggart's claims, Vere responded, "I believe you, my man." But Vere's understanding of Billy's innocence could make no difference. As Melville summarized the principle involved: "The essential right and wrong involved in the matter, the clearer that might be, so much the worse for the responsibility of a loyal sea commander, inasmuch as he was not authorized to determine the matter on that primitive basis." Like the simple seamen, Captain Vere told his officers, "in receiving our commissions we in the most important regards ceased to be natural free-agents."[60]

Billy understood as well as Vere that because he had struck down an officer of the king's navy in time of war, he must hang. Billy's last words on the morning he was hung were "God bless Captain Vere." Though we can, along with Billy and Vere, understand the importance of rules and discipline in a military setting, we still resist the obvious injustice of a man falsely accused being hung for striking down his accuser. But Hamilton, Cooper, and Melville urge us to think again. Hamilton knew that the whiskey rebels of western Pennsylvania were just aggrieved farmers, but when they bore rifles against the federal government, he was for swift punishment lest others get the idea that resistance of law might work. Cooper knew that as soon as Natty trained his rifle on the magistrates, he was headed for the stocks and jail. Melville pointed out that even in the absence of natural depravity, freedom unconstrained by tradition and law would be chaotic and perhaps barbaric.

Conclusion

The Founders offered a view of human nature, society, and government that has charmed many from their day to ours. Jefferson spoke for the rising nation's best self, saying that "all men are created equal, that they are endowed by their Creator with certain unalienable Rights, that among these are Life, Liberty, and the pursuit of Happiness." In his less poetic moments he declared that society had a natural aristocracy of wealth and education and that it would be well if they led. More broadly, the best social science of the day, faculty psychology, declared that all men were moved by reason, passions, and interests, but that only a few well-cultured men consistently allowed reason to guide their passions and interests. Madison thought that well-built institutions would sift for society's best men and check and balance the powers of government to produce stability and prosperity.

At the elite level, Hamilton challenged Jefferson's very attractive vision, warning that men were seldom moved by the common good, and that, far more frequently, they were driven by personal passions and interests. Self-interest might lead men to work, save, and invest, but when it led them to unlawful behavior, as when the whiskey rebels challenged the nation's tax laws, force was Hamilton's recourse. Jefferson disagreed, warning against breaking the spirit of a free people, but Washington knew that freedom and order were always in a delicate balance.

Outside and below the elite debate between Jeffersonians and Hamiltonians rose a chorus of voices that challenged Jefferson's bucolic vision. Abigail Adams, though she liked Jefferson far better than she did Hamilton, agreed with Hamilton's psychology in her opinion that "all Men would be tyrants if they could." Moreover, a series of novels set in the early national period rejected the complacency of faculty psychology, denied the claim that among a white governing elite reason would guide and control passions and interests. William Wells Brown's *Clotel*, aimed directly at Jefferson and the southern elite, showed passion overwhelming reason and conscience as wealthy white men bid for and drooled over light-skinned women at auction. Two novels by Herman Melville, *Benito Cereno* and *Billy Budd*, highlighted the dangerous presence of evil in the world. In *Benito Cereno*, Captain Amasa Delano was described as a good, warmhearted, trusting man unaccustomed to thinking ill of others. Blacks he saw as limited creatures requiring firm but gentle guidance. These Jeffersonian assumptions blinded him to the horrific slave revolt and massacre that had befallen Captain Cereno and his crew. Even more strikingly, *Billy Budd* made the point that natural depravity stalked the world. Some men, like Master-at-Arms Claggart, seemed moved by reason but were actually sociopaths whose only use for reason was to further the pursuit of evil ends. Of what use, then, were Jefferson's confidence and Madison's careful checks and balances if malevolence could mask its presence until it was too late for good men to defend themselves?

Melville's defense against the presence of evil in the world, as it had been Hawthorne's in *The Scarlet Letter* and Cooper's in *The Pioneers* and *The Prairie*, was law forcefully applied. Captain Vere knew that Billy was an innocent, if not innocent of striking Claggart dead, but, regretfully, he hung him anyway, for a violation of military law in time of war. Similarly, Judge Temple, thinking of the aging Natty Bumppo as a kind of innocent as well, moved to protect him from harsh legal consequences for killing a deer out of season. But when Natty lowered his rifle on officials come to investigate the crime, Judge Temple, like Captain Vere, and like Washington and Hamilton in regard to the whiskey rebels, felt that they had to stand up and defend law and order. In fact, very late in his long life, even Natty came to understand the need for law. He told both Ellen and her betrothed, Paul Hover, that while the law was troublesome to the man alone, it represented protection for the young, the weak, and women.

As the new nation moved deeper into the nineteenth century, the day of the "upright barbarian," the man alone, even an open, honest, and trustworthy one, was receding. Natty Bumppo and Billy Budd were natural, untrammeled men, loved and admired until they ran afoul of the law; then they were seen as limited and anachronistic. Natty explained to Hover that in taking Ellen, he gave up his natural right to roam beyond the reach of law and civilization. The lure of the forest and the trail had always been paramount for Natty, but he counseled Paul, like Natty in many ways, that "the girl would be more like a flourishing flower in the sun of a clearing, than in the winds of a prairie. Therefore, . . . turn your mind on the ways of the inner country." One assumes, though the story does not say, that Paul Hover, like Jasper Western, did look to "the inner country"—to the settlements, with their peace and security, their farms, their schools, and their churches—to build a life and family.

4 | Democracy and Melancholy: The Visions and Fears of Emerson, Melville, and Lincoln

Society is full of excitement: competition comes in place of monopoly; and intelligence and industry ask only for fair play and an open field.
—Daniel Webster, 1823–1824

The middle decades of the nineteenth century, from the rise of Andrew Jackson to the assassination of Abraham Lincoln, spanned the boisterous adolescence of the American Dream. Jackson (1767–1845) promised that every white man willing to earn bread by the sweat of his brow would enjoy a full and honorable role in the civic life of his community. While land in the woods was still the dream of most, the sense of agrarian limits began to fall away as men looked to new opportunities in business, trade, and manufactures. Americans saw an endlessly promising future in a nation that was both pushing steadily westward and pulling the three great regions, North, South, and West, together with bands of water and steel.

The progress of Abraham Lincoln (1809–1865)—from rail-splitter to store clerk to law student and political candidate on his way to becoming a successful railroad lawyer and candidate for the nation's highest offices—seemed a glowing vindication of Jackson's promise. But the mature Lincoln saw further than Jackson and sought to use government to expand opportunity into new realms. Lincoln believed that men and women who sweat for bread, irrespective of their color, deserved the full benefit of their labor. Yet even Lincoln was not ready to endorse social equality for blacks.

Despite Lincoln's slow coming to support of black freedom, antebellum America was a white man's nation. Indians were driven beyond the Mississippi during the 1830s. Slavery's grip was tightened as the Civil War approached, and every social, political, and legal effort was made to teach free blacks, northern and southern, that they were not Americans in any meaningful sense of the word. Women won a few legal victories beginning in the late 1830s, mostly on property rights, but were denied full civic and suffrage rights. The broad achievement of freedom and opportunity for white men made the exclusion of women and minorities even more glaring as Lincoln rose to the task of redefining human rights in America.

Perhaps not surprisingly, the decline of traditional hierarchies weakened the limits that faith and community had earlier placed on competition. The consequent scramble and rude separation of winners and losers produced a broad melancholy not previously seen in American life. In politics, the struggle and sadness of Jackson's life, especially after the death of his beloved wife, Rachel, and the pathos so frequently noted as a major element of Lincoln's personality suggest the tensions in antebellum life. In literature, the American Renaissance posed the enthusiasts, Walt Whitman, Ralph Waldo Emerson, and Henry David Thoreau, against the brooders, Nathaniel Hawthorne, Herman Melville, and Emily Dickinson. We focus on Emerson's essays, Thoreau's *Walden* (1854), and Melville's novels, including *Moby Dick* (1851) and *Bartleby, the Scrivener* (1853). In regard to the role of race and slavery, we highlight Mark Twain's *Adventures of Huckleberry Finn* (1883) and *Pudd'nhead Wilson* (1894) and William Faulkner's *Absalom, Absalom!* (1936). In Tocqueville, Emerson, Lincoln, and Melville, among others, we find a melancholy new to American politics and literature.

The Democratic Vision from Jefferson to Jackson

John Adams at ninety and Thomas Jefferson at eighty-three, the second and third presidents of the United States, died within hours of each other on July 4, 1826. The symbolism of these two great men succumbing together on the fiftieth anniversary of the nation's independence produced a sustained period of national introspection and analysis.[1] Massachusetts congressman, soon to be senator, Daniel Webster spoke for a national consensus that the Founders had done their work well. Like so many American leaders, before and after, Webster was certain that the world was watching, declaring, "The world turns hither its solicitous eyes. . . . It cannot be denied . . . that with America, and in America, a new era commences in human affairs. . . . If we cherish the virtues and the principles of our fathers, Heaven will assist us to carry on the work of human liberty and human happiness."[2]

Though widely praised and deeply admired, Jefferson and Adams passed from a world that had become increasingly foreign to them. Just eighteen months before his death, Jefferson lamented in correspondence with an old friend, "All, all dead, and ourselves left alone amidst a new generation whom we know not, and who knows not us."[3] Jefferson still viewed the world through the lens of faculty psychology, which held that only a few superior men were guided by reason while most were at the mercy of their interests and passions. Hence, he was deeply dismayed by the rise of a raucous partisan politics that seemed to deny the very existence of a natural aristocracy and perhaps even of a common good or public interest. Martin Van Buren and those around him in the Jackson movement were the first to understand that well-organized political parties could be permanent vehicles for contesting elections, winning office, and enacting the views of the majority, even a narrow partisan majority, into law.

The Jeffersonian dream had been of a bountiful country that would provide sufficiency and even plenty to all who were willing to work. A productive agricultural economy, in which land was cheap and easily available, also ensured good wages for young laborers and a market for the products of village craftsmen and urban merchants. Once Jefferson made peace with the idea that manufacturing, as well as commerce and agriculture, was required to make America a self-sufficient society, his domestic vision became one of a balanced and diversified economy of competitive small producers. Decentralized competition promised widespread opportunity without runaway jealousy, competition, and greed. Foresight, planning, and careful accumulation might lead beyond sufficiency to comfort and even plenty, but sufficiency was the promise and the general expectation.[4]

The Jacksonians tried to hold to these traditional Jeffersonian ideals, but they were overwhelmed by the onrush of a vastly more competitive and entrepreneurial age. Antebellum America was a place of immense energy. Most Americans were confident that the day of the common man had arrived, that the world was new, and that the opportunities for growth, improvement, and achievement had no limits near enough that a man need worry about them. Encomiums to the boundless optimism and enthusiasm of the age filled the popular press and found resonance in the elite opinion and literature of the day. A long article published in the *New York Sun* in 1838 celebrated the new age of equality and individualism. "Boys . . . are educated in the belief that every man must be the architect of his own future. . . . Dreams of ambition or of wealth" danced in the head of every American boy. "There is scarcely a lad of any spirit who does not, from the time that he can connect the most simple ideas, picture to himself some rapid road to wealth."[5] Richard Hofstadter has described "the typical American" of the second quarter of the nineteenth century as "an expectant capitalist, a hardworking, ambitious person for whom enterprise was a kind of religion, and everywhere he found conditions that encouraged him to extend himself."[6]

Jackson himself rose from obscurity. Orphaned early and thinly educated, he arrived in Nashville, Tennessee, at twenty-one and immersed himself in the western scramble for wealth, prominence, and prestige. While the economic turmoil of the frontier left Jackson in debt well into his forties, prominence and prestige came early. He was a congressman, a federal judge, and a senator in his thirties and the architect of the smashing American victory in the Battle of New Orleans in his forties. Thereafter, he was simply known as "the hero" by his friends and supporters. As the revolutionary generation passed from politics, the nascent democratic forces of the day rallied around Jackson. Once he was elected president, "the hero" was referred to simply as "the government."[7]

Jackson believed that all that stood in the way of the hopeful and expectant many were the pampered and privileged few.[8] "The real people" or "the producing classes" were the planters and farmers, small merchants and businessmen, craftsmen and mechanics, who raised, made, or sold real goods, usually in the local marketplace. These virtuous citizens were simple, hardworking, frugal, honest, and self-reliant. Their wealth grew incrementally. Opposed to "the producing classes" were the "non-producing classes" who lived by promotion, trade, and speculation in paper representations of real assets. These were men with soft hands and hard hearts. They were the bankers, merchants, land speculators, and corporate stockjobbers who benefited by the mysteries of finance at the expense of those who grew the crops and built the machines. President Jackson also believed that the nonproducing classes, with their command of the economic and social high ground of corporations, colleges, and churches, bent politics, law, and policy to their advantage. He declared in the famous message vetoing the recharter of the Bank of the United States that "it would be an unqualified blessing" if government "would confine itself to equal protection, and, as Heaven does its rains, shower its favors alike on the high and the low, the rich and the poor."[9]

Orestes A. Brownson, Jacksonian minister, author, and editor, summarized the major political and policy turn of the period by declaring, "We believe property should be held subordinate to man, and not man to property, and therefore that it is always lawful to make such modifications of [property's] constitution as the good of Humanity requires."[10] But as Brownson well knew, property had the means to defend itself and win advantages. Brownson's image of a balance between human rights and property rights, between the man and the dollar, would be a continuous theme in partisan politics for the next century and more. The Jacksonian dream was of free white men, competing on a fair field, without artificial penalty or privilege, for the benefits held out by a boundlessly wealthy continent.

The Democratic Party of Andrew Jackson and his lieutenants, Martin Van Buren and James K. Polk, tried to adhere to the Jeffersonian vision. Jackson moved systematically, much as Jefferson had three decades earlier, to kill the Bank of the United States, reduce the tariff, and limit federal spending on internal improvements. The Democrat's Whig opponents carried forward Hamilton's vision of a more dynamic, complex, and differentiated economy of farmers, merchants, and mechanics. The Whigs' principal leader in the second quarter of the nineteenth century was congressman and then senator Henry Clay of Kentucky. Clay advocated the more open, entrepreneurial ethic then rising in society. He described a sharper social and economic conflict in which an open continent welcomed the efforts of the talented and hardworking and in which those who failed had only themselves to blame.[11]

In the decades before the Civil War, free white men, both native and immigrant, saw opportunity everywhere. Moreover, opportunity existed on a modest scale that common men approached with confidence. Most men were farmers, and land was always available in the West. Most businesses were sole proprietorships or partnerships, and the owners provided the capital. Proprietors were usually merchants or master craftsmen, and their employees were, formally or informally, apprentices learning the business or trade before launching out on their own. But by midcentury disruptive changes were afoot. Technological developments allowed businesses that had been local, or at most regional, to move goods more cheaply and at greater speeds over long distances and to communicate instantaneously with distant suppliers and buyers.

Bigger businesses required more capital and new forms of organization. The corporate form allowed multiple investors to pool their capital for a particular business endeavor without encumbering all their assets or being fully and personally responsible for the conduct or financial fate of the business.

Fundamentally, life sped up in antebellum America, and the forces active in society got bigger, stronger, and more complex. To some the new size and speed spelled opportunity, but for many it was disturbing, even threatening. Farmers and craftsmen who worked on their own account, owned their own tools, and set their own schedules were proud of their independence and autonomy. They felt a threatening loss of control when shops and factories set their hours, owned the machines on which they worked, paid them a fixed wage, and fired them when they were no longer needed. To many, the very equality that characterized the age of Jackson seemed endangered by these developments. It was not just that the nation was booming; the scale of business, the ferocity of competition, and the rewards of winning were all burgeoning. Hence, equality of opportunity came under pressure from the growing inequality of results. Everyone dreamed big, a few won big, and many, perhaps most, worried that they might be left behind. Not surprisingly, the noisy dynamism of America captured European attention. Governments, investors, and potential immigrants all wanted to know what was happening in America and what it might mean for them.

Alexis de Tocqueville on America and Democracy

Alexis de Tocqueville's *Democracy in America* (1835) has long been seen as the most insightful book ever written on the American society and democracy. Tocqueville (1805–1859) was a young French nobleman sent by his government to study American prisons, but he interpreted his mandate broadly. He spent nine months, from May 1831 through February 1832, covering a 7,000-mile circuit that took him throughout the East, as far west as Green Bay, and as far south as New Orleans. Tocqueville believed that America and Europe were destined for democracy; America had arrived in the democratic future first, but France and the rest of Europe would surely follow, and the path might be smooth or rocky depending upon whether the Europeans learned from the American experience. Tocqueville hoped that if Europe learned well, it might produce a fuller and richer democracy than the one he studied in America.

Tocqueville declared equality to be America's "ruling passion." In Jacksonian America, Tocqueville said, "equality is the distinguishing characteristic of the age. . . . It creates opinions, gives birth to new sentiments, founds novel customs, and modifies whatever it does not produce."[12] Tocqueville also coined the word "individualism" to help describe what he saw in America. He defined individualism as "a mature and calm feeling, which disposes each member of the community to sever himself from the mass of his fellows and to draw apart with his family and his friends, so that . . . he willingly leaves society at large to itself." Individualism produced in Americans "the habit of always considering themselves as standing alone, and they are apt to imagine that their whole destiny is in their own hands."[13]

Unfortunately, Tocqueville thought, the majestic image of America as a land of unlimited opportunity put great pressure on individuals to succeed in visible, even dramatic, ways. If everyone was on the move, even though there was a continent to be won, those who did not move quickly might be left behind. Tocqueville marveled, "It would be difficult to describe the avidity with which the American rushes forward to secure this immense booty that fortune offers. . . . Before him lies a boundless continent, and he urges onward as if time pressed and he was afraid of finding no room for his exertions." The fear of failure, Tocqueville thought, "may be said to haunt every one of them . . . and to be always flitting before his mind."[14] In the absence of social hierarchy, only wealth gave status, so men worked with dreary determination to acquire and maintain wealth. Tocqueville observed, "It is strange to see with what feverish ardor the Americans pursue their own welfare, and to watch the vague dread that constantly torments them lest they should not have chosen the shortest path which may lead to it." He concluded, "In democratic times . . . man's hopes and desires are oftener blasted, the soul is more stricken and perturbed, and care itself more keen."[15] Tocqueville was among the first to note that as equality and competition spread throughout society, dread and melancholy spread as well. American observers saw this disturbing connection, too.

The American Renaissance: Dreamers and Doubters

The three decades from 1830 to 1860 have been called the American Renaissance because they saw the flowering of a distinctly American, as opposed to British or European, literature. But within the American Renaissance, there were stark differences about what today we would call American exceptionalism. Ralph Waldo Emerson (1803–1882) and Walt Whitman (1819–1892) believed that freedom allowed men to set their own goals as high as they might, while Nathaniel Hawthorne (1804–1864) and Herman Melville (1819–1891) warned that human nature had a darker side that too regularly erupted. Henry David Thoreau (1817–1862) agreed with both, but his memorable solution—to withdraw to Walden Pond—flew in the face of the go-get-'em culture of his day.

The essayist and poet Ralph Waldo Emerson was the preeminent mid-nineteenth-century literary exponent of freedom, opportunity, and wealth, but he shared many of Tocqueville's misgivings about American individualism. In an essay entitled "The American Scholar" (1837), Emerson joined Tocqueville in declaring that a leading "sign of our times . . . is the new importance given to the single person. Every thing . . . tends to insulate the individual,—to surround him with barriers of natural respect, so that each man shall feel the world is his."[16] In "Self-Reliance" (1841), Emerson praised "the self-helping man. For him all doors are flung wide; him all tongues greet, all honors crown, all eyes follow with desire."[17] Emerson believed that American individualism and self-help were underpinned by a universal appreciation of and commitment to work. In Europe, the distain of a leisured elite made work seem an unfortunate necessity of the lower classes. In America, Emerson sang, "I hear . . . with joy . . . of the dignity and necessity of labor to every citizen. . . . Labor is everywhere welcome; always we are invited to work." He assured Americans that "the day is always his who works in it with serenity and great aims."[18] Emerson extolled "the open future expanding here before the eye of every boy to vastness."[19]

Yet like Tocqueville, Emerson worried that with high expectations come keen disappointments. Emerson noted in his diary that "history gave no intimation of any society in which despondency came so readily to heart as we see it & feel it in ours. Young men, young women at thirty & even earlier seem to have lost all spring & vivacity, & if they fail in their first enterprize the rest is rock & shallow."[20] Elsewhere, Emerson explained, though seemingly without knowing it, why failure was so keenly feared and felt in antebellum America. In an essay entitled "The Young American" (1844), he suggested that markets set a fair price on human talent: "Trade goes to . . . bring every kind of faculty of every individual that can in any manner serve any person, *on sale.*"[21] In an essay entitled "Wealth" (1860), he observed, "There is always a reason, *in the man,* for his good or bad fortune, and so in making money."[22] Tremendous opportunity, a continent to be tamed, a world to be built, and achievement all around left no easy place for failure. Individualism and self-help made success a personal triumph, but they just as certainly made failure excruciatingly personal.

Moreover, thoughtful people in the nineteenth century were concerned that failure might befall the strong as well as the weak. Decision and destiny, choice and chance, reason and fate were irrevocably intertwined. A man might choose his course and work toward it with might and main, but accident and fate might intervene to make failure inevitable. Emerson, but also Lincoln and Melville, asked what the interaction of free will and fate meant for choice, planning, effort, and personal responsibility. Emerson preceded his essay "Experience" (1844) with a poem in which he described the "lords of life" as towering above dazed and awed mankind. An abbreviated version of the poem reads

> The lords of life, the lords of life,— . . .
> They marched from east to west:
> Little man, least of all,
> Among the legs of his guardians tall,
> Walked about with puzzled look:—
> Him by the hand dear Nature took; . . .
> Whispered, "Darling, never mind!
> To-morrow they will wear another face,
> The founder thou! These are thy race![23]

In "Experience," Emerson clarified, just a bit, how he saw decision and fate interacting and what he meant by the "lords of life." Emerson described life as "a mixture of power and form." Power Emerson described as "the largest and solemnest things, . . . commerce, government, church, marriage, and so with the history of every man's bread, and the ways by which he is to come by it." Form he described as "Illusion, Temperament, . . . Surprise, Reality, Subjectiveness,—these are threads on the loom of time, these are the lords of life."[24] Today we might call these power and ideology, but either way the "lords of life" were the distribution of power in the world and the construction of our ideas about the world. Emerson described the context within which life is lived as a mixture of power and form, "sweet and sound" only when an ever-elusive, fine balance was maintained. Emerson did not say how "dear Nature" could assure "Little man" that the lords of life would "wear another face," a kinder face, tomorrow.

Henry David Thoreau was one of the singular figures in American letters and quite consciously presented a systematic challenge to Franklin and Emerson and to society's focus on hard work, accumulation, and material success. Thoreau went to Walden Pond to conduct an experiment in minimizing the demands of everyday life in order to clear the mind and expand the soul. In the first paragraph of the first chapter of *Walden*, entitled "Economy," Thoreau said, "I lived alone, in the woods, a mile from any neighbor, in a house which I had built myself, on the shore of Walden Pond, in Concord, Massachusetts, and earned my living by the labor of my hands only. I lived there two years and two months" (March 1845 to May 1847). Thoreau reported that "if one would live simply and eat only the crops which he raised, and raise no more than he ate, . . . he could do all his necessary farm work as it were with his left hand at odd hours in the summer." The "lords of life" thus limited and controlled, Thoreau wrote that "every morning was a cheerful invitation to make my life of equal simplicity, and I may say innocence, with Nature herself." But "Nature herself" was not the main point; nature was the setting, the background, that allowed the mind to clear. In the final chapter of *Walden*, Thoreau advised readers to "be rather the . . . Lewis and Clark . . . of your own streams and oceans; explore your own higher latitudes. . . . Nay, be a Columbus to whole new continents and worlds within you, opening new channels, not to trade, but to thought. . . . Explore the private sea, the Atlantic and Pacific Ocean of one's being alone."[25]

Thoreau's challenge to Franklin's "Way to Wealth" and Emerson's call to work was, in fact, a broader challenge to the Protestant ethic's celebration of work—but Thoreau seemed especially to enjoy skewering Franklin as the exemplar of that ethic. The following are just a few of Thoreau's challenges to Franklin, Emerson, and his fellow citizens:

> Some are "industrious," and appear to love labor for its own sake, . . . to such I have at present nothing to say.

It is not necessary that a man should earn his living by the sweat of his brow, unless he sweats easier than I do.

I love a broad margin to my life.

The day advanced as if to light some work of mine; it was morning, and lo, now it is evening, and nothing memorable is accomplished. . . . I silently smiled at my incessant good fortune.

Why should we be in such desperate haste to succeed . . . ? If a man does not keep pace with his companions, perhaps it is because he hears a different drummer.[26]

Making light of the work ethic was intellectual brush clearing, preparing the ground for his positive message. Thoreau explained that he "went to the woods because I wished to live deliberately, to front only the essential facts of life, and see if I could not learn what it had to teach." What Thoreau learned was "to stand on the meeting of two eternities, the past and the future, which is precisely the present moment; to toe that line." Thoreau recommended "the discipline of looking always at what is to be seen. . . . Read your fate, see what is before you, and walk on into futurity." His point was not that the past and future were not important, but that each moment—the present—must be well used to draw value from the past and prepare for the most fulfilling future. Late in *Walden*, Thoreau concluded, "I learned this, at least, by my experiment: that if one advances confidently in the direction of his dreams, and endeavors to live the life which he has imagined, he will meet with a success unexpected in common hours. . . . If you have built castles in the air, your work need not be lost. . . . Now put the foundations under them."[27]

Hawthorne and Melville rejected Emerson's promise that tomorrow the "lords of life" would wear a more benign, less compulsive face and Thoreau's sense that the world's hurry and bustle could be quieted to allow the mind and spirit to breathe. For them, the transcendental promises of personal definition and development were false. Choice, volition, and agency were too often overwhelmed by the shaping forces of the world—nature, culture, faith, power, law, and chance. Better, Hawthorne and Melville thought, for humans to live within their culture, community, and laws. Obedience was no guarantee of security, but disobedience would eventually be punished—the scales would be rebalanced.

Of Melville's early books, *Typee* (1846) and *Omoo* (1847) were successes, but *Moby Dick* was a magnificent failure. The sprawling and obscure *Moby Dick*, with its long and detailed descriptions of the variety of whales, of sperm whale anatomy, of the details of whaling ship construction, and of the whaling culture, left reviewers and readers cold.[28] *Moby Dick* sold just 1,600 copies in the first two years and then fell into more than a half century of obscurity. A Melville renaissance beginning in the 1920s has allowed *Moby Dick* to outstrip the likes of *The Last of the Mohicans* and even *Uncle Tom's Cabin* to stand nearly alone, perhaps with *The Scarlet Letter* and *The Adventures of Huckleberry Finn*, as a truly great American novel. While *Moby Dick* has always seemed actively to spurn first-time readers, those who persevere through multiple readings are rewarded with remarkable insights into human nature, sanity and insanity, free will, fate, democracy, God, and the world. Frederic Carpenter argued that the dark fatalism so prominent in Melville's novels made him "the greatest critic of the American dream."[29]

Moby Dick described the interplay between Ahab, the captain of the whaling ship *Pequod*; Starbuck, the first mate; the crew; and Moby Dick, the great white whale. Ahab, in his middle to late fifties, with forty years of whaling experience, and Moby Dick, a legend among whalers around the world, had met before. On Ahab's previous voyage, he had harpooned Moby Dick, only to have the enraged leviathan overturn his boat and sever one of his legs. Ahab had recovered physically, though not psychologically, when, with a new crew, he set out on a quest to find and slay Moby Dick. Captain Ahab was the central human figure against whom others were defined and defined themselves. Ahab was a dominant, even colossal, personality driven by an overwhelming, grim determination. Even before the *Pequod* left port, Captain Peleg, one of the owners of the ship, described Ahab as "a grand, ungodly, god-like man." Once the ship was under way, Ishmael, an experienced seaman on his first whaling voyage and the principal narrator of the first half of the book, noted that "the whole grim aspect of Ahab" covered "an infinity of firmest fortitude, a determinate, unsurrenderable willfulness" flowing from "the nameless regal overbearing dignity of some mighty woe."[30]

Ahab's mighty woe arose from having been confronted, defeated, and mangled by Moby Dick. Ahab responded by "yielding up all his thoughts and fancies to his one supreme purpose; that purpose, by his own sheer inveteracy of will, forced itself against gods and devils into a kind of self-assumed, independent being of its own." Ahab knew that he had become deeply, helplessly, obsessed, saying, "I'm demoniac, I am madness maddened!" Starbuck tried to reason with him, as did Captain Boomer of the whaler *Samuel Enderby*, who had lost an arm to Moby Dick and hence had given up the chase. Ahab listened to the captain's advice that the white whale was "best let alone" and responded, "What is best let alone, that cursed thing is not always what least allures." So powerful was the allure that "all the subtle demonisms of life and thought; all evil, to crazy Ahab, were visibly personified, and made practicably assailable in Moby Dick."[31]

Crazy Ahab had made his decision and set his course in pursuit of the white whale, but Melville taught that men's choices were only half, at best, of what determined outcomes; luck, chance, fortune, and fate had a hand as well. He wrote, "Aye, chance, free will, and necessity—no wise incompatible—all interweavingly work together." As a result, Melville warned, "the mingled, mingling threads of life are woven by warp and woof: calms crossed by storms, a storm for every calm. There is no steady unretracing progress in this life; . . . ifs eternally." Not surprisingly, Ahab himself thought fate, not free will, the dominant power. About to lower for the final confrontation with the white whale, Ahab declared, "By heaven, men, we are turned round and round in this world, like yonder windless, and Fate is the handspike."[32]

With fate so likely to overwhelm free will, the caliber and character of officers and crew on a voyage as dangerous as a whaling trip would seem critical. In fact, Ishmael knew it to be so and, unable to meet and gauge Captain Ahab before signing for the voyage, said, "I did but half fancy being committed this way to so long a voyage, without once laying my eyes on the man who was to be absolute dictator of it, so soon as the ship sailed out upon the open sea." Ishmael and the crew had good reason to fear because "the paramount forms and usages of the sea," embedded in maritime law and tradition, made captains at sea unchallengeable. And with Ahab in particular, "that certain sultanism of his brain, . . . through those forms . . . became incarnate in an irresistible dictatorship." Given the advantages of fixed purpose, position, and tradition, Ahab had little trouble converting the crew to his obsession: the pursuit of Moby Dick. Once the crew had declared their support for the quest, Ahab declared, "I do not order ye; ye will it." But had they willed it? No, thought Melville, because the "forms and usages" that magnify power easily overwhelm men, even when some good men are mixed among the thoughtless multitude. The weakness of democracy, especially against the willful would-be tyrant, was in the moral failings of the people—in this case, "a crew . . . morally enfeebled also, by the incompetence of mere unaided virtue or right-mindedness in Starbuck."[33]

Of the three officers of the ship below Ahab, Starbuck, Stubb, and Flask, Starbuck was senior, the first mate, and the most interesting. Starbuck was an experienced officer, brave, steady, and dependable, with a wife and young son back in Nantucket. Ahab was obsessed, maybe crazy, but he was a galvanizing, powerful personality, which Starbuck early acknowledged: "My soul is more than matched, she's over-manned; and by a madman. . . . I think I see his impious end; but feel that I must help him to it. . . . Horrible old man!" Starbuck made several impassioned pleas to Ahab, calling upon him to break off the fight, forget the white whale, and sail for home. Ahab could not and was heard to say, "Some one thrusts these cards into these old hands of mine; swears that I must play them, and no others." But he did hear Starbuck on home and family. In the final confrontation with the white whale, Ahab ordered Starbuck to remain on board in command of the *Pequod*, saying, "Stay on board, on board!—lower not when I do; when branded Ahab gives chase to Moby Dick. That hazard shall not be thine. No, no! not with the far away home I see in that eye." Starbuck's emotional response, recognizing Ahab's sad grandeur, was "Oh, my Captain! My Captain! Noble soul! Grand old heart, after all."[34] Grand as Ahab's gesture may have been, he was not in charge; the whale and fate were. Moby Dick scattered and sank the lowered boats, killing their crews, including Ahab, and in a final burst of vengeance the great whale rammed and sank the *Pequod*, killing Starbuck and all the crew, save Ishmael, the lone survivor.

The sea and Moby Dick were the great forces of nature against which Ahab and the crew of the *Pequod*, and other whaling ships they met at sea, pitted themselves. The whalers generally got the better of the fight, as the jubilant crew of the *Bachelor*, headed home with a hull full of valuable whale oil, would testify. But dangers were many; the *Pequod* also met the *Goney*, at sea almost four years; the *Jeroboam*, with disease on board and a crew in revolt; and the *Rachel*, whose captain's own son had been lost. And certainly, the whales were massive and dangerous, particularly when wounded, but, as dumb beasts, they were generally harvested when found. Moby Dick was fearfully different. Legend noted "the White Whale's infernal aforethought of ferocity, that every dismembering or death that he caused, was not wholly regarded as having been inflicted by an unintelligent agent." Rather, there was a "malicious intelligence ascribed to him." In the final moment of the confrontation between Ahab's *Pequod* and Moby Dick, "retribution, swift vengeance, eternal malice were in his whole aspect, and spite of all that mortal man could do, the solid white buttress of his forehead smote the ship's starboard bow. . . . Through the breach, they heard the waters pour. . . . Oh, lonely death on lonely life!"[35]

The confident hopes of the Founding period and the first decades of the new nation's history were compromised by the middle decades of the nineteenth century. Lincoln's famous melancholy was not simply personal; to some extent it was social as well, noted by Tocqueville and Emerson and epitomized in literature and life by Melville. Melancholy and fate were personified, jointly and severally, by Ahab and Moby Dick, and both sources of gloom pervade the book. When Ishmael first glimpsed the *Pequod*, he declared it "a noble craft, but somehow a most melancholy!" But then he mused, "All noble things are touched with that." And in great men, Ishmael warned, one always found "a certain morbidness. Be sure of this, O young ambition, all mortal greatness is but disease." So has history said of Abraham Lincoln.

Melville warned that the world and life were futility. Ishmael was concerned about going to sea under a captain he did not know, but Melville told us that we were all in Ishmael's position; "the world's a ship on its passage out, and not on a voyage complete," so we know not what may befall. Even more sobering, Melville declared that it is always thus: "One most perilous and long voyage ended, only begins a second; and a second ended, only begins a third, and so on, for ever and for aye. Such is the endlessness, yea, the intolerableness of all earthly effort."[36] So much for the humanism of Jefferson and the transcendentalists.

Bartleby, the Scrivener exudes futility, the futility of a good man trying to live a calm and secure life and the still greater futility of a fragile man simply trying, ultimately unsuccessfully, to survive. What does the good and compassionate man do with the emotionally crippled man, the incapable man, in his path? The lawyer, who goes unnamed in the story, was a corporate and bond attorney on Wall Street who hired several copyists, or scriveners, to assist with his work. Two original employees, Turkey and Nippers, had their quirks, their strengths and weaknesses, and their abilities and shortcomings, but they did the close and critical work of legal copyists adequately. As the work of the office increased, the lawyer hired a third scrivener, Bartleby, and soon his grander quirks emerged to threaten the lawyer's peace of mind and business.

The lawyer and narrator introduced himself first, saying, "I am a man who, from his youth upwards, has been filled with a profound conviction that the easiest way of life is the best." This rejection of Emerson and the boosterism of the age is no adoption of Thoreau. The easiest life is not the one with the least labor; rather, it is the calm, well-ordered, professional routine of the bond lawyer's office. No wretched murderers for clients, no impassioned trials, just the detailed and orderly work that brings prosperity. "I am one of those unambitious lawyers who never addresses a jury, . . . but, in the cool tranquility of a snug retreat, do a snug business among rich men's bonds, . . . consider me an eminently *safe* man."[37] Into this snug world comes Bartleby. Bartleby was slight, pallid, and forlorn—a scrivener—but he was in the office before anyone else, working steadily through the day, and staying late into the evening. A copying phenomenon, Bartleby was amazingly productive. But just three days into his employment the lawyer called Bartleby to assist him in proofreading an important document; Bartleby's polite but firm reply—"I would prefer not to"—stunned the lawyer and set the denouement of the story in train.

For a time, Bartleby continued to do his work, but he declined to be interrupted for other tasks with his polite but firm reply—"I would prefer not to." As the scrivener withdrew further into himself, eventually ceasing all work and staring blankly at the wall, the lawyer discovered that Bartleby had been living in the law offices, apparently without warm food, a bed, or toilet facilities and without companionship of any kind. The lawyer reported that his "first emotions had been those of pure melancholy and sincerest pity; but just in proportion as the forlornness of Bartleby grew . . . did that same melancholy merge into fear, that pity into revulsion."[38] When the lawyer finally asked Bartleby to quit his offices, the scrivener replied, "I would prefer not to." Soon the kind but timid lawyer decided that all that was left to him was to seek new offices for himself and to abandon Bartleby in the old offices.

The new tenants, more decisive and less understanding than the lawyer, called the police on Bartleby when he would not leave. The kindly lawyer reported, "As I afterwards learned, the poor scrivener, when told that he must be conducted to the Tombs [jail], offered not the slightest obstacle, but, in his pale, unmoving way, silently acquiesced." The lawyer visited Bartleby in jail and arranged for the delivery of good meals to him, but when he checked back a few days later, he found that Bartleby had refused all meals. The lawyer found Bartleby in the jail yard, apparently sleeping but in fact dead. Bartleby was dead of sadness, isolation, and undoubtedly much more. For Bartleby, and for Melville, the world was a sad and uninterpretable place. The final words of the novel are "Ah, Bartleby! Ah, humanity!"[39]

Abraham Lincoln, Opportunity, and the American Dream

Abraham Lincoln came to see freedom and opportunity in America more broadly than any of his predecessors, most of his contemporaries, and many of ours. Yet he shared with Melville a sad sense that flawed man might never realize them. The Lincolns, poor farmers out of North Carolina, arrived in Illinois in 1830, by way of Kentucky and Indiana. The Lincolns were part not of the first wave of immigrants, explorers, hunters, and trappers, but of the second wave, small farmers, storekeepers, and traders in a still very raw frontier environment. Though the Lincolns were overwhelmingly Jacksonian Democrats, the young Abraham Lincoln cast his first vote against Jackson and for Henry Clay in 1832. Lincoln shared with Clay the sense that it was better to throw the doors of economic growth and opportunity open than to worry that a few men might be getting richer than their fellows.[40]

One of Lincoln's first major political speeches, entitled "The Perpetuation of Our Political Institutions," was delivered before the Young Men's Lyceum of Springfield, Illinois, in January 1838. Just days before his twenty-ninth birthday and in his second term in the Illinois House, Lincoln was at the beginning of his political career. In this remarkable speech, delivered more than a decade before Melville wrote *Moby Dick*, Lincoln asked what dangers a "great man"—not an Ahab at sea, but a man like Alexander, Caesar, or Napoleon—posed to freedom and democracy.

Lincoln claimed that the Founders had won everlasting glory by establishing a stable and prosperous republic of free men. Men of his and later generations had open to them only the more modest but still critical responsibility of perpetuating those institutions. Lincoln warned that the threat to the nation's institutions came not from foreign powers but from within. He pointed to racial violence and vigilantism, and he warned that lawbreaking, if unchecked, might force good, law-abiding citizens to look for peace and order in dangerous places. If law and normal politics could not protect citizens, "men of ambition and talents" might seek glory by exploiting the unrest. Lincoln declared that in times of peace and stability, "many great and good men . . . would aspire to nothing beyond a seat in Congress, a gubernatorial or a presidential chair, *but such belong not to the family of the lion, or the tribe of the eagle.*" In times of tumult, on the other hand, when citizens might call out for a Caesar or a Napoleon, "towering genius distains a beaten path."[41] Lincoln's teaching was that only strong and respected laws and institutions could hold towering genius in place. Democracy was still new enough in Lincoln's day, and would still be in Melville's, that both men shared George Washington's dedication to law-abidingness.

But disorder grew, and ultimately fate required Lincoln to choose a course he did not want. He would not enslave free men, and he tried to avoid dividing the country by freeing the slaves. He chose law-abidingness for as long as he could, but ultimately he freed the slaves and, in doing so, joined the pantheon of American Founders as the equal of any one of them. Several prominent intellectual and cultural traditions came together in Lincoln and emerged from him transformed and energized. Jefferson and Jackson thought government was commonly a tool of the wealthy and the well positioned, so they sought to keep it small and unobtrusive. Hamilton and Clay were eager to use the power of government, but mostly to expand commerce and manufacturing, leaving the little man to scramble for whatever wages the market made available. Lincoln was the first major public figure in American history to use government both to expand the economy and to ensure that "all men" could pursue the resulting benefits and opportunities. Abraham Lincoln, like Theodore Roosevelt and Franklin D. Roosevelt after him, pursued Jeffersonian ends, the benefit of the small man, through Hamiltonian means, the aggressive use of government to expand economic opportunity.[42]

Lincoln rarely failed to remind audiences of his own humble origins and of the self-help ideology that he shared with them. To one audience Lincoln said, "Twenty-five years ago I was a hired laborer. The hired laborer of yesterday labors on his own account today, and will hire others to labor for him tomorrow. Advancement—improvement in condition—is the order of things in a society of equals."[43] Elsewhere, Lincoln described his social ideal as one in which "men, with their families . . . work for themselves, on their farms, in their houses, and in their shops, taking the whole product to themselves, and asking no favors of capital on one hand nor of hired labor or slaves on the other."[44] Lincoln spoke to and for the great middling range of working Americans, and they trusted him because they knew he had risen from among them.

Lincoln made the mythic ideals of the Declaration of Independence the foundation for his political career. He believed that "the principles of Jefferson are the definitions and axioms of free society" but that they had never been fully applied; he wrote, "The Jefferson party were formed upon its supposed superior devotion to the *personal* rights of men, holding the rights of *property* to be secondary only, and greatly inferior." Hamilton's Federalists and Clay's Whigs had made similar charges before pledging themselves to property, always forgetting that there were too few men of wealth and position to win elections. Lincoln was shrewder; he charged that Jackson's Democrats had abandoned Jefferson by concluding that the property rights of southern slaveholders completely eviscerated the human rights of slaves. Lincoln concluded by seizing the traditional Democrat claim to value the man over the dollar, declaring that "Republicans . . . are for both the *man* and the *dollar*, but in cases of conflict, the man *before* the dollar."[45]

Like Cotton Mather, Penn, Jefferson, and many in the Founding generation, Lincoln hoped that Americans would not just strive and compete but also build themselves as full and rounded human beings. Echoing Emerson's hope that power and form, the outer and the inner worlds, might be finely balanced, Lincoln wrote, "Let us hope . . . that by the best cultivation of the physical world, beneath and around us; and the intellectual and moral world within us, we shall secure an individual, social, and political prosperity and happiness, . . . which, while the earth endures, shall not pass away."[46] As Michael Illuzzi noted, "Lincoln's formulation makes the self-made individual dependent on political practices and institutions."[47] Lincoln understood that if opportunity were to be broadly available in America, especially to common citizens, both individual and social goals had to be well designed and aligned. Faith and community needed to limit competition and accumulation, but in the emerging world of the mid-nineteenth century they seemed less and less capable of doing so.

And as always, slavery was the great exception to the nation's stated principles.[48] Most white men were confident that God had distinguished between the races and the genders, giving different virtues, capacities, and roles to each. Even northern leaders approached issues of race hesitantly. Lincoln rarely spoke about race as an Illinois state legislator or during his one term, 1847–1849, in the U.S. House of Representatives. Lincoln's Whig Party was ambivalent about slavery, and the Republican Party had not yet been born. Out of office and seemingly out of political options, Lincoln's first public statement in opposition to slavery came in a speech on October 16, 1854. It is almost pitiful to read, but it portrays vividly the deep ambivalence of northern white Americans toward slavery and blacks. Of slavery, Lincoln said, "I hate it because of the monstrous injustice of slavery itself." He then proceeded immediately to say, "If all earthly power were given me, I should not know what to do, as to the existing institution. My first impulse would be to free all the slaves, and send them to Liberia,—to their own native land." If freedom and removal proved untenable, "What next?—Free them, and make them politically and socially, our equals? My own feelings will not admit of this, and if mine would, we well know that those of the great mass of white people will not."[49] Lincoln knew that slavery was deeply embedded in the South and that racism was just as deeply embedded throughout the nation.

The Democrats promoted both the geographic expansion of slavery and the legal expansion of slaveholders' property rights. The U.S. Supreme Court held, in *Dred Scott v. Sandford* (1857), that southern slave owners could carry their slaves into free states and hold and use them there. Writing for the court, Chief Justice Roger B. Taney declared that blacks, slave or free, could not be citizens of the United States and had "no rights which the white man was bound to respect." The *Dred Scott* decision gave Lincoln the opening he needed; he could return to politics not as an enemy of slavery but as an opponent of its expansion. In 1858, Senator Stephen A. Douglas, the powerful incumbent Democratic senator from Illinois, was up for reelection, and Lincoln declared against him. Douglas attacked Lincoln on the issue of equality between the races. Douglas was unequivocal in his support for white supremacy. Douglas said in Chicago, "I am opposed to Negro equality. I repeat that this nation is a white people—a people composed of European descendants—a people that have established this government for themselves and their posterity."[50]

While Douglas stood for white supremacy, Lincoln had concluded that in his "right to eat the bread, without leave of anybody else, which his own hand earns," the Negro "*is my equal and the equal of Judge Douglas, and the equal of every living man.*"[51] Elsewhere, Lincoln extended the same right to the benefits of one's labor to the black female slave, saying, "In her natural right to eat the bread she earns with her own hands without asking leave of anyone else, she is my equal, and the equal of all others."[52] Douglas won the election, but Lincoln won a national audience for his views. Lincoln's American Dream was of a nation in which every man, by which he came almost to mean men and women of every color, had an unobstructed chance to rise in society by dint of his or her own preparation, strength, and sagacity. But Lincoln confronted a world in which racism was pervasive even among those who opposed slavery.

Faulkner, Twain, Race, and Slavery in Antebellum America

Absalom, Absalom!, one of the great gothic novels of the American South, was published by William Faulkner in 1936. The novel was mostly set in Jefferson, Mississippi, and its events mostly occurred between 1833 and the era of the Civil War and Reconstruction, but it spanned the nineteenth century, as its central character was born in 1808 and one of its principal narrators recounted parts of the story in 1906. Though there were multiple narrators, one of the most important was Quentin Compson, a native of Jefferson, Mississippi, studying at Harvard in 1906 and trying to explain to his Canadian roommate the South's background and mental baggage. Each narrator laid down a layer of recollection, rumor, and interpretation, revising the story as remembered or as told to the narrator by others, to leave a cobweb of possible events and meanings rather than a historical narrative.[53] For Faulkner, as for Melville, life and history were not linear; rather, they were a complex mixture of purpose, choice, and decision crosscut and infused by fortune, fate, and chance.

The meaning in *Absalom* was in the multiple tellings, retellings, and interpretations of Thomas Sutpen's life and its impact on those around him. Sutpen started poor, strove mightily, achieved greatly, and saw it all collapse in the muck and mire of unmoored ambition, miscegenation, and betrayal. The first Sutpen into Virginia arrived on a prison ship, and several generations later the impoverished family was ensconced deep in the hills of what would become West Virginia. Thomas Sutpen was born about 1808 and grew to late boyhood as deeply illiterate and benighted as the backwoods could make him. Faulkner wrote that "Sutpen's trouble was innocence," by which he meant a near-total lack of knowledge, perspective, and context concerning the world beyond his cabin. When young Sutpen was ten, the family moved out of the mountains and nearer to civilization, where he learned not only the difference between white men and black men but also that there were differences, just as big and momentous, among white men. At thirteen, these differences were made starkly clear in a way that set Thomas Sutpen's course in life. Thomas's father, who had a shack and some kind of work on a plantation, sent him to the plantation house with a message. Sutpen, ragged and barefoot, carried the message to the front door, where a "monkey-dressed nigger butler" physically blocked him from entering and ordered him around to the back door.[54]

Sutpen's initial "innocence" evaporated as a humiliating reality became clear to him. Some whites—poor, landless, ignorant whites like himself and his family—were distained by rich whites and were not fit to enter their homes because they were lower than "niggers." He knew that being treated peremptorily by the "monkey . . . butler" required some response. He thought of shooting the monkey butler but realized the snub was not the butler's fault, as behind him stood the rich white man—Pettibone, the plantation owner. Sutpen soon concluded, "This ain't a question of rifles. So to combat them you have got to have what they have that made them do what the man did. You got to have land and niggers and a fine house to combat them with. . . . He left that night . . . to the West Indies."[55]

Sutpen's new "innocence" took the form of single-minded— monomaniacal, Ahabian—pursuit of "his dream and his ambition" of having everything that Pettibone had and more.[56] To get what he wanted, he did not grow and improve, he did not educate himself, but instead he hardened himself, determined to get what his "dream" demanded: land, slaves, a mansion, wealth, and a wife to provide an heir. Faulkner did not tell us much about Sutpen's time in the West Indies, but what he did tell us was striking and shaped the rest of the novel. As Sutpen grew to adulthood, he became the overseer of a sugar plantation owned by a Frenchman, his wife, and his daughter and worked by slaves. A slave revolt, in which the family and Sutpen were trapped for days in the main house, ended when Sutpen went into the jungle in the dead of night. When he emerged in the morning, the slave revolt was over, and the family was saved. How Sutpen accomplished this astounding result was never told, but the assumption was powerful that he had outsavaged the savages, awed and intimidated them back into their chains. As a reward for his strength and valor, Sutpen married the daughter, thereby becoming heir to the plantation, and produced a son and heir, and so it looked as if his "dream" was realized. Soon, he discovered that the plantation owner's wife, the mother of his wife, who had initially been described as Spanish, actually had black blood—and so, then, did his wife and son. Sutpen responded as most southern-bred white men of his day would have, by abandoning his tainted wife and child. After arranging with her father for the care of his repudiated family, Sutpen took just twenty slaves, renounced all other claims, and appeared at twenty-five years old in Jefferson, Mississippi.

Sutpen's sudden arrival, his wild, barely broken slaves, and his mysterious acquisition from Indians of 100 square miles of prime land unsettled the town and set it sullenly against him. He was unmoved; he turned himself with single-minded purpose to preparing the land, putting in cotton, and building and ultimately furnishing a mansion. Finally, at thirty, five years after he arrived, Sutpen took Ellen Coldfield for his wife, and they soon had two children, a daughter, Judith, and, two years younger, a son, Henry. Also in the household and secondarily acknowledged was Clytemnestra, "Clytie," born earlier to Sutpen and one of his female slaves. Clytie was set to serve Judith, sleeping in her room on a pallet while Judith slept in the bed. Much later in the book, when Sutpen was leaving for the Civil War, his last words to his daughters were "Well, Clytie, take care of Miss Judith."[57]

Marriage and family changed Sutpen little, and though Ellen struggled, she adapted herself to him. Sutpen's dominant personality, and the personalities and characters of those around him, was displayed in one of the book's great scenes: the barn fight. Before he was married and while the mansion was being built, he had men from the town out for bouts of drinking and gambling. After he was married and the children ranged in age from Henry's seven to Clytie's fourteen, men still came overland through the fields to the barn on some nights. Ellen asked no questions, assuming Sutpen was holding fights among the slaves for the amusement of neighbors. One night the men were in the barn and the children were not to be found, so Ellen went looking for them. Entering the barn, she saw "not the two black beasts she had expected to see but instead a white one and a black one, both naked to the waist and gouging at one another's eyes as if they should not only have been the same color, but should have been covered with fur too." Ellen demanded a stop to the fight and the return of the children. Slowly a group of the observers parted to "permit her to see Henry plunge out from among the negroes who had been holding him, screaming and vomiting." She demanded Judith too, but Sutpen denied having brought Judith to the barn, and perhaps he had not, but as Ellen escorted Henry from the barn, she failed to see "two Sutpen faces this time—once on Judith and once on the negro girl beside her [Clytie]—looking down through the square entrance to the loft."[58] Thomas Sutpen was a force of nature to which others always gave way. Ahab in Mississippi, Sutpen had breasted every challenge to stand at the pinnacle of his dreams. But clouds of doom arose from individual and collective sins.

Unbeknownst to Sutpen, his first wife, Eulalia Bon, and their son, Charles Bon, had left the West Indies for New Orleans. Eulalia raised Charles to wealthy, hedonistic, indolent, cultured manhood with a purpose that she did not share even with him. Charles had an octoroon mistress and, with her, a young son. At twenty-eight, for reasons mysterious to him, Eulalia dispatched Charles to college at the new University of Mississippi. There he met and became something of an older guide and mentor to Henry Sutpen. Henry invited Charles home, where he met and developed an ill-fated mutual attraction with Judith. Thomas Sutpen himself went to New Orleans to find out more about Charles and confirmed what had he feared, that Eulalia and Charles were back in the family.

Only Eulalia put a plan in motion; everyone else chose not to plan or even to take deliberate action, but to act only as required by unfolding fate. Upon returning from his New Orleans inquiries, Sutpen told Henry that Charles was a half brother to him and Judith, though with black blood; Henry knew that it was true but claimed not to believe it, and Sutpen said nothing to Charles directly. The Civil War, in which Thomas, Henry, and Charles all served, provided a four-year hiatus but no resolution to the looming tragedy—incest and miscegenation— should Charles and Judith marry. As Henry and Charles rode back to Sutpen's Hundred (as Thomas had named his plantation) after the war, "Henry would say, 'But must you marry her? Do you have to do it?' and Bon would say, 'He should have told me. He should have told me, myself, himself. I was fair and honorable with him. I waited. You know why I waited. I gave him every chance to tell me himself." As they rode on, ever closer to the inevitable reunion with Judith, Charles said, "He sent me no word? He did not ask you to send me to him? No word to me, no word at all? That was all he had to do. . . . He would not have needed to ask it, require it, of me. I would have offered it."[59] Finally, as they approached the gates of Sutpen's Hundred, Charles pulled a revolver from his pack and held it out, butt first, to Henry. Both knew that the only way to stop an impossibly unacceptable fate from playing out was for Henry to fire—and he did. Charles fell dead, and Henry fled, some said to California, to avoid the probable murder charge.

Ellen had died during Sutpen's absence at war, so he returned to a house in which Clytie, Judith, and Ellen's much younger sister, Rosa, had been trying to hold things together with the assistance of Wash Jones, "a gangling, malaria-ridden white man whom [Sutpen] . . . had given permission . . . to squat in the abandoned fish camp." Judith, after Charles's killing, withdrew further into herself and never married. Rosa, Ellen's younger sister by twenty-seven years, four years younger even than Judith, had been called to Sutpen's Hundred as Ellen lay dying to look after her children. With Ellen largely isolated on the plantation, Rosa grew up in town, thinking Sutpen an ogre. Yet the war had left her destitute, without family or purpose, so when Sutpen declared that they would be married, she said neither yes or no, which he took as acquiescence. Two months after his declaration, he appeared with a modified proposal, "that they should breed together for test and sample and if it was a boy they would marry."[60] Rosa fled back to town to stew over her "moral affront" and remained an old maid to the end of her days. The demon, Sutpen, turned without apparent hesitation to the fifteen-year-old granddaughter of Wash Jones to bear him a son and heir. She failed, bearing him a daughter, and Sutpen was killed by Wash Jones, a scythe to the chest, when he tried to walk away again.

In *Absalom, Absalom!*, even dominant men like Thomas Sutpen (let alone women or weaker men) do not act. Rather, they are borne along on strong currents of history, culture, and fate. Thomas Sutpen, a poor and ignorant child of the mudsill South, had gone to the West Indies to make his fortune. While barely twenty, having shown indomitable strength and courage, he ran afoul of one of the South's most powerful "lords of life": race and race mixing. Sex with a black woman was not the problem—that was common, even mundane—but allowing black blood to enter the white family line was impermissible. From the moment his violation became known to him, he did what he had to do and others did what they had to do, and the resulting chaos brought the destruction of "his dream and his ambition." As Sutpen sent Henry off to the University of Mississippi, he was Pettibone's equal in every way. He was at "that peak which all the different parts that make a man reach, where he can say *I did all that I set out to do . . .* and maybe this is the instance which Fate always picks out to blackjack you, only the peak feels so sound and stable that the beginning of the falling is hidden for a little while." Rosa Coldfield was less charitable; she blamed "the very dark forces of fate which he had evoked and dared."[61]

Given the darkness of Faulkner's vision of race and slavery in the mid-nineteenth century, one might look, vainly, to Mark Twain for a brighter vision. Race was an element in much of Twain's writing, most obviously in the relationship between Huck and the escaped slave Jim in *The Adventures of Huckleberry Finn*. Huck and Jim famously shared a raft and got to know each other as people on a trip down the Mississippi River. Readers fondly remember Jim for his determination to be free and to free his family, but also for his kindhearted dedication to Huck, as when he stood extra watch to let Huck sleep. Huck struggled against the legal and social conventions of the day and against his own conscience to help Jim escape. But the only extended and overt treatment of race in *Huckleberry Finn* was from a white perspective, most memorably that of Pap, Huck's reprobate father. His was the perspective of illiterate white trash, but it was memorably stark. Many a modern classroom has barred the book for just these passages.

Huck recounted that when Pap got drunk he almost always "went for the . . . govment" and for "niggers." Pap thought that any white man, even himself, especially himself, was better than any black man and that the "govment" should do everything in its power to uphold that truth. In an extended drunken diatribe, Pap reported, "There was a free nigger there [in town], from Ohio; a mulatter, most as white as a white man. . . . And what do you think? they said he was a p'fessor in a college, and could talk all kinds of languages, and knowed everything. And that ain't the wust. They said he could *vote*, when he was at home. Well, that let me out. Thinks I, what is the country a-coming to? It was 'lection day, and I was just about to go and vote, myself, if I warn't too drunk to get there; but when they told me that there was a State in this country where they'd let that nigger vote, I drawed out. I says I'll never vote agin."[62]

Twain's most extended and most nuanced treatment of race was in *Pudd'nhead Wilson*. Written late in Twain's career, almost two decades after *The Adventures of Tom Sawyer* and a decade after *The Adventures of Huckleberry Finn*, *Pudd'nhead Wilson* was a darker book. David Wilson, a twenty-five-year-old lawyer, trained in the East, arrived in 1830 in Dawson's Landing, a small, sleepy, town on the Mississippi. On his first day in town, Wilson said something odd in response to a howling dog: "I wish I owned half of that dog." When someone asked why, he answered, "Because I would kill my half."[63] Townspeople puzzled over this strange remark, wondered whether he realized that killing his half would leave the whole dog dead, and finally concluded that he must be addled. Hence, the nickname "Pudd'nhead." No legal business ever came his way, so he scraped by for two decades on a little bookkeeping and some odd hobbies, like collecting people's fingerprints. Wilson was always liked, was vaguely respected for his education, but was never taken seriously in the town. Wilson's stock began to rise as he participated in the investigation of a murder and ultimately solved the mystery with his fingerprints—simultaneously revealing the real mystery at the heart of the book.

The central character in the book was Roxana, or Roxy, a twenty-year-old slave with two new babies to care for, one her own, and the other her master Percy Driscoll's. Mrs. Driscoll died soon after giving birth, so Roxy raised both children in the Driscoll home. Roxy was beautiful, just one-sixteenth black, almost white, but illiterate, with the diction and mannerisms of a slave. When three other slaves in the Driscoll house were accused of stealing, Mr. Driscoll threatened to sell them all down the river. Terrified for her infant son, Roxy executed a plan to switch the two baby boys, who looked identical, especially to the harried and grieving Percy Driscoll. Thomas a Becket Driscoll, Percy Driscoll's white son, was switched in the cradle with Roxy's son, Valet de Chambre, called Chambers.[64] We find later that the father of Roxy's son was a prominent white man in the town, making Chambers one-thirty-second black, white to the eye but a slave by law and culture. After the switch, Thomas (now called Chambers) was the slave and Chambers (now called Thomas) was the privileged son of a prominent white family.

These stylized facts set up fascinating questions of race, class, law, and culture that appeared as fully nowhere else in Twain's work. First, as we saw in *Uncle Tom's Cabin* and *Clotel*, the idea of white slaves, especially white female slaves, fascinated nineteenth-century Americans. Twain told us that "to all intents and purposes Roxy was as white as anybody, but the one-sixteenth of her which was black outvoted the other fifteen parts and made her a negro. She was a slave, and salable as such. Her child was a thirty-one parts white, and he, too, was a slave, and by a fiction of law and custom a negro."[65] Race, this "fiction of law and custom," was extraordinarily powerful, controlling what and how both whites and blacks thought and could think—they were the load-bearing beams and walls of their mental architecture. Tom was white and Chambers was black, by culture and law, at birth, but after the switch in the cradle,

Chambers was raised white, with all the attendant privileges, and Tom was raised black and a slave.

Roxy's sense of race and the qualities attendant on race were fascinating. As the story opened, Roxy was young and beautiful, white by appearance but black by dialect and demeanor because a slave from birth. Walking the two new babies, Roxy was hailed by a slave acquaintance named Jasper. After a friendly exchange, Jasper said, "I's gwine to come a-court'n you bimeby, Roxy," to which she responded, "*You* is, you black mudcat! Yah, yah, yah! I got somep'n better to do den 'sociat'n wid niggers as black as you is!"⁶⁶ The merry exchange continued, with no apparent offense taken by Jasper, and highlighted the value that Roxy put on color, on skin tone, even among, maybe especially among, slaves. Even more strikingly, after Tom mistreated Roxy, his mother, when she appealed to him for emotional and financial support, Roxy retaliated by declaring that he was her son—Chambers—by law a Negro and a slave. Roxy shouted, "You's a *nigger*! *Bawn* a nigger en a *slave*!—en you's a nigger en a slave dis minute; en if I opens my mouf ole Marse Driscoll'll sell you down de river befo' you is two days older den what you is now!" Tom was immediately undone, feeling the truth of her charge: "'Oh,' groaned Tom, 'I more than believe it; I *know* it.'"⁶⁷

Knowing that he had black blood, even just one-thirty-second of black blood, changed Tom's sense of his own worth. Once Tom knew who he truly was, "he dreaded his meals; the 'nigger' in him was ashamed to sit at the white folks' table, and feared discovery all the time; and once when Judge Driscoll said, 'What the matter with you? You look as meek as a nigger,'" Tom felt weak, felt discovered, and left the table. Roxy had earlier explained to Tom, actually her son Chambers, that his father was Colonel Cecil Burleigh Essex, a former Virginian and a leader in the town before his death. When Tom was rudely kicked in public, he sought redress in court rather than thrashing his assailant or challenging him to a duel. Tom's cowardice brought this reprimand from Roxy: "What would yo' pa think of you? . . . Whatever has come o' yo' Essex blood? . . . En it ain't just Essex blood dat's in you, not by a long sight—deed it ain't. My great-great-great gran'father was Ole Cap'n John Smith, de highest blood dat Ole Virginny ever turned out. . . . En here you is, a-slinkin' outen a duel. . . . Yes, it's de nigger in you!"⁶⁸ Roxy was one-sixteenth black and her son, Tom, was one-thirty-second black—but she attributed any cowardice in him to his "nigger" blood.

Finally, when the baby switch was discovered, the fake Tom was undone; in fact, as a slave, he was sold down the river. But the real Tom, the white heir to the Driscoll name and estate, raised a slave, was undone too: "The real heir suddenly found himself rich and free, but in a most embarrassed situation. He could neither read nor write, and his speech was the basest dialect of the negro quarter. His gait, his attitudes, his gestures, his bearing, his laugh—all were . . . the manners of a slave. Money and fine clothes could not mend these defects . . . ; they only made them the more glaring and the more pathetic."[69] The social role of slave was so powerful that it blotted out all effect of character, attributes, and effort. Chambers, the real Tom, had been raised a faithful slave in the Driscoll household, and though freedom came he remained slavish in every social and psychological sense. No one knew better than Abraham Lincoln the depth and strength of American opinion on race.

Lincoln, Douglas, and the End of Slavery

Abraham Lincoln was elected president of a nation tumbling toward the Civil War. When Lincoln reached Washington as the newly elected president, several of the southern states had already gone. He moved immediately to define the coming struggle in the broadest terms, declaring, "On the side of the Union, it is a struggle for maintaining in the world, that form, and substance of government, whose leading object is, to elevate the condition of men—to lift artificial weights from all shoulders—to clear the paths of laudable pursuit for all—to afford all, an unfettered start, and a fair chance, in the race of life."[70] A little more than two years into the war, Lincoln set the end of slavery in train with the Emancipation Proclamation. He put the critical word "all" back in Jefferson's declaration that "all men are created equal." In so doing, he opened America's "door of mercy" to persons whom society had previously rejected even in their humanity, and he changed the debate about America's promise and meaning forever.

Lincoln was the prism through which the light of the American Dream passed to become a purer, broader, beam. The American Dream of equality, opportunity, and justice was clear from first settlement, but it was narrowly conceived in the beginning. Lincoln used the Gettysburg Address (1863) to define the Civil War as the next great battle in the ongoing struggle to live up to the nation's values:[71] "Four score and seven years ago our fathers brought forth on this continent, a new nation, conceived in Liberty, and dedicated to the proposition that all men are created equal. . . . Now we are engaged in a great civil war, testing whether that nation, or any nation so conceived and so dedicated, can long endure." His conclusion, essentially, was that such a nation could endure not by standing still but only by pressing forward. Hence, he declared, "we here highly resolve that . . . this nation, under God, shall have a new birth of freedom—and that government of the people, by the people, for the people, shall not perish from the earth."[72]

Lincoln believed that the embedded presence of slavery in the South had prevented the Founding generation from writing the ideals of the Declaration fully into the Constitution. The Declaration's core principle, that "all men are created equal," was compromised in the Constitution's acceptance of slavery, but the principle had not been debased or rejected. The Founders "meant simply to declare the *right*, so that the *enforcement* of it might follow as fast as circumstances should permit. They meant to set up a standard maxim for free society, which could be familiar to all, and revered by all; constantly looked to, constantly labored for, and even though never perfectly attained, constantly approximated, and thereby constantly . . . augmenting the happiness and value of life to all people of all colors everywhere."[73]

Lincoln was determined to reaffirm the promises of the Declaration of Independence and to embed them more firmly in the Constitution. Moreover, he knew that it would take more time, treasure, and blood to make the Declaration's promise good for all Americans. Hence, his second inaugural address exuded quiet determination to proceed with the work in hand beyond the war and into the nation's future. Lincoln called on his fellow citizens to persevere in the pursuit of justice: "With malice toward none; with charity for all; with firmness in the right, as God gives us to see the right, let us strive on to finish the work we are in; to bind up the nation's wounds; to care for him who shall have borne the battle, and for his widow, and his orphan—to do all which may achieve and cherish a just and lasting peace."[74] Sadly, Lincoln's assassination on April 15, 1865, just one week after General Ulysses S. Grant accepted the surrender of General Robert E. Lee at the Appomattox Court House, left the new peace without its wisest advocate.

Once the war was over and nearly 4 million slaves were free, the Republican Congress had to decide what freedom meant in real terms. Were the freedmen free in the same sense that white men were free, free to do the same things, enjoy the same privileges, exercise the same rights, and pursue the same opportunities? As Congress mulled these questions, congressman and future president James A. Garfield asked, "What is freedom? Is it the bare privilege of not being chained?"[75] Most Republicans believed that the answer had to be no, that freedom had to mean more than not being held in chains. But few white Americans could conceive that freedom meant equality. The battle over the meaning of freedom was fought out in the adoption and implementation of the Thirteenth, Fourteenth, and Fifteenth Amendments to the Constitution and the Civil Rights Acts that followed. Freedom was grudgingly upheld, but equality was rejected.

The Thirteenth Amendment, which went into effect on December 18, 1865, completed emancipation; it read, "Neither slavery nor involuntary servitude, except as a punishment for crime whereof the party shall have been duly convicted, shall exist within the United States, or any place subject to their jurisdiction." Senator William Stewart, representing the new state of Nevada, warned that Congress "must see to it that the man made free by the Constitution of the United States . . . is a freeman indeed."[76] The Fourteenth Amendment sought to do precisely that. The Fourteenth Amendment declared, "All persons born or naturalized in the United States, and subject to the jurisdiction thereof, are citizens of the United States and the state wherein they reside. No state shall make or enforce any law which shall abridge the privileges and immunities of citizens of the United States; nor shall any State deprive any person of life, liberty, or property, without due process of law; nor deny to any person within its jurisdiction the equal protection of the laws." This broad and generous language, explicitly overturning the Supreme Court's ruling in *Dred Scott*, went into effect on July 28, 1868.

Nonetheless, southern resistance to black freedom was broad and determined. Whites needed the labor of their former slaves and believed that blacks would not work unless coerced. Hence, southern legislatures quickly passed laws and regulations, generally called Black Codes, that threatened former slaves with arrest and punishment if they were not satisfactorily employed. Congress reacted by passing the Reconstruction Act of March 1867, establishing military rule in the South and requiring that states approve the Fourteenth Amendment and adopt state constitutions treating blacks and whites equally before being allowed to rejoin the Union and regain their representation in Congress.

A major debate was initiated in Congress early in 1869 about how to protect voting rights and implement equality in America. Massachusetts senator Henry Wilson took the broadest view, saying, "Let us give to all citizens equal rights, and then protect everybody in the United States in the exercise of those rights. When we attain that position we shall have carried out logically the ideas that lie at the foundation of our institutions."[77] Republican senators Simon Cameron of Pennsylvania and Oliver Morton of Indiana also argued for a broad suffrage amendment and against excluding voters on the basis of race, ethnicity, property, religion, or education. They failed. Democrats, of course, wished to limit black voting, but many Republicans were just as determined to exclude the Democrat-leaning Irish, as well as the Chinese, Native Americans, illiterates, and itinerants. Neither party envisioned female suffrage. Hence, on February 26, 1869, the Republican majority in Congress passed a narrow version of the Fifteenth Amendment, which read, "The right of citizens of the United States to vote shall not be denied or abridged by the United States or any State on account of race, color, or previous condition of servitude." Freedom had expanded in the crucible of the Civil War, but constitutional equality still glimmered in the distant future.

It took a terrible Civil War to produce an end to slavery and the promise of legal equality for black Americans. Within a few short years, white Americans were exhausted, troubled, and doubtful. Many had become convinced that the war had carried them too far, and they yearned for the ideals of a simpler and more orderly time. The critical proposal to distribute seized and abandoned property in the South to former slaves was blocked in Congress. Without the promised "forty acres and a Mule," that is, land and the tools to work it, the freed slaves were without the means to survive on their own. Within the space of a few short years, most southern blacks had fallen back under the control of their former owners. Vagrancy laws and the sharecropping or crop-lien system tied indebted black farmers to the land only slightly less securely than had slavery. The late nineteenth century was largely dedicated to retracting many of the promises made during and immediately after the war in order to re-create, as much as could be, the antebellum social order. Black Americans had to wait a century more for freedom.

Conclusion

Jackson and his followers sought to leave behind Jefferson's republican elitism while expanding his promise of equality for white men. The raucous partisanship of Jacksonian democracy left the aging Jefferson concerned for his country and feeling that he had outlived his time. The quarter century following Jefferson's death in 1826 found Democrats and Whigs struggling to understand and guide a nation in which life had sped up, businesses had grown in size and complexity, and equality left many exposed, vulnerable, and uncertain.

The focus on equality that Tocqueville and so many others saw defining the second quarter of the nineteenth century promised that every white man could compete for wealth and position. Energy and enthusiasm characterized the culture, all could compete and perhaps win big, but not all did. So a new concern, barely evident in the colonial, Founding, and early national periods, emerged and spread throughout society. Opportunity was widespread, but everyone was pursuing it, and no one had a better claim to win than anyone else. So, if a man failed, he had no one to blame but himself. Tocqueville was the first to notice and describe the fear of failure, the "feverish ardor," the "vague dread," and the blasted hopes that accompanied the new and more naked individualism of the age.

Tocqueville was by no means alone in linking equality and democracy to doubt and melancholy. Both Emerson and Thoreau described the same competitive excitement and grim determination in society, though they reacted to it in different ways. Emerson urged Americans, especially young people, into the fray; he urged them to celebrate their equality by pursuing wealth. Nonetheless, like Tocqueville, Emerson was concerned that young people who failed in their first endeavor would lose all hope, "all spring & vivacity," and he urged them to try again. Thoreau, however, gave radically different counsel. Thoreau saw the competitive hustle in society and advised withdrawal—such as his retreat to Walden Pond—where physical needs could easily be met and nature, quiet, and calm allowed the exploration of inner oceans and continents. Few could follow Thoreau's course; most had to follow Emerson's and judge themselves as the market did.

Melville was convinced that equality, competition, and the results of the marketplace did not serve society or the people well. Melville thought that men differed profoundly in character, determination, preparation, advantages, and ability and that turning them loose, unfettered, on each other invited domination, conflict, and chaos. Rather, people and society needed and benefited by the limits and restraints of culture, tradition, and law. Competition among men as disparate as the "ungodly, god-like" Ahab, the merely virtuous Starbuck, the compliant Ishmael or Billy Budd, and the radically incapable Bartleby invited the monomaniacal to tyrannize over the multitude. Melville saw democratic life as "Ifs eternally" unless checked by culture, tradition, and law.

Lincoln shared many of Melville's instincts and concerns, even though his view of human nature was less dark. Lincoln thought men often benighted and wrong but educable, capable of being led, slowly and carefully, to higher ground. Lincoln's "The Perpetuation of Our Political Institutions" counseled a civil religion of respect for the Constitution and laws as the best check against lawlessness and political instability. Two decades later, when lawlessness had overwhelmed the nation and brought civil war, Lincoln worked to hold the nation together and then, only as northern public opinion seemed slowly to allow, to extend the promise of the Declaration, always his guiding light, to the freedmen.

The delicacy and complexity of Lincoln's challenge in moving toward freedom, if not quite equality, for blacks was evident in his famous debate with Douglas and in the novels of Twain and Faulkner. Twain and Faulkner, though in very different ways, focused on the white supremacy pervasive in mid-nineteenth-century America. Twain's *Pudd'nhead Wilson* highlighted the power of cultural presumptions and laws to shape lives. A white baby and a baby one-thirty-second black, with bloodlines running back to Virginia's Captain John Smith, were switched at birth, and both were ruined by the cultural impact, one of being raised black and a slave, though white, and the other of discovering black blood after being raised white and privileged. Faulkner's *Absalom* was a compelling story of a family built on and ultimately destroyed by cultural assumptions about race, miscegenation, and vengeance. In the face of these deep cultural presumptions of white supremacy and black inferiority, Lincoln ended slavery and the post–Civil War Republican Party passed the Thirteenth, Fourteenth, and Fifteenth Amendments to the Constitution before losing momentum. The final decades of the nineteenth century, to which we now turn, saw the return of white supremacy both in the South and nationally, the restoration of the antebellum social and economic status quo, and the loss of promise and hope in black America.

5 | Individualism and Combination in the Age of the Robber Barons

> The law of competition . . . insures the survival of the fittest.
> . . . We accept and welcome, therefore, . . . the concentration
> of business, . . . in the hands of a few, . . . as being not only
> beneficial, but essential for the future progress of the race.
> —Andrew Carnegie, "Wealth"

Adding ideas drawn from Charles Darwin to the intellectual stock earlier drawn from Protestant theology, liberal individualism, and laissez-faire economics gave the social theory of the second half of the nineteenth century an unusually sharp edge. Darwin (1809–1882) declared in his seminal book *On the Origin of Species* (1859) that life in the plant and animal kingdoms evolved through natural selection, a process in which competition and struggle led to the survival of the fittest and the progressive improvement of the species. Darwin declared that "natural selection acts by competition" in which "the most vigorous individuals . . . successfully struggled" to dominate "their conditions of life." He assured the reader that "the great and complex battle of life" redounded to the general good, saying, "When we reflect on this struggle, we may console ourselves with the full belief . . . that the vigorous, the healthy, and the happy survive and multiply."[1] Darwin concluded that the laws of nature that governed plant and animal life displayed the same underlying processes as those discovered by Sir Charles Lyell in geology and Thomas Malthus in population economics and social theory. Strikingly, this meant that the best physical, biological, and social science of the day agreed that natural processes, working unimpeded over time, led inexorably to improvement in individuals, societies, and species.

By the late 1860s Darwinian ideas had permeated the nation's corporate boardrooms and university classrooms and were generally familiar to the literate public. British sociologist Herbert Spencer and an American disciple, Yale sociologist William Graham Sumner, with Darwin's acquiescence and occasional cooperation, applied these themes to human society in a theory that came to be called social Darwinism. Social Darwinists employed analogies to the natural world to suggest that social change, like biological and geological change, occurred by processes too detailed, complex, and multifaceted for man to fully understand, let alone control and direct. Better simply to clear the social terrain of obstacles and allow competition to decide the struggle for wealth and status. In 1868 E. L. Godkin, editor of the *Nation* and one of the leading literary arbiters of the last half of the nineteenth century, declared that competition was "the law by which Providence secures the progress of the human race. . . . It is a law of human nature."[2] Sumner summarized this view in the striking declaration "This is a world in which the rule is, 'Root, hog, or die.'"[3]

Thoughtful Americans worried that the emerging Darwinian framework undermined traditional American ideals and attitudes concerning freedom, individual rights and liberties, the common good, and much more. Competition, natural selection, and survival of the fittest seemed to comport easily with American conceptions of individualism, opportunity, hard work, and personal responsibility, but they seemed just as certainly to strip away commitments to equality, fairness, and the good of one's fellow man. Many worried that if competition overwhelmed compassion, if property held unmediated sway over man, the American Dream would be no more.

But change was coming on in a rush. A nation of scattered farms and small villages was transformed during the middle decades of the nineteenth century into a nation of cities, corporations, factories, and wage laborers. Especially in the North, the Civil War accelerated the expansion of transportation, communication, and mass production. The victors in this battle for economic ascendency—John D. Rockefeller, J. P. Morgan, Andrew Carnegie, Cornelius Vanderbilt, Leland Stanford, Jim Fisk, Jay Gould, Philip Armour, and their peers—came to be known as "captains of industry," the "robber barons" of the Gilded Age. Immensely competitive, unrestrained by government regulation, and buttressed by the Darwinism of the age, these men and others of their class and station exercised nearly unchecked power. Clearly, the scope and scale of opportunity in America had changed dramatically. Just as clearly, with the stakes so high, few men could play this game, and fewer still could win.

The American Commonwealth (1891), by the British lawyer, historian, and diplomat Lord James Bryce, has long been accounted second only to Tocqueville's *Democracy in America* as an insightful outsider's view of American society. Bryce famously titled one of the early chapters in his book "Why Great Men Are Not Chosen President." He argued that "in America, . . . much of the best ability, both for thought and for action, . . . rushes into . . . the business of developing the material resources of the country."[4] As a result, while few Americans could name a president between Abraham Lincoln and Theodore Roosevelt, many could name at least a few of the great robber barons of the age.

The voices of the nation's elected leaders may have been weak, but those of the new captains of industry, Carnegie, Rockefeller, Vanderbilt, Stanford, Morgan, and their like, were strong. Moreover, great wealth had its advocates in the academy, the pulpit, and the arts. The showman P. T. Barnum praised "money getting," and Horatio Alger Jr. labored for decades, most notably in *Ragged Dick* (1868), to transmit Poor Richard's lessons to new generations. As always, most of the great novelists of the period and great novelists writing later about the period criticized the winners and pointed with sympathy to the losers and the excluded. Mark Twain's classics *The Adventures of Tom Sawyer* (1876) and *The Adventures of Huckleberry Finn* (1883) were explicit assaults on Alger. They were, of course, much more than that; they introduced an American vernacular that quickly became standard in our national literature. William Dean Howells's most important books, *The Rise of Silas Lapham* (1885) and *A Hazard of New Fortunes* (1890), explored the conflict between the traditional American values of the first half of the nineteenth century and the no-holds-barred competition and concentration of the second half of the century. Traditional values, even the American Dream, were under intense pressure and seldom fared well in these novels.

Finally, several important novels focused on the excluded. Toni Morrison's *Beloved* (1987) described how thoroughly pulverized, physically and psychologically, blacks were by slavery and its immediate aftermath. The Darwinian ethic of the age explained black failure to compete and thrive as incapability; Morrison disagreed, saying it was the entirely understandable result of being nearly destroyed, body and soul, by white oppression. Three novels, Alger's *Helen Ford* (1866), Stephen Crane's *Maggie: A Girl of the Streets* (1893), and Theodore Dreiser's *Sister Carrie* (1900), highlighted the narrow choices and deep vulnerability of women, especially young women alone, at the close of the nineteenth century.

Andrew Carnegie and John D. Rockefeller:
Benefactors of Mankind

P. T. Barnum (1810–1891), the great entrepreneur, showman, and lecturer, narrowed and sharpened the lessons that Benjamin Franklin and Ralph Waldo Emerson taught young Americans. Barnum was universally known for his New York museum, the massively successful American tour that he organized for the great European singer Jenny Lind, and his traveling circus. Barnum's most popular lecture, entitled "The Art of Money Getting," delivered first in 1858 and innumerable times thereafter, read like a condensation of the wisdom of Franklin and Emerson. Barnum began with the assurance that "those who really desire to attain an independence, have only to set their minds upon it, and adopt the proper means . . . and the thing is easily done."[5] Hard work and perseverance were the keys. Barnum advised his listeners to pick the right goal and then to "work at it, if necessary, early and late, in season and out of season, not leaving a stone unturned, and never deferring for a single hour that which can be done just as well *now*." In words that Franklin could very easily have uttered, Barnum reminded his listeners that "ambition, energy, industry, perseverance, are indispensable requisites for success in business."[6] Barnum also listed a number of "Maxims" for success in money getting, one of which he attributed directly to Franklin and all of which echoed Poor Richard and Father Abraham. Barnum advised that "the maxim of Dr. Franklin can never fail to be true—that 'honesty is the best policy.'" Barnum's other maxims included

> Perseverance is sometimes but another word for self-reliance.
> Learn something useful.
> Let hope predominate, but be not too visionary.
> Do not scatter your powers. Engage in one kind of business only.
> Be systematic.[7]

Clearly, Barnum looked back to the Protestant ethic of the Puritans and Franklin, but he also reflected a coarsening of that tradition evident in Emerson and gaining decisive momentum. The coarsening involved a new praise of "money getting" per se and a dismissive treatment of those who lost out in the race for wealth. Barnum declared that "the desire for wealth is nearly universal, and none can say it is not laudable." Responsible and humane "money-getters are the benefactors of the race." Barnum always closed his lecture on "Money Getting" with the story of a "vagabond" who claimed, "I have discovered there is money enough in the world for all of us, if it was equally divided; this must be done, and we shall all be happy together." When he was pressed—"if everybody was like you, it would be spent in two months, and what would you do then?"—he replied, "Oh! divide again; keep dividing, of course."[8] Audiences roared at the vagabond's suggestion that society's wealth be divided and redivided among all citizens. They knew better because wealthy "benefactors" of the race, led by Carnegie and Rockefeller, explained that society was best served when its "fittest" members controlled its wealth.

Andrew Carnegie (1835–1919), born to grinding Scottish poverty and an immigrant at age thirteen, made the most famous argument for the discretion and independence of society's wealthiest members in an article entitled simply "Wealth" (1889). Carnegie saw the men who controlled the monopolies and trusts as winners in a Darwinian competition for dominance. He declared that while "the law of competition . . . may be sometimes hard for the individual, it is best for the race, because it insures the survival of the fittest in every department. We accept and welcome, therefore, . . . the concentration of business, industrial and commercial, in the hands of a few, and the law of competition between these, as being not only beneficial, but essential for the future progress of the race."[9] John D. Rockefeller (1839–1937), perhaps the preeminent robber baron of the age, the architect of the Standard Oil Trust, and the most hated man of the half century spanning the beginning of the twentieth century, declared, "The day of combination is here to stay. Individualism has gone never to return."[10] He agreed with Carnegie that "the growth of a large business is merely a survival of the fittest." So too did the railroad baron James J. Hill, who said, "The fortunes of railroad companies are determined by the law of the survival of the fittest."[11] Carnegie, Rockefeller, and their fellow captains of industry assumed that Charles Elliott Perkins, president of the Chicago, Burlington, and Quincy Railroad, was merely posing a rhetorical question when he asked, "Are not the great benefactors of mankind the men who organize industry and help to cheapen the necessaries and conveniences of life?" Perkins admitted, "Their motives may be selfish . . . but are they not benefactors all the same?"[12]

Not only did the concentration of power and wealth reward society's fittest for their successful competitive efforts, but it also kept power and wealth out of the hands of the unfit. Once again, Carnegie made the point in greatest detail and drew the most direct connection to the social Darwinism of the day. Carnegie simply declared, "One of the serious obstacles to the improvement of our race is indiscriminate charity. It were better for mankind that the millions of the rich were thrown into the sea than so spent as to encourage the slothful, the drunken, the unworthy. . . . He is the only true reformer who is as careful and as anxious not to aid the unworthy as he is to aid the worthy."[13] Carnegie, standing on Darwin's shoulders, proudly served the race by denying the unworthy poor. Carnegie and Rockefeller were leading spokesmen for the business elite, but there were many others in the higher citadels of academe, the arts, and the church eager to support their case that the competition of social Darwinism worked in the general interest.

One clear example of how Darwinian ideas changed the way people thought and expressed themselves politically juxtaposes words spoken by Abraham Lincoln and by William Torrey Harris, one of the nation's leading educators. Lincoln, speaking to the Wisconsin State Agricultural Society in 1858, said, "As the Author of man makes every individual with one head and one pair of hands, it was probably intended that . . . [that] particular head, should direct and control that particular pair of hands. . . . And that being so, every head should be cultivated and improved, by whatever will add to its capacity for performing its charge."[14] Harris was the superintendent of the St. Louis Public Schools from 1868 to 1880 and U.S. commissioner of education from 1889 to 1906. Just a dozen years after Lincoln's speech, speaking to the 1870 meeting of the National Education Association of the United States, he warned, as Lincoln never would have, "An edict has gone forth to the New World in our Declaration of Independence: 'Woe unto that head which cannot govern its pair of hands.' Unto the lower races who fail in this, it reads the sentence: 'If you cannot direct your own hands by your own intelligence you only encumber the ground here, and can remain by sufferance in this place only so long as land is cheap.'"[15] Lincoln's generous point was that since heads must direct hands, we had better educate those heads. Harris's much less generous point was that if hands fail to fulfill a body's needs, the head must be incapable and that body must make way for its better.

Horatio Alger, Mark Twain, and the American Dream

Within America a debate raged over how to ensure that freedom, equality, and opportunity remained healthy and vibrant in a rapidly changing society. Horatio Alger passed the traditional wisdom of Franklin and Lincoln on to new generations. For Alger, the American Dream continued to counsel that study, industry, frugality, and saving and investing for the future, leavened with sympathy and generosity toward the less fortunate, were the surest path to security and respect. Mark Twain trained his devastating wit on Franklin and Alger, making their old virtues a laughingstock for the next generation, though without offering serious counsel or guidance of his own. Twain's destruction of Alger left the door open for others who stressed competition, striving, and struggle to the detriment and even the exclusion of charity, benevolence, public service, and attention to the common good. Increasingly, society's elites presented a description of American freedom that the common man and his representatives found difficult to dispute but that left them only the slimmest chance of competing successfully against much more powerful actors.

Horatio Alger Jr. (1832–1899) wrote more than a hundred novels describing how young men might follow the road to success. His most popular book and his only real best seller, *Ragged Dick; or, Street Life in New York with the Boot Blacks*, was initially serialized in a periodical for schoolchildren and then published in book form. There followed over the next three decades a steady stream of books with titles like *Strive and Succeed*, *Slow and Sure*, *Struggling Upward*, and *Luck and Pluck*. Alger sought to update the American Dream for a late nineteenth-century world that was increasingly urban and hence fast moving, complex, and morally ambiguous. He did not laud the new robber barons; in fact, he almost never mentioned, and never positively, the mines, factories, canneries, and slaughterhouses of the new economy. The economic world in Alger's novels was still one of small businesses and commercial partnerships, in which the personal and business reputations of the proprietors were one and in which a hand up to a promising young man was a Christian duty. As he wrote on through the closing decades of the nineteenth century, the world he described and the world around him increasingly diverged.[16]

Richard Hunter, the Ragged Dick of the title, was orphaned early and had survived on the streets of New York, first by selling matches and fruit and then as a bootblack (shoe-shine boy), into his early teens. Homeless, living in a cardboard box, possessing a single set of soiled clothes, Dick affected a carefree and blustery but tenuous self-sufficiency. He smoked, drank a little, gambled, and wasted money on going to P. T. Barnum's circus and treating his friends to chowder. Dick Hunter was honest and dependable, smarter and harder working than most, kind and generous, but he could not read or write, lacked foresight, and had no idea how to better his situation. Dick's transformation began with a chance sidewalk encounter. Dick was working the streets of New York, blacking boots enough to feed himself that day and keeping a sharp eye out for other opportunities. Outside one of the city's swank hotels, Dick overheard a distinguished gentleman, a Mr. Whitney, explain to his nephew Frank that he did not have time to show him the city. Dick, with dirty face and hands, ill-fitting clothes, and a swagger that neither Mr. Whitney nor Frank found reassuring, offered to act as Frank's guide. After talking with Dick, cleaning him up and putting him in a spare set of Frank's much nicer and cleaner clothes, Mr. Whitney agreed and paid Dick a modest sum to guide Frank around the city.

The day that Dick spent with Frank was instructive for both. Frank, a well-educated but sheltered rural boy, was impressed by Dick's ability to avoid and even outsmart all the urban hustlers, con men, and crooks they encountered. Dick, on the other hand, began to glimpse the clean, comfortable, literate, middle-class life that Frank enjoyed. In his new clothes, and in Frank's good company, Dick was treated with a deference and respect that he had not known before. Soon Dick confided to Frank that he would "like to be a office boy, and learn business, and grow up 'spectable."[17] Frank assured Dick that his future was in his own hands. "A good many distinguished men have once been poor boys. There's hope for you, Dick, if you'll try. . . . If you'll try to be somebody, and grow up into a respectable member of society, you will. You may not become rich—it isn't everybody that becomes rich, you know—but you can obtain a good position, and be respected." Dick promised to try, and later Frank explained what it would take to succeed, telling Dick, "You must manage to get as good an education as you can. Until you do, you cannot get a position in an office or counting-room, even to run errands."[18]

Frank taught Dick by example and encouragement, but Dick's most authoritative teacher was Frank's uncle. Alger intended Mr. Whitney to conjure up images of Benjamin Franklin and the great inventor Eli

Whitney. After Frank and Dick returned to the hotel and Mr. Whitney heard about their day, he thanked Dick, paid him a bonus, and they talked. "How did you get up in the world?" Dick asked. Mr. Whitney replied, "I entered a printing-office as an apprentice. . . . [shades of Franklin] Then my eyes gave out. . . . I went into the country, and worked on a farm. After a while I was lucky enough to invent a machine, which has brought me in a great deal of money. [Eli Whitney's cotton gin?] But there was one thing I got while I was in the printing-office which I value more than money." Dick asked what that was, and Whitney replied, as Franklin would have, "A taste for reading and study. During my leisure hours I improved myself by study. . . . If you ever expect to do anything in the world, you must know something of books."[19] Whitney concluded his advice to Dick Hunter by telling him, "Save your money, my lad, buy books, and determine to be somebody, and you may yet fill an honorable position. . . . Don't forget what I have told you. Remember that your future position depends mainly upon yourself." Dick doubled his effort at boot blacking, saved his money, and avoided extravagance, and before long he rented a permanent place, learned to read and write, found a church, and planned for the future. Most important, Dick's hard work, frugality, and foresight led him to open a bank account to secure his small but growing fortune. He observed that "it was wonderful how much more independent he felt whenever he reflected upon the contents" of that account.[20] In Jeffersonian America, independence rested on possession of land; in Alger's increasingly urban post–Civil War America, independence rested on money in the bank.

As it always did in Alger novels, determination to improve paid off through a combination of preparation, pluck, and luck. After a year of intensive study, Dick could "read well, write a fair hand, and had studied arithmetic, . . . grammar, and geography. . . . He knew that it would take a long time to reach the goal which he had set before him, and . . . that he had only himself to depend upon, and he determined to make the most of himself,—a resolution which is the secret of success in nine cases out of ten."[21] Dick's big break, landing a job in a counting room, the first or apprenticeship stage in a business career, came unexpectedly as a result of both luck and pluck. One afternoon Dick decided to accompany his new roommate and tutor, Henry Fosdick, on an errand that required taking a ferry from Manhattan to Brooklyn. During the trip, a young boy of six slipped away from his father and sister and fell over the side and into the water. The father, unable to swim, cried out in anguish, "Who will save my child? A thousand—ten thousand dollars to anyone who will save him!" Dick, an excellent swimmer reacting instinctively, was in the water to save the boy even before hearing the father's promise of a reward. While Alger did not record that the child's father, Mr. James Rockwell, actually gave Dick a reward of $10,000, Mr. Rockwell did give him a new suit of clothes and his dream job, $10 a week as a clerk in Mr. Rockwell's business.

For Dick Hunter and Henry Fosdick, as well as for other working- and middle-class boys in the Alger novels, a "position" in a store, a business, or a counting room, a "clerkship" with the opportunity to move up, was the middle and late nineteenth-century urban equivalent of Jefferson's fifty-acre freehold. It was the minimum basis for security and independence and the foundation from which future opportunity might be sought. Dick's American Dream was a comfortable sufficiency, a place to sleep, enough to eat, an extra suit of clothes or two, some savings to fall back on, and a chance, not a guarantee but a chance, to better himself.[22] Alger's boys aspired to a position, maybe a business of their own someday, but they did not aspire to control national monopolies and command thousands of nameless workers.

Mark Twain (1835–1910) read Alger's advice to boys and made no attempt to stifle his laughter and derision. Twain has often been described as the most original American author of the nineteenth century. He rejected the formal standards of Europe and New England and instead developed a distinctive American voice. The class and race dialects in which Twain wrote became the standard American literary voice, a voice that lasted well into the twentieth century. Alger's formula of honesty, education, preparation, hard work, and saving and investing to earn security and, hopefully, prosperity was rejected by Twain's characters in literally every particular. Twain's first thrust, just two years after Alger's publication of *Ragged Dick*, was a short piece entitled "The Story of the Good Little Boy Who Did Not Prosper" (1870). Over the next few years, Twain teased the original tale into two, the original, now entitled "The Story of the Good Little Boy," and a new one entitled "The Story of the Bad Little Boy" (both 1875). Nothing turned out well for the good little boy, while the bad little boy, remaining bad all his life, "got wealthy by all manner of cheating and rascality; and now . . . belongs to the Legislature."[23] Twain's most famous novels, *The Adventures of Tom Sawyer* and *The Adventures of Huckleberry Finn,* tell the same story.

Tom Sawyer and Huckleberry Finn were Twain's two most beloved characters; both were rascals, though Huck was more thoroughly so. Tom Sawyer was orphaned, but he lived with his good and well-meaning Aunt Polly. He was well cared for, fed, and clothed; he went, grudgingly, to school and church; but he had a raging imagination and lacked foresight, so his adventures frequently went awry. Huck, on the other hand, was homeless, ill-clothed, and ill-fed; did not go to school or church, except very occasionally; and was subject to the emotional and physical abuse of a drunken father. Huck resembled Ragged Dick: homeless, illiterate, and vulnerable. While Alger tutored Dick in society's values and led him to security, Twain led Huck through a joyous romp in which "sivilization" itself was rejected as "smothery."

In *The Adventures of Tom Sawyer*, Twain, like Alger, identified "model boys." In Alger, these boys and their habits and choices were to be emulated, but in Twain they were models that adults might appreciate but that no real boy could possibly admire. The model boys in *Tom Sawyer* were Tom's cousin Sid and Willie Mufferson. Twain told us that Tom "was not the model boy of the village. He knew the model boy [Sid] very well though—and loathed him." Sid was described as "a quiet boy, and had no adventurous, troublesome ways." To Tom, Willie was even worse. On Sunday mornings, as the congregation filed in, "last of all came the model boy, Willie Mufferson, taking as heedful care of his mother as if she were cut glass. He always brought his mother to church, and was the pride of all the matrons. The boys all hated him, he was so good; and besides, he had been 'thrown up to them' so much."[24]

Tom was full of devilment but he was not mean, and any harm that might befall him or those around him resulted from a chronic lack of foresight and an inability to consistently separate fact from fantasy. Twain introduced Tom with the famous scene in which Aunt Polly had ordered him to whitewash the front fence. She observed, ruefully, that "he hates work more than he hates anything else," and Tom confirmed that as he faced the fence: "The gladness went out of nature. . . . It seemed to him that life was hollow, and existence but a burden." Tricking other boys into doing his work lifted his spirits, but the thought of Sunday school and real school on Monday cratered them again. On Sunday, "the three children set out for Sunday school, a place that Tom hated with his whole heart; but Sid and Mary were fond of it." In church, "the prayer, he only endured it—if he did that much." And "Monday morning found Tom Sawyer miserable. Monday always found him so, because it began another week's slow suffering in school."[25]

Huckleberry Finn was the more complicated and the more fascinating character. Huck, like Ragged Dick, started outside society and "sivilization," but unlike Dick, who worked to enter society and adopt its rules, Huck rejected them outright. Initially, Huck and Dick had much in common, including their wardrobe and their casual freedom;

> Huckleberry was always dressed in cast-off clothes of full-grown men . . . his coat, when he wore one, hung nearly to his heels. . . . Huckleberry came and went at his own free will. He slept on door-steps in fine weather, and in empty hogsheads in wet; he did not have to go to school or to church, . . . or obey anybody: he could go fishing or swimming when and where he chose, . . . nobody forbade him to fight; . . . he never had to wash, nor put on clean clothes; he could swear wonderfully. In a word, everything that goes to make life precious, that boy had.[26]

Huck knew that his freedom had costs, which he occasionally bemoaned but ultimately agreed to pay. Near the end of *Tom Sawyer*, Huck and Tom get an Alger-like lucky break; they discover a treasure box containing more than $12,000. In an Alger tale, the boys would already have learned the right virtues and habits, so the story would have ended with the benediction that both boys were secure on the path to respectability and prosperity. But Twain had a different lesson to teach. Judge Thatcher, at Aunt Polly's request, put Tom's money out at 6 percent interest, and the Widow Douglas took Huck into her home and invested his money as well. "Huck Finn's wealth, and the fact that he was under the Widow Douglas's protection, introduced him into society—no, dragged him into it, hurled him into it. . . . The widow's servants kept him clean and neat, combed and brushed. . . . He had to eat with knife and fork, he had to use napkin, cup, and plate; he had to learn his book; he had to go to church." After about three weeks, Huck broke for the woods. Tom found him hiding out in some old hogsheads; Huck explained,

> The widder's good to me, and friendly; but I can't stand them ways. . . . It's awful to be tied up so. . . . And besides, that schools going to open, and I'd a had to go to it; well, I wouldn't stand that, Tom. Looky here, Tom, being rich ain't what it's cracked up to be. It's just worry and worry, and sweat and sweat, and a-wishing you was dead all the time. . . . No, Tom, I won't be rich, and I won't live in those cussed smothery houses. I like the woods, and the river, and hogsheads, and I'll stick to 'em, too.[27]

The Adventures of Huckleberry Finn made Huck the principal character, along with the runaway slave Jim, and made Tom secondary. Rafting down the Mississippi, Huck was running from "sivilization" and Jim was running from the prospect of being sold away from his family. On the river, they were outside society, civilization, and the law, living by their wits, come what may. Alger's Dick Hunter prided himself on never lying or stealing and on protecting the weak and unaware from sharpers and con men. Huck decided that since he had grown up outside law and morality,

> it warn't no use for me to try to learn to do right; a body that don't get started right when he's little, ain't got no show—when the pinch comes there ain't nothing to back him up. . . . Well, then, says I, what's the use you learning to do right, when it's troublesome to do right and ain't no trouble to do wrong, and the wages is just the same? . . . So I reckoned I wouldn't bother no more about it, but after this always do whichever come handiest at the time.[28]

Not surprisingly, Huck treated the truth with suspicion. In a puzzling situation, he observed, "I reckon a body that ups and tells the truth when he is in a tight place, is taking considerable many resks." Even when the truth seemed the only way, it struck Huck as "most like setting down on a kag of powder and touching it off just to see where you'll go to." Moreover, Huck rarely blinked at dishonesty, even theft, and did not see it as his responsibility to save the untutored from fraud. When Huck wanted to go to the circus, he "loafed around the back side till the watchman went by, and then dived in under the tent. I had my twenty-dollar gold piece and some other money, but I reckoned I better save it." Huck explained, "I ain't opposed to spending money on circuses, when there ain't no other way, but there ain't no use in *wasting* it on them." When two con men that Huck and Jim had fallen in with sought to steal the inheritance of two blameless sisters, Huck observed, "I see what *he* was up to; but I never said nothing, of course."[29] Ultimately, Huck did step in to help the sisters, but his normal stance was that of disengaged outsider.

Huck Finn concluded with Tom, Huck, and Jim all safe and free. Tom gave Jim forty dollars and Jim's thoughts turned to his family, but Tom's turned to the next adventure. He proposed that the three of them "slide out of here, one of these nights, and get an outfit, and go for howling adventures amongst the Injuns, over in the Territory, for a couple of weeks or so." Huck raised the question of money to buy "an outfit" and was told that his $6,000 remained in the bank and that his father, who he feared had gained control of that money, was dead. Huck was unmoved by his father's death—understandably, as the man had been a drunken scoundrel—and by the fact that he was still rich. He decided "to light out for the Territory ahead of the rest, because Aunt Sally she's going to adopt me and sivilize me, and I can't stand it. I been there before."[30] Lawrence Buell wrote that Tom Lutz, author of *Doing Nothing: A History of Loafers, Loungers, Slackers, and Bums in America* (2006), called "'the slacker' the 'necessary twin' of the model American workaholic. By that logic Huck's vicarious appeal then and now as counterforce, as the most ingratiating slacker in national literature, seems all the more irresistible."[31]

William Dean Howells: The Moral Challenges of Business and Wealth

The novelist, editor, literary critic, and cultural arbiter William Dean Howells was one of the nation's leading cultural figures of the late nineteenth century. His novels now are less read than Mark Twain's, but in their day, Howells was an equally influential figure. His two most important novels, *The Rise of Silas Lapham* and *The Hazard of New Fortunes*, explored the practical and ethical rules of business competition. Carnegie, Rockefeller, Gould, Fisk, and others claimed that good Christian men building companies, and thus creating wealth and employment, were the nation's greatest benefactors. Novelists like Howells—and, a little later, Upton Sinclair and Frank Norris—saw greater complexity; they had questions and doubts, and they told stories that raised them sharply.

The Rise of Silas Lapham began after Silas had risen; in fact, he had risen high enough that the novel opened with him being interviewed for a business profile. He described his family and early life in classic terms: not rags to riches, but insecurity to security and then wealth. Silas told the journalist that his parents "were quiet, unpretentious people, religious, . . . and of sterling morality, and they taught their children the simple virtues of the Old Testament and Poor Richard's Almanac." Of himself, Silas said, "I'm fifty-five years old; and I've *lived* 'em, too; not an hour of waste time about *me*, anywheres!" About forty when the Civil

War broke out, Silas enlisted, took a ball above the knee at Gettysburg, and upon returning home, "found that I had got back to another world. The day of small things was past, and I don't suppose it will ever come again in this country."[32] At his wife Persis's suggestion, even insistence, Silas took a partner, Milton K. Rogers, with more capital than he, to expand a paint business he inherited from his father.

The business relationship with Milton Rogers was the flaw, the small crack at the base of Silas Lapham's life story, and a source of tension and sorrow between Silas and Persis. Persis always thought that Silas had treated Rogers unfairly when the partnership dissolved, and Silas always bristled at the mention of it. Just as the Laphams were about to build a fine new house on the Boston Back Bay, Rogers reappeared unexpectedly. Persis raised the old doubts, and Silas responded, "I tell you, . . . it was a perfectly square thing. And I wish, once for all, you would quit bothering me about it. My conscience is easy as far as he's concerned, and it always was." But, in fact, his conscience was not easy, and Persis responded, "No; you had better face the truth, Silas. . . . You crowded him out. A man that saved you! No, you had got greedy, Silas. You had made your paint your god, and you couldn't bear to let anybody else share its blessings."[33]

Silas's doubts, despite his protestations, plagued him. When Rogers appeared again at Silas's business, it was to seek his financial help. Upon returning from work that day, Silas told Persis, "Rogers . . . came to borrow money of me, and I lent him it. . . . We settled our business, and then we went into the old thing, from the very start. And we talked it all over. And when we got through we shook hands. Well, I don't know when it's done me so much good to shake hands with anybody." Persis was immensely relieved, saying, "You've taken the one spot—the one *speck*—off you that was ever there, and I'm satisfied."[34]

The relief felt by both Laphams, especially Silas, made him forget briefly that Rogers was a rolling business disaster. Rogers borrowed from Lapham to extricate himself from his latest difficulties, and he gave Lapham stock in some midwestern mills as collateral for the loan. The stock was trading too low for banks to loan on them, but Silas thought he could hold them until they rose. In fact, his conscience diverted him from the due diligence he would otherwise have exercised; the stocks fell further, and Silas had to loan Rogers more money to keep the investment from going under altogether. Silas explained to Persis, "I had to help him to try to get my money back. I might as well poured water into a sieve." As his own finances tightened, Silas sought to recoup by taking aggressive positions in the stock market. Again, he told Persis, "I began to buy and sell on a margin—just what I told you I never would do. . . . I began to lose, and then I began to throw good money after bad."[35]

The deflated price of the mill stock reflected the expectation that the G.L.&P. Railroad, the only transportation link to the mills, intended to build railcar works nearby and might want to buy the mills themselves. The railroad could make a lowball offer, and given their transportation leverage, the owners, now including Lapham, would have to sell. Rogers had some English buyers, either unaware that the G.L.&P. might force a low price or for some unscrupulous motive, willing to buy the mills at a premium. Selling to the English buyers would save both Rogers and Lapham. Rogers did not care why the English buyers were willing to overpay for the mills; he wanted to sell before the railroad moved. Silas, facing bankruptcy, was tempted, but Persis was adamantly opposed, and Silas sadly agreed that she was right. Simultaneously, a competing paint company discovered new means to reduce their costs, underselling Silas's paint in the marketplace, and he was forced to shut down. In this perfect storm of financial calamity, Lapham struggled unsuccessfully to survive. Deeply in debt, Silas sold most of his paint business to his competitors, except for a specialty line named for Persis, and paid those creditors he could.

Money had led Silas Lapham to behave sharply once, pushing Rogers from the business, and fear of losing his fortune tempted him to do so again, but he resisted and eventually did right—this, not the accumulation of wealth, was the rise of Silas Lapham, actually the recovery of his real self. "All those who were concerned in his affairs said he behaved well, and even more than well, when it came to the worst. The prudence, the good sense, which he had shown in the first years of his success, and of which his great prosperity seemed to have bereft him, came back."[36] Now an old man, Silas struggled halfheartedly to rebuild his business, but he eventually sold out completely to his competitors and took a small share in their company to pay off his remaining debts. Silas lost his fortune, perhaps too aggressively gained, but regained the character that his parents had taught him from *Poor Richard's Almanac*.

Howells's second great novel, *A Hazard of New Fortunes*, was more sharply drawn. Basil March, in his forties, had had literary aspirations when young but had gone into insurance to support his family. He was a careful man, lacking in confidence but buttressed by his wife and confidante, Isabel. When he lost his insurance job, he was offered the editorship of a new literary magazine, *Every Other Week*, by a journalist and advertising entrepreneur named Fulkerson. The Marches, lifelong Bostonians, reluctantly relocated to New York for the new job. Over time, it became clear to March that Fulkerson depended upon a financial backer, a midwestern natural gas mogul and Wall Street investor, and tensions developed.

Jacob Dryfoos; his wife; his son, Conrad; and his two daughters, Christine and Mela, were simple farm folk, made quickly and fabulously wealthy by the discovery of natural gas on their farm and, after a move to New York, by a series of winning financial investments. Mrs. Dryfoos mourned the loss of their old life, but Jacob had the bit in his teeth. He intended to turn the bookish Conrad, intent on the ministry, to business and finance and to use his money to make a place for his daughters among the New York elite.[37] Conrad's titular position as publisher of *Every Other Week* was to be his introduction to business, though Fulkerson and March effectively ran the magazine. After the magazine got off to an unexpectedly strong start, Jacob Dryfoos visited the offices and talked with Conrad, Fulkerson, and March. All were pleased with their success until Jacob asked them how much the magazine should earn in the first year; he was told $25,000. Dryfoos responded dismissively, "Humph! And you are all going to work a year—editor, manager, publisher, artists, writers, printers, and the rest of 'em—to clear twenty-five thousand dollars? . . . I see it made in half a minute in Wall Street, sometimes."[38]

Basil and Isabel March, subject as they were to Dryfoos's whims, struggled to understand his motivations. Basil suggested that Dryfoos "must have undergone a moral deterioration, an atrophy of the generous instincts. . . . He has sharpened, but he has narrowed; his sagacity has turned into suspicion, his caution to meanness, his courage to ferocity. . . . I am not very proud when I realize that such a man and his experience are the ideal and ambition of most Americans."[39] Howells explained, in the narrator's voice, that "there had been a time in Jacob's life when other things besides his money seemed admirable to him. He had once respected himself for the hardheaded, practical common sense which first gave him standing among his country neighbors. . . . His moral decay began with his perception of the opportunity of making money quickly and abundantly. . . . For money that had been earned painfully, slowly, and in little amounts he had only pity and contempt."[40]

Jacob's money did not bring peace and security; rather, it brought sadness and death. Jacob's attempt to make Conrad a hardheaded businessman only drove the young man away, toward charitable activities and the needs of the poor. Conrad was accidentally shot and killed while present, but not participating, in a labor riot, really a police attack on strikers and demonstrators. Jacob's vision and the valuation that he put on money shattered, but it was the Marches again who voiced Howells's message. About the labor unrest and the broader class conflict they saw around them, Basil said, "What I object to is this economic chance world in which we live and which we men seem to have created. . . . No one is sure of finding work; no one is sure of not losing it. . . . And so we go on, pushing and pulling, climbing and crawling, thrusting aside and trampling underfoot, lying, cheating, stealing."[41]

The din of economic growth drowned out the opponents of social Darwinism for decades. Opponents were always present, but they struggled well into the 1880s to marshal effective counterarguments. Among late nineteenth-century novelists, Howells analyzed the problem of rampant individualism, unrestrained competition, and an absence of social security and regulation as well as anyone. But as a pillar of the East Coast literary establishment, he barely suggested solutions. Solutions came from journalists like Ida Tarbell and Lincoln Steffens and intellectuals like Henry George. Slowly an argument took shape asserting that the competition, destruction, and carnage of nature, whereby a thousand fertilized eggs might produce a single fruit fly or pollywog that survived to adulthood, was no model for human life. Reason, intelligence, and invention could control, channel, and improve natural processes. Among novelists, the most thoroughgoing reform program came from Edward Bellamy.

Edward Bellamy (1850–1898) thought that individualism needed to be balanced by community and that humans were shaped more by nurture than by nature, by circumstances and conditions more than by genes and evolution, and that hence society could change rapidly for the better as a result of thoughtful reform. Bellamy's influential novel *Looking Backward, 2000–1887* (1888) sold more than 300,000 copies in its first two years. Bellamy died young, at just forty-eight, but he powerfully shaped the late nineteenth-century critique of laissez-faire industrial capitalism.

The literary device employed in *Looking Backward* was to transport a wealthy, well-educated Bostonian named Julian West from the Boston of 1887 to the Boston of 2000, where he marveled at and inquired into the tremendous changes that had taken place. West found himself in the year 2000 after a fire in 1887 destroyed his Boston home and put him in a coma, in which the passage of time produced no ill physical or mental effects. He lay undiscovered in a buried basement vault until awakened in 2000. Attention soon turned to the differences between the Boston of 1887 and that of 2000. Julian's interlocutors were Dr. Leete, a social historian of 2000 familiar with the 1880s, and the doctor's daughter, Edith.

Dr. Leete was interested to know how men of the late nineteenth century understood and accepted the poverty, class prejudice, and industrial conflict of the period, and West was interested to know how those seemingly natural and inevitable social, political, and economic realities had been resolved. *Looking Backward* opened with a wonderful analogy that West offered to explain late nineteenth-century society. West sketched the picture of "a prodigious coach," drawn over a hilly terrain of loose and rocky soil, to which most of humanity was harnessed. Atop the coach, and never getting down no matter how sandy the soil or steep the hill, were society's elite—the wealthy, educated, and prominent. Those harnessed to the coach were very hard-pressed; "the desperate straining of the team, their agonized leaping and plunging . . . , the many who fainted at the rope and were trampled in the mire, made a very distressing spectacle." Those atop the coach, by no means bereft of sympathy, "would call down encouragingly to the toilers at the rope, exhorting them to patience, and holding out hopes of possible compensation in another world for the hardness of their lot, while others contributed to buying salves and liniments for the crippled and injured. It was also agreed that it was a great pity that the coach should be so hard to pull."[42] Yet for three critical reasons, those atop the coach did no more than commiserate with their less fortunate fellows on the ropes. First, "it was firmly and sincerely believed that there was no other way in which Society could get along, except that the many pulled at the rope and the few rode." Second, it was so pleasant atop the coach and so fearsome below that the favored few held on as tight as they could. And third, those who rode on top shared "[a] singular hallucination . . . that they were not exactly like their brothers and sisters who pulled at the rope, but of finer clay, in some way belonging to a higher order of beings who might justly expect to be drawn."[43]

Leete responded that the basic intellectual error of the nineteenth century had been an "excessive individualism" that fueled mindless, destructive competition. The poverty, strikes, and violence had been produced by the struggle of working men and women against the concentration of capital. Nonetheless, while few recognized it at the time, this very process pointed the way to an unseen future; "the tendency toward monopolies, which had been so desperately and vainly resisted, was recognized at last, in its true significance, as a process which only needed to complete its logical evolution to . . . a single syndicate representing the people, to be conducted in the common interest for the common profit." Leete likened this economic evolution to the political revolution of 1776.[44] Allowing robber barons to dominate the economy, Leete argued, made no more sense than allowing the English monarchy to dominate politics had made a century earlier.

Under the people's syndicate, everyone would work, but the nature of the employment would be determined by choice and natural capacity, and the desirability of jobs would be equalized by varying time and benefits. All citizens, irrespective of their individual capabilities of body or mind, would receive an equal share of society's wealth. Leete explained to West that "the right of a man to maintenance at the nation's table depends on the fact that he is a man, and not on the amount of health or strength he may have. . . . The solidarity of the race and the brotherhood of man, which to you were but fine phrases, are, to our thinking and feeling, ties as real and as vital as physical fraternity."[45] The unquestioned right to an equal share of the social wealth removed all hunger, fear, and vulnerability among citizens and all the crime and violence that they produced.

Blacks and Opportunity in Late Nineteenth-Century America

One of the most powerful and long-lasting effects of Darwinian social theory was to undermine the ability of excluded groups to claim an equal share of society's opportunities and benefits. Darwin had been quite clear in the famous chapter on "Natural Selection" in *On the Origin of Species* that competition led not just to individual winners and losers but to survival and extinction for species. In nature, including that corner of nature that is human society, "the struggle for existence" produced "a constant tendency . . . to supplant and exterminate" in which "one large group [read white Anglo-Saxons, or simply whites] will slowly conquer another large group [read Africans, Asians, Indians, and so on], reduce its numbers, and thus . . . small and broken groups will finally tend to disappear."[46]

Darwinian social theorists argued that though freedom and equality were formally granted to black men in the wake of the Civil War by the Thirteenth, Fourteenth, and Fifteenth Amendments to the Constitution, real freedom and equality had to be earned in the open competition of the marketplace. Success in the marketplace demonstrated freedom and equality, while failure to thrive announced inability and inferiority. Most whites resolutely ignored the fact that blacks were freed with no land, no income, and few skills. Whites looked only to the results of the competition. If the freedmen failed to thrive, as most did, the immediate conclusion was that the gift of freedom and the related assumption of equality had been ill-advised. Soon the U.S. Supreme Court sanctioned state-mandated and state-enforced separation of the races in public places.

How blacks should respond to segregation and exclusion was a subject of heated debate within the black community and among black leaders. Frederick Douglass, the foremost black leader in nineteenth-century America, called for the fulfillment of the egalitarian vision to which he had coaxed Abraham Lincoln. Douglass held that "all that any man has a right to expect, ask, give, or receive in this world, is fair play. When society has secured this to its members, and the humblest citizen of the republic is put into the undisturbed possession of the natural fruits of his own exertions, there is really very little left for society and government to do."[47] Douglass knew that such a day had not yet come, and to his dying day in 1897 he decried the unwillingness of a great nation to live up to its values.

No novelist has focused more intently on the world as blacks experienced it in slavery and after slavery than Toni Morrison. The core of Morrison's Pulitzer Prize–winning *Beloved* was the magical realist tale of the return from the dead of a baby, Beloved, murdered by her mother to save her from the abuses of slavery and sexual exploitation. Eighteen years later, the murdered baby, now about nineteen, returned to her mother's home to learn why she had been murdered and to exact revenge. The action in *Beloved* occurred mostly in the 1870s, but with frequent flashbacks and remembrances to slavery in the antebellum period. Morrison's message was that slavery and racism left black Americans broken, with no personal or emotional security, no sense of individuality or autonomy, no hope, no future, barely a willingness or ability to love.

Morrison explored the devastation of black lives, especially black women's lives, and from whence that devastation had come. The physical exploitation that black men suffered in slavery was compounded among black women by sexual exploitation. Most of the adult black women in *Beloved* had been sexually abused. Sethe, the focus of the novel, escaped from slavery in Kentucky, giving birth to a daughter, Denver, in flight. She made her way across the Ohio River, guided by Stamp and Ella Paid, to the Ohio home of her slave husband's mother, Baby Suggs. Sethe's flight from the Sweet Home plantation had been sparked by sexual assault followed by a severe whipping when she told. But most graphically, Sethe was told of her mother's serial rape on the passage from Africa and thereafter. When Sethe was a child, Nan, an older slave woman, told Sethe that she and her mother "were together from the sea. Both were taken up many times by the crew. 'She threw them all away but you. The one from the crew she threw away on the island. The others from more whites she also threw away. Without names, she threw them. You she gave the name of the black man. She put her arms around him. The others she did not put her arms around.'" Sethe knew, both from her mother's story and her own, that "anybody white could take your whole self for anything that came to mind. Not just work, kill, or maim you, but dirty you. Dirty you so bad you couldn't like yourself anymore. Dirty you so bad you forgot who you were."[48]

While black women were particularly vulnerable during and after slavery, all blacks were physically vulnerable and, as Morrison displayed, emotionally stunted. Morrison wrote, "All of Baby's life, as well as Sethe's own, men and women were moved around like checkers. Anybody Baby Suggs knew, let alone loved, who hadn't run off or been hanged, got rented out, loaned out, bought up, brought back, stored up, mortgaged, won, stolen or seized." Paul D, the Sweet Home slave who had known Sethe as a girl and found her eighteen years later in the hope of starting a life with her, remembered, "During, before, and after the War he had seen Negroes so stunned, or hungry, or tired or bereft . . . who, like him, had hidden in caves and fought owls for food; who, like him, stole from pigs; who, like him, slept in trees in the day and walked by night; . . . to avoid regulators, raiders, paterollers, veterans, . . . and merrymakers."[49]

Paul D, Baby Suggs, and Sethe knew, all blacks knew, that all this deprivation and misery came from white people. As Baby Suggs lay broken and dying, she said, "Those white things have taken all I had or dreamed, . . . and broke my heartstrings too. There is no bad luck in the world but whitefolks." On the last day of her life, "she announced to Sethe and Denver the lesson she had learned from her sixty years a slave and ten years free: that there was no bad luck in the world but white people. 'They don't know when to stop.'"[50] Stamp Paid and Paul D were equally overwhelmed and uncomprehending. Stamp Paid wonderingly observed, "Eighteen seventy-four and whitefolks are still on the loose. Whole towns wiped clean of Negroes; eighty-seven lynchings in one year alone in Kentucky. . . . What *are* these people? You tell me, Jesus. What *are* they?" Later, Paul D asked, and Stamp Paid answered, "'Tell me this one thing. How much is a nigger supposed to take? Tell me. How much?' 'All he can,' said Stamp Paid. 'All he can.'" Paul D's plaintive response was "Why? Why? Why? Why? Why?"[51]

Paul D's relationship with Sethe was a study in the attempt, mostly failed, to reconstruct broken hearts, to allow long-stifled emotions to flow, and to dare to hope, to dream again. Initially, their emotional reservoirs were dry. Paul D had come, haltingly and over many years, looking for her, and she was deeply pleased and moved to see him. As they came together, "it was over before they could get their clothes off. . . . His dreaming of her had been too long and too long ago. Her deprivation had been not having any dreams of her own at all." Soon, Paul D and Sethe were sleeping together and having frequent, rewarding sex, but the emotional channels remained blocked. Sethe wondered, "Would it be all right? Would it be all right to go ahead and feel? Go ahead and *count on something*?" Paul D was uncertain as well, but he was willing to try, if only tentatively: "The best thing, he knew, was to love just a little bit; everything just a little bit." Paul D told Sethe, "We can make a life, girl. A life." But Sethe remained unsure, saying, "I don't know. I don't know." Paul D responded soothingly, "See how it goes. No promises, if you don't want to make any. Just see how it goes. All right?" Slowly, Sethe rose to the warmth, finally thinking, "A life. Could be."[52]

Could be, but probably not! Paul D remembered that in slavery, "you protected yourself and loved small. . . . A woman, a child, a brother—a big love like that would split you wide open." But after slavery, he thought it was at least possible "to get to a place where you could love anything you chose—not to need permission for desire—well now, *that* was freedom." But freedom, freedom and hope, brought the possibility, even the likelihood for battered blacks, of failure. When the past split Paul D and Sethe, he observed, "Wanting to live out his life with a whole woman was new, and losing the feeling of it made him want to cry and think deep thoughts that struck nothing solid."[53]

As *Beloved* concluded, there were only two real survivors, Paul D and Denver, and only one of them had a future. In the novel's closing pages, Paul D returned to Sethe, but like Baby Suggs, she had collapsed under the weight and consequences of white oppression, and nothing in the book suggested recovery. Denver, though, was young. As a child, she attended school for a year, until one of the other children, Nelson Lord, asked about her mother, the murderer, and she never went back—in fact, she remained mute for two years as a result of that trauma. As the battle with Beloved sapped Sethe's strength, Denver could only watch, but in watching, she grew stronger.

As Denver prepared to face the future, she remembered the warning of her grandmother, Baby Suggs, and her mother, Sethe, that in the broader world "were whitepeople [*sic*] and how could you tell about them?" Standing frozen on the front porch, knowing she needed help but afraid to go in search of it, Denver heard Baby Suggs, long dead, laugh "clear as anything." She reminded her grandmother that she had said "there was no defense" against white people, to which Baby responded, "There ain't." When Denver asked what, then, she could do, Baby answered, "Know it, and go out the yard. Go on." Thus empowered, Denver went to her old teacher, looking for help and asking for food. Nelson Lord, now grown too, was glad to see her, and neighbors stepped up and provided food, and Denver planted a garden. "It was a new thought, having a self to look out for and preserve. . . . Weeding the garden, pulling vegetables, cooking, washing, she plotted what to do and how." The Bodwins, old-line abolitionists, had helped her grandmother and mother, providing the house in which they lived, and soon, Denver, "thinner, steady in the eyes," went to work for them and thrived. "Miss Bodwin taught her stuff. . . . 'She says I might go to Oberlin. She's experimenting on me.'"[54]

The Bodwins had experimented on Baby Suggs and Sethe, welcoming them out of slave Kentucky and providing them a home to live in, but they had been too broken. Now Denver, a third generation, appeared on their porch, and they took her in to try again, a new experiment, education that might lead to Oberlin College. Maybe this experiment succeeded; the novel does not say. But being experimented on in a way that might lead to Oberlin, or anywhere else, was not pursuing a dream so much as it was following where led. In Morrison's *Sula* (1973), which I survey in chapter 7, several more generations crumble under the weight of white oppression.

White Women, Individualism, and Opportunity in the Gilded Age

Elizabeth Cady Stanton, Susan B. Anthony, Lucretia Mott, and many others hoped that the end of slavery would bring legal and constitutional recognition of equality for all Americans, irrespective of race or gender. But within months of the end of the war, Republican Party leaders and their male abolitionist allies, led by Wendell Phillips, began shrinking from the political challenge of confronting race and gender discrimination simultaneously. Phillips summed up the male leadership consensus: "One question at a time. . . . This hour belongs to the Negro."[55]

The nation's centennial celebration in 1876 seemed an obvious setting in which women might renew their demands for equal rights. Though denied space in the official Philadelphia exhibit halls, Elizabeth Cady Stanton and others prepared a Declaration of Rights for Women reminiscent of the 1848 Seneca Falls Declaration of Sentiments. The Declaration of Rights read, "We declare our faith in the principle of self-government; our full equality with man in natural rights; . . . We ask justice, we ask equality, we ask that all the civil and political rights that belong to citizens of the United States, be guaranteed to us and our daughters forever."[56] As women's demands for equality continued to be unheeded, a new brand of feminism arose. It was hoped that some who found the idea of equality between men and women unacceptable could accept the idea that though nature made men and women different, women had distinctive virtues and capabilities that deserved respect and could work a positive influence on society. The call for a "maternal commonwealth" reflected the special virtues and vision—of a peaceful, sober, nurturing, and family-centered community—of the nation's women.

Women, even white women, in the last third of the nineteenth century had few options outside the home. The lucky ones were kept comfortably by their fathers until they were transferred to husbands, though poor women found even this path to be rocky and uncertain. Single women had few ways to maintain themselves beyond domestic service, shop and factory work, piecework sewing, or, at least in novels, singing. Women alone were frequently presented as balanced on a knife's edge between poverty and the street. Sometimes miracles happened, fate intervened, and vulnerable women were saved in the nick of time. When miracles failed, women might fall to the street, through their own errors or those of others, where they faced degradation or death. Three novels, Horatio Alger's *Helen Ford*, Stephen Crane's *Maggie*, and Theodore Dreiser's *Sister Carrie*, showed fictional paths available to women—but none of these paths led to competence, security, and prosperity.

Horatio Alger generally wrote for boys. *Helen Ford* was the only one of Alger's more than 100 novels that featured a girl as the leading character.[57] As the story opened, Helen was the fourteen-year-old daughter and caregiver for her befuddled, often disoriented, inventor father. Robert Ford was estranged from his family because of a misunderstanding over his marriage to Helen's mother, the love of his life. The death of his wife left him emotionally and practically dependent on his young daughter. Though they lived very frugally, Robert Ford's lack of practical focus left it up to Helen to respond as their resources slipped to just a few dollars.

Helen was attractive and friendly, "a truthful, unsophisticated child, perfectly transparent and straightforward, and imagined that others were equally so."[58] Like many Alger heroes, Helen was praised for honesty, integrity, forthrightness, generosity, empathy, and a vague religiosity. But unlike Ragged Dick and other boy heroes, Helen did not prepare systematically for success. She had a modest education and no preparation for a trade, so her first attempt to buttress the family finances was piecework sewing. Helen had become friends with Martha Grey, a resident in the same boardinghouse who maintained herself by sewing full-time. Martha "was one of a large family, who had never known sorrow or separation till the death of her parents . . . turned them all adrift upon the world." Martha was quiet and dignified, working steadily over long hours, and "in spite of her humble circumstances, Martha would have been recognized by anyone possessing discernment as a lady."[59] Martha served as something of a big sister to Helen, but also as an object lesson as she struggled under the strain of her poorly paid work.

Martha's fate was very instructive. Alger explained, "Perhaps no employment is more confining and more poorly compensated than that of sewing. The narrow choice allowed to women, who are compelled to labor for their livelihood, leads to an unhealthy and disastrous competition . . . and enables employers to establish a disgracefully low scale of prices. Fifteen hours out of twenty-four are sometimes spent in unremitting labor, the results of which will scarcely keep soul and body together." Strikingly, Horatio Alger, the name most frequently connected to the rags-to-riches myth, here declared that the formula did not work for women because they had such narrow choices. It certainly did not work for Martha; she weakened, sickened, collapsed, and was discovered by Helen "lying insensible on the floor."[60] Helen's fate, while often uncertain, never sank as low as Martha's because, as in so many Alger novels, luck and fate intervened.

Helen sewed just briefly, until it became clear that the pay would not sustain them. Among the "narrow choice[s] allowed to women," in Alger's phrase, natural women's work—sewing, cooking, cleaning, laundry—might be done for low pay, but other avenues were few. One opened for Helen when Martha's cousin, more secure in the world, invited them to the theater. The next day, when Martha longed to hear again one of the songs from the show, Helen offered to sing it for her. Helen had been "gifted with a voice of extraordinary flexibility and compass, whose natural power had evidently been improved by cultivation."[61] Martha encouraged Helen to apply to the theater, but for a lady to display herself publicly was morally ambiguous and physically dangerous. Nevertheless, Helen had few choices, so, without her father's knowledge, she timidly approached the theater manager, auditioned, and was hired at the sum of six dollars per week. This was financial stability; she and her father were saved. And as her talents brought bigger roles and more money, she could help Martha and Herbert Coleman, a young artist also living in the boardinghouse. On the street after performances, Herbert regularly protected Helen from entitled and wealthy young men who would press their attentions on the teenager.

Helen's rise to financial security had little to do with the early hard work and preparation that led to success in other Alger novels. Helen was honest and determined, but she succeeded by a natural gift, her voice. More important, as soon as she was financially able, she was relieved to quit the theater and a public career for good. Helen said to the theater manager, "I should like to have you release me from my engagement, if you please, Mr. Bowers. . . . I . . . am willing, . . . to refund the whole amount of wages that I have received from you. . . . I do not wish to sing any more in public. . . . I have had a fortune left me."[62]

How the fortune came to Helen, actually to her father, was the main story line of *Helen Ford*. Robert Ford's estrangement from his father, Mr. Rand, was orchestrated by his evil cousin, Lewis Rand, in pursuit of the old man's wealth. Mr. Rand had long repented his fight with Robert, had searched for him, but had been misled by newspaper reports planted by Lewis of Robert's death. Eventually, after many twists and turns involving unscrupulous lawyers, private investigators, and forgers, Robert discovered his father, was reunited with the old man as he lay dying, and slowly began to recover his wits and bearing. A lawyer, Richard Sharp, forced Lewis Rand to sign half the estate over to Robert and served as Robert's legal and financial adviser thereafter. Robert's share of the estate, amounting to more than half a million dollars, brought security to many, though not by the traditional route of preparation, hard work, and steady accumulation of the American Dream.

A stroke of good fortune saved Helen and all those around her from a life of drudgery and poverty. Martha, recovered from her exhaustion and illness, was invited to share the home of Robert and Helen Ford (now Rand). "No longer obliged to toil for her daily bread, she would henceforth live in affluence." Unremitting hard work had brought her poverty and collapse; good fortune brought her affluence. Herbert Coleman, unable to sell his paintings and on the verge of being forced back to a small Vermont town to run the family store, was saved. Herbert moaned to Helen, "It is money that rules the world. Before its sway we must all bow, willing or unwilling. It is the want of money that drives me to abandon that which is the chief joy of my life. . . . Helen, it is bread and butter that must decide this question."[63] When her father came into his fortune, Helen encouraged him to buy one of Herbert's paintings for $150, saving him for a time, and then to send him to Italy for a deeper education in art. After more than three years in Italy, Herbert's return was expected to be followed by marriage to Helen. Herbert's work, like Martha's, brought him poverty, but good fortune brought him formal training as an artist and marriage to an heiress.

On the other hand, Lewis Rand's scheming, forgery, and lying had brought him half his uncle's fortune, but no peace. An unrepentant crook, Lewis had early observed that "he who aims to be successful in his undertakings, must not scruple to employ the means best suited to advance his interests." He also said, "I never do anything without a motive. I don't believe in disinterestedness." Finally, on the novel's last page, Alger asked, "But does he find in his riches the full satisfaction which he anticipated? I answer, no. He finds, too late, that happiness must be earned; it can never be bought."[64] To be sure; but waiting for lightning to strike, although occasionally the road to success, is not a common route to the American Dream. In fact, *Helen Ford* made plain that the path to the American Dream for nineteenth-century women, outside a stable family, was blocked.

Helen's worrisome circumstances, with money dwindling and a helpless adult to care for, were secured by her fine voice and a timely inheritance. Poor girls faced greater dangers and had little chance of good fortune saving them. Poor girls' dreams, when disappointed, left them with only the most personal of assets to barter to the world. The protagonist of *Maggie: A Girl of the Streets*, the first novel by a twenty-three-year-old Stephen Crane, started life poor, and when her dreams were dashed, her respectability and then her life were quickly forfeit. *Maggie* was a critical and commercial failure, its urban realism panned as too harsh a depiction of tenement life and opportunities. Crane's literary reputation and personal finances were saved the next year by his best-selling *Red Badge of Courage*, but he continued to believe *Maggie* important. Crane rejected the anodyne depiction of poor girls' options in *Helen Ford*, of uncertainty but no indignity, and anticipated the urban realism of Theodore Dreiser's *Carrie*.

Maggie was "a small ragged girl" who, over the course of a few years, "blossomed in a mud puddle. She grew to be a most rare and wonderful production of a tenement district, a pretty girl."[65] What made Maggie rare was that she grew up in a harsh and unsupportive environment; her parents were crude, combative, and often drunk, while her older brother Jimmie survived on the street by strengthening and hardening himself. Maggie's choices as she approached physical if not emotional maturity were few, and Jimmie outlined them starkly for her. Jimmie warned her, "Mag, I'll tell yeh dis! See? Yeh've edder got teh go teh hell or go teh work!" So Maggie went to work: "By a chance, she got a position in an establishment where they made collars and cuffs. She received a stool and a machine in a room where sat twenty girls of various shades of yellow discontent." Like the piecework sewing regime that Martha Grey endured in *Helen Ford*, Maggie's factory work was hard and depleting. "Yellow discontent" came quickly, particularly as factory girls saw more privileged girls and women on the street. Maggie "began to note, with more interest, the well-dressed women she met on the avenues. . . . Studying faces, she thought many of the women and girls she chanced to meet, smiled with serenity as though forever cherished and watched over by those they loved."[66] Maggie's dilemma was how to exchange the instability and drudgery of her life for the security and variety she imagined in the lives of the women she met on the avenues.

Through Jimmie, Maggie met Pete. To her untutored eye, Pete seemed handsome, confident, and secure. Pete's occupation, she thought, as "a very elegant and graceful bartender," always immaculately dressed and smoothly conversant, "brought him, no doubt, into contact with people who had money and manners." The more Pete's elegance attracted her, the more "she began to have an intense dislike for all her dresses. . . . She speculated how long her youth would endure. She began to see the bloom upon her cheeks as valuable."[67] For a turn-of-the-century factory girl, as for Judith, the beauty on the lake of more than a century before, the bloom on her cheeks was a diminishing asset; how and when to offer it in the marketplace was a perilous decision.

A booming fight at home, parents raging drunk and at each other's throats, and Pete at the door framed Maggie's choices. Remain a flower in a mud puddle, soon to fade, or take up Pete's offer to "come ahn we'll have a hell of a time." With her mother raging drunkenly that she was a disgrace to the family, Maggie, fatefully, chose Pete and the world. Initially, Pete was attentive, even tender, but Maggie sensed her vulnerability; she became "timid, as if fearing his anger or displeasure. She seemed to beseech tenderness of him." Soon Pete's attention began to wander; eventually he abandoned Maggie at a bar to go off with a more sophisticated girl, Nell. Maggie tried to go home, only to be rejected again by her mother; she tried Pete one last time, but he felt harried and put upon. He had offered fun, no more. Maggie pled, "But where kin I go?"[68]

The answer soon emerged that when one falls from society's lower rungs, there is nowhere to land but the streets. Though Crane depended exclusively upon allusion, it was clear that Maggie fell immediately to the streets, where her only assets, youth and beauty, "the bloom upon her cheeks," drew their market price. "Upon a wet evening, several months after . . . a girl of the painted cohorts of the city went along the street. . . . She smiled squarely into the face of a boy who was hurrying by. . . . He turned his head and smiled back at her, waving his hands. 'Not this eve—some other eve!'" Maggie disappeared into the "gloomy districts near the river," and soon reports reached the family that "Mag's dead." The novel ended with neighbors pleading with Maggie's drunken mother, the ignorant cause of much of her early suffering, "Yeh'll fergive her now, Mary, won't yehs, dear, all her disobed'ence," and her mother replying, "Oh, yes, I'll fergive her! I'll fergive her."[69] Too late, "Mag's dead."

Theodore Dreiser's first novel, *Sister Carrie*, appeared less than a decade after Crane's *Maggie* and received much the same chilly reception. *Sister Carrie* had miserable initial sales, fewer than 500 copies, but its reputation grew, and it now is seen as an important window on the ambiguous place of women in urban America at the turn of the century. Unlike Maggie, Carrie Meeber had a stable and loving small-town upbringing that helped her, just a little, to find her way. Many aspects of Carrie's story were similar to those of Helen Ford and Maggie. Carrie did not suffer Maggie's dire fate, though she made some of the same choices, but neither did she enjoy Helen's pleasant security and fulfillment.

The novel opened on Carrie, eighteen years old, a small-town midwestern girl, on her way to Chicago to find a job and a future. Just as Jimmie warned Maggie, Dreiser warned on the first page of the novel that Carrie was at a moment in life fraught with danger, saying, "When a girl leaves her home at eighteen, she does one of two things. Either she falls into saving hands and becomes better, or she rapidly assumes the cosmopolitan standard of virtue and becomes worse." A third option, the one that Alger stressed to boys, rising by determination and hard work, seemed not available to girls; girls fell into saving hands or, as Jimmie told Maggie, they went "teh hell." Fortunately, Carrie had an older sister living with her husband in Chicago, so she had a place to land until she could find a job.

On the train to Chicago, Carrie, exuding equal measures of excitement and trepidation, was befriended by a salesman named Charles Drouet (pronounced *Drew-eh*). Drouet was open, buoyant, gregarious, and ready to help; he gave her his card. Carrie was eager, expectant, open to all the good things, new experiences, and fresh insights that might present themselves. Dreiser described her as "a half-equipped little knight . . . venturing to reconnoitre the mysterious city and dreaming wild dreams of some vague, far-off supremacy." But her early experience of the city was sobering. Her sister's life was poor and mean, her husband worked long, hard hours in the stockyards, money was tight, and he was sullen and uncommunicative toward Carrie. Carrie and her sister hoped that she would find nice, clean work in a store or shop: "A shop girl was the destiny prefigured for the newcomer. She would get in one of the great shops and do well enough until—well, until something happened. Neither of them knew exactly what. They did not figure on promotion. They did not exactly count on marriage. Things would go on, though, in a dim kind of way until the better thing would eventuate."[70] But all she found was factory work, almost exactly the kind of work that Maggie found and hated, and most of the money she made went to her sister and husband for room and board.

As with Maggie, what fueled Carrie's growing discontent was what other women seemed to have and to take for granted: security, sufficiency, even plenty. "A flame of envy lighted in her heart. She realized in a dim way how much the city held—wealth, fashion, ease—every adornment for women, and she longed for dress and beauty with a whole heart." Dreiser confided, "Her imagination trod a very narrow round, always winding up at points which concerned money, looks, clothes, or enjoyment." Carrie's longing for more and better made her receptive to Drouet's beckoning when they met again. As a salesman, Drouet's fashionable clothes were a business necessity, and he had money to spend. He took Carrie to fine restaurants, he bought her nice clothes, and when she needed money, "he gave her . . . money out of a good heart." When her sister's home and husband became oppressive, Drouet offered solace, saying, "I'll tell you what you do, . . . you come with me. I'll take care of you. . . . I won't bother you—you needn't be afraid."[71]

Initially, Drouet was true to his word. He did take care of Carrie, providing a nice apartment, furniture, and food, and he did not bother her; they slept apart. Drouet provided and Carrie accepted. Her "average little conscience" worried what "the good girls" might think if they knew she had "been weak," failed before she had even tried. Several times Carrie said, "Why don't we get married?," and each time Drouet said, essentially, "We will, . . . just as soon as I get this little deal of mine closed up." Soon they were no longer sleeping apart. With the chase concluded, Drouet's attention, like Pete's, began to drift. He enjoyed Carrie, he was even proud of her in a self-centered way, but "this goodly drummer carried the doom of all enduring relationships in his own lightsome manner and unstable fancy. He went merrily on, assured that he was alluring all, that affection followed tenderly in his wake, that things would endure unchanging for his pleasure." Meanwhile, secure for the time being, Carrie made friends who had more, husbands, money, clothes, and furnishings. Her own rooms then seemed comparatively insignificant; she rocked by her window, "sad beyond measure, and yet uncertain, wishing, fancying."[72] While Carrie rocked and wished, an associate of Drouet's, George H. Hurstwood, a married man of about forty, the manager of a prominent gentleman's club, set his sights on Carrie.

Carrie and Hurstwood understood each other almost immediately. Hurstwood was not a member of the moneyed elite, but he was Drouet's visible superior, a member of the managing class just below leisured wealth. When Hurstwood entertained Drouet and Carrie, "it was driven into Carrie's mind that here was the superior man." Still, Carrie did not pursue Hurstwood; she was passive, weakly loyal to Drouet, but open to Hurstwood's visits when Drouet was on the road. Hurstwood read Carrie easily; during one visit he observed, "You are not satisfied with life, are you?" "'No,' she answered, weakly."[73] Hurstwood yearned for Carrie, but he had a wife, two teenage children, a home, and a position—he was well-known. One night, unexpectedly, the safe at the club he managed was left open, exposing $10,000 in cash. Hurstwood removed the money, hefted it, thought of the new life it might permit him, closed the door to the safe, and immediately repented his folly but did not have the combination and could not return the money without notice. So he decided to keep the money, trick Carrie onto a train, and make a break for Canada. Once it became clear to Carrie that the train was bound for Canada, he promised that she could just see Montreal and New York and then return to Chicago if she wished. "You won't need to do anything but travel with me. I'll not trouble you in any way." With little to return to in Chicago, she elicited a promise of marriage from Hurstwood; they were married, though this too would later turn out to be a ruse, and she threw her lot in with Hurstwood. Dreiser observed, "Being of a passive and receptive rather than an active and aggressive nature, Carrie accepted the situation. . . . She seemed ever capable of getting herself into the tide of change where she would be easily borne along."[74] But the tide of change was running hard out for Hurstwood in New York, and Carrie's passivity meant that she shared his demise, at least for a time.

Having been forced to return most of the stolen money, Hurstwood had only modest capital to invest. He put it into a New York saloon well below the level of the Chicago gentleman's club he had managed, and he lost that investment. Moreover, Carrie again made friends of higher station and more means; she felt that "she had not lived, could not lay claim to having lived, until something of this had come into her own life. Women were spending money like water."[75] As Hurstwood spiraled down, they fought, and he declared that they were not married and had never been married. With money nearly gone, Carrie's instinct for self-interest returned. After a long and humiliating search, Carrie found a job as a member of a theater chorus line at twelve dollars a week. Carrie did well and rose to lead the chorus and then the company, but Hurstwood's decline gathered speed, and finally Carrie abandoned him. She and a fellow actress, Lola, less accomplished but wise in the ways of the theater, took modest rooms together, but when Carrie's success led to a year's contract at $150 a week, they moved into a suite at the Wellington, a new hotel on Broadway.

Even at the height of her success, having everything she had once craved—gowns, carriages, money, and acclaim—"it struck her that the door to life's perfect enjoyment was not open. . . . She was lonely. In her rocking-chair she sat, when not otherwise engaged—singing and dreaming." Dreiser concluded that Carrie, led by her insatiable emotions, was incapable of settled happiness, of satisfaction. He explained, "In life there is ever the intellectual and the emotional nature—the mind that reasons and the mind that feels. . . . Sitting alone, she was . . . still waiting for that halcyon day when she should be led forth among dreams become real." The novel's final sentences sound judgment on Carrie's future: "Oh, Carrie, Carrie! Oh, blind strivings of the human heart! . . . Know, then, that for you is neither surfeit nor content. In your rocking-chair, by your window dreaming, shall you long, alone. In your rocking-chair, by your window, shall you dream such happiness as you may never feel."[76] A woman alone, whether securely rich like Madeleine Lee, newly rich like Carrie, or poor and vulnerable like Maggie, was empty and incomplete. Waiting to retire on an inheritance, as Helen Ford did, was not an option for most.

Conclusion

The colonial period, from John Winthrop to Cotton Mather to William Penn and beyond, taught that the outer world of social, political, and economic life must not be allowed to compromise the inner life of the heart and soul. The Founding era consensus highlighted proportion and balance; in man reason should guide and limit passions and interests, and in politics and society well-built institutions should check and balance power. During the first half of the nineteenth century, from Jefferson to Lincoln, a national consensus called for a steadily wider conception of natural rights and liberties.

By the early 1840s, Emerson had begun, tentatively at first, to explore the idea that equality and individualism limited the traditional roles of community and charity. But it was the publication of Darwin's *On the Origin of Species* and the cultural coming to terms with its implications over the next couple of decades that changed American thought deeply and permanently. Jefferson and Lincoln had talked of natural rights, self-evident truths, and inalienable rights to life, liberty, and the pursuit of happiness. Darwin and his acolytes said that nature knew nothing of rights and equality. Nature was a field of competition, red in tooth and claw, in which only the strong survived. These ideas, that competition led to the survival of the fittest and the steady progress of the species, were elaborated by scholars like Sumner, promoters like Barnum, and confident robber barons like Carnegie, Rockefeller, and Morgan. The best science and social science of the day pointed to them as the great benefactors of mankind, and they rose proudly to accept the accolades.

Horatio Alger, whose name became synonymous with rags-to-riches narratives, luck and pluck, and the right to rise by the dint of one's own effort, carried a message of modest opportunity and success well earned. He neither praised nor even acknowledged the robber barons. Nonetheless, Alger and the whole Franklin tradition of the American Dream became a fat, rich target for Twain. A great humorist and literary stylist, Twain rejected and scorned every element of the Franklin-Alger program of education, preparation, work, thrift, and steady accumulation. Tom Sawyer and, more so, Huck Finn gleefully rejected "sivilization" and all its "smothery" demands. The more serious Howells highlighted the stress that gathering great wealth, especially new wealth quickly achieved, put on the traditional values of honesty, charity, and community. Both Silas Lapham and Jacob Dryfoos had been good, solid, well-respected rural men until wealth made them proud, sharp, and hard. Lapham lost his money but recovered his values; Dryfoos lost his values and his son, and his money provided no solace.

Sharp as the new competition was for those white men fortunate enough to be engaged in it, most blacks and women were not in the game at all. They took what white men allowed, the leftovers, and often that was too little to survive. Morrison's *Beloved* was set in the mid-nineteenth century, the 1870s and before, and showed how shattered and bereft blacks were for decades after the formal end of slavery. The Darwinian, that is to say white, interpretation was that the freed slaves failed in competition with whites and that their poverty testified that they were less fit, even unfit. Morrison's point was that the failure of blacks to thrive for generations after slavery was a simple reflection of the devastation resulting from slavery, segregation, and ongoing discrimination.

Similarly, *Helen Ford*, *Maggie*, and *Sister Carrie* all showed that women not fortunate enough to be raised in or married into stable, prosperous families had few paths to security. As often happened in Alger novels, a stroke of good fortune just in the nick of time saved Helen from hard choices and danger. In most Alger novels, boy heroes like Dick Hunter had to learn, work, save, and plan before their lucky break put them on the path to security and perhaps prosperity. As a nice but lightly educated young woman, Helen's work was singing, which she quit as soon as her circumstances permitted. Maggie and Carrie, a poor girl and a lower-middle-class girl, respectively, both teenagers, sought a man to protect and provide for them. Maggie's circumstances at home were dire, so in a crisis she chose Pete. Pete promised a good time, used her until he became bored, and then felt put upon when she begged to stay. She fell to the streets, to prostitution, and soon she was dead. Carrie started a few rungs further up the social ladder, had a little more family support, but was ill-prepared to make it on her own. She accepted help from Drouet and then from Hurstwood, pleading for marriage from both, and paying for their support with the coin available. When she did succeed on her own, like Helen, by singing, she was alone, empty, and disconsolate.

Both Maggie and Carrie looked at the wealthy and secure women they met on the street, in their fine clothes and carriages, with money to spend, confident in the love and support of their fathers and husbands, and dreamed of walking among them. These women had not earned their enviable position in the Algeresque way, but fortune had smiled on them all the same. They were secure, but like Madeleine Lee, they were probably unfulfilled. How, at the turn of a new century, a woman might find her own fulfillment, pursue her own dreams, remained unclear.

6 | The Dream in Prosperity and Depression

Our job was to preserve the American ideal of economic as well as political democracy, against the abuse of concentration of economic power that had been insidiously growing up among us in the past fifty years.
—Franklin Roosevelt, Campaign Address, 1936

Modern America became recognizable in the early years of the twentieth century. The commercial application of electricity in the first decade of the century powered lights, mass transit, and round-the-clock use of factories. Soon came telephone, radio, and movies. In the second decade of the century, railroad building declined and road building increased, reflecting and promoting growth in the oil, gas, and auto industries. Through the first third of the century, consumer goods continued to displace capital goods as the leading products of American business. Advertising and marketing became increasingly important as white America became a mass-consumption society.

Despite rapid social and economic change, conservatives argued for adherence to the competitive individualism that they believed underlay the nation's evident growth and prosperity. Alternatively, reformers argued that careful thought and detailed planning would be required to assure order and efficiency in the face of rapid social and economic change. Some reforms were achieved; the role of government expanded under Theodore Roosevelt and Woodrow Wilson, with new independent boards and commissions created to oversee activities in areas like health, education, taxation, corrections, and natural resources. But broader reform initiatives were defeated or weakened by conservative opposition. Indeed, many hailed the Republican ascendancy of the 1920s as a "return to normalcy" because it restored business priorities, market principles, and a "night watchman" view of government. Not until the Great Depression shattered the basic assumptions of nineteenth-century political economy were most Americans receptive to new ideas about the relationships among business, government, society, and citizens. Franklin Roosevelt embodied some of those new ideas in his New Deal program, but he did so tentatively because both he and his constituents, the American people, had been raised on the old laissez-faire individualism, and they came to doubt it only reluctantly.

Novelists were less reluctant. Frank Norris's *The Octopus* (1901) and Upton Sinclair's *The Jungle* (1906) warned that neither established white elites, like the big wheat farmers of California, nor immigrants, like those struggling in the Chicago meatpacking plants, could stand against the trusts and monopolies of the new industrial economy. In the 1920s, Sinclair Lewis explored the comfortable but empty lives of the new professionals. Lewis's *Babbitt* (1922) was the depiction of George F. Babbitt, a conservative businessman both comforted and strangled by a smug upper-middle-class consensus. In the 1930s, John Steinbeck's *Grapes of Wrath* (1939) challenged Franklin Roosevelt's promise that the American Dream could be restored even for poor whites. Finally, Richard Wright's *Native Son* (1940) and Ralph Ellison's *Invisible Man* (1952) showed that the American Dream was just for privileged whites and that blacks had no dreams at all.

Defining the Problem: *The Octopus, The Jungle,* and the Threat of Monopoly

The rapid social and economic change that occurred during the two decades on either side of 1900 left Americans frightened and uncertain. Economic entities of unprecedented size, the new corporations and trusts seemed beyond the control of individuals and even of governments.[1] Two important books, Henry Demarest Lloyd's *Wealth versus Commonwealth* (1894) and Ida Tarbell's *History of the Standard Oil Company* (1904), laid bare the unscrupulous business practices and political chicanery that accompanied the oil trust's rise to power. Novelists used the discretion available in their medium to make similar points even more strikingly. Norris's *The Octopus* and Sinclair's *The Jungle* galvanized the public and the government.

Norris and Sinclair were leading practitioners of the late nineteenth-century and early twentieth-century realist or naturalist literary genre. They sought to place their protagonists in real and detailed social positions and to describe the broader forces that put and held them there. *The Octopus* was the story of one white elite group, big ranchers in California, being dispossessed by another white elite entity, the railroad, the octopus of the title. *The Jungle* told the compelling, if less surprising, story of hard-pressed immigrants ground up by the unregulated urban capitalism of the Chicago stockyards. Both novels highlighted forces in the new economy against which no man, rich or poor, citizen or immigrant, could stand.

The protagonist in *The Octopus* was Magnus Derrick, a former candidate for governor of California and owner of the 10,000-acre Los Muertos ranch. The antagonist, Derrick's evil enemy, was S. Behrman, the local banker and real estate broker and, most important, the legal representative and agent of the Pacific and Southwestern Railroad (P&SW). The story was set in the San Joaquin Valley of central California. Since the railroad's arrival, the valley had become the state's breadbasket, with huge wheat farms or ranches stretching for thousands of acres. The P&SW carried their grain to market. In introducing Derrick and Behrman, Norris gave every authorial advantage to Magnus Derrick.

At six feet tall and sixty years of age, the owner of the largest ranch in the region, Derrick was a commanding figure. Born and raised in North Carolina, he had made two unsuccessful runs for the U.S. Senate before striking out for California. There he quickly established himself and won the Democratic Party nomination for governor but lost the general election. Norris described Derrick as a romantic figure, though not without flaws: "Magnus was in every sense the 'prominent man.' In whatever circle he moved he was the chief figure. Instinctively other men looked to him as the leader." S. Behrman was as loathsome as Derrick was attractive: "Behrman . . . was a large, fat man, with a great stomach; his cheek and the upper part of his thick neck ran together to form a great tremendous jowl. . . . A roll of fat . . . protruded over the back of his collar."[2]

Despite the positive portrayal of Derrick and the negative portrayal of Behrman, Norris was clear that they were merely representatives of two great privileged forces; Derrick represented the big wheat-growing ranchers, and Behrman, behind the shadowy Mr. Shelgrim, president of the P&SW, represented the railroad. The ranchers were wealthy white men, the acknowledged leaders of their community and, in Derrick's case, known and respected statewide. Moreover, they produced one of the world's staple crops. Wheat traded in San Francisco, Chicago, and

Liverpool; it was demanded in the world's rich nations and cried for in the poor nations. But the individual wheat farmers, and maybe especially big farmers like Magnus Derrick, had pride but not power. Derrick and the ranchers were "price-takers"; they sold into a world market at the price available that day. The words used to describe the railroad, on the other hand—"colossus," "cyclops," "octopus"—were uniformly threatening. The octopus's rail-line tentacles were spread throughout the valley, throughout the state.[3] The railroad, in all its local markets, was a monopolist and a "price-giver." Even more galling to the ranchers was that when global wheat prices rose, the railroad raised freight rates to soak up all the gain, leaving the ranchers always struggling.

The ranchers, though, were prominent men, and they had a plan. They were convinced that if they organized and stood together, they could defeat the railroad. The ranchers, independent men like Derrick, had fought and lost before when they failed to stick together. As the pressure built and the fight came on, "a sense of impending calamity, oppressive, foreboding, gloomy," came over them. They lost at the ballot box and in the courts until all that was left were a few ranchers with rifles guarding their homes when Behrman, the sheriff, and the sheriff's deputies arrived to evict them. In the ensuing gun battle, most of the ranchers were killed, and their ranches were forfeit. As Norris summarized, "The Railroad had prevailed. The ranches had been seized in the tentacles of the octopus."[4]

Behrman's personal share of the spoils was Los Muertos and its wheat, which he contracted directly to a grain ship bound for Asia. He oversaw his wheat transported, at favorable freight rates on the railroad for which he was agent, to his grain elevator and onto the grain ship. Shockingly, but predictably, as he leaned over the open hatch to watch the endless stream of grain disappear into the hold, "his foot caught on a coil of rope, and he fell headforemost into the hold." The grain broke his fall, "but search as he would, he could find no outlet. . . . And all the while without stop, incessantly, inexorably, the wheat, as if moving with a force all its own, shot downward."[5] With Behrman submerged, dead beneath his wheat, the ship, unknowing, sailed for Asia.

Two explanations were offered for the results of the battle between the ranchers and the railroad, one involving human agency, the other not. One explanation was that those who understood and practiced the "New Finance" and the "New Politics" defeated those who did not. The New Finance, of course, was simply "the reorganization of capital, the amalgamation of powers, the consolidation of enormous enterprises." The names identified with the New Finance were Rockefeller, Carnegie, and Hill (Shelgrim in the book) and their integrated financial empires. The masters of the New Finance had also mastered, even if they had not invented, the New Politics of "bribery and corruption in high places, . . . the devious intrigues of the unscrupulous." When the battle was over and the war was lost, the ranchers and their supporters, novices in the New Finance and New Politics, could only cry, "They own us, these task-masters of ours. . . . We are told we can defeat them by the ballot-box. They own the ballot-box. We are told that we must look to the courts for redress; they own the courts. We know them for what they are,—ruffians in politics, ruffians in finance, ruffians in law, ruffians in trade, bribers, swindlers, and tricksters."[6]

A second explanation, just as troubling, though in a different way, was offered by Shelgrim, the president of the P&SW. In his view, men like Derrick, Behrman, and himself were only tangentially involved; instead, he says, "You are dealing with forces, . . . when you speak of Wheat and the Railroads, not with men. . . . The Wheat is one force, the Railroad, another, and there is the law that governs them—supply and demand. Men have only little to do in the whole business. . . . I run my road, as a business proposition."[7] Shelgrim's point, of course, was that as a business proposition, when the price of wheat rose, the railroad was responsible to its shareholders, to its own financial health, to capture some or all of that increase by raising freight rates on that product. A railroad that declined to act thus would be beaten and bought by one that did, so he had no choice but to operate his road so as to be buyer rather than bought. Men, their preparation, their dreams, counted for little when great forces clashed.

While the consolidation of vast financial empires attracted great attention, the public also worried about social and cultural turmoil. A million immigrants, mostly from southern and eastern Europe, mostly poor and illiterate, and mostly Catholics and Jews, arrived every year from 1900 to 1914. Far fewer, averaging less than 100,000 each year, came from northern Europe. Both the large numbers and the unfamiliar cultures of the new immigrants concerned traditional elites. World War I and its aftermath, especially the rise of communism in Russia and the subsequent Red Scare in America, produced deep concern about how to "Americanize" these foreign hordes. Sinclair's *The Jungle* followed the vicissitudes of Jurgis Rudkus and his extended family of twelve, Lithuanian immigrants newly arrived in the United States in 1900, as they battled forces they did not comprehend and could not overcome. Sinclair, just twenty-six when he began the novel and twenty-eight when it was published, dedicated it "TO THE WORKINGMEN OF AMERICA."

Rudkus and his family found Chicago and America to be big, boisterous, and booming. With no English and little money but with a profound willingness to work, Jurgis was about twenty, powerfully built, with all the confidence of youth. His betrothed, Ona, was not quite sixteen, small and frail, but literate, buoyant, and happy. Jurgis's father was past his prime but determined to work, and Ona's stepmother, Elzbieta, was expected to manage the home and younger children. Ona's cousin Marija, a little older and much stronger than Ona, and Elzbieta's brother Jonas and his children completed the family. Once Jurgis and Ona were married, they quickly had a son, Antanas.

Jurgis's physical prowess and his youth, strength, energy, and determination meant that the family's security depended on him, and he exuded confidence. His first visit to the stockyards, called Packingtown, where he expected to work, left him exultant; "it seemed a dream of wonder, with its tale of human energy, of things being done, of employment for thousands upon thousands of men, of opportunity and freedom, of life and love and joy." Standing among hundreds of men seeking employment, Jurgis was selected almost immediately for his size, strength, and desire. Ona was more cautious and farsighted than Jurgis. When sometimes she tried to slow him down, urging him to be a little more careful, he responded, admirably but irresponsibly, "Leave it to me; leave it to me. I will earn more money—I will work harder." Initially, Jurgis excelled in the hard, fast, physical work of the cattle-killing beds and had no patience for those who complained. Jurgis "would not have known how to pronounce 'laissez-faire'; but he had been round the world enough to know that a man has to shift for himself in it."[8]

Work in Packingtown inexorably took its toll on Jurgis's imagination, his hopes and dreams, and then his body. Jurgis saw diseased cows, "slunk" or as yet unborn calves, "downer" cows, and "steerly" or ulcerated cattle, pushed right through with the healthy animals. "When he came home that night he was in a very sombre mood, having begun to see at last how those might be right who had laughed at him for his faith in America."[9] While Jurgis remained healthy, he stood some chance of keeping his head above water; but just as Jurgis and Ona began to pull even financially, pay off debts, and start a bank account, Jurgis was injured at work. A plunging, frantic steer crashed into Jurgis and injured his ankle. Knowing that he had to support the family, he returned to work too soon, aggravated the injury, and was off for three months.

When Jurgis's injury did heal and he sought to return to work, his job had been filled and he was no longer the fresh, strong, healthy young man he had been. He was used, if not used up, and new men stood for the same jobs. Instead of being the first chosen, he was passed over time after time; meanwhile, the family's circumstances steadily worsened. The women in the family sought or kept work, and the children down to age eight were set to work selling newspapers. Jurgis concluded, "It might be true, then, after all, what others had told him about life, that the best powers of a man might not be equal to it! It might be true that, strive as he would, toil as he would, he might fail, and go down and be destroyed!"[10] Finally, Jurgis got work in the Packingtown fertilizer plant, the worst job in Packingtown, leaving him choked, coughing, and smelling, inside and out, of fertilizer. Ona, never strong, pregnant with a second child, gave way. Jurgis, enduring terrible, dirty, unhealthy work himself, did not notice as Ona became increasingly nervous and emotional, then hysterical.

The fate of Ona and her cousin Marija is a focus of the novel. Needing her job and more money if she could find it, Ona worked overtime, but really her boss, Miss Henderson, and the boss of the loading dock, Phil Connor, forced her into prostitution. Connor threatened Ona with the firing of Jurgis and Marija, raped her, and prostituted her. When Jurgis found out, Ona begged him to forgive her, to understand, as she explained, "I only did it—to save us. It was our only chance."[11] But Jurgis was outraged; he hunted Connor, beat him mercilessly, and was sent to jail. Emerging from jail, Jurgis found that he had been blackballed at the stockyards and that his family was near starvation. Without money for a doctor or even a midwife, Ona went into premature labor. The child was stillborn, and Ona, barely eighteen, died. Jurgis vowed to pull himself together and find work for Antanas's sake. As Jurgis began to get his feet under him again, Antanas died horribly, drowning in the mud of the street in front of the tenement. Jurgis fled, jumping a freight train headed south. During the spring and summer on the road, working as needed, he regained his mental and physical health and then returned to Chicago for the winter.

Jurgis had become convinced that "he saw the world of civilization then more plainly than ever . . . ; a world in which nothing counted but brutal might, an order devised by those who possessed it for the subjugation of those who did not." In such a world, participating in political corruption, thuggery, and crime made more sense than doing the kind of hard, poorly paid, dirty work he had done in Packingtown. After bouncing around the city for a time, Jurgis found Marija in a house of prostitution. Strong and resilient, she had been in and out of work in Packingtown until she turned, purposefully, to prostitution. Marija told Jurgis, "I had to live, . . . and I couldn't see the children starve." But as Marija, at peace and comfortable with her decision, went deeper, Jurgis was forced to confront both his own beliefs and his treatment of Ona. Marija said, "'We were too ignorant—that was the trouble. . . . If I'd known what I know now we'd have won out.' 'You'd have come here?' said Jurgis. 'Yes,' she answered; 'but that's not what I meant. I meant you—how differently you would have behaved—about Ona. . . . When people are starving . . . and they have something with a price, they ought to sell it.'" Jurgis had concluded for himself that life was a war of all against all, dog-eat-dog, with the devil take the hindmost, a world of street crime, political corruption, whatever it took. And at that point, having lost so much, he understood Marija's choice, but Ona! Ona, young, pretty, not quite eighteen, his wife and the mother of his son, was now dead; he listened as Marija concluded, "Ona could have taken care of us all, in the beginning!" Jurgis responded, "I—yes, I guess so."[12]

The shock value of *The Jungle*, then and now, was both in the human casualties, the babies drowned in the mud, teenage boys eaten by rats, and their cousins and sisters reduced to gratitude for prostitution, and in the commercial horrors of Packingtown, the diseased animals, filth, and chemicals delivered to the nation's dinner tables. The untrammeled greed, the unequivocal valuation of the dollar over the man, and the lack of social and political response cried out for change. Sinclair closed *The Jungle*, much as Edward Bellamy had closed *Looking Backward* two decades earlier, with a powerful call for socialism; socialize the means of production so the people benefit from the people's work.

Despite the dire picture that novelists painted of the powerful forces confronting individuals, most Americans still thought that the old ideas of equality, opportunity, and competition had merit. Tentatively, public intellectuals like Herbert Croly and Walter Lippmann and political leaders like Theodore Roosevelt and Woodrow Wilson suggested that government might have to limit powerful economic actors so that individuals again had space to find a place for themselves and their efforts.

Reconceiving Old Ideas for New Times

Intellectual and political leaders struggled to think clearly of social Darwinist assumptions about human nature, individual motivation, social evolution, and progress to better understand how the future might be shaped. As novelists like Norris and Sinclair highlighted the vulnerability of everyone, rich and poor, before the new corporate leviathans, an increasingly influential cluster of public intellectuals, led by Herbert Croly and Walter Lippmann, argued that government action might regulate the economy and shape the social environment so that opportunity and justice might flourish. Leading politicians, even leading progressive politicians like Theodore Roosevelt and Wilson, moved carefully because they and many of the voters they courted retained strong commitments to ideals of competition, individualism, and self-help. Politicians had to balance every suggestion that government take a wider role with assurances that this would promote rather then inhibit individualism, opportunity, and competition.

Herbert Croly wrote an influential book, *The Promise of American Life* (1909), that described industrial concentration as an immediate and general threat to American public life and values. Croly argued, "The big corporations have become too wealthy and powerful for their official standing in American life. . . . Children, as they are, of the traditional American individualistic institutions, ideas, and practices, they have turned on their parents and dealt them an ugly wound." He concluded, ominously, "Either these economic monsters will destroy the system of ideas, institutions, and practices out of which they have issued or else be destroyed by them."[13]

Croly described an American Dream that had been in place since the Founding. Croly's "promise of American life" was J. Hector St. John de Crevecoeur's "dream." Croly said, "No more explicit expression has ever been given to the way in which the Land of Promise was first conceived by its children than in the 'Letters of an American Farmer.'" Croly believed, just as Crevecoeur had 130 years before, that "the Promise of America has consisted largely in the opportunity which it offered of economic independence and prosperity. . . . This conception of American life and its Promise is as much alive today as it was in 1780. . . . The Promise . . . is a promise of comfort and prosperity for an ever increasing majority of good Americans."[14]

But as the new century dawned, it was clear that America had changed; the frontier was closed, the continent was owned, and workers were flowing both from abroad and from the countryside to the cities to take jobs in the burgeoning factories. What would independence, autonomy, and opportunity mean for them? Croly described what they should mean—must mean—if America were to maintain its historic promise: "What the wage-earner needs, and what it is to the interest of a democratic state he should obtain, is a constantly higher standard of living. . . . The American state is dedicated to such a duty, not only by its democratic purpose, but by its national tradition. . . . The American people, particularly those of alien birth and descent, have been explicitly promised economic freedom and prosperity," and that requires "a constantly higher standard of living."[15]

How would the new urban, industrial America of the early twentieth century restore the promise of American life? Croly argued that American history had been dominated by "two different and, in some respects, antagonistic groups of political ideas—the ideas which were represented by Jefferson, and the ideas which were represented by Hamilton."[16] Croly's distinctive insight was to "unite the Hamiltonian principle of national political responsibility and efficiency with a frank democratic purpose"—that is, to deploy Hamiltonian means in pursuit of Jeffersonian ends. Croly believed with Hamilton that economic opportunity was best protected by authoritative national action. But he also believed that the ends toward which national powers were to be directed should be distinctively Jeffersonian—the rights, opportunities, and benefits of the common people.

Finally, Croly reached back to Lincoln's famous analogy of democratic competition to a fairly run race. Croly observed, "The democratic principle requires an equal start in the race, while expecting at the same time an unequal finish." But a fair start to the race required more than legal equality. Croly argued that an economic competition that began with gross inequalities in wealth between the competitors "is as if a competitor in a Marathon cross country run were denied proper nourishment or proper training, and was obliged to toe the mark against rivals who had every benefit of food and discipline. Under such conditions . . . it would be absurd to claim that, because all the rivals toed the same mark, a man's victory or defeat depended exclusively on his own efforts."[17]

Croly's book and President William Howard Taft's reversion to traditional Republican policies radicalized Theodore Roosevelt. In July

1910, former president Roosevelt wrote to Croly saying, "I do not know when I have read a book that profited me so much. . . . I shall use your ideas freely in speeches I intend to make." Those speeches announced Roosevelt's return to national politics. Between August 23 and September 11, 1910, he traversed the country, giving dozens of speeches and interviews in fourteen states on a program for rejuvenating the American society. *The New Nationalism*, made up mostly of selected speeches from the tour, was published late in 1910 and served as the manifesto of Roosevelt's 1912 Bull Moose campaign to regain the presidency.

Roosevelt's "New Nationalism" still put a high premium on individual effort, but he saw a broader and deeper role for government than he had previously allowed. Roosevelt declared in the maiden speech of his tour, "I stand for the square deal. But when I say that I am for the square deal, I mean not merely that I stand for fair play under the present rules of the game, but that I stand for having those rules changed so as to work for a more substantial equality of opportunity and of reward for equally good service." Later in the trip, he advised his listeners to shape their political action with two things in view: "In the first place, try to get by legislation, national and state, a better chance for the average man, a greater equality of opportunity for that man." Again though, he reminded his audience of the importance of individual effort and the limits to government action. "Now, the second part is this: . . . remember that the fundamental factor in any man's success in life must be that man's own character. The wisest laws and the best government will not help a man who will not work, or who cannot work well and wisely."[18]

Roosevelt was always careful to assure his audiences that while he demanded the right of the average man to equal opportunity, he was not hostile to wealth or property. Again, reaching back to Jackson and Lincoln, he demanded a better balance between the interests of the dollar and the man—between property rights and human rights. "We grudge no man a fortune which represents his own power and sagacity, when exercised with entire regard to the welfare of his fellows." In fact, he said, "We cordially believe in the rights of property. . . . But we feel that if in exceptional cases there is any conflict between the rights of property and the rights of man, then we must stand for the rights of man."[19] Throughout the tour, Roosevelt reminded audiences, "Our republic has no justification unless it is a genuine democracy—a democracy economically as well as politically—a democracy in which there is a really sincere effort to realize the ideal of equality of opportunity for all men."[20] No two

words rolled off Roosevelt's tongue more frequently than those quintes-
sentially American words "opportunity" and "democracy."

Guaranteeing genuine political *and* economic democracy was a far
broader mandate than any American president had sought before, and
Roosevelt knew that he had to address the issue of government size and
intrusiveness. "We who work for the New Nationalism," he declared,
"believe in the hearty encouragement and reward of individual excellence, but we believe also in steadily using the power of the government
to secure economic democracy as well as political democracy." Roosevelt knew that this was new ground and that many would be uneasy.
He said, "This, I know, implies a policy of far more active governmental
interference with social and economic conditions in this country than
we have yet had, but I think we have got to face the fact that such an
increase in governmental control is now necessary."[21]

Roosevelt promised that he was not proposing new ideals, just new
means to secure old ideals. He declared, "The New Nationalism really
means nothing but an application to new conditions of certain old and
fundamental moralities." "Our ideal," he said, "is to secure . . . a reasonable approximation to equality of opportunity for all men, so that
. . . each man shall have the chance to start fair in the race of life and
show the stuff that is in him." This was the standard American ideal
of equal opportunity and self-help. But elsewhere Roosevelt described
the "ideal" of the New Nationalism more broadly and hence, for some,
more disconcertingly. He said, "Our ideal should be a rate of wages
sufficiently high to enable workmen to live in a manner conformable to
American ideals and standards, to educate their children, and to provide for sickness and old age."[22]

Croly's analysis underpinned Roosevelt's New Nationalism in the
election of 1912, but it was Woodrow Wilson's "New Freedom" that carried the day. Roosevelt, coming to progressivism out of the Republican
Party, adopted a broad vision that reflected and built upon the earlier
nationalist strains of Hamilton, Clay, Lincoln, and William McKinley.
Wilson, coming to progressivism out of the Democratic Party, sought to
reclaim and protect equal opportunity, competitive markets, and popular democracy in the tradition of Jefferson, Jackson, and Grover Cleve-
land. Americans had always bragged that their nation was uniquely
open to talent and effort. Wilson was convinced that America would
"insist upon recovering in practice those ideals which she has always
professed."[23]

How America would be brought back in line with its highest ideals was the topic of Wilson's first inaugural address, on March 4, 1913. As Jefferson and Lincoln had done before him, Wilson sought to place the present moment within the broader flow of American history. Wilson declared that the economy was "incomparably great in its material aspects, in its body of wealth, in the diversity and sweep of its energy, in the industries which have been conceived and built up by the genius of individual men and the limitless enterprise of groups of men." The cost of America's economic progress had been levied against both principles and people. Property rights had been allowed to rise far above the rights of men. As if speaking directly to Jurgis Rudkus and his family, Wilson said, "we have not hitherto stopped thoughtfully enough to count the human cost, the cost of lives snuffed out, of energies overtaxed and broken, the fearful physical and spiritual cost to the men and women and children upon whom the dead weight and burden of it all has fallen pitilessly the years through." Wilson closed his analysis and critique of the current state of affairs by remarking, "There has been something crude and heartless and unfeeling in our haste to succeed and be great. Our thought has been 'Let every man look out for himself; let every generation look out for itself,' while we reared giant machinery which made it impossible that any but those who stood at the levers of control should have a chance to look out for themselves." Wilson moved immediately to assure his listeners that men should look out for themselves, but that in the new industrial era they could only do so when the competition was fair and the rules applied equally to everyone in the game. Wilson declared, "We have made up our minds to square every process of our national life again with the standards we so proudly set up at the beginning and have always carried at our hearts. Our work is a work of restoration."[24]

While politicians like Roosevelt and Wilson had to speak reassuringly of change as "restoration," intellectuals like Walter Lippmann and John Dewey sought not only to restore but to enlarge old ideals. Lippmann's *Drift and Mastery* argued that industrialization had so changed the scope and scale of American society that its traditional ideas and ideals no longer served it well. The Jeffersonian vision of the sturdy yeoman farmer, standing free and independent on his own land, did not fit, and could never again be made to fit, the emerging order. The American Dream of unfettered individualism had passed.[25] But Lippmann was not rejecting the American Dream; he was merely demanding that it be made worthy of the new century. "Our business," he declared, "is not to lay aside the dream, but to make it plausible." That demanded that one "drag dreams out into the light of day, show their sources, compare them with fact, transform them to possibilities."[26]

Lippmann proclaimed education, innovation, and science to be the saving forces of the new century. He identified "the scientific spirit" as "the discipline of democracy" and "the outlook of a free man." Rejecting the Darwinian complacency of the previous generation, Lippmann said, "Rightly understood science is the culture under which people can live forward in the midst of complexity, and treat life not as something given but as something to be shaped."[27] He wrote with a touching confidence that would soon be gone from American public life. The horrors of World War I (1914–1917) brought an end to the progressivism of Roosevelt and Wilson and left Americans thirsting for domestic security and prosperity.

Postwar America was comfortably Republican. Republican presidents Warren G. Harding (1921–1923) and Calvin Coolidge (1923–1929) governed with a confidence born of more than six decades of political and economic success. Presidents Harding and Coolidge both named financier Andrew Mellon, one of America's richest men, to Hamilton's old post at the Treasury. Coolidge famously reminded his exuberant countrymen that "the business of America is business," and then he used his 1924 State of the Union message to make the then-novel argument that steep tax cuts would both spur growth and increase government revenues. Coolidge argued that "the larger incomes of the country would actually yield more revenue to the Government if the basis of taxation were scientifically revised downward."[28] Secretary Mellon explained that "high rates tend to destroy individual initiative and enterprise and seriously impede the development of productive business."[29] The booming economy of the 1920s seemed to fully validate the Republican economic model of low taxes, deregulation, and individual initiative. Many celebrated the new energy and freedom of modern life, spectacularly including speakeasies, flappers, and ragtime, while others worried that this all threatened traditional American values. The novelists F. Scott Fitzgerald and Sinclair Lewis explored these alternative interpretations of the American condition in the fictional characters of Jay Gatsby and George F. Babbitt.

Gatsby, Babbitt, and the Return of Normalcy

No one represented the Roaring Twenties in the public mind, then or now, better than F. Scott Fitzgerald. Fitzgerald, born in the Midwest, stylishly educated through private schools and Princeton, served as a stateside aide-de-camp during World War I before marrying his aristocratic, southern-belle sweetheart and achieving national acclaim and wealth at twenty-two. Fitzgerald's wealth, fame, and marriage to Zelda Sayre were all secured by the dramatic success of his first book, *This Side of Paradise* (1920). There followed in rapid succession *The Beautiful and the Damned* (1922) and his masterpiece, *The Great Gatsby* (1925). *Gatsby* confirmed his status as a luminary in Europe and America; he was an exemplar and arbiter of important aspects of his times. Yet by the early 1930s, both Scott and Zelda Fitzgerald were spent, intellectually and emotionally drained, and in 1940 Scott Fitzgerald died, at forty-four.

The Great Gatsby was the story of a young man from the American Midwest, James Gatz, who created a glamorous life out of whole cloth and saw it collapse tragically around him. At seventeen Jim Gatz changed his name to Jay Gatsby and was taken into service by Dan Cody, a millionaire world traveler. In a five-year tour of Europe, Gatsby added a veneer of knowledge and sophistication to his native wit and charm. Cody's death and the outbreak of World War I led Gatsby into the army. While training as a young officer at Camp Taylor, near Louisville, Gatsby met, courted, and fell deeply in love with Daisy, the pampered daughter of one of the city's leading families. Though they pledged themselves to each other, family pressure and Gatsby's absence in Europe led to Daisy's wedding to Tom Buchanan, of a prominent and wealthy Chicago family. Gatsby's memory of Daisy, refined and elaborated through five years of singular obsession, became the center of an existence dedicated to reclaiming her. After leaving the army, Gatsby achieved wealth, through shady means, bought a mansion near Daisy and Tom Buchanan's Long Island estate, and prepared for the past to unfold anew.

Gatsby's marvelous mansion was appointed with fine furniture, his closets were filled with English suits and shirts, and his lavish parties, attended by dozens of anonymous guests, ran late into summer nights. Society crackled with wild rumors about Gatsby's origins, character, and wealth. When Gatsby's hope that Daisy would be drawn to one of his famous parties was unfulfilled, he launched a scheme through neighbors and acquaintances to lure Daisy to his house. He assumed, reasonably enough within the confines of the story, that Daisy would be drawn to his wealth and glamour and choose to complete their life together as he had long envisioned it. Gatsby had everything, looks, money, and glamour, and his name was on everyone's lips; why shouldn't his dream of having Daisy too come true?

The Great Gatsby has sometimes been seen as a derisive commentary on and even a profound critique of the American Dream. It seems more reasonable to say that Gatsby reminded us that not every American dreams the American Dream. Gatsby dreamed, to be sure, but his dream lacked reality, substance, and worth. Moreover, Gatsby pursued his dream through deception, deceit, and theft.[30] Hence, Nick Carraway, Gatsby's young neighbor and the book's narrator, said of Gatsby that while "there was something gorgeous about him, some heightened sensitivity to the promise of life, . . . an extraordinary gift for hope," some "foul dust floated in the wake of his dreams."[31] The collision between illegitimate means and ill-conceived ends was bound to conclude badly.

Gatsby's life story, as well as his personality and its projection into the world, was more a hologram than a human life grounded in effort and reality. Hence, its power rested in his confidence that others would accept it, believe it, and willingly act on it. When his dream seemed to be coming alive, as when he saw Daisy again and she seemed to respond to the old memories they shared, "he literally glowed; without a word or gesture of exaltation a new well-being radiated from him." But Gatsby's glow was dependent both upon Daisy's continued belief in him and his own confidence in her belief. Doubt and rejection killed the dream and brought Gatsby's complete collapse. In the direct personal confrontation between Gatsby and Tom Buchanan over Daisy, Tom went straight for Gatsby's constructed self. Gatsby had claimed roots in a prominent and wealthy midwestern family. Tom connected him to Jewish underworld figures, asking Gatsby, "Who are you, anyhow?," accusing him of being "one of that bunch that hangs around with Meyer Wolfsheim," and telling the assembled party, "I picked him for a bootlegger the first time I saw him." Tom was more right than he knew; Gatsby's money came from bootlegging, securities fraud, and more. And when Nick later asked Wolfsheim whether he had given Gatsby his start, Wolfsheim responded, "Start him—I made him."[32]

Gatsby, of course, knew and feared all of this, so when Tom challenged him, Gatsby "began to talk excitedly to Daisy, denying everything, defending his name against accusations that had not been made.

'Jay Gatsby' had broken up like glass against Tom's hard malice."[33] The dream was punctured, both Gatsby and Daisy knew it, and all that remained was reality. Daisy had to chose between the vaporous gangster she had once loved and her hard, cruel, but predictable millionaire husband; it was no choice. Carraway concluded that "Gatsby . . . paid a high price for living too long with a single dream."[34] Perhaps, but a more reasonable conclusion would be that Gatsby paid a high price for living too long with the wrong dream; the dream of adolescent romance proved an insufficient basis for later stages of adult life and accomplishment. In all Fitzgerald's stories, and certainly in *The Great Gatsby*, wealth either existed as the story opened or was attained quickly and mysteriously. In fact, in the worlds that Fitzgerald created, there were no paths to success, no means by which wealth and security were created, no virtues maintained and employed to good and growing effect over time.

Despite Fitzgerald's contributions, the most prominent American novelist of the 1920s was Sinclair Lewis. In a remarkable torrent of creativity, Lewis wrote *Babbitt*, *Arrowsmith* (1925), and *Elmer Gantry* (1927). He won the Pulitzer Prize for *Arrowsmith* in 1926. He declined that prize, declaring all prizes a threat to literary excellence, but he accepted the Nobel Prize for Literature in 1930. The first American novelist to win the Nobel Prize, Lewis joined the politicians and pundits, from Wilson and Theodore Roosevelt to Croly and Lippmann, who argued that the nineteenth-century dream was inadequate to the more complex twentieth century. Sinclair Lewis subjected the Chamber of Commerce boosterism that underpinned the individualist message to a derision similar to Twain's disdain for Alger.

Lewis's George F. Babbitt was a successful businessman, in his midforties, with a wife and three children, a nice house, and a secure though only moderately prominent place in Zenith, a midsize industrial city in the fictional midwestern state of Winnemac. Lewis made Babbitt such a compelling character that "Babbitt" has come to mean, according to Merriam-Webster.com, "a person and especially a business or professional man who conforms unthinkingly to prevailing middle-class standards." George Babbitt was a booster, 100 percent American, who took his views from solid newspaper editorials, club mates, and community leaders. He stood with the go-getters and the producers against the losers and the socialists.

In the wake of a mayoral election in which Babbitt had done yeoman service for the business candidate and against the labor-socialist candidate, he was asked to deliver the annual address to the Zenith Real Estate Board. Babbitt declared to his fellow realtors that Zenith, America, in fact, had been and was being built by men just like them: "the fellow with four to ten thousand a year, say, and an automobile and a nice little family in a bungalow on the edge of town, . . . a God-fearing, hustling, successful, two-fisted Regular Guy, who belongs to some church with pep and piety to it, . . . up-standing, lend-a-handing Royal Good Fellows, who plays hard and works hard, and whose answer to his critics is a square-toed boot."[35]

Still, after two decades of working successfully and becoming a respected member of the Zenith business community, he was, at middle age, unsure that all he had was all there was. He confided to his best friend, Paul Reisling, "Here I've pretty much done all the things I ought to; supported my family, and got a good house and a six-cylinder car, and built up a nice little business. . . . And I belong to the church, and play enough golf to keep in trim, and I only associate with good decent fellows. And yet, even so, I don't know that I'm entirely satisfied."[36]

Babbitt's vague dissatisfaction led him into a number of fantasies, which he worked halfheartedly to fulfill. His two most frequently recurring fantasies involved the "fairy-girl" and running off to the woods to get away from it all. Myra Babbitt, George's wife, was described as "definitely mature. . . . She was a good woman, a kind woman, a diligent woman." George's fairy-girl was definitely not mature; rather, she was young, lithe, and eager. George sought, somewhat awkwardly, to realize his fantasy with Miss McGoun, a young secretary in his office; with a manicurist named Ida Putiak, who eluded him; and with a widow in her early forties, Tanis Judique. George and Tanis did start a romance, which burned hot for a time, until her demands and expectations became oppressive.[37]

For George Babbitt, and in much of American literature, women are necessary to security and comfort but also ever present, confining, and burdensome. George's reaction to Myra, his wife, was to be brief, presumptuous, and dismissive, while Tanis's attempt to keep him close caused claustrophobia. As he tired of Tanis and sought to distance himself from her, he complained, much as Pete had when Maggie would not go, "Darn these women, the way they make demands! . . . Why can't women ever learn a fellow hates to be bulldozed?"[38] George's feeling of being constrained and limited extended beyond women and family to job and friends—to all the ties that bound him to middle-aged, middle-class life.

Babbitt's sense of freedom was "to beat it off to the woods right now. And loaf all day." In fact, Babbitt and Reisling planned a trip to the Maine woods, arranging to go several days before their families so they could "just loaf by ourselves and smoke and cuss and be natural." Elsewhere, the shimmering vision of freedom was to "wear old pants, and loaf, and cuss." In Maine, George met a half-white, half-Indian fishing guide named Joe Paradise. Joe was young, strong, handsome, and capable in the woods. George idolized Joe and imagined, dimly, a future in which he and Joe, buddies, returned to nature and lived in the woods. On a return trip, George sought out Joe and hired him for a fishing trip. When George proposed to hike in, Joe demurred, saying, "Most of the sports go by boat." George insisted on hiking, and Joe agreed, though he remained silent the whole way. George arrived exhausted but exultant. Feeling manly and vital in the woods, George asked Joe about his aspirations: "Joe, what would you do if you had a lot of money?" Joe's response was crushing to George: "I'd go down to Tinker's Falls and open a swell shoe store."[39] No fairy-girl, no buddy.

Slowly, George realized "that he could never run away from Zenith and family and office, because in his own brain he bore the office and the family and every street and disquiet and illusion of Zenith." George's insight still left him dissatisfied, empty, and without direction, but Myra's sudden illness restored his sense of her importance to him and began his turnaround. More clarity came when his son, Ted, unhappy in college but in love with Eunice, eloped and married. Ted explained, "Dad, I can't stand it any more. . . . Maybe I'll want to go back some day. But me, I want to get into mechanics. I think I'd get to be a good inventor." George responded, "Well— . . . I've always wanted you to have a college degree. . . . But I've never—Now, for heaven's sake, don't repeat this to your mother . . . I've never done a single thing I've wanted to in my whole life!"[40]

George's advice to Ted was good, healthy, even admirable: know your own mind, chart your own course, follow your passion. But George Babbitt became a byword in American literature and culture precisely because he was unable to follow his own good advice. He was unable to channel his rebellion back into a more independent posture in life, where family, work, and associations reflected rather than dictated his values and choices. Instead, he gave up his brief quest for independence of mind; "within two weeks no one in the League was more violent regarding . . . the crimes of labor unions, the perils of immigration, and the delights of golf, morality, and bank accounts than was George F. Babbitt."[41] Thereafter, George F. Babbitt wore Chamber of Commerce conformity like a warm winter coat.

Hoover, Roosevelt, Steinbeck, and the Great Depression

No political leader epitomized the Chamber of Commerce view of American life better than Herbert Hoover, the longtime secretary of commerce and the Republican nominee for president in 1928. Born in West Branch, Iowa, but orphaned at nine, Hoover was raised by an uncle in Oregon, worked his way through the new Stanford University, and became an internationally famous and wealthy civil engineer and construction executive before turning to public service in his forties. He became a tireless spokesman for the Republican Party's program and vision. In 1922 Hoover wrote *American Individualism: The Challenge to Liberty* to defend free-market values from collectivist urges that he saw rising in Europe and at home. Hoover assured Americans that "while we build our society upon the attainment of the individual, we shall safeguard to every individual an equality of opportunity to take that position in the community to which his intelligence, character, ability, and ambition entitle him; . . . while he in turn must stand up to the emery wheel of competition."[42] Hoover's view was that within the broad confines of the rule of law and protection of private property, initiative and competition produced individual fairness and social justice. "The emery wheel of competition" exposed unmerited claims and scraped away artificial advantages to leave the energetic and talented members of society in possession of society's top spots and best rewards.

Late in his campaign for president, Hoover gave a series of speeches that laid out his sense of the majestic stability of the American Dream even in light of the tremendous changes that had taken place during his lifetime. The most famous of these speeches was given at his boyhood home near West Branch, Iowa. Hoover remembered a bucolic boyhood on a nearly self-sufficient family farm. In the intervening half century, Hoover informed the crowd, both rural and urban life had improved dramatically. In the countryside, he said, "we have improved seed and livestock; we have added a long list of mechanical inventions for saving labor; we have increased the productivity of the land." Over the same period, electricity, telephones, automobiles, radios, and movies had transformed urban life. These discoveries and inventions enhanced productivity and expanded plant capacity and profits, permitting increased wages and a better life for most Americans. Moreover, free citizens exercising personal initiative within a political order of limited government had achieved all this. This "self-reliant," "rugged" individualism imparted "a genius to American institutions" that was "the real basis of American democracy."[43]

Hoover's August 11, 1928, address accepting the Republican nomination for president again made the case that individualism and equal opportunity produced American growth and prosperity. He declared, "Equality of opportunity is the right of every American—rich or poor, foreign or native-born, irrespective of faith or color. It is the right of every individual to attain that position in life to which his ability and character entitle him. . . . Only from confidence that this right will be upheld can flow that unbounded courage and hope which stimulate each individual man and woman to endeavor and to achievement." He then turned to Lincoln's famous comparison of equal opportunity to a fairly run footrace to help communicate his vision. Hoover wanted both to bathe in Lincoln's sense that fair competition made unequal outcomes legitimate and to reject Croly's criticism that economic inequality rigged the race in favor of the privileged to the detriment of new men seeking to move up. Hoover posited that "the ideal of individualism based upon equal opportunity to every citizen is . . . as if we set a race. We, through free and universal education, provide the training of the runners; we give to them an equal start; we provide in the government the umpire of fairness in the race. The winner is he who shows the most conscientious training, the greatest ability, and the greatest character."

Hoover entered into his term as president in March 1929 convinced that he and his party represented the great American political tradition of individualism, enterprise, limited government, laissez-faire, progress, and prosperity. Hence, he was perfectly equipped by experience and temperament to govern in a period of Republican growth but was ill-equipped to govern in, or even understand, its collapse. The stock market crash of October 1929 paralyzed the American economy, and the Great Depression of the 1930s slowly strangled prosperity for most Americans. Virtually every measure of national and individual wealth and well-being in the United States plummeted in 1929, reached its nadir in 1932–1933, and then climbed slowly and unevenly back over the remainder of the decade. Along with opportunity and prosperity, the American Dream suffered greatly in the 1930s. Most Americans stopped dreaming altogether. Instead, they lay awake at night worrying about what new horrors tomorrow would bring.

Franklin Delano Roosevelt faced the daunting task of rebuilding the American economy and the national confidence, and not simply on the old foundations. FDR rightly declared, "All our great Presidents were leaders of thought at times when certain historic ideas in the life of the nation had to be clarified." Times of crisis and uncertainty provided a "superb opportunity for reapplying, applying in new conditions, the simple rules of human conduct to which we always go back."[44] Franklin Roosevelt redefined the American Dream for an urban industrial society in which most men, and women increasingly, worked for wages and in which old ideas of rural autonomy and independence seemed remote. In the twentieth century, economic stability and a healthy job market were the context within which workers could start small, learn, work, save, and seek to move up over time.

In the fall of 1932, before the Commonwealth Club of San Francisco, FDR gave what would become the most famous speech of the campaign. The Commonwealth Club speech began with a broad description of American political development from the Founding period, through the tremendous economic expansion of the nineteenth century, through the progressive reforms of the early twentieth century, to the Republican heyday of the 1920s that ended in the collapse of 1929. He traced the broad outlines of the traditional American Dream to Jefferson's commitment to the autonomy and independence of the yeoman farmer. "So began," Roosevelt declared, "the day in which individualism was made the great watchword of American life. The happiest of economic conditions," a growing population in a rich and fertile continent, "made that day long and splendid. On the western frontier, land was substantially free. No one, who did not shirk the task of earning a living, was entirely without opportunity to do so." Ideas and reality, the traditional American Dream of hard work applied to extensive opportunity, reflected each other perfectly.

As the nation developed, railroads, industries, and cities spread across the landscape. Roosevelt told his audience, "It was in the middle of the nineteenth century that a new force was released and a new dream created. The force was what is called the industrial revolution. . . . The dream was the dream of an economic machine, able to raise the standard of living for everyone; to bring luxury within the reach of the humblest." Government and citizens wanted this new economic machine and the wealth it promised to grow as quickly as possible. "There was, however, a shadow over the dream. To be made real, it required the use of the talents of men of tremendous will and tremendous ambition." These men built great corporations and produced great wealth, but the costs imposed on common men and on society were greater than had been anticipated. "In retrospect," FDR declared, "we can now see that the turn of the tide came with the turn of the century. We were reaching our last frontier; there was no more free land and our industrial combinations had become great uncontrolled and irresponsible units of power within the State." The builders of the great industrial enterprises of the nation had become threats more than benefactors. Hence, just as Theodore Roosevelt and Wilson had before him, Franklin Roosevelt argued, "Our task now is not . . . producing more goods. It is the soberer, less dramatic business of administering resources and plants already in hand, . . . of adapting existing economic organizations to the service of the people. The day of enlightened administration has come."

But what ends, what goals, what values, were enlightened administrators to pursue? From the nation's earliest days, the values that had guided it through the darkest times were the natural rights, the human rights, set forth in the Declaration of Independence. FDR declared, "The task of statesmanship has always been the re-definition of these rights in terms of a changing and growing social order." The terms of the American social contract, he declared, "are as old as the Republic, and as new as the new economic order." Life was the first human right for both Locke and Jefferson. In the new day, Roosevelt declared, "every man has a right to life; and this means he has also a right to make a comfortable living. . . . Our Government formal and informal, political and economic, owes to everyone an avenue to possess himself of a portion of that plenty sufficient for his needs, through his own work. . . . The final term of the high contract," Roosevelt explained, "was for liberty and the pursuit of happiness." The old liberty of being left alone, of "drift," as Lippmann called it, was no longer sufficient. "We have learned a great deal . . . in the past century. . . . We know that liberty to do anything which deprives others . . . is outside the protection of any compact; and that Government in this regard is the maintenance of a balance, within which every individual may have a place if he will take it; in which every individual may find safety if he wishes it." Roosevelt concluded the Commonwealth Club speech with a solemn promise: "We recognize the new terms of the old social contract. We shall fulfill them."[45]

When Franklin Roosevelt assumed the presidency in March 1933, the nation was mired in a depression nearly four years old. FDR was determined to move immediately and decisively on a number of fronts, all intended to rebalance, reorganize, and rejuvenate the American economy. Roosevelt knew that the American people expected action, government action, but he also knew that old commitments to individualism and self-help, while shaken, were alive. Throughout his presidency, but particularly in the early days, he groped for the right balance, in rhetoric and policy, between government activism and personal responsibility. In the sixth of his famous Fireside Chats, delivered on September 30, 1934, FDR assured the American people that his New Deal respected traditional American values even as the New Deal looked beyond unconstrained individualism and unregulated laissez-faire to a "broader definition of liberty under which we are moving forward to greater freedom, to greater security for the average man than he has ever known before in the history of America."[46]

By the spring of 1936, as the Depression dragged on, President Roosevelt was increasingly emboldened to state the case for a strong and consistent government presence in American social and economic life. He personally drafted the Democratic Party platform of 1936. FDR again drew on the powerful image of Jefferson's Declaration of Independence, declaring on behalf of the Democratic Party, "We hold these truths to be self-evident—that government in a modern civilization has certain inescapable obligations to its citizens, among which are: (1) Protection of the family and the home. (2) Establishment of a democracy of opportunity for all the people. (3) Aid to those overtaken by disaster."[47] In a powerful speech accepting the Democratic nomination for president on June 27, 1936, Roosevelt continued his project of refining and redefining America's core values. Before a crowd of 100,000 in Philadelphia's Franklin Field stadium, he explored the meaning of liberty in America, declaring, "Liberty requires opportunity to make a living—a living decent according to the standard of the time, a living that gives man not only enough to live by, but something to live for." Without the opportunity to make a living, "life was no longer free; liberty no longer real; men could no longer follow the pursuit of happiness."[48]

Though Roosevelt labored mightily throughout the 1930s, the Depression held on and even took a turn for the worse in the late 1930s before preparations for World War II brought the economy fully back. Many Americans, including John Steinbeck, lost patience. Steinbeck's 1939 classic, *The Grapes of Wrath*, set in California late in the Depression, highlighted the impossibility of the American Dream for many Americans, especially those on the social and economic fringes, transients, the old, and the disabled. *The Grapes of Wrath* won the Pulitzer Prize in 1940, and in 1962 Steinbeck won the Nobel Prize for Literature.

The Grapes of Wrath was the story of the Joad family, semiliterate white sharecroppers pushed off the land in Oklahoma by the Dust Bowl, the Great Depression, and the banks. Though they had once owned the land they farmed, hard times had cost them ownership, and harder times had pushed them west in search of security and dignity in a new life. The Joad family, like so many others, struggled to survive but slowly broke up under the pressure of poverty, dislocation, sadness, and confusion. Grandpa and Grandma Joad, old as the family prepared to leave Oklahoma, died on the way to California. Tom Joad Sr., called Pa, cracked under the pressure of the trip and under the disappointment at what they found in California, and Ma had to work to hold the family together without completely displacing Pa. Of the Joad children, the oldest, Noah, big, gentle, but mentally challenged, was overwhelmed by the trip and just walked off; he disappeared down the river never to be seen again. Rose of Sharon's new husband, Connie Rivers, abandoned his pregnant wife, and Al, the youngest of the grown children, prepared to marry and leave the family late in the novel. Tom, one of the central characters of the novel, just out of prison as the family left Oklahoma, was forced into hiding and away from the rest of the family when his struggle to defend them brought more trouble with the law. Finally, Jim Casy, another leading character, traveled with the Joads and increasingly became part of the family and its fate, until he was killed for standing up to oppressive authority. The novel ended with the family broken and scattered, but wiser, even enlightened, with a knowledge of society's evils more likely to get them killed than to help them prosper.

When Tom Joad reached home after being released from prison, where he had served four years of a seven-year term for an understandable but unjustifiable murder, he found the house pushed off its foundation and the family off at Uncle John's, picking cotton to earn money so they could "shove on west." When Tom caught up with the family, he found Pa optimistic and Grandpa absolutely giddy. Pa said, "We had hard times here. 'Course it'll be all different out there—plenty work, an' ever'thing nice an' green, an' little white houses an' oranges growin' aroun'." Grandpa, who ultimately had to be made drunk and forced onto the truck, had been euphoric, telling Tom, "Jus' let me get out to California where I can pick me an orange when I want it. Or grapes. There's a thing I ain't never had enough of. Gonna get me a whole big bunch of grapes off a bush, or whatever, an' I'm gonna squash 'em on my face an' let 'em run off my chin." Steinbeck used the grape imagery, so idyllically attractive to Grandpa, to symbolize the bitter disappointment, the wrath, of those who found only grief and ashes.[49]

When the family reached California, they found little work, low pay, squalid camp life, and hostile, sometimes violent, communities. Tom Joad and Jim Casy puzzled over the hostile reception and over how they might respond. Tom said to Casy, "Look, . . . this ain't no lan' of milk an' honey. . . . They's a mean thing here. The folks here is scared of us people comin' west; an' so they got cops out tryin' to scare us back."[50] Casy had been thinking about issues of humanity, religion, good and evil, God and nature. A former itinerant minister who had lost the call when his own ideas drifted too far from orthodoxy, Casy had joined the Joad's westward quest to stay close to what the people, the nation's least and lost, were thinking and saying. Under increasing pressure, Casy, Tom, and Ma struggled to formulate a new sense of what dignity should mean for people like themselves.

Casy explained his conversion road to Tom Joad, saying, "I went off alone, an' I sat and figured. The sperit's strong in me, on'y it ain't the same. I ain't so sure of a lot of things." As Casy sat and figured, a very American idea occurred to him, similar to what Emerson in 1841 had called "the Over-Soul." Casy's thought was unrefined but closely related: "I figgered about the Holy Sperit and the Jesus road. I figgered, 'Why do we got to hang it all on God or Jesus? Maybe,' I figgered, 'maybe it's all men an' all women we love; maybe that's the Holy Sperit—the human sperit— . . . Maybe all men got one big soul ever'body's a part of.' . . . I knew it was so deep down that it was true, and I still know it."[51]

Ma Joad had known inequality, class tensions, and the use of public and private force to protect property and the existing order in Oklahoma. When Tom arrived home from prison to find the family uprooted, Ma warned him, "Tommy, don't you go fighten' 'em alone. They'll hunt you down like a coyote." But times were changing, and by the time they reached California Ma was wondering whether the decision to fight might not be coming, saying, "Tommy, I got to thinkin' an' dreamin' an' wonderin'. They say there's a hun'erd thousand of us shoved out. If we was all mad the same way, Tommy—they wouldn't hunt nobody down—." Tom asked, "Many folks feel that way?," and she replied, "I don' know. They're jus' kinda stunned." Steinbeck completed Ma Joad's thought, writing, "And some day—the armies of bitterness will all be going the same way. And they'll all walk together, and there'll be a dead terror from it." Later, Steinbeck sharpened the point to a near future certainly, writing, "When property accumulates in too few hands it is taken away. . . . And the little screaming fact that sounds through all history: repression works only to strengthen and knit the repressed."[52]

Being pushed off the land in Oklahoma was traumatic for the Joads, but it took the experience of California—the sullen resistance to their presence, the scarce work, the low pay, the bad housing, and the violence—to radicalize them. When strike-breaking vigilantes killed Casy and pushed Tom into hiding, he told Ma it was time to resist, "long as I'm an outlaw anyways." She worried that he might be killed and she would not even know. Tom reassured her that if Casy had been right, if there was just one big soul that everyone participated in, "Then it don' matter. Then I'll be all aroun' in the dark. . . . Whenever they's a fight so hungry people can eat, I'll be there. Whenever they's a cop beaten' up a guy, I'll be there. . . . I'll be in the way kids laugh when they're hungry an' they know supper's ready."[53] What made *The Grapes of Wrath* so striking was the picture of poor white families—poor white men and their wives and children—disinherited of their nation's promise and ready to resist and, if need be, to die.

Women and Minorities: Vulnerability and Exclusion

Popular assumptions about and standards for women began to change in the opening decades of the twentieth century. In the cities and among the comfortable classes, traditional standards loosened to accept a more public, active, sexualized view of women. Recreational opportunities expanded women's public presence in movie theaters, amusement parks, speakeasies, and dance halls. Economic change opened jobs for women in fields such as clerical work and sales; even medicine, law, and the professions began to open. Still, the great protection for women, as it had always been, remained marriage and family. Poor women, black women, and women alone remained deeply vulnerable.

Steinbeck made the roles of men and women in families, in good times and bad, a major focus of *The Grapes of Wrath*. He observed that when times were good, men were proud, the land was theirs, and they worked it to secure their independent place in the community and to take care of their families. The women were proud too that their men were strong, their home secure, and their children safe. When hard times came, the men promised that it would be all right and that they would work harder. Sometimes, not often but sometimes, when times were very hard, the men cracked, their pride shattered, and they were broken. When the men cracked, they drank or they ran, but they seldom were whole again, and the women and children were alone and exposed.

The Joads and their neighbors had slipped a long way, many of them from landowners to sharecroppers, but the women deferred to their men. Occasionally, if the men were particularly prideful or short-sighted, women would step forward to effect a change and then step back. When their men stumbled and the women moved to break their fall, they were careful of the men's pride, apologizing for getting in the way. They knew that only when the fight was over, when all chance of winning had been lost and the men were beaten, could they organize the retreat and bury the dead. So Steinbeck opened and closed *The Grapes of Wrath* with the women, quiet and sullen, watching for signs that their men had broken.

In the opening paragraphs, Steinbeck described the worst of the Dust Bowl conditions in Oklahoma. Families held on, certain that at some point the rains would come and the earth would again be green. As the men studied the cloudless sky and the parched fields, "the women came out of the houses to stand beside their men—to feel whether this time the men would break. . . . After a while the faces of the watching men lost their bemused perplexity and became hard and angry and resistant. Then the women knew that . . . there was no break. . . . Women and children knew deep in themselves that no misfortune was too great to bear if their men were whole." But when the end came in Oklahoma for the Joads, when the land and the house were gone, the household goods and farm implements had been sold for pennies on the dollar, and the family headed west, Ma "seemed to know, to accept, to welcome her position, the citadel of the family, the strong place that could not be taken."[54]

On the way to California and in the unwelcoming new land, Ma occasionally had to confront Pa, once threatening him with a tire iron, but usually she advised and deferred. Even near the end, when Pa was effectively broken and had acknowledged as much, Ma was careful not to step in front of him. When once she did, she apologized, saying, "I didn't mean no harm." Pa replied, "I know. . . . I ain't no good any more. Spen' my time a-thinkin' how it use' ta be. Spen' all my time thinkin' of home, an' I ain't never gonna see it no more. . . . Woman takin' over the fambly. Woman sayin' we'll do this here, an' we'll go there. An' I don' even care." Ma worked hard to comfort Pa and to urge him forward, telling him women handle change better and naturally take the long view and that next year would be better. Women worked hard to save their men from irrecoverable damage. As Steinbeck noted again in the novel's penultimate paragraph: "The women watched the men, watched to see whether the break had come at last. The women stood silently and watched. And where a number of men gathered together, the fear went from their faces, and anger took its place. And the women . . . knew it was all right—the break had not come; and the break would never come as long as fear could turn to wrath."[55] But as he was at pains to point out, it's a long way from fear and wrath to the American Dream.

Richard Wright's *Native Son*, set in Depression-era Chicago, was a radical tale in which murder provided the unifying conclusion to a black life of denial and exclusion. Bigger Thomas, one of American fiction's most compelling characters, at just twenty was alienated, sullen, filled with confusion and rage, and without direction or hope. Wright's presentation of Bigger's sense of self, of race relations, and of the lack of opportunity in a deeply divided and unequal society was a direct challenge to the American Dream from the black perspective. Wright wrote in the bleak and gritty urban realist tradition of Sinclair, Crane, and Dreiser. *Native Son* sold well—250,000 in the first year—because the terrors of the Great Depression made Americans more receptive to dark readings of society.

Still, many readers were jarred by Wright's description of the utter alienation and hopelessness of black life, at least Bigger's black life, and of violence as its natural product. Bigger Thomas, still a young man, was already defeated by a "world he feared" as "too big and too strong for him." He asked, as Stamp Paid and Paul D had in *Beloved*, though with more self-doubt, "Why did he and his folks have to live like this? What had they ever done? Perhaps they had not done anything. Maybe they had to live this way precisely because none of them in all their lives had ever done anything, right or wrong, that mattered much."[56] Stamp Paid and Paul D suffered defeat but had little self-doubt because they knew clearly that white folks were the source of their misery. Bigger knew that too, but three or four more generations of broken black lives led him to question himself and his folks.

For Bigger, whites, especially wealthy whites, were a strange, exalted, uninterpretable people who controlled their world and his. Bigger was thrust, unprepared and scared, into that foreign white world when the relief agency offered him a job as a driver for Mr. and Mrs. Dalton and their twenty-three-year-old daughter Mary. He took his gun and knife to the interview because he did not know what to expect and he wanted to feel himself the equal of anyone he met. Entering the Dalton neighborhood, he found "a cold and distant world; a world of white secrets carefully guarded. He could feel a pride, a certainty, and a confidence in these streets and houses." The Daltons, like the Bodwins in *Beloved,* were liberals, friends of the Negro people; Mr. Dalton said to Bigger, "I want you to know why I am hiring you. . . . You see, Bigger, I'm a supporter of the National Association for the Advancement of Colored People. Did you ever hear of that organization?" Bigger responded, "Nawsuh." Bigger's experience of Mr. Dalton was that he "was somewhere far away, high up, distant, like a god."[57] Mrs. Dalton, though blind, was also very solicitous of Bigger.

Bigger's sense of the white world was that it was dangerous, mysterious, and closed, that its promises were illusory. When considering the job at the Daltons, Bigger thought, "He could take the job . . . and be miserable, or he could refuse it and starve. It maddened him to think that he did not have a wider choice of action." But he had no doubt whom to blame for his limited options. In talking with his friend Gus, Bigger said, "They don't let us do *nothing.*" Gus asked who he meant, and Bigger replied, "The *white* folks. . . . Everytime I think about it I feel like somebody's poking a red-hot iron down my throat. Goddammit, look! . . . We black and they white. They got things and we ain't. They do things and we can't. It's just like living in jail. Half the time I feel like I'm on the outside of the world peeping in through a knothole in the fence."[58] Still, his choice was to either serve those white people or starve, and his anger built.

Mary's conduct toward Bigger, open and kind but presumptuous, was deeply disturbing and disorienting to him. Mary "responded to him as if he were human, as if he lived in the same world as she," but the "hard fact" was "that she was white and rich, a part of the world of people who told him what he could and could not do."[59] An entitled young liberal, Mary demanded that Bigger drive her to meet her socialist paramour, Jan. Mary and Jan then pressed Bigger to take them into his neighborhood and to select a café where he and people like him ate. As they drove past rows of tenement apartment buildings, Mary mused that she had always wanted to go into such rooms to see how black people lived. When they arrived at the café, they pushed Bigger to eat and drink with them—with white people in public. Mary and Jan drank more in the car and had a tryst in the back seat as Bigger drove slowly through a park, and then Jan left and Bigger drove Mary home. By the time they reached the house it was past midnight and Mary was stumbling drunk; by the time he got her to her room she had passed out. Her soft, sweet, pliant body aroused him; he kissed her, caressed her breasts, and kissed her harder before sensing the blind Mrs. Dalton in the room. Bigger put his hand and then a pillow over Mary's mouth to keep her quiet. Scared, he pressed down, she went limp, dead, and her mother soon left, thinking she was drunk but home safe. In a panic, Bigger took the body to the basement, thinking to dispose of it in the furnace. He beheaded the corpse to make it fit in the furnace, cleaned up, and hoped the fire would destroy all traces of her. A few small, white, bone fragments survived and were his undoing.

Once caught and on trial for murder, Bigger explained to his lawyer, "Mr. Max, we're all split up. . . . All I knew was that they kill us for women like her. We live apart. And then she comes and acts like that to me." Mary and Jan had treated Bigger "as if he were human," eating and drinking with him, but also as if he were much less than human, mere furniture, making love in the backseat as Bigger drove. He told Max, "White folks and black folks is strangers. We don't know what each other is thinking." When Max asked Bigger what his goals in life had been before the murder, he responded, "I reckon I wanted to do what other people do," but then he thought a bit more and said, "Why should I want to do anything? I ain't got a chance. I don't know nothing. I'm just black and they make the laws." Asked if he had ever hoped for anything, Bigger replied, "What for? I couldn't get it. I'm black. . . . They don't give black people a chance, so I took a chance and lost."[60]

Strikingly, Bigger's murder of Mary, and subsequently of his girlfriend Bessy, fearing that she might talk, gave his life a purpose, weight, and meaning that it had never had before. Bigger felt that "he had murdered and created a new life for himself. It was something that was all his own, and it was the first time in his life he had anything that others could not take from him." As Bigger sought to cover up the crime, then to evade the police and perhaps to escape, "he felt that he was living upon a high pinnacle . . . that his life was his, that he held his future in his hands." While still on the run, "there remained to him a queer sense of power. *He* had done this. *He* had brought all this about. In all his life these two murders were the most meaningful things that had ever happened to him. . . . Never had his will been so free as on this night and day of fear and murder and flight."[61]

The shocking idea that black Americans might be so outside the social and economic mainstream as to feel powerless until driven to strike out—to murder—was a dramatic challenge to the American Dream. Max's closing statement at Bigger's murder trial asked the judge to "remember that men can starve from a lack of self-realization as much as they can from a lack of bread! . . . Did we not build a nation, . . . in the name of a dream to realize our personalities and to make these realized personalities secure!" Bigger was convicted and faced death with equanimity, feeling that he had lived, if only briefly, saying, "I didn't know I was really alive in this world until I felt things hard enough to kill for 'em. . . . But I'm all right. I feel all right when I look at it that way."[62] But Bigger had not killed because he felt things hard, unless his objectification by Jan and Mary made him feel so; he felt things hard, sharp, and deeply only after he killed. He killed Mary and Bessy out of a soul-deadening sadness, out of an enervating sense of exclusion, that his country had no place, outside the ghetto or prison, for him.

Wright wrote *Native Son* to dramatize the exclusion of blacks from "the promise of American life," in Croly's phrase, and the psychological consequences of that social exclusion. In a 1940 article entitled "How Bigger Was Born," Wright wrote, "We live by an idealism that makes us believe . . . that every man and woman should have the opportunity to realize himself, to seek his own individual fate and goal." Wright challenged that idealism—the American Dream—with the literary realism of Bigger's contracted life. Wright concluded, "We have in the oppression of the Negro a shadow athwart of national life dense and heavy enough to satisfy even the gloomy broodings of a Hawthorne."[63] Wright forced racial exclusion into the twentieth-century American consciousness in a darker and more threatening shape than it had taken before. *Native Son* was blunt and powerful, but it did not soon lead to change in American life, at least not for the Bigger Thomases of our culture.

Like *Native Son*, Ralph Ellison's *Invisible Man* was set during the Depression, in the 1930s. The protagonist and narrator of *Invisible Man*, who goes nameless because he was figuratively invisible, was born and remained in the South until about age twenty, and he then fled to New York City. While *Native Son* was written in the sad and gritty urban realist tradition, *Invisible Man* anticipated the magical realism of Toni Morrison's work, especially *Beloved*. The invisible man was an intelligent, hard-working, hopeful young man. A top graduate in his high school, he won a "scholarship to the state college for Negroes." At college, he was comfortably in his element; he observed, "Here within this quiet greenness I possessed the only identity I had ever known. . . . I became aware of the connection between these lawns and buildings and my hopes and dreams."[64] He hoped that he might one day teach in and perhaps lead the college. But he was naive, unknowing, unaware, unfamiliar with the world around him and the motivations and incentives that moved men in it. As a result, his desire to pursue his academic dreams, to study, work, contribute, and make something of himself, was checked, time after time, by people, rich and poor, black and white, who seemed simply not to see him, not to account for him, as a worthy person in the world. *Invisible Man* was the story of his recognition of, response to, and strategy for addressing his marginality—his invisibility.

The invisible man remained naive throughout the book, thinking he might make himself into an individual. But his naivety was jolted at every turn by successful blacks and whites who seemed determined to make no room for him. When he disappointed and embarrassed the head of his Negro college, President Bledsoe, by mishandling a visiting trustee, Bledsoe expelled him from the college and declared, "You're nobody, son. You don't exist—can't you see that?" Bledsoe then provided supposed letters of recommendation addressed to prominent men, trustees, donors, and others in New York. The letters actually warned against him, which he soon discovered. After landing a job with a mysterious organization, called the Brotherhood, a communist front of sorts, and doing very well in gathering a following and organizing public demonstrations, he again thought the path to success was open: "It was no dream, the possibility existed. I had only to work and learn and survive in order to go to the top." Soon, his boss, Jack, drew him up short, declaring, "You were not hired to think. Had you forgotten that? . . . We furnish all ideas." He concluded that visibility and individuality were not available to him: "I AM AN invisible man . . . simply because people refuse to see me. . . . That invisibility . . . occurs because of a peculiar disposition of the eyes of those with whom I come in contact. A matter of the construction of their inner eyes."[65] As a black man, the culture simply refused to "see" him.

That blacks should be invisible to whites was no great shock; neither was it a great shock that prominent blacks like President Bledsoe should treat powerless blacks badly. But the narrator wondered whether blacks in general lacked individuality, especially when compared to more luminous whites. In a photo gallery of the college's founding, he saw "photographs of men and women in wagons drawn by mule teams and oxen, dressed in black, dusty clothing, people who seemed almost without individuality, . . . and among them the inevitable collection of white men and women in smiles, clear of features, striking, elegant, confident." But the real luminosity shone from the white trustees that visited the campus. Just as Bigger had seen Mr. Dalton as "high up, distant, like a god," the invisible man said of the trustees, "And oh, oh, oh, those millionaires!" Later, he noted, "The black rite of Horatio Alger was performed . . . , with millionaires come down to portray themselves; not merely acting out the myth of their goodness, and wealth and success and power and benevolence and authority . . . , but themselves, these virtues concretely!"[66] But a slip with one of those benefactors led to the narrator's expulsion from the Eden of college.

Other blacks in the novel also saw whites as omnipotent, often maliciously so. As the narrator was leaving college for New York, a disturbed but insightful veteran that he had met earlier tried to explain to him the power of whites, saying "they" do this and "they" do that. When he was asked, "Man, who's this *they* you talking so much about?," the vet responded, "They? Why, the same *they* we always mean, the white folks, authority, the gods, fate, circumstances—." Later, in New York, as an elderly black couple was being evicted in winter from their longtime tenement apartment, all their worldly goods in a heap on the sidewalk, the old woman said, "These white folks, Lord. These white folks." When her husband tried to fix blame on "the agent," she would have none of it, saying, "It's all the white folks, not just one. They all against us. Every stinking low-down one of them."[67] Many blacks, including Bigger, the vet, and this old woman, saw whites as Ahab saw the white whale: as a force denying their lives and dreams.

The invisible man also came to believe, though only after having been told so a number of times and in a number of ways, that the white

THE DREAM IN PROSPERITY AND DEPRESSION | 187

world and its opportunities were not open to him. He was haunted by and never quite understood his grandfather's deathbed instruction to his father, which he had overheard: "After I'm gone I want you to keep up the good fight. I never told you, but our life is a war. . . . Live with your head in the lion's mouth. I want you to overcome 'em with yeses, undermine 'em with grins, agree 'em to death and destruction." President Bledsoe gave the invisible man much the same instruction as he was being ejected from campus, saying, "My God, boy! You're black and living in the South—did you forget how to lie? . . . Why, the dumbest black bastard in the cotton patch knows that the only way to please a white man is to tell him a lie." And as he was departing for New York, the vet, equally exasperated, said, "For God's sake, learn to look beneath the surface. . . . Come out of the fog, young man. . . . Play the game, but don't believe in it—that much you owe yourself."[68]

In New York, the invisible man began, slowly, to emerge from the fog, from the mistaken sense that the classic white American Dream of study, work, and upward mobility applied to him. With the cold linearity of the white world foreclosed, the invisible man asked what options and possibilities the black world allowed. As he looked within the black community, his community, he saw a few potential models that he might emulate. Ras the Exhorter, who became Ras the Destroyer as the novel progressed, was a black nationalist who became increasingly shrill and confrontational as the Depression and white oppression pushed down on blacks. While the invisible man wondered whether Ras's path was the right one, he ultimately took another figure, Rinehart, as the better model.

Rinehart, never actually introduced but rumored, discussed, and admired throughout the book, was a hustler, a grifter, a man of many parts, many roles, making him a prominent if opaque member of the black community. The invisible man became aware of Rinehart in multiple guises, even being mistaken for him on the street, before he realized that the guises all hid a single person: "Could he be all of them: Rine the runner and Rine the gambler and Rine the briber and Rine the lover and Rinehart the Reverend? . . . His world was possibility and he knew it. . . . The world in which he lived was without boundaries. A vast seething, hot world of fluidity, and Rine the rascal was at home." If Benjamin Franklin's and Horatio Alger's linearity were foreclosed, then Rinehart's fluidity had to be embraced. The community knew that linearity was denied, so no adverse judgments were made about a man like Rinehart who could be, simultaneously, gambler and minister. The narrator concluded that "somewhere between Rinehart," all fluidity and motion, "and invisibility were great potentialities." This insight—much like the insight that Baby Suggs's spirit delivered to Denver as she stood on the porch afraid to go into the world and confront the dangers posed by white people, "Know it, and go on out the yard"—allowed the invisible man to conclude, "I'm coming out, no less invisible . . . , but coming out nonetheless."[69]

Conclusion

As the new century opened, the problems of the late nineteenth century, including immigration, urbanization, and the concentration of corporate power and control, were unresolved. Social Darwinism counseled that small government, low taxes, and limited regulation fostered competition that allowed the fittest to emerge as the benefactors of society. Progressives called for more regulation of the powerful and more security and support for the weak and vulnerable. President Theodore Roosevelt initiated a series of trust-busting suits against predatory monopolies, but he was quick to say that successful competitors, no matter how big and wealthy, were to be admired rather than feared.

Norris's *The Octopus* and Sinclair's *The Jungle* highlighted corporate excess, and Roosevelt responded. He rejected the socialist policy prescriptions of Norris and Sinclair, but he moved against both the railroads and the meatpackers. The U.S. Supreme Court's decision in the *Northern Securities* case (1904) broke up a railroad monopoly between Chicago and Seattle constructed by Rockefeller, E. H. Harriman, Morgan, and Hill. At Roosevelt's urging, Congress passed in 1906 the Pure Food and Drug Act and the Meat Inspection Act. Only after Roosevelt read Croly's *Promise of American Life* and decided to try to recapture the presidency in 1912 did he adopt a broader, more progressive sense of the average man's need for government to ensure equality of opportunity. Roosevelt never got a chance to implement his new program because his challenge to the Republican incumbent, William Howard Taft, split the Republican vote and allowed the election of the Democrat Woodrow Wilson.

Wilson's first term as president saw passage of a wave of progressive regulation, including the federal income tax and the federal-reserve banking system, both passed in 1913. In 1914 Congress created the Federal Trade Commission and passed the Clayton Anti-Trust Act to better balance the roles of business and labor in American life. Soon though, American entry into World War I brought government and business, especially the large corporations, into partnership and slowed reform. The Republican postwar ascendency of the 1920s was called a "return to normalcy" and brought a decided shift back in favor of business priorities. Republican presidents Coolidge and Hoover lauded traditional American values of independence, work, and saving as the path to security and prosperity. Hoover's *American Individualism* was an encomium to Chamber of Commerce, free-market, Republican principles.

The stock market crash of late October 1929, which began the Great Depression, the worst and most sustained economic collapse in American history, cast a dark shadow over Republican Party principles. Franklin Roosevelt easily defeated Hoover for the presidency in 1932 and then won three more elections, in 1936, 1940, and 1944. Despite an activist administration that implemented back-to-work programs and farm-support programs, as well as Social Security, unemployment compensation, insurance for bank deposits, and much more, the Depression's grip relaxed only slowly. Every president, Republican and Democrat, from Theodore Roosevelt through Franklin Roosevelt felt compelled to pay obeisance to American individualism and the self-help tradition even as they moved carefully to craft a federal government capable of addressing the issues and problems of the new, urban, industrial, and increasingly global twentieth century.

Even as Franklin Roosevelt expanded the federal government's role in American society and economy, first to confront the Depression and then to fight World War II, the nation's great novelists declared that the country's problems were much deeper and more intractable than any of the elected officials had allowed. The publication of Steinbeck's *Grapes of Wrath* in 1939 and Wright's *Native Son* in 1940 pointed to groups for whom the American Dream had receded or had never been available at all. The fact that *The Grapes of Wrath* chronicled the dispossession and destruction of a white family by the Depression hit even more fortunate Americans with an immediacy and power that said, There, but for the grace of God, go I. That the Joads and hundreds of thousands of their rural, lower-class, white peers had been driven from their homes and made itinerant drifters on the verge of starvation announced that, no matter what the politicians said, for many people the American Dream no longer had meaning.

Both Wright's *Native Son* and Ellison's *Invisible Man* declared that blacks had never had access to the American Dream and that that fact was taking an increasingly fearsome toll on them. Bigger Thomas was enraged by his exclusion from the opportunities and benefits that whites enjoyed. Murder alone salved the hurt and made him feel, if only briefly, that he understood and controlled his own life. The invisible man held on to the prospect of preparing himself, through education and hard work, for an independent and responsible place in society. His grandfather, President Bledsoe, and the deranged veteran all told him, bluntly and in their different ways, that no such path existed for a black man in this white society. Enlightenment, both as knowledge of self and society, was the invisible man's recognition that his future was to be found not in the cold linearity of the white world but in the hot, vibrant fluidity of the black community. Nearly a century after the end of slavery, blacks were still clear that the American society had no honorable, or even visible, place for them.

7 | The Dream Unmoored: The Rise of Entitlement from Truman to LBJ

I say to you, my friends, that . . . I still have a dream. It is a dream deeply rooted in the American Dream, that one day this nation will rise up and live out the true meaning of its creed,— . . . that all men are created equal.
—Martin Luther King Jr., "I Have a Dream," 1963

The Depression and World War II changed the way Americans thought about individuals, communities, and society. Hoover failed to recognize, but FDR was instinctively aware, that the Depression had laid bare the great changes that technology, industrialization, and urbanization had produced in the American society. The transition from rural to urban life, the diversification of the economy, and the increasing importance of education, science, and technology—the falling importance of strong backs and the rising importance of strong minds—had changed the meanings of freedom, equality, and opportunity.

The United States emerged from World War II as the dominant cultural, political, military, and economic power in the world. In 1946, an exuberant young Texas congressman named Lyndon Baines Johnson spoke for many in saying, "We in America are the fortunate children of fate. From almost any viewpoint ours is the greatest nation; the greatest in material wealth, in goods and produce, in abundance of the things that make life easier and more pleasant. . . . Nearly every other people are prostrate and helpless. . . . If we have excuse for being, that excuse is that through our efforts the world will be better when we depart than when we entered."[1]

Congressman Johnson was right; the United States of America was the wealthiest and most powerful society the world had ever known. Most Americans were comfortable and confident about using that power and wealth to support freedom in the world. Many were even comfortable with opening rights and opportunities to Americans who previously had been excluded. Moderates, both Democrats and Republicans, admitted that more justice demanded to be done, but they warned that equality, absent the striving and competition that had always characterized American life, might be an attractive dream, but it was not *the* American Dream.

As American leaders exulted in the nation's economic strength and military dominance and as many even promised to open opportunity to those previously denied it, the nation's most prominent novelists pointed to deep and intractable problems that would have to be overcome. Toni Morrison's *Sula* (1973) declared that the American Dream had always been and remained illusory for blacks. John Updike dedicated his four-book Rabbit series, published a book a decade, in 1960, 1971, 1981, and 1990, to tracing the angst and futility of small-town middle-class life. *Rabbit, Run* (1960) and *Rabbit Redux* (1971) present a sense of entitlement, an absence of striving and achievement, that rendered life enervating. Norman Mailer's *An American Dream* (1965) showed the danger, even horror, of striving and achieving without moral or social purpose. And finally, Kurt Vonnegut's *Slaughterhouse-Five* (1969) highlighted the overwhelming forces, including war and fate, that made preparation, planning, choice, and purpose futile or worse. The broad message of these novels was that few Americans lived lives of preparation, striving, and competition. Most women, minorities, low-income people, and small-town people lived lives of narrow choices and tight constraints.

The Future of Striving in a World of Plenty

As Depression memories faded, the American Dream came to focus on a comfortable, high-consumption, leisure-oriented private life. For the white middle and working classes this meant securing and enjoying single-family homes, cars, televisions, washing machines, refrigerators, and lawn mowers. Modern amenities such as indoor water and plumbing, electricity, central heat, and later air conditioning became common in American homes. Men provided the principal income, and women, even when they supplemented family income, managed the private domain of home and family. But much had changed; most workers toiled within large organizations. The blue-collar worker gave long, hard hours on an assembly line without ever feeling the autonomy, security, and personal pride of the master craftsman. The white-collar worker climbed the corporate ladder, taking on more responsibility and gaining more income and prestige but rarely achieving the independence and control that goes with ownership. Increasingly, middle- and working-class Americans put in their time at work but focused their attention and expectations on free time after work.

Scholars were deeply concerned about the changes that modern society encouraged in American character, virtues, and aspirations. David Riesman's classic work *The Lonely Crowd* (1950) argued that conformist professionals were displacing the entrepreneurs of the Protestant ethic. The social critic C. Wright Mills, in his prominent book *White Collar: The American Middle Classes* (1951), described the decline of independent entrepreneurialism in the face of bureaucratic and corporate management. Mills continued his analysis with an extraordinarily influential book, *The Power Elite* (1956), describing a new interlocking set of governing elites that were closing off the paths that generations of entrepreneurs had traveled to opportunity, success, and status in America. William Whyte's *Organization Man* (1956) worried that "belongingness," the safety and predictability of the large corporation, threatened the individuality and creativity of the white-collar worker.[2] Scholars worried that security and plenty had sapped the initiative, verve, and creativity shown by previous generations of workers and entrepreneurs. Politicians largely ignored these analyses while novelists expanded upon them in their own métier.

The Search for Purpose in Postwar Prosperity

While intellectuals struggled to explain and common citizens strove to understand the changes taking place in American society, politicians articulated a familiar vision of America's past accomplishments and future prospects. Throughout the 1950s the dominant Republican voice was that of Dwight Eisenhower, and the dominant Democratic voice was that of Adlai Stevenson. That Eisenhower defeated Stevenson in the presidential elections of 1952 and 1956 indicated that his voice rang through most clearly. Eisenhower and Stevenson both sensed that the balance between the material and the spiritual in American life was shifting. Eisenhower complimented Americans on what they had achieved, while Stevenson challenged them to do more. Voters accepted the compliment but not yet the challenge.

Late in the 1952 campaign, Eisenhower promised that if he were elected, "The world will again recognize the United States of America as the spiritual and material realization of the dreams that men have dreamt since the dawn of history."[3] Just four months later, in his first inaugural address, Eisenhower reminded his listeners that America could only be an example to others, a "city on a hill," if it was true to its own best values: "Whatever America hopes to bring to pass in the world must first come to pass in the heart of America. The peace we seek, then, is nothing less than the practice and fulfillment of our whole faith among ourselves and in our dealings with others." The new president called upon his fellow citizens to "proclaim anew our faith. This faith is the abiding creed of our fathers. . . . It establishes, beyond debate, those gifts of the Creator that are man's inalienable rights, and that make all men equal in His sight." Moreover, Eisenhower was at pains to say that these treasured rights belonged to all men. The American faith "warns that any man who seeks to deny equality among all his brothers betrays the spirit of the free and invites the mockery of the tyrant." Elsewhere in the speech, Eisenhower declared, "We hold all continents and peoples in equal regard and honor. We reject any insinuation that one race or another, one people or another, is in any sense inferior or expendable."[4]

The Eisenhower administration's policy was challenged, and in critical cases it failed, to live up to its egalitarian rhetoric. In the landmark case of *Brown v. Board of Education* (1954), Chief Justice Earl Warren urged the U.S. Supreme Court to confront directly the constitutionality of segregation in public education. After extensive consideration, Warren, writing for a unanimous court, declared, "In the field of public education the doctrine of separate but equal has no place. Separate educational facilities are inherently unequal. . . . The plaintiffs . . . have been deprived of the equal protection of the laws guaranteed by the Fourteenth Amendment." While the states of the Deep South dug in for a decade-long contest called "massive resistance," Eisenhower repeatedly refused to endorse *Brown*. The president counseled patience while the public mind, especially the southern public mind, came around. The conservative coalition in Congress, led by southern Democrat committee chairs, actively obstructed enforcement of the court's ruling. For many whites, the 1950s were a return to peace and prosperity, a bucolic time, but for blacks they were a time of preparation and early skirmishing for civil rights.

Eisenhower easily won reelection in 1956, and in his second inaugural address, as in the campaign, he celebrated the nation's power and wealth. He said, "We live in a land of plenty. . . . In our nation work and wealth abound. Our population grows. Commerce crowds our rivers and rails, our skies, harbors and highways. Our soil is fertile, our agriculture productive. The air rings with the song of our industry—rolling mills and blast furnaces, dynamos, dams and assembly lines—the chorus of America the bountiful."[5] Eisenhower celebrated America's material success. Adlai Stevenson, though defeated a second time, called upon Americans to look beyond work and even wealth. Stevenson declared, "I believe with all my heart that, under democracy, this country is going forward to an uplifting of all its citizens, not just in terms of new goods and gadgets, but even more in terms of a broadening and deepening of the mind and heart of the nation."[6] The nation's leading novelists, including John Updike, painted a far grittier picture of life in 1950s America.

John Updike (1932–2009) was one of the leading American novelists of the second half of the twentieth century. Updike was born in Reading, Pennsylvania, and lived in nearby Shillington and Plowville through high school. After graduating from Harvard with a degree in English, he spent a year at Oxford before joining the staff of the *New Yorker* in 1956. Though he maintained a lifelong association with the *New Yorker*, he left its full-time employ after two years and moved to Ipswich, Massachusetts, to focus on his writing. *Rabbit, Run*, his second novel, was set in the fictional towns of Brewer and Mt. Judge, Pennsylvania, stand-ins for Reading and Shillington. Ultimately, the Rabbit series extended to four books, the last two of which won the Pulitzer Prize for fiction.

The Rabbit series followed the life of Harry "Rabbit" Angstrom from his midtwenties to his death in his midsixties. The series explored in fiction the concerns of such intellectuals as David Riesman, C. Wright Mills, William Whyte, and others that the prosperity of middle-class life had sapped the drive and danger, or at least insecurity, from American life. Rabbit's life was not a robust pursuit of the American Dream so much as an aimless and often futile struggle to find and hold security and meaning in middle-class life. The high point of Rabbit's life came early. As a six-foot-three forward, Rabbit broke the county high school basketball scoring record in his junior year and then broke it again as a senior. He was young, strong, quick, and handsome—he was a winner—and nothing afterward quite compared to that feeling. His scoring record stood for four years; his sense of winning easily for less than that.

In the book's opening pages, Rabbit, then twenty-six, happened across a group of teenagers shooting baskets and asked to join in. They were skeptical but agreed, and Rabbit soon warmed up and was elated that he still had the touch: "He feels liberated from long gloom. . . . Naturals know. It's all in how it feels."[7] Rabbit's life through the decades was a halfhearted quest to get that feeling back. Updike explored the narrow choices, modest opportunities, and shifting social and economic life of small-town America in the second half of the twentieth century.

Rabbit's feeling of early triumph dominated his young life. He explained to anyone who would listen how he felt when he was on top—in the zone. Others seemed slow, even plodding, while he got "this funny feeling . . . , just drifting around, passing the ball, and all of a sudden I know, you see, I *know* I can do anything." But that incomparable feeling had been gone for a long time; Rabbit talked about it in the past tense, saying, "I *was* great. It's the fact. I mean I'm not much good for anything now, but I really was good at that."[8] One is reminded of Emerson's observation that young Americans, failing in their first endeavor, despair. But Rabbit had not failed; he had succeeded blissfully as a teenager, a high school basketball star, and nothing filled him up like that again.

Janice Springer Angstrom was Rabbit's wife and the mother of his son, Nelson. Janice and Rabbit met and became lovers after she was out of high school and he was back from service in the army. Both were working at Kroll's, a department store, and sneaking off for sex at a friend's apartment. In those early days, Janice was bashful but easy and eager, and Rabbit was thoughtlessly happy. Updike explained that Rabbit and Janice were married "when he was twenty-three and she was two years out of high school, still scarcely adult. . . . Nelson was born seven months after the Episcopal service."[9] Married and pregnant, Janice became bored, unkempt, sedentary, and, frequently, drunk. Rabbit increasingly felt limited, constrained, trapped; like so many male characters in American fiction, marriage was experienced as a burden, an end to excitement, spontaneity, and freedom.

In a particularly telling scene, Janice and Rabbit interrupted their squabbling when their attention was captured by the Mouseketeers Club on television. The leader of the Mouseketeers, Jimmie, had mentioned God. "Janice and Rabbit became unnaturally still; both are Christians. God's name makes them feel guilty." While no longer children, they were still childish, not just watching the Mouseketeers but looking to Jimmie for life lessons. Jimmie presented them with the old Puritan idea of a calling, of developing one's God-given talents, as the path to the American Dream. Jimmie advised his young audience, "God wants some of us to become scientists, some of us to become artists, some of us to become firemen and doctors. . . . And He gives to each of us the special talents to become these things, *provided we work to develop them.* We must *work*, boys and girls. . . . Learn to understand your talents, and then work to develop them. That's the way to be happy."[10] Janice and Rabbit treated Jimmie's wisdom with brief respectful awe and then returned to their squabbling.

Rabbit responded to life's demands by running away. Early in his marriage, he took the car and headed to Philadelphia and points south, where it was warm and the girls were barefoot. He got lost and ended up back in Brewer, parked in front of his old coach's apartment. Initially, Mr. Tothero played the responsible adult, advising Rabbit not to be harsh after he characterized Janice as an alcoholic. Tothero promised him a place to sleep if he would try to work it out with Janice; he agreed, but said, "I don't think I can. I mean I'm not that interested in her. I was, but I'm not." Soon Rabbit was telling a minister, Jack Eccles, who had befriended him and tried to counsel him, that he was not going back: "I don't know what she feels. I haven't known for years. All I know is what's inside *me*."[11] Here we have the key to Harry "Rabbit" Angstrom; he was as completely and continuously self-absorbed, self-referential, and oblivious to the feelings and needs of others as any character in American fiction.

Tothero's role as the responsible adult guiding Rabbit back to Janice lasted only until he had a couple of drinks. Tothero pulled Rabbit along to a bar where they met Tothero's sometime girlfriend, a hard, worn hooker named Margaret, and her younger friend, a part-time hooker named Ruth Leonard. Rather than returning to Janice, again pregnant, and Nelson, Rabbit went home with Ruth and stayed for two months. Ruth was a diamond in the rough, jaded and saddened by her life, still alive inside, but more clear-eyed than hopeful. She saw Rabbit's self-absorption very clearly. When Rabbit blamed Janice for his flight, saying, "There's something about her, . . . she's a menace," Ruth responded, "This poor wife you left? *You're* the menace, I'd say." Reverend Jack Eccles saw Rabbit just as clearly. Eccles, initially Rabbit's counselor and confidant, became a golfing buddy. They spent significant time together but made no progress; Rabbit resisted returning to his family and enjoyed the easy availability of Ruth. Eccles told him, "The truth is, . . .

you're monstrously selfish. You're a coward. You don't care about right and wrong; you worship nothing except your own worst instincts."[12]

Rabbit's childish Mouseketeers-Club understanding of life was again on display in an exchange with Ruth about religion. Ruth's apartment, where she entertained her clients, overlooked a large church. With the congregation flowing in, Ruth said that Sunday morning made her sick. Rabbit asked her,

> "Why don't you believe anything?"
> "You're kidding?"
> "No. Doesn't it ever, at least for a second, seem obvious to you?"
> "God, you mean? No. It seems obvious just the other way. All the time."
> "Well now if God doesn't exist, why does anything?"

Ruth's hard fatalism responded, "Why? There's no why to it. Things just are."[13]

Rabbit had taken a different lesson from his experiences than the ones Ruth and Eccles thought he should have learned. Rabbit told Ruth, "When I ran from Janice I made an interesting discovery. . . . If you have the guts to be yourself, . . . other people'll pay your price." Rabbit was too self-absorbed and shortsighted to realize that the price, and not just for others, might be very high. Rabbit's discovery that Ruth—who, after all, had been a part-time prostitute—had slept with Ronnie Harrison, his high school teammate and competitor for athletic glory, made him leave her and return to Janice. Janice was in delivery, having their second child, Rebecca June. The reunited family, Rabbit, Janice, Nelson, and Rebecca June, returned to their old apartment and resumed life. Soon, the old tensions and disappointments returned, and they were right back where they were before Rabbit left. Janice's father, Mr. Springer, owned several used-car lots and had given Rabbit a job, so he was gone during the day and not very helpful or supportive when he was home. Janice was tired, listless, and overwhelmed. On a particularly bad day, both children fussy, Rabbit and Janice fought, and Rabbit again prepared to leave. Janice pleaded, "Why can't you try to imagine how I feel?" Rabbit's response, classic narcissism, was, "I can. I can but I don't want to, it's not the thing, the thing is how *I* feel. And I feel like getting out."[14] Janice was alone with the children, drinking; her father was looking for Rabbit; her mother was berating her over the phone. Janice took the baby for a bath in the hope of quieting her. The tub was too full; Janice lost the baby beneath the water and could not recover her; Rebecca June, days old, drowned.

The death, of course, brought Rabbit home, but tensions between him and Janice and between the Angstroms and the Springers remained high. At the funeral, Rabbit's narcissism again emerged as he feared being blamed, even indirectly, for the death. Rabbit blurted out, "Don't look at *me*, . . . I didn't kill her. . . . You all keep acting as if *I* did it. I wasn't anywhere near. *She's* the one." Everyone is appalled; "even his own mother is horrified. . . . He turns and runs." Predictably enough, his flight led him directly to Ruth's door. Her response, even though she had cried when he left, was self-protectively harsh: "Go away, . . . go *away*." When he persisted, again blaming Janice for the death, taking no responsibility himself, she responded, "Boy, you really have the touch of death, don't you? . . . You're Mr. Death himself."[15] The distance between Updike's picture of the grimy meaninglessness of American life and the shimmering descriptions of leading politicians was immense.

What Did Prosperity Mean for Women?

Janice Springer Angstrom was born at an inflection point for women in American history. Many women of the previous generation had been drawn into the workforce by World War II, but most returned to private life after the war. Like about 80 percent of young white women, Janice worked for wages before marriage, but only a quarter of women worked outside the home after marriage. But times were changing, and, as we shall see later in this chapter and in the next, Janice would be part of that change. Nonetheless, major economic and social changes are never smooth; the gears grind ominously before they begin to catch and pull again. Cultural assumptions about the role of women changed more slowly than did their economic opportunities in the 1960s and 1970s, exaggerating existing tensions over gender roles, home life, and family authority.

The 1960s were a time of great dynamism and change, but most middle-class women were caught midway between the stultifying safety of the home and the exciting uncertainty of the marketplace. Then a truly formative event occurred: in 1960 the U.S. Food and Drug Administration approved the first birth-control pill. "The pill" gave women direct and personal control over the decision to bear children and, just as important, over the timing and spacing of pregnancy and childbearing. While the pill made it possible to separate sex and childbearing, thereby helping give women control over one major issue in their lives, it only made the question of how to use that control more pressing. What goals should women pursue in their lives?

As middle-class white women groped to understand and articulate their place in the American society, Betty Friedan's *Feminine Mystique* (1963) emerged as definitive. Friedan's famous first chapter, "The Problem That Has No Name," described a malaise that millions of women recognized in their lives. Historian Sara Evans described Friedan's problem with no name as a "passive and infantilizing domesticity."[16] Millions of talented and educated middle-class suburban women were trapped in increasingly comfortable, electrified, user-friendly homes without important outside work and responsibility to give their lives independent meaning. The culture advised femininity and domesticity while the abilities, inner needs, and objective interests of women advised education, preparation, and accomplishment.

Few black women, of course, had such high-class problems. Married black women shared the low-wage economic fate of their husbands, and when they worked too, which they always did in far larger numbers than white married women, their wages were lower still. Black women alone, with or without children, were on the economy's periphery and struggled to get by. The novelist Toni Morrison always sought to portray black life, especially black women's lives, from a perspective internal to the black community. The goal was to enlighten for black people, more than for whites, why black life was so difficult and failure and defeat so common.

Morrison's novel *Sula* was the story of black life in "The Bottoms" of the fictional Medallion, Ohio, from the end of World War I through the mid-1960s. The novel focused on the relationship between two girls, Sula Mae Peace and Nel Wright, together from youth, through tumult and separation, to maturity and the beginnings of understanding. More broadly, *Sula*, the novel and the character, highlighted the limited options available to black men and women, especially women, into the middle of the twentieth century and the impact that those limits had on their social and moral horizons. In a classic line, Morrison said of Sula and Nel that by the age of twelve, both "had discovered years before that they were neither white nor male, and that all freedom and triumph was forbidden to them."[17]

Black families and black lives had always been fragile. Sula's grandmother, Eva Peace, had three children: Sula's mother Hannah; Eva, called Pearl; and Ralph, called Plum, with her husband, BoyBoy, before he abandoned them. With BoyBoy gone and no money, Eva left the children with a neighbor, Mrs. Suggs, just for the day. She returned to collect the children eighteen months later, with cash, a monthly insurance payment of twenty-three dollars, and one leg. Facing long odds, Eva had deliberately let a train take off one of her legs. Eva presided over a large ramshackle house, built with the insurance money, holding her extended family and renters. Pearl married and left at fourteen, Plum returned from the war a drug addict, and "Hannah married a laughing man named Rekus who died when their daughter Sula was about three years old, at which time Hannah moved back to her mother's big house." Hannah "had a steady sequence of lovers, mostly the husbands of her friends and neighbors." She "taught Sula that sex was pleasant and frequent, but otherwise unremarkable."[18]

Nel's mother, Helene Sabat, had been born to a "Creole whore" in New Orleans before being taken and raised by her grandmother. At sixteen, Helene married her middle-aged cousin Wiley Wright, and nine years later Nel was born. Helene was a cautious, even rigid, religious woman determined that both she and Nel should escape her low origins. Nel was raised in a stable, clean, orderly home. The marriage of Wiley and Helene Wright, while formal and cool, was the only stable marriage in *Sula*. Nel matured into a woman much like her mother, not as beautiful but careful, calm, and faithful. At seventeen, she was the choice from among all the girls of Mount Zion Church for the wife of the choir's principal tenor, twenty-year-old Jude Greene.

Black men faced great difficulty in getting good, steady, work. Jude Greene, Nel's husband, was a particularly poignant example. Jude initially worked in the dining room of the Medallion Hotel. He made enough to help his family while he was single, but not enough to support a wife. When hiring was being done for construction on the New River Road, he was excited. In line every day, he "longed more than anybody else to be taken. Not just for the good money, more for the work itself," the physical work of measuring, digging, building; "he was full of such dreams." When it became clear that few if any blacks would be hired, "it was rage, rage and determination to take on a man's role anyhow that made him press Nel about settling down. He needed some of his appetites filled, some posture of adulthood recognized, but mostly he wanted someone to care about his hurt." After "his burst dream of road building," Jude became disheartened and sullen. When he returned home one day to find Nel and Sula talking in the kitchen, Sula hailed him, "Hey, Jude. What you know good?" Jude responded, "White man running it—nothing good" and ended with the observation "that a Negro man had a hard row to hoe in this world."[19] Disconsolate and weak, Jude fell to Sula's blandishments, lost his home and family, and bought a ticket for Detroit.

Black women had it even harder; they usually had children, and their job options were no better and often at lower pay. When BoyBoy left Eva with three children under four, she concluded that she "would have to scrounge around and beg through the winter. . . . Then she could plant and maybe hire herself out to valley [white] farms to weed or sow or feed stock." These bleak prospects led Eva to maim herself for an insurance settlement and a monthly stipend. Those moneys and rent from boarders fed her family. When Hannah, Eva's oldest child, was about twelve, she asked, "Mamma, did you ever love us?" Eva responded, "No. I don't reckon I did. Not the way you thinkin." Hannah clarified her question, saying, "I know you fed us and all. . . . Did you ever, you know, play with us?" Eva responded that they were very poor, living at one time for a week on just three beets. Hannah responded, as a twelve-year-old might, "I know 'bout them beets, Mamma. You told us that a million times." Eva, exasperated, said, "Yeah? Well? Don't that count? Ain't that love? . . . I stayed alive for you can't you get that through your thick head . . . heifer?"[20]

Sula and Nel, despite very different home environments, shared the debilities of being black and female. Nel sought security in a husband and family; Sula sought freedom in a life alone, though lived in the serial and simultaneous presence of many men. When Sula arrived home, unexpectedly after a decade's absence, Eva confronted her immediately, saying, "When you gone to get married? . . . It ain't right for you to want to stay off by yourself." And as Sula lay dying, Nel sought her out and made up with her about Jude, and they debated women's options and best course in life one last time. Nel said, "You *can't* do it all. You a woman and a colored woman at that. You can't act like a man. You can't be walking around all independent-like, doing whatever you like, taking what you want, leaving what you don't." Sula disagreed, saying, "I got my mind. And what goes on in it. Which is to say, I got me." Nel responded, "Lonely, ain't it?"[21]

Each generation of American blacks had found for itself that despite official rhetoric, the country did not see them and did not envision a place, or certainly not an equal place, for them. Yearn as they might for full inclusion in the good and bad of America, a chance to compete and either win or lose, it did not come. In *Notes of a Native Son,* James Baldwin wrote, "It comes as a great shock to discover that the country which is your birthplace, and to which you owe your life and your identity, has not in its whole system of reality evolved any place for you."[22] Still, white politicians continued to promise change.

John F. Kennedy, Camelot, and the American Dream

John F. Kennedy won the presidency in 1960 by offering a refurbished "city on a hill" called Camelot. The legendary Camelot was a utopia, a realm in which the good King Arthur, having warred for decades to defeat evil, promised peace, justice, and beauty to his grateful subjects. When Kennedy was elected president in 1960, there were still battles to be fought, powerful forces of evil still ruled over large parts of the globe, and stubborn injustice was visible at home, but the wealth and power to suppress them seemed to be at hand. Reaching back beyond his Massachusetts forebear, the Puritan governor John Winthrop, to Pericles, the fountainhead of the western democratic tradition, president-elect Kennedy promised to pursue freedom and justice, at home and abroad, with energy and verve.

Kennedy used a speech to a joint session of the Massachusetts legislature on January 9, 1961, and his inaugural address on January 20, 1961, to rally the nation to a renewal of its fundamental principles. To an appreciative Massachusetts audience, Kennedy declared, "What Pericles said to the Athenians has long been true of this commonwealth: 'We do not imitate—for we are a model to others.'" Kennedy reminded his listeners, just as Winthrop had reminded his listeners on the deck of the *Arabella* more than three centuries before, "We must always consider that we shall be as a city upon a hill—the eyes of all people are upon us." Kennedy warned his sober colleagues, "We are setting out upon a voyage in 1961 no less hazardous than that undertaken by the *Arabella* in 1630. We are committing ourselves to tasks of statecraft no less awesome than that of governing the Massachusetts Bay Colony, beset as it was then by terror without and disorder within."[23]

Kennedy developed these themes in his famous inaugural address. Kennedy began by reminding his listeners that America stood guard over "beliefs for which our forebears fought. . . . We dare not forget today that we are the heirs of that first revolution." Then he intoned the famous declaration, "Let the word go forth from this time and place, to friend and foe alike, that the torch has been passed to a new generation of Americans— . . . Let every nation know, whether it wishes us well or ill, that we shall pay any price, bear any burden, meet any hardship, support any friend, oppose any foe to assure the survival and success of liberty."

Like Pericles, Kennedy warned his countrymen that a free people must defend its liberties. Freedom grown too comfortable becomes lazy, and lassitude invites loss of liberty. "In your hands, my fellow citizens, more than mine, will rest the final success or failure of our course. Since this country was founded, each generation of Americans has been summoned to give testimony to its national loyalty. . . . Now the trumpet summons us again." Kennedy closed his charge to the American people by promising, "The energy, the faith, the devotion which we bring to this endeavor will light our country and all who serve it—and the glow from that fire can truly light the world. . . . And so, my fellow Americans: ask not what your country can do for you—ask what you can do for your country."[24]

As Kennedy assumed the presidency, the two gravest problems facing America were international communism and domestic racial discrimination. Each posed a serious threat to human freedom and dignity. There was broad bipartisan commitment to oppose communism with every element of national power. No such consensus existed in regard to civil rights. Kennedy was painfully aware that the Democratic Party, with its electoral dependence on southern votes and with the legislative sway of powerful southern committee chairs in Congress, was an unlikely vehicle for confronting racism. Events forced Kennedy to move forward despite the difficulties.

Kennedy made two major speeches to the nation about civil rights. The first was on September 30, 1962, in response to James Meredith's struggles to be admitted to the University of Mississippi, and the second was on June 11, 1963, when the National Guard was called out to help manage the desegregation of the University of Alabama. The Mississippi speech was a cool and almost dispassionate lecture on judicial process and the importance of the rule of law. The president closed to echoes of Winthrop and Lincoln by reminding Mississippians, "The eyes of the

Nation and of all the world are upon you and upon all of us, and the honor of your University and State are in the balance. . . . Let us preserve both the law and the peace and then healing those wounds that are within we can turn to the greater crises that are without and stand united as one people in our pledge to man's freedom."[25]

Mississippi and the South chose to resist, tensions grew, and the Freedom Summer of 1963 saw violence and death as the nation and the world watched. Kennedy responded with a powerful call, the first such presidential call in nearly a century, for the nation to live up to its founding values. Kennedy opened his national radio and television address on the evening of June 11, 1963, by reminding his countrymen, "This Nation was founded . . . on the principle that all men are created equal, and that the rights of every man are diminished when the rights of one man are threatened." "It ought to be possible," the president said, "for every American to enjoy the privileges of being American without regard to his race or color. . . . But this is not the case."

Other presidents, including FDR, Harry S. Truman, and Eisenhower, had acknowledged and even criticized racism, but they had seen the social and political resistance to equality as too great to overcome. Kennedy posed the issue differently, saying, "This is not a sectional issue. . . . Nor is this a partisan issue. . . . This is not even a legal or a legislative issue alone. . . . We are confronted primarily with a moral issue. It is as old as the scriptures and is as clear as the American Constitution." He said that racism impugned the integrity of every American and of the nation itself. No president since Lincoln had said quite as much; none had said that America simply cannot be like this. "One hundred years of delay have passed since President Lincoln freed the slaves, yet their heirs . . . are not fully free. . . . And this Nation," Kennedy continued, "for all its hopes and all its boasts, will not be fully free until all its citizens are free."[26]

Kennedy, initially quite timid on civil rights, declared from the White House that the nation had not lived up to its most cherished principles and that its rhetoric was hollow so long as the reality of black lives remained so bleak. Hence, he declared, "Now the time has come for this Nation to fulfill its promise. . . . A great change is at hand, and our task, our obligation, is to make that revolution, that change, peaceful and constructive for all." "Next week," he announced, "I shall ask the Congress of the United States to act, to make a commitment it has not fully made in this century to the proposition that race has no place in American life or law."[27] The president then outlined a bill to provide equality of access to public accommodation and services and desegregation of schools and of voting.

Just two and one-half months after Kennedy defined civil rights as a challenge to the nation's moral integrity, Martin Luther King Jr. led the March on Washington for Jobs and Freedom and delivered his famous "I Have a Dream" speech to a quarter million people assembled before the Lincoln Memorial and to tens of millions more in the nation beyond. The Kennedy administration had bargained with King and others to forestall the march and, when that proved impossible, to control the rhetoric of those allowed to address the crowd. The Kennedy administration did not want the speakers to diminish support for the proposed civil rights bill then before Congress.

Not only did King's "I Have a Dream" speech hew to Kennedy administration wishes, but also King elaborated and built upon several themes from the president's June 11 speech. Standing in the shadow of the Lincoln Memorial, King echoed Kennedy's observation that 100 years after the Emancipation Proclamation, "the Negro still is not free." King also echoed Kennedy's observation that the promise of the American Founding had still not been fulfilled for blacks. King said, "In a sense we've come to our nation's capital to cash a check . . . a promissory note. . . . This note was a promise that all men would be guaranteed . . . the 'unalienable Rights of Life, Liberty, and the pursuit of Happiness.'"

King also joined Kennedy in calling for redress of public discrimination against blacks. Kennedy had called for equal access to public accommodations and for voting rights; King declared, "We can never be satisfied as long as our bodies, heavy with the fatigue of travel, cannot gain lodging in the motels of the highways and the hotels of the cities. . . . We cannot be satisfied as long as the Negro in Mississippi cannot vote and the Negro in New York believes he has nothing for which to vote." King declared, quoting the Bible, that black Americans "will not be satisfied until 'justice rolls down like waters, and righteousness like a mighty stream.'"

King closed by tying black demands firmly, but reverentially, not just to the promises of the Declaration of Independence and the Emancipation Proclamation but to the broader American Dream. In a closing that built to a powerful crescendo, King said, "I say to you today, my friends. . . . even though we face the difficulties of today and tomorrow, I still have a dream. It is a dream deeply rooted in the American dream.

I have a dream that one day this nation will rise up and live out the true meaning of its creed: 'We hold these truths to be self-evident, that all men are created equal.'" Only when the dream had been made reality would all of America's citizens, "black men and white men . . . be able to join hands and sing in the words of the old Negro spiritual: 'Free at last! Free at last! Thank God Almighty, we are free at last!'"[28]

Just ten weeks after King spoke in the shadow of the Lincoln Memorial about the unrequited dreams of black Americans a century after emancipation, Kennedy, like Lincoln, was shot and killed by an assassin. Kennedy and Camelot still hold a mythic place in the American mind. But there was a darker side to the Kennedy myth, which included illicit wealth, political corruption, the Mafia, marital infidelity, and elite entitlement. While one side of the Kennedy myth suggested Camelot, peace, and justice for all, another side suggested a rawer, darker, more self-indulgent, no-holds-barred quest for the summit.

Norman Mailer, *An American Dream*

Norman Mailer's fascinating novel *An American Dream* made the not-very-surprising point that *an* American Dream might be far from *the* American Dream. An American Dream, achieved without character, even if made up of all the outward elements of the classic American Dream, as in *Absalom, Absalom!* or *The Great Gatsby*, would weaken and collapse, even "fester" and "stink like rotten meat," as Langston Hughes famously wrote. Interestingly, there were two Jay Gatsby/Thomas Sutpen figures in Mailer's *American Dream*. Both, like Fitzgerald's Gatsby and Faulkner's Sutpen, were self-made men who rose through vice rather than virtue and who were emotionally hollow. Stephen Richards Rojack, the book's central figure, and Rojack's father-in-law, Barney Oswald Kelly, were fascinatingly complex characters—Gatsby on the surface and Sutpen beneath.

Stephen Rojack was a man of great ability but no character. The ability carried him a long way; he received the Distinguished Service Cross for his actions in World War II, he was a congressman at twenty-six and an intimate of Jack Kennedy before leaving Congress for graduate school in psychology. He completed graduate school and rose to full professor in just seven years. He had a television show based on his academic theories concerning memory, dreams, and death, and he was married to a beautiful, wealthy heiress. Rojack remembered, "Those became the years when the gears worked together, the contacts and the insights, the style and the manufacture of oneself. It all turned together very well." Rojack stood, and not just briefly, at the pinnacle; he was a striking figure, a mélange of Jay Gatsby and Jack Kennedy, attractive, accomplished, prominent, and wealthy. But the beast of Thomas Sutpen lurked just beneath the polished surface. The early and rapid success was unsteady and vulnerable because, as Rojack observed, "I remained an actor. My personality was built upon a void."[29] Moreover, his marriage of eight years had been slipping for five. The end of that marriage, in which Stephen strangled his wife, Deborah, and threw her body from a hotel window to the street below in an attempt to suggest suicide, opened exploration of the character of all those involved.[30]

Everyone agreed that Deborah was an elemental force, beautiful, but driven to dominate, harsh and unyielding, but Stephen too thrived on violence and physical domination. Rojack, a biased observer to be sure, said of his marriage, "I wanted to withdraw, count my dead, and look for love in another land, but she was a great bitch, Deborah, a lioness of the species: unconditional surrender was her only raw meat." Deborah herself, in pillow talk with Stephen, wondered, "I know that I am more good and more evil than anyone alive, but which was I born with, and what came into me?" A moment's reflection led her to conclude, "I'm evil if truth be told. But I despise it, truly I do. It's just that evil has power." Stephen explained, "It was horror this edge of madness to lie beside Deborah in a marriage bed and wonder who was responsible for the cloud of foul intent which lifted on the mingling of our breath."[31] Mailer's phrase "cloud of foul intent" is readily reminiscent of F. Scott Fitzgerald's declaration that "foul dust floated in the wake of his [Gatsby's] dreams."

Deborah's awareness that she had chosen evil over good and that there would be costs was explained by her father, Barney Oswald Kelly. As he told it, Deborah was conceived in a literally Faustian bargain that he had initiated, sometimes repented, but could not undo. Kelly described to Rojack his own sad marriage to Leonora, Deborah's mother. Leonora was a pale, lifeless, religious girl who provided Barney access to networks of wealth and opportunity. A sexually unsatisfying marriage culminated in intercourse characterized more by rage and disgust than by love or even lust. Barney promised, "Satan, if it takes your pitchfork up my gut, let me blast a child into this bitch!" Both knew immediately that his wish had been granted: "'What the *hell* have you done?' she screamed at me, which was the only time Leonora ever swore. That was it. Deborah was conceived. . . . 'Oh God,' I used to pray before sleep 'have mercy on this child growing in her womb, for I have damned the creature before it began.'"[32]

So Rojack's killing Deborah, the bitch lioness of her breed, the devil's spawn, was no great surprise, but his actions and reactions after the murder were surprising; he was drunk with energy to the point of ecstasy. Like a more articulate and intelligent Bigger Thomas, Stephen explained, "I was floating. I was as far into myself as I had ever been and universes wheeled in a dream." As he mellowed, he said, "I was weary with a most honorable fatigue, and my flesh seemed new. . . . It seemed inconceivable at this instant that anything in life could fail to please. . . . I was feeling good, as if my life had just begun."[33] Rojack, like some other brilliant psychopaths, might have been smart enough to get away with his crime, but he found help from a surprising quarter, Deborah's father.

Barney Oswald Kelly was a Jay Gatsby toughened up and gone global, or a civilized Thomas Sutpen who had leashed his inner demons. Barney was born into a large, poor, Irish family in Minnesota. Just after World War I, he stole the family's savings, $3,000, and fled to Philadelphia. There, in one year, he grew the $3,000 into $100,000, "speculating" in army surplus. He sent $5,000 to his family to make them whole, and in gratitude for not reporting his theft, and he ran the $95,000 into a million in two years. While speculating in grain futures and stocks in Kansas City, he met and married Leonora. She was from an aristocratic Sicilian family named Mangaravidi. Joining Leonora's father internationalized Barney's social, economic, and political contacts and rendered mysterious two decades of his life. Coming out of World War II he was extraordinarily wealthy, respected, and feared among global elites and was assumed to be connected to both the Sicilian Mafia and the American CIA. Deborah had become aware of Barney's connections and was maybe involved somehow, but she was so unpredictable that Barney and the intelligence services of most major powers were concerned. Hence, Barney had been watching her closely, to the point of inserting a spy into her household, and upon her death he was more interested in putting the matter quickly to rest than in pursuing her murderer, who he soon came to know was Stephen.

In managing Deborah's funeral, Barney demanded that he and Stephen stand together, shoulder to shoulder. Standing together would not wipe away the suspicions and rumors that Stephen had killed Deborah, but as Barney explained, "It doesn't matter whether people think you killed Deborah, it matters only whether people are given the opportunity to recognize it's being swept under the carpet, and you and I together are in control of the situation." Kelly knew that power and the fear it inspired could make appearances all that mattered. In fact, Kelly knew that power could be enhanced by making people look away from reality—Stephen killed Deborah—making them look down, look at their feet, and avert their gazes, and when their eyes came back up, they would be unable to meet Stephen's gaze, let alone that of Barney Oswald Kelly. In one of the most extraordinary moments in the literature of the American Dream, Barney told Stephen, "God and the Devil are very attentive to the people at the summit. . . . There's nothing but magic at the top . . . , but that, my friend, is one reason it's not easy to get to the very top. Because you have to be ready to deal with One or the Other, and that's too much for the average good man on his way. Sooner or later, he decides to be mediocre."

Barney and Stephen succeeded in clouding the circumstances of Deborah's death. Once the funeral was over, Stephen "packed the car, and started on a long trip to Guatemala and Yucatan," and Barney, we assume, returned to his life as a global financier and man of mystery.[34] But as they schemed together, Barney schooled Stephen in the costs and benefits of playing for the highest stakes. Stephen was very smart, a psychopath; he won, but everything was destroyed in the process. He ended up by himself on the road to Guatemala—where's the sophistication there? Barney expected to win in place, still wealthy and influential, his enemies routed and awed. Still, Mailer's message was that *the* American Dream that the average good man pursued was nothing to those who played for the highest stakes.

LBJ and Equality of Results

John Kennedy's assassination made Lyndon Baines Johnson president and released a legislative flood that came to be known as the Great Society. Johnson quickly appointed seventeen task forces to develop program proposals across the full range of domestic policy. Joseph Califano, Johnson confidant and secretary of the Department of Health, Education, and Welfare, recalled that Johnson submitted and Congress approved more than 100 major programs in both the Eighty-Ninth (1965–1966) and Ninetieth (1967–1968) Congresses. These major programs accounted for more than 500 separate social programs, including "such important policy departures as Medicare, Medicaid, the Voting Rights Act of 1965, the Elementary and Secondary Education Act, the War on Poverty, the Air Pollution Control Act, and legislation to establish the Department of Transportation and the Department of Housing and Urban Development."[35] LBJ did what Truman and Kennedy had been unable to do: move beyond FDR's "economic bill of rights" to provide education, health care, housing, legal aid, and much more to the nation's poor.

Just five days after Kennedy's assassination, President Johnson addressed a joint session of the Congress about the slain president's dreams and about his intention to fulfill them. Johnson sought to mythologize the fallen president in order to fuel passage of an agenda larger than Kennedy had ever thought it plausible to pursue. Johnson told a grieving Congress and country, "The ideas and the ideals which he so nobly represented must and will be translated into effective action. . . . We have talked long enough in this country about equal rights. . . . It is time now to write the next chapter, and to write it in the books of law."[36]

President Johnson sought first to move forward stalled elements of the Kennedy agenda, but then to build well beyond that agenda. Johnson dramatically strengthened Kennedy's civil rights bill. The new bill was passed into law as the Civil Rights Act of 1964. Its critical Title VI held that "no person in the United States shall, on the ground of race, color, or national origin, be excluded from participation in, be denied the benefit of, or be subjected to discrimination under any program or activity receiving Federal financial assistance." Title VII of the act prohibited discrimination by employers and labor unions in businesses with 100 or more employees; prohibited segregation or denial of service in any public accommodation, including motels, restaurants, movie theaters, or sports facilities; and permitted the U.S. attorney general to represent citizens attempting to desegregate state facilities, including public schools. Another centerpiece of Johnson's Great Society program was the War on Poverty. In Johnson's view, the New Deal had secured the position of the white working class within American society and economy. What remained was to focus intently on the poor, the bottom 20 percent, many of whom were minorities, and develop programs designed to prepare them for successful inclusion in American life.

But Johnson had more than civil rights in view. On May 22, 1964, he famously urged students at the University of Michigan to join him in making America a "Great Society." Like Theodore Roosevelt, Wilson, and Franklin Roosevelt, Johnson tried to place his vision of a Great Society within the broader sweep of American history. He began his speech by noting that America had been founded to protect and foster the life, liberty, and property of its people. "For a century we labored to settle and subdue a continent. For half a century we called upon unbounded invention and untiring industry to create an order of plenty for all of our people. The challenge of the next half century," he declared, "is whether we have the wisdom to use that wealth to enrich and elevate our national life, and to advance the quality of our American civilization."

Unbridled growth, Johnson told his audience, was not the solution. "The Great Society rests on abundance. . . . But that is just the beginning. The Great Society . . . serves not only the needs of the body and the demands of commerce but the desire for beauty and the hunger for community. . . . It is a place where men are more concerned with the quality of their goals than the quantity of their goods." Johnson closed his address by calling the next generation of Americans to the great task of their forebears. The president declared, "Those who came to this land sought to build more than just a new country. They sought a new world. So I have come here today . . . to say that you can make their vision our reality. . . . Will you join in the battle to build the Great Society, to prove that our material progress is only the foundation on which we will build a richer life of mind and spirit?"[37]

Johnson's aspirations continued to soar through the winter of 1965. His remarkable State of the Union address, delivered to a joint session of Congress and a national radio and television audience on January 4, 1965, laid out a broad domestic program to take Americans beyond the material to the moral. As the booming 1960s buried memories of the Depression, LBJ advised Congress and the American people to "turn increased attention to the character of American life." Wealth was present in abundance, so the pressing issue was how best to use it in the interest of the country and its people. "The Great Society asks not how much, but how good; not only how to create wealth but how to use it; not only how fast we are going, but where we are headed." Fascinatingly, Johnson suggested to the Congress and the country that these questions, at first glimpse perhaps disconcertingly broad, had standing answers in America. Johnson assured the Congress that a dream had always guided the nation's development and that it was the patrimony of all: "It existed when the first settlers saw the coast of the new world, and when the first pioneers moved westward. It has guided us every step of the way. . . . There was a dream—a dream of a place where a free man could build for himself, and raise his children to a better life—a dream of a continent to be conquered, a world to be won, a nation to be made." This dream, Johnson reminded his listeners, "sustains every President. But it is also your inheritance," he reminded each congressman and woman, "and it belongs equally to all the people that we all serve."

Johnson closed by reminding his colleagues and country, just as FDR had more than three decades earlier, that the American Dream did not stand still. The American Dream "must be interpreted anew by each generation for its own needs; as I have tried, in part, to do tonight. . . . This, then, is the state of the Union: Free and restless, growing and full of hope. So it was in the beginning. So it shall always be, while God is willing, and we are strong enough to keep the faith."[38] Two weeks later, Johnson again addressed a joint session of Congress in his inaugural address. Again, he closed with a call to Congress and to the American people to join him in fulfilling the nation's promise, saying, "I will lead and I will do the best I can. But you, you must look within your own hearts to the old promises and to the old dream. They will lead you best of all."[39]

Johnson extended his promise of black inclusion beyond equality of opportunity to equality of results in a June 4, 1965, commencement speech at Howard University. Johnson drew on Lincoln's century-old justification for the fairness of open competition: the justice of the fairly run race. He began by saying, "Freedom is the right to share, share fully and equally, in American society—to vote, to hold a job, to enter a public place, to go to school. It is the right to be treated in every part of our national life as a person equal in dignity and promise to all others. But freedom is not enough," he continued. "You do not wipe away the scars of centuries by saying: Now you are free to go where you want, and to do as you desire. . . . You do not take a person who, for years, has been hobbled by chains and liberate him, bring him up to the starting line of a race and then say, 'you are free to compete with all the others,' and still justly believe that you have been completely fair." The president declared that America had reached "the next and the more profound stage of the battle for civil rights. We seek not just freedom but opportunity. We seek not just legal equity but human ability, not just equality as a right and a theory but equality as a fact and equality as a result."

Johnson closed his Howard University speech by reiterating the basic right of blacks to a full share in the American Dream. "From the first," he said, "this has been a land of towering expectations. . . . It was a rich land, glowing with more abundant promise than man had ever seen. Here, unlike any place yet known, all were to share the harvest. . . . Each could become whatever his qualities of mind and spirit would permit—to strive, to seek, and, if he could, to find his happiness." Again he sought to summon the next generation to the work of extending the American Dream, saying, "So, it is the glorious opportunity of this generation to end the one huge wrong of the American Nation, and, in so doing, to find America for ourselves, with the same immense thrill of discovery which gripped those who first began to realize that here, at last, was a home for freedom."[40]

But Johnson's dreams were about to be dashed as black hope and aspiration became disappointment and rage. In the summer of 1965, in the midst of the Great Society's sweeping legislative triumphs, Watts, a neighborhood in Los Angeles, erupted in rioting. One of the Johnson administration's top black officials, Roger Wilkins, explained, "In earlier decades, the overwhelming majority of Negroes retained a profound faith in America, her institutions, her ideals. . . . Now, however, there is a growing and seriously held view . . . that white people have embedded their own personal flaws so deeply in the institutions that those institutions are beyond redemption."[41] During the four summers from 1965 to 1968, 250 American cities experienced rioting, violence, arson, and theft, much of it televised. White Americans, even many who had supported the early stages of the civil rights movement and of LBJ's Great Society, withdrew support from Johnson, the Democratic Party, and the movement culture that seemed to threaten the nation.

Johnson's focus on civil rights and the escalating demands of blacks and other minorities left many whites concerned that their interests and ideals were being challenged directly. The American Dream had always required hard work, steadily applied, in a climate where success was possible, even common, but still uncertain. While the dream culminated in autonomy, success, and security, it was the uncertainty that prodded Americans to the hard and steady work. But once Kennedy, Johnson, and the Democratic majorities in Congress declared—in law—that blacks did deserve equality of opportunity and, Johnson claimed, equality of results, many whites became deeply alarmed. Prosperity threatened to change the American Dream of equal opportunity into an expectation that society would guarantee success and that if success could not be fully guaranteed, failure would be well cushioned.

Race, Gender, and Alienation

As *Rabbit Redux* opened, ten years had passed in the lives of Harry and Janice Angstrom. The drowning death of their infant daughter, Rebecca June, had devastated Janice initially, as she was the immediate cause, and Harry more completely over time as it killed intimacy and their marriage. At thirty-six, no one called Harry "Rabbit" anymore. He was soft, heavy, stooped, and passive. Janice, on the other hand, at thirty-two, had begun to come to life. Once small, weak, and incapable, drinking for escape, she had become stronger, more demanding of involvement and consideration, more forward looking and eager. In addition to working accounts for her father's car business, now a Toyota new-car dealership, Janice had taken a lover; she was energized, blooming, and she would continue to grow. As Harry spiraled down, Janice prepared for life.

A decade earlier, in the wake of Rebecca June's death, Mr. Springer had fired Harry from his job at the car lot. Harry's father, Earl, had gotten him one as a Linotype operator at the printing shop where he worked. The job paid a middle-class wage but was blue-collar, dirty, and depressing. Harry's physical energy and, even more dramatically, his emotional energy had waned. He concluded, "The trouble with caring about anybody, you begin to feel overprotective. Then you begin to feel crowded." So Harry's response was to squelch the feeling, the emotion, so as not to feel crowded, and he advised others, including Janice, to be radically independent, self-contained. When Harry found that Janice was working late every night at the car lot because she had a lover there, the salesman Charlie Stavros, he reacted violently, though he cooled quickly. Soon, Harry asked her,

"Are you going to tell him?"
"I suppose I must."
"Why? Wouldn't you like to keep him?"
"What are you saying, Harry?"
"Keep him, if he makes you happy. I don't seem to, so go ahead. . . . "
"Harry, he loves life. . . . "
"*O.K.* Relax. I said, keep the son of a bitch."[42]

To Harry, caring was vulnerability, feeling crowded, and he preferred his wife to keep her lover than need anything from him.

While Harry had died inside, assuming he had ever been alive in there, Janice had come to life, and she was unwilling to risk losing her chance to be fulfilled and happy—with Harry or without. "I love him. Damn you, Harry. We make love all the time. . . . It's been going on for *months*. . . . I do things for him, . . . I never do for you." Part of Janice's fury was that she had watched her husband, the Rabbit of his earlier days of triumph, die. She told Harry bluntly, "I'm trying to look honestly into myself, to see who I am, and where I should be going. I want us both, Harry, to come to a decision we can live with."[43] Janice ultimately left Harry and their son, Nelson, to live with Stavros. Stavros was good to her, excited her, fulfilled her, but he did not intend to marry, and she worried about Nelson.

While Janice was gone, Harry descended into a shocking level of depravity, even though Nelson, just twelve, was in the house. Harry and a black coworker, Buck Buchanan, went to a mixed but mostly black bar where they met Skeeter, a black activist, petty criminal, and pimp, and Jill, an eighteen-year-old white runaway from a wealthy Connecticut family. Jill drove a white Porsche, a vestige of her privileged upbringing, but she had renounced all that completely, even radically. Skeeter spouted black nationalism to anyone who would listen, and he pimped Jill out as a display of his personal black power. Skeeter told Harry, "The thing about these Benighted States . . . is that it was never no place [*sic*] . . . where this happens because that happens, and some men have more luck than others . . . ; no, sir, this place was never such a place it was a *dream*, it was a state of mind from those poor fool pilgrims on, right?" Harry, part of the "silent majority" that brought Richard Nixon to power, rejected the black critique as "pure self-pity" and told Skeeter, "The real question is, Where do you go from here? . . . Hell, you're just ten per cent. The fact is most people don't give a damn *what* you do. This is the freest country around, make it if you can, if you can't, die gracefully. But Jesus, stop begging for a free ride."[44] Skeeter was a caricature of late-sixties black nationalism, eventually killed by police in Philadelphia, but Jill was more interesting.

Jill was doing personal penance for the sins of capitalism and inequality. She was pale, thin, and, before she left home, pampered and cultured. Booze and drugs had been widely available in high school, but money and class had made their use, even abuse, safe. Away from home,

Jill had given herself, literally and unreservedly, to the lowest of the low. Jill was emptier than Harry, and this repelled him initially; he said, "You rich kids playing at life make me sick, throwing rocks at the poor dumb cops protecting your daddy's loot. You're just playing. . . . You're all sucked out and you're just eighteen. You've tried everything and you're not scared of nothing and you wonder why it's all so dead. You've had it handed to you, sweet baby, that's why it's so dead."[45]

But Harry being Harry, soon his needs asserted themselves, and he took Jill for himself, though not exclusively. Skeeter soon joined them in Harry's house and was allowed to ply Jill with drugs, which she feared and pleaded with Harry to limit, and to use her sexually. Both Jill and Nelson appealed to Harry, as the adult and the owner of the home, to expel Skeeter and save Jill, if only for his own exclusive use. Harry responded, despite the chaos around him and Jill's evident distress, "People aren't property. I can't control what they want to do together. We can't live Jill's life for her." Nelson, just twelve, but deeply concerned, responded, "We *could*, if you wanted to. If you cared at all."[46] But Harry didn't care, maybe couldn't care. Soon Jill was dead in a fire caused by Skeeter that burned Harry's home.

The fire punctuated Harry's decline and began to force his life back toward its former channels. Janice concluded her affair with Stavros in satisfaction and fulfillment; she walked away with a smile on her face. She concluded, "Miracles are granted but we must not lean on them. . . . Spirits are insatiable but bodies get enough." She had had enough, and so she left empowered. Still, Janice knew that she was stepping back into the cage, knew she was giving up a great deal, but did it willingly. Back with Harry, Janice suggested stopping at a motel for sex. Harry demurred, suggesting they go to his parents' house to meet Nelson after school. She teased him, asking,

"Who matters more to you, me or Nelson?"
"Nelson."
"Nelson or your mother?"
"My mother."
"You are a sick man!"[47]

Yep!

The Diffusion of the New Deal Coalition

Novelists like Updike and scholars like Riesman listened with skepticism to Johnson's declaration that Americans, all Americans, should be entitled to look beyond the material to the moral content and character of their lives. They saw a society increasingly adrift. Could the "vague dread" that Tocqueville and Emerson had noted more than a century before actually be banished from American life? And if so, would an American Dream that stretched beyond the material to the psychological and philosophical, that promised Americans a certain quality of life beyond abundance, still be the American Dream?

Many were uncertain. It had been more than a century since Penn's vision of a balance between the inner and outer plantations and Jefferson's vision of a widespread agrarian sufficiency had given way to the materialism of the Gold Rush and the Gilded Age. Work, creativity, and competition had made the United States a very wealthy society. But how society might grant more opportunity to the formerly excluded, encourage a more wholesome balance between work and private life for the comfortable, and maintain the characteristic American commitments to hard work, determination, and productivity was unclear. Once change sparked instability, conservatives had little difficulty in convincing the comfortable that a firm defense of work and wealth was the only way to keep the needy at bay. Republicans promised to slow the change, but many Democrats, including Minnesota's Senator Eugene McCarthy, thought to push through the turmoil to a New Politics of social justice. Just months before "Clean Gene" McCarthy stepped forward to challenge LBJ for the Democratic presidential nomination in 1968, he described the turmoil wracking the nation as "a special kind of insurrection . . . by the poor and the exploited—those who have been denied their part in the American Dream."[48]

The civil rights movement supplied the template for two related but distinct sets of movements in the late 1960s and the 1970s. The first set of movements, directly related to the civil rights movement and using many of the same arguments, organizational structures, and strategies, was the Chicano movement, the women's movement, the Native American movement, and the gay rights movement. In each case, distinct racial, ethnic, gender, and sexual preference groups organized to demand improved access and opportunity. The second set of movements, using the same organizational techniques and strategies as the civil rights movement but claiming to represent the public interest, was the antiwar movement, the environmental movement, and the consumer movement. These movements produced a flowering of public interest groups, including the Consumer Federation, Common Cause, Environmental Action, Friends of the Earth, and the Natural Resources Council. Openness in government and participatory democracy were key demands of these new social movements. The cacophony of new groups, interests, and demands posed a threat to and were perceived as a threat by traditional white elites and their middle-class supporters.

As the social movements of the 1960s pushed the rights revolution beyond opportunity to outcomes, the rhetoric of freedom, individualism, and responsibility was ceded to the Republicans. Democrats became identified with a panoply of rights claims that seemed to require intrusive regulation, high taxes, and expansive bureaucracy. Moreover, Democrats seemed to reject traditional requirements for hard work, frugality, self-help, and personal responsibility as unfair, demeaning, and probably racist. A resurgent Republican Party gleefully scooped up the abandoned pieces of America's traditional values and claimed them as their own. The prominent black conservative Shelby Steele complained that after the sixties, "and to this day the liberal looks at black difficulties—high crime rates, weak academic performance, illegitimacy rates, and so on—and presumes them to be the result of victimizing forces beyond the control of blacks." Standards to which others are held, based on "principles of merit, excellence, hard work, delayed gratification, individual achievement, personal responsibility, and so on—principles without which blacks can never achieve true equality," were not to be expected of victims.[49] Many conservatives saw in Kurt Vonnegut's *Slaughterhouse-Five* not just a powerful antiwar novel but also a dystopian argument against the very existence of the American Dream.

Kurt Vonnegut, *Slaughterhouse-Five*

Kurt Vonnegut, born in 1922, served as a young man in World War II and, as a prisoner of war (POW), experienced the Allied firebombing of Dresden, Germany. Vonnegut's construct in *Slaughterhouse-Five*, Billy Pilgrim, was unhinged by his experiences in war; he was wounded, captured, held in a psych ward as a POW, and treated in a facility for nonviolent mental patients after the war. But the novel was less about Billy as a person than it was about the forces that buffeted him and about his inability, anyone's, everyone's inability, to respond to them. In fact, well more than halfway through the novel, Vonnegut as narrator explained, "There are almost no characters in this story, and almost no dramatic confrontations [no Stephen throwing Deborah from the hotel window], because most of the people in it are so sick and so much the listless playthings of enormous forces."[50] *Slaughterhouse-Five* described the fracture of an American innocent—Billy Pilgrim—and made clear that it could not have been otherwise. The values and expectations that had long been central to the American Dream had no place in Pilgrim's world.

Billy Pilgrim was born in 1922 in the fictitious town of Ilium, New York, the only child of a barber and his wife. Billy was raised comfortably, though he was tall, thin, and awkward and a loner. He graduated in the top third of his high school class and started night school in optometry before being drafted to serve in World War II. In the war, Billy served as a chaplain's assistant rather than as an active combatant, so he was treated by his fellow soldiers as useless if not worse. In a general Allied retreat, Billy became disoriented and was abandoned and eventually captured by the Germans. As a prisoner, Billy was held in Luxembourg until he was moved to Dresden, where he witnessed the general destruction of the city and its inhabitants, combatants, and civilians by Allied bombing. Despite this introductory chronology, *Slaughterhouse-Five* was told through flashbacks, often by troubled and untrustworthy observers, so we learn about Billy piecemeal throughout the book.

After the war, Billy returned to optometry school and married the daughter of the school's founder and owner. Billy had a family and, with the help of his father-in-law, built a thriving practice. He was a success; he appeared, even to himself, to be living the American Dream. In his midforties, "Billy owned a lovely Georgian home in Ilium. He was rich as Croesus, something he had never expected to be, not in a million years. He had five other optometrists working for him. . . . In addition, he owned a fifth of the new Holiday Inn out on Route 54, and half of three Tastee-Freeze stands."[51] Early in 1968, Billy and a group of optometrists chartered a plane to fly to a conference in Montreal. The plane clipped the top of Sugarbush Mountain in Vermont and went down. Billy was the only survivor, though he experienced a head injury that opened doors to new dimensions, mentally, temporally, and galactically.

Billy's head injury convinced him that he was a time traveler and a released captive of an advanced extraterrestrial civilization called the

Tralfamadorians. While those around him thought him unhinged by the plane crash and perhaps by his wartime experiences, Billy's time travel and extraterrestrial adventures were very real and deeply meaningful to him. Vonnegut explained in the first sentence of the novel, "Billy Pilgrim had come unstuck in time." Soon Billy found himself bouncing from the war to the mental ward after the war to the hours before the plane crash. Billy could see his life in total, backward and forward, but "among the things Billy Pilgrim could not change were the past, the present, and the future"; he could change nothing. He knew everything but could do nothing. For example, Vonnegut wrote that one moment Billy was in Dresden, and the next he was boarding the ill-fated plane with his fellow optometrists. "Billy Pilgrim got onto a chartered airplane. . . . He knew it was going to crash, but he didn't want to make a fool of himself by saying so."[52] Hence, the most famous recurring phrase—observation really—in *Slaughterhouse-Five* was "So it goes."

Billy learned two great lessons about goals, will, motivations, and dreams from two unusual teachers. The lessons conflicted profoundly, but both drew the American Dream of preparation, hard work, striving, and determination into deep sociological and epistemological question. The sociological point was made by Howard W. Campbell Jr. In *Slaughterhouse-Five*, Campbell was an American cowboy–become–Nazi propagandist. Campbell wrote to shake the conviction of American soldiers in their nation, saying, "America is the wealthiest nation on Earth, but its people are mainly poor. . . . Americans . . . will not acknowledge how in fact hard money is to come by, and, therefore, those who have no money . . . blame themselves. This inward blame has been a treasure for the rich and powerful, who have had to do less for their poor . . . than any other ruling class."[53]

Not surprisingly, the freshest insights in *Slaughterhouse-Five* came from Billy's interactions with the Tralfamadorians. Naturally, when Billy found himself on Tralfamadore, his first question was, from the Earthling perspective, the natural one: "How—how did I get here?" This elicited an eye roll from the Tralfamadorians, one of whom only semipatiently responded, "It would take another Earthling to explain it to you. Earthlings are the great explainers, explaining why this event is structured as it is, telling how other events may be achieved or avoided. I am a Tralfamadorian. . . . All time is all time. It does not change. It does not lend itself to warnings or explanations." From the Tralfamadorian perspective, one can run time forward and backward, see all time as all time, subject to knowing but not changing. Billy was, of course, perplexed, saying, "You sound to me as though you don't believe in free will," to which the Tralfamadorian response was dismissive: "Only on Earth is there any talk of free will."[54] The full extent to which complete knowledge precluded choice, volition, and alternative outcomes was driven home to Billy when his Tralfamadorian host said, "We know how the universe ends . . . and Earth has nothing to do with it, except that *it* gets wiped out too." Billy asks how and is told, "We blow it up, experimenting with new fuels for our flying saucers. A Tralfamadorian test pilot presses a starter button, and the whole universe disappears." So it goes. Billy wanted to know whether they could keep the pilot from pressing the button, but the weary Tralfamadorian response was "He has *always* pressed it, and he always *will.* . . . The moment is *structured* that way."[55] So if Earth is part of a universe in which events are structured one way and not another, what of choice, free will, alternative paths—what of the American Dream? The very question would elicit another Tralfamadorian eye roll.

Conclusion

American politicians celebrated peace, prosperity, and, they claimed, the revival of the American Dream in the wake of World War II. National wealth and productivity were unprecedented, but scholars and novelists sensed something seriously amiss. The outer plantation of the world was rich and vibrant, but the inner plantation of the heart and soul seemed increasingly diffuse, doubtful, and lacking a sense of purposeful direction. Unmoored from traditional expectations and standards, Americans seemed to know how but not why. They were rich, but to what end?

The novelists John Updike and Toni Morrison described an increasingly disoriented white American mainstream and the continuation of old traumas in black America. Updike's Harry and Janice Angstrom graduated from high school and entered married life without plan or purpose. They were representative of their time; the entertaining scene in which Jimmie, the leader of the Mouseketeers, replaced Mather, Penn, and Franklin in teaching the lessons of work, success, and purpose to the next generation of Americans highlighted the enervating impact of prosperity. In *Rabbit, Run*, Harry and Janice seemed without purpose or direction, but they were young, yet in *Rabbit Redux*, all the major characters, Harry, Janice, Skeeter, and Jill, were intensely self-absorbed. Their selfishness was not economic or competitive; worse, it was emotional—an inner void. Morrison described blacks, no matter what road they took, as excluded from the mainstream society and its dreams. Nel chose church and family, but like so many black families, hers succumbed to the disappointment and despair of exclusion from social and economic opportunity, from wages that would support a man and his family in dignity. Rage threatened to explode.

The explosion came, but not immediately. Before the explosion came Camelot. Kennedy was young, just forty-three, handsome, seemingly vibrant, with a beautiful wife and two small children when he was elected president. After the staid Eisenhower years, Kennedy promised to get the country moving again, and the nation thrilled to him and his promises. Yet Kennedy proceeded cautiously, particularly on civil rights, until his hand was forced by southern resistance to racial integration. Then he spoke boldly about the nation's original promise of freedom and equality for all citizens, but he was assassinated before the daunting work of passing legislation over southern resistance in Congress could be achieved. Kennedy's death made him a mythic figure in American public life, but the myth had a darker side explored by Norman Mailer in *An American Dream*. Mailer described a Kennedyesque figure, Stephen Richards Rojack, as promising, able, and accomplished but morally empty. Rojack's unprincipled abilities produced great accomplishments and great tragedies. Remarkably, Rojack's father-in-law, Barney Oswald Kelly, declared the American Dream irrelevant to most men and women. To get to the pinnacle, Kelly said, you had to strike a deal with God or the devil, and most people did not have it in them, so they settled for mediocrity. Even more troublesome, most theologians would say, though Mailer did not, is that God does not make such deals, only the devil does.

President Johnson promised a Great Society in which all Americans, irrespective of race, would have equal opportunity. As Johnson described the parameters and contours of his Great Society, equality of opportunity seemed to become equality of results, and economic security seemed to become a promise of personal fulfillment, where the "needs of the spirit" and the "quality of their goals" held equal weight with work and productivity. Conservatives, and soon most white Americans, grew increasingly concerned that promises of equality, if seen as promises of wealth without work, success without insecurity and doubt, weakened and betrayed the traditional American Dream.

Kurt Vonnegut put an exclamation point on these growing doubts. Billy Pilgrim was a high school nerd, radically unlike Rabbit Angstrom, the high school basketball star, but Billy knew he wanted to be a dentist. Despite the horrors of World War II, Billy lived the American Dream, becoming a wealthy dentist and investor with a nice house and family. But Billy came "unstuck in time" and was convinced that he was a released captive of advanced extraterrestrials, the Tralfamadorians. The Tralfamadorians taught Billy that time could be run backward and forward, known from beginning to end, but not changed in any way. The Earthling sense of free will—the feeling that men decide, make choices, succeed or fail, win or lose, based on their decisions and choices—was meaningless Earthling chatter to the Tralfamadorians. They knew all time, backward and forward, and they knew it did not change, so their summary observation was "So it goes." And so it seemed to go for Rabbit Angstrom, Nel and Sula, Stephen Rojack, and Billy Pilgrim; struggle as they might, time did not bring the future they hoped for. The one exception, perhaps, was Barney Oswald Kelly, but then, he had made a bargain with the devil, and there would be a price to pay.

8 | The Dream in Doubt: Opportunity to Uncertainty from Reagan to Obama

Tonight . . . there are communities in this country where no matter how hard you work, it is virtually impossible to get ahead: factory towns decimated from years of plants packing up. Inescapable pockets of poverty, urban and rural. . . . America is not a place where the chance of birth or circumstance should decide our destiny.
—Barack Obama, State of the Union address, February 12, 2013

For most of American history the American Dream promised opportunity, a fair shot to compete for the good things that society had to offer. Success required hard work, perseverance, frugality, and dedication in a competitive environment where failure, whether due to insufficient attention and effort or to simple bad luck, was an ever-present possibility. Running scared was just a part of working hard and exercising reasonable foresight in the open, competitive, volatile environment of democratic capitalism. During hard times, Americans might do everything right and still lose, but hard times rarely lasted, and when good times returned they expected and were expected to try again.

Ronald Wilson Reagan, William Jefferson Clinton, and Barack Hussein Obama all defined themselves as defenders of the American Dream. They spoke of the sanctity of the American Dream early, often, and in the most prominent public settings, including the six inaugural addresses that they delivered among them. While Reagan, Clinton, and Obama each oversaw an extended period of economic growth, none succeeded in restoring confidence and opportunity broadly throughout the society and economy—none reestablished the American Dream. Moreover, while the dream rhetoric still moved most Americans, an underlying dread pervaded society as rhetoric and reality seemed steadily to diverge. Especially in the wake of the Great Recession, Obama warned more insistently than any president since Franklin Roosevelt that the American Dream was endangered for many.

The Dream in Doubt

Lyndon Johnson's vision for the Great Society reflected the tremendous prosperity of post–World War II America. The power and plenty of postwar America suggested the plausibility of an American Dream that offered, perhaps guaranteed, economic security, social equality, and personal development. LBJ declared that a nation as wealthy as ours was bound to expand equality of opportunity toward equality of results. Moreover, the Great Society promised not just a nation in which people were well fed and safe, but one in which they were allowed and encouraged to nurture and develop their intellectual and artistic abilities and talents as well.

Others worried, as they had since the nation's earliest days, that prosperity might compromise and weaken traditional American values. Would people really work hard, save, and plan for the future in the presence of plenty? Would prosperity and ease unwind the tight springs of faith, responsibility, and virtue? Among the keenest analysts of post-sixties America was the sociologist Daniel Bell, author of *The Coming of Post-Industrial Society* (1973) and *The Cultural Contradictions of Capitalism* (1976). Bell explained that the nation's economy was evolving from an industrial configuration in which manual labor produced goods to a postindustrial configuration in which mental labor produced services like information and entertainment. Bell warned that the transformation of work from physical labor to creativity and innovation might leave average Americans with too few good jobs and the best educated and most creative with a sense of privilege and entitlement.

New and threatening dynamics emerged within the American economy just as Bell issued his warnings. Economic growth slowed and income inequality rose as the economy distinguished between winners and losers, the successful and the unsuccessful, ever more starkly. Median family income grew by 63 percent from 1950 to 1970, then slowed to just 16 percent growth from 1970 to 1990, and 4.5 percent growth between 1990 and 2013. In fact, between 2000 and 2013, median family income in the United States fell by 7.1 percent.[1] A prominent book by the French economist Thomas Piketty, entitled *Capital in the Twenty-First Century* (2014), reported that between the late 1970s and the early 2010s, a period of almost four decades, the "richest ten percent appropriated three-quarters of the growth" in U.S. national income. As a result, the richest 10 percent's share of national income "increased from

30–35 percent . . . in the 1970s [to] 40–45 percent in the 2000s." For the bottom 90 percent of wealth holders, "income growth was less than 0.5 percent per year."[2] Similarly, Berkeley economist Emmanuel Saez reported that 95 percent of real income growth between 2009 and 2012 went to the top 1 percent of earners, with the bottom 99 percent sharing the remaining 5 percent.[3] Many have asked what the American Dream means when a select few seem to harvest most of prosperity's benefits.[4]

As politicians continued to promise a revival of the American Dream and as economists charted its steady decline, novelists understood instinctively that the driving dynamics and assumptions of American society and economy were changing. Completion of John Updike's Rabbit series with two Pulitzer Prize–winning novels, *Rabbit Is Rich* (1981) and *Rabbit at Rest* (1990), captured the malaise coming to surround the dream for many. Richard Russo's *Empire Falls* (2001), another Pulitzer Prize–winner, might well have been a fifth volume in the Rabbit series, as it too explored the limited and shrinking options available in small-town America in the final decades of the twentieth century. Philip Roth's *American Trilogy* (1997–2000), including the Pulitzer Prize–winning *American Pastoral* (1997) and *The Human Stain* (2000), described the tumult in America as the hope and prosperity of the 1950s and 1960s collapsed into the doubt and ennui of subsequent decades. Jonathan Franzen's *Freedom* (2010) extended the story of the dream's demise both into urban America and into the twenty-first century.

Ronald Reagan and Morning in America

Ronald Reagan promised to restore both the old opportunity and its accompanying discipline by lowering taxes and reducing government regulation, thus freeing the economy to reward education, experience, talent, hard work, dedication, imagination, and creativity. Once again, Americans were reminded that good character led to success, bad character led to failure, and that was as it should be. No one claimed new ideas for Reagan, but some did claim that he put force and energy back into America's oldest ideas—its founding principles. Hugh Heclo argued, "The important point is not that Reagan ever said anything fundamentally new, but that in the new context created by the Sixties Reagan continued to uphold something old."[5] Reagan refocused the American Dream on individual responsibility, work, and striving in a way that it had not been since the 1920s. Campaigning for Barry Goldwater for president in 1964, Reagan called for less government and lower taxes as "a start toward restoring for our children the American Dream that wealth is denied to no one, that each individual has the right to fly as high as his strength and ability will take him."[6] Government should ensure that the rules are clear and the game is fair, but who wins the game and what they do with their winnings are none of the government's business. Those who lose should be encouraged to try again and to depend on their church, their neighbors, and their family in the meanwhile.

Reagan's great strength was that he believed in the American Dream with every fiber of his being. Others thought the world complicated: America was now an advanced industrial society, a superpower, and surely that required adjusting old ideas, if only to make them relevant to the new age. Reagan thought the old ideas were relevant just as they were and that, in fact, earlier attempts to adjust them were mistakes best undone. Reagan believed that the pattern of American history had been well set in the beginning; hence, staying on course was the goal, changing course was decay, disorder, and declension.

Reagan ran for president in 1980 on the promise that limiting the role of government, removing regulations, and depending on free markets to reward work and productivity would expand the economy and benefit every American. Reagan challenged the premises of post–New Deal American politics. Whereas for half a century the role of government in managing and directing the economy and society had grown, Reagan declared his determination to reduce the role of government and return freedom, opportunity, and choice to the individual citizen. The key to individual freedom, Reagan thought, was to cut taxes and regulations and thereby limit the size and intrusiveness of government. He was convinced that if his program was adopted, private initiative would flourish, businesses would grow, profits would rise, new jobs would be created, and the poor could compete for jobs rather than wait by the mailbox for government checks and benefits.

Throughout his mature political life, Reagan taught that free men should look to themselves and not to government for their liberties, hopes, goals, and aspirations. Reagan's first inaugural address (1981) warned against a bigger and more active national government. Reaching back beyond LBJ and even FDR, Reagan declared, "In this present crisis, government is not the solution to our problem; government is the problem. From time to time we've been tempted to believe"—by previous, Democratic presidents, Reagan might have said—"that society has become too complex to be managed by self-rule, that government by an elite group is superior to government for, by, and of the people. Well," Reagan asked, "if no one among us is capable of governing himself, then who among us has the capacity to govern someone else?" He reminded listeners that "we are too great a nation to limit ourselves to small dreams" or to be satisfied with the safety and comfort of government handouts. "We have every right to dream heroic dreams."[7]

During the 1984 reelection campaign, the Republican National Convention film that reviewed Reagan's first term reminded delegates that during Jimmy Carter's presidency, "people were losing faith in the American Dream," but that the dream was now restored. Campaign ads declared that it was "morning in America" once again: "Today, the dream lives again. Today, jobs are coming back. The economy is coming back. And America is coming back, standing tall in the world again." The ads closed with the simple declaration, "President Reagan, rebuilding the American dream."[8] Reagan won the 1984 election in a landslide.

Reagan saw much of government from the New Deal to the Great Society as a mistaken and unnecessary burden on the openness, dynamism, and richness of American society and economy. When Reagan spoke of an "economic bill of rights" on Independence Day 1987, echoing FDR's phrase of almost half a century earlier, Reagan did not mean FDR's government supports and guarantees. Reagan's four freedoms were "the freedom to work. The freedom to enjoy the fruits of one's labors. The freedom to own and control one's property. The freedom to participate in a free market."[9] Reagan's "economic bill of rights" was a set of guarantees that persons would be let alone to make their way in the free market. Calvin Coolidge or Herbert Hoover could easily have made these commitments, and both Reagan and his opponents knew it.

Much of Reagan's Farewell Address was dedicated to clarifying what he meant when he talked about the American Dream, or America as "a city on a hill." Reagan reminded his listeners that he had used the phrase "shining city upon a hill" many times over the decades but had never put the vision into words, "but in my mind it was a tall, proud city built on rocks stronger than oceans, wind-swept, God-blessed, and teeming with people of all kinds living in harmony and peace; a city with free ports that hummed with commerce and creativity. And if there had to be city walls, the walls had doors and the doors were open to anyone with the will and the heart to get here. That's how I saw it, and see it still." Reagan closed, as he so often did, with striking imagery, this time of the "shining city" still playing its historic role of beacon and promise to men everywhere who would be free. "After 200 years, two centuries, she still stands strong and true on the granite ridge. . . . And she's still a beacon, still a magnet for all who must have freedom, for all the pilgrims from all the lost places who are hurtling through the darkness, toward home."[10]

Reagan harkened back to the original vision of the American Dream, the city on the hill, as envisioned and described by conservatives from John Winthrop to Calvin Coolidge and Herbert Hoover. Heclo noted, "More than any other politician in the last half of the 20th century, Reagan continued to speak the vision boldly and with deep personal conviction."[11] Reagan never doubted, never reconsidered, never even imagined that the American Dream might need to be updated for the new era. He believed that the American Dream had always been in place, that all one had to do was aspire to it, strive for it, reach out and grasp it. It was the natural right of all Americans.

John Updike and Richard Russo on Reagan's America

The last two novels, the third and the fourth, in Updike's Rabbit series bookended Reagan's presidency. *Rabbit Is Rich* and *Rabbit at Rest* each won the Pulitzer Prize for fiction. As Harry Angstrom expressed it in *Rabbit at Rest*, "Reagan . . . had that dream distance; the powerful thing about him as President was that you never knew how much he knew, nothing or everything, he was like God that way, you had to do a lot of it yourself."[12] In *Rabbit Is Rich*, published as Reagan was settling into the presidency convinced that an overgrown government was strangling opportunity and innovation, Updike shared some of Reagan's concerns but not his confidence that American vibrancy could easily be restored. *Rabbit Is Rich* found Harry Angstrom middle-aged, forty-eight, as secure and happy as his personality and character would permit but convinced that the world was going to hell around him.[13]

Harry and his generation believed that America had become a harsher, more difficult place, especially for young people. In the opening paragraph of *Rabbit Is Rich*, Harry looked at the world around him and thought, "The people out there are getting frantic, they know the great American ride is ending." High gas prices still drove them into the Toyota showroom, but Harry was sobered by the knowledge that "they're running scared out there." Harry observed to Charlie, Janice's former lover and now a coworker at the Toyota lot, "Seems funny to say it, but I'm glad I lived when I did. These kids coming up, they'll be living on table scraps. We had the meal." Harry observed to a young couple looking at a base Corolla that he liked to help those just getting started because "I think it's a helluva world we're coming to, where a young couple like yourselves can't afford to buy a car or own a home. If you can't get your foot on even the bottom rung of a society geared like this, people are going to lose faith in the system." Janice, talking to Harry about their son Nelson and his generation, observed, "They seem to have so many choices and yet they don't. They've been taught by television all their lives to want this and that and yet when they get to be twenty they find money isn't so easy to come by after all. They don't have the opportunities even we had."[14]

Harry believed in a thin version of the American dream, and he saw himself pursuing it, reaching for it, but never fully and securely achieving it. Nelson believed in the desiccated view of the dream against which both Daniel Bell and Ronald Reagan had warned. In *Rabbit at Rest*, soon after Nelson too had gone to work at the Toyota dealership, he and Harry talked about money. Nelson wanted more than Harry thought reasonable for a junior salesman, so Nelson said, "People don't make money an hour at a time anymore; you just get yourself in the right position and it *comes*. I know guys, lawyers, guys in real estate, no older than me and not as smart who pull in two, three hundred K on a single transaction. . . . It's *easy* to be rich, that's what this country is all about." Harry spurned Nelson's pressure for more money, but when he and Janice spent time at their Florida condo, Harry and his golfing buddies shared views not too different from Nelson's. In one golf cart chat, Bernie opined to Harry, "There are two routes to happiness. . . . Work for it, day after day, like you and I did, or take a chemical shortcut. With the world the way it is, these kids take the shortcut. The long way looks too long." Harry responded, "Yeah, well it *is* too long. And then when you've gone the distance, where's the happiness?" Bernie answered, "Behind you." Later in the novel, Harry pinpointed another source of dissatisfaction. The climb never brought the quiet satisfaction of having achieved the summit—achieved the dream—because "no matter how hard you climb, there are always the rich above you, who got there without effort. Lucky stiffs, holding you down, making you discontent so you buy more of the crap advertised on television."[15]

No theme was more evident in the Rabbit series than Harry's emptiness. Harry was not completely unaware; he sensed "some limitation within him really, a failure or refusal to love any substance but his own." Nelson felt the distance between Harry and himself keenly, saying, "I keep trying to love you, but you don't really want it. You're afraid of it, it would tie you down. You've been scared all your life of being tied down." Harry's heart doctor told him, "The best thing for a body is a healthy interest in life. Get interested in something outside yourself, and your heart will stop talking to you."[16] He couldn't.

His marriage to Janice dead, Nelson troubled by drugs, Harry tried to recover the good feeling that had once filled him up. Alone in Florida and taking Nitrostat (nitroglycerin tablets) for his heart, Harry begged a pickup basketball game from an eighteen-year-old black player called Tiger. Though Tiger was skeptical, he agreed to a game of twenty-one. Harry popped a Nitrostat; Tiger started slow, but Harry worked at it, so Tiger picked it up. When Harry began to labor, Tiger asked if he was OK, and he said that he was even though he felt a heaviness and then a spread of pain across his chest. He pushed on, in the zone, exultant when a shot went in from half-court. When he rebounded Tiger's next miss and tried to go back up, his heart gave out and he crumpled to the court. Tiger picked up his ball and walked calmly away. Janice and Nelson reached the hospital before Harry died. He shared a tender moment with Janice, though they did not speak, and to his son, all he had to say was "Well, Nelson, . . . all I can tell you is, it isn't so bad."[17] Alone and empty, he had chosen his exit and had been more than ready to go.

As noted above, Richard Russo's *Empire Falls*, might easily have been the fifth book in Updike's Rabbit series. Though he set his book in central Maine, as opposed to Updike's central Pennsylvania, Russo also dealt with the limited and shrinking choices faced by the denizens of small-town America in the late twentieth century. *Empire Falls* revolved around the relationship between Francine Whiting, the matriarch of the town's leading family, and the once promising but now trapped and enervated Miles Roby. Whiting, the novel's antagonist, while not evil, was entitled, demanding, and controlling—and she kept score. Roby, the novel's protagonist, while a good and gentle man, was passive and accepting of circumstances and events that, with a little foresight and effort, he might have influenced and perhaps controlled.

Throughout its early history, Empire Falls had been a Whiting company town. The family owned a textile plant, a shirt factory, a paper mill, and most of the commercial real estate in town. Even though, beginning in the late 1960s, the mills had all been sold to multinational corporations, looted, and closed, the Whiting family, in the formidable person of Francine, still owned much of the town, including the Empire Grill that Miles had operated for the preceding twenty years. The Whiting family role in Empire Falls was akin to that of Judge Marmaduke Temple in Cooper's *Pioneers*: the founding family, guiding development, taking the civic lead, foreclosing the best land and opportunities, and, sometimes intentionally and sometimes not, shaping the fate and reaping the resentment of all in the town.

The emotional dynamics of the story were complex; hurt and revenge, softened but not assuaged by proximity and time, became patronage, though not friendship. In brief, Francine Robideaux, from a poor and scorned local family, the first of that family to go to college, graduated from Colby and returned to marry Charles Beaumont "CB" Whiting. CB, a dreamy, poetical young man, sensual, profligate, and weak, had been living in Mexico. He was called home to assume his responsibilities in the family business operations and met and married Francine, but she was too much for him, a force of nature, not impetuous like Deborah in Mailer's *American Dream* but prepared, determined, and unremitting. CB eventually fell in love with Grace Roby, Miles's mother, but Francine intervened, and soon CB was on his way back to Mexico and Grace, guided by her faith and her priest, went to Francine to seek forgiveness. Over time, Francine seemed to grant the forgiveness; she took Grace into her employ to serve her and to care for her crippled daughter, and Grace became completely dedicated to them. Grace also had high hopes for Miles, first that he would get out of Empire Falls and then that he would graduate from college, which she could not bring to fruition.

An intergenerational sense of defeat pervaded Empire Falls. The grandparents' generation had become universally fatalistic. Preparation, planning, striving were all futile. Miles's ex-wife Janine was told by her mother, Bea, that her fairly shallow attempts to improve herself through exercise and weight loss were just "shoveling shit against the tide. A person is what she is." Mrs. Walsh, the housekeeper for the Catholic church and the priests, put the same point a bit more traditionally, noting, "To aspire to that which is beyond one's designated station in life was a sin, . . . and in the end, all the strivers and enviers would come to know the Truth, that . . . there was but one duty and that was to do God's will." A contemporary and boyhood neighbor of Miles's, Jimmy Minty, was given an earthier version of the same lesson by his father, a drunk, wife beater, poacher, and small-time thief. Mr. Minty opined, "Ambition . . . it'll kill you every time." Better, he thought, to keep one's head down, fly under the radar, steal small so the establishment wouldn't be a bother, and ignore the establishment's lies. Warming to his lesson, he told Jimmy, "In school they tell you it's a free country, I bet. . . . Yeah, well, don't you believe it. They got the whole thing figured out, believe me, and they've thought of everything. . . . All of it. You think *you* got a say? Think again."[18]

Miles's generation, including Miles, had largely concluded that their elders were right, even if they were not yet ready to tell their children. After another of his fraught conversations with Jimmy Minty, Miles echoed Melville: "After all, what was the whole wide world but a place for people to yearn for their heart's impossible desires, for those desires to become entrenched in defiance of logic, plausibility, and even the passage of time." Miles's ex-wife Janine, attending a high school football game, was saddened to think how soon life would press down on the slim, lithe young cheerleaders and the quick, powerful athletes on the field. She envisioned graduation, "the quick marriage . . . followed by relentless house and car payments and doctor's bills and all the rest. . . . Their jobs, their marriages, their kids, their lives—all of it a grind."[19] The depression that settled over Rabbit Angstrom was resonant in the concerns of the parents of Empire Falls.

The central examples of parents' concerns for their children's futures and fates were Grace Roby's concern for Miles and Miles's concern for his daughter, Tick. Grace planned for Miles not just to go to college but to go away, to go out of state so, as she said, he could not "come running back to Empire Falls." As Grace lay dying, when Miles had, at Mrs. Whiting's call, returned home in the midst of his senior year of college to help care for his mother, she shrieked over and over, "Go away, Miles. You're killing me. Can't you understand that? Your being here is killing me. Killing me." For two decades after their mother's death, Miles's brother David worked to break him out of his long reverie, reminding him, "Mom never wanted you to come back. Your getting out of here was her life's work." Miles agreed, saying, "I'm sure you're right that she'd be disappointed"—though, the author noted, "'Brokenhearted' was more like it." Miles continued, "No doubt I've shamed her. I feel like I have, believe me." With Miles, acknowledging that he had settled for life at the Empire Grill against his mother's wishes and against his own hopes and goals was not a prelude to action. David continued the pressure, saying, "You claim you're sticking it out for Tick, but do you know what that kid's going to be if you aren't careful? She'll be the next manager of the Empire Grill."[20]

Miles's passivity was best understood in relation to Francine Whiting's resolve. She was alert, purposeful, and determined from an early age. In conversation with Miles, she noted that her late husband, CB Whiting, hadn't been "the sort of man you'd notice, unless you knew he had money." Miles pointed out that she had noticed him, to which she responded, "True . . . and I just explained why." A little later in the same conversation, she elaborated on her accomplishment, saying, "Still, I've always believed that people largely make their own luck. . . . You think I married my luck. . . . There's a world of skill and timing involved in marrying the right person. Especially when the girl in question comes from the Robideaux Blight."[21] Francine's strengths were such that she could savor Miles's noting what might be considered weaknesses.

Francine, infinitely stronger and more capable than CB, had ushered him to his suicide and then enjoyed the management of the family holdings for decades. She did so through a calculating strategy that her opponents—many of whom, like Miles, barely suspected that they were opponents—could not match. As Miles came to understand, her approach to problems large and small was systematic and rigorous; she thought so far ahead of others that she seemed to them omniscient. "She possessed a marvelous ability to divide the chore into smaller, more manageable, tasks. . . . Each day Mrs. Whiting had a 'To Do' list, and the brilliance of that list lay in the fact that she was careful never to include anything undoable. . . . In this fashion, the woman never experienced anything but success. . . . She might be delayed, but never deterred." Late in the novel, Francine and Miles again played at assessing her strengths and weaknesses. To his suggestion that she knew little of passion, she mused, "It's true I'm seldom swept away like those with more romantic temperaments. . . . But we are what we are, and what can't be cured must be endured. . . . Payback is *how* we endure, dear boy."[22] Francine Whiting had made her pact with the devil and commanded all she surveyed; Miles had chosen mediocrity, but there would be a final totaling of accounts.

Bill Clinton and the New Covenant

Like Reagan, Arkansas governor Bill Clinton had an ear wonderfully at-
tuned to the tones and rhythms of American politics. Born in the small,
rural town of Hope in one of the nation's poorest states, Clinton worked
his way through Georgetown, Oxford, and Yale to become both attorney general and governor of Arkansas. Clinton pursued and caught his
American Dream, but across Arkansas and beyond he saw the sadness
and doubt that Updike and Russo had painted on the faces of Harry
Angstrom, Miles Roby, and many others in the rural areas and small
towns of postindustrial America.

When Bill Clinton stepped out onto the front portico of the Old
State House in Little Rock, Arkansas, to announce his candidacy for
the presidency, he declared his campaign to be "a commitment to . . .
preserving the American dream, restoring the hopes of the forgotten
middle class, reclaiming the future of our children." He declared that
he, like most Americans, "was raised to believe in the American dream,
in family values, in individual responsibility, and in the obligation of
government to help people who were doing the best they could."[23] Clinton ran for president in 1992 on a promise to even the playing field and
insure that a greater share of the society's benefits went to those who
showed up, worked hard, and played by the rules.

For Reagan, government was a burden that slowed Americans' pursuit of their dreams; for Clinton, government created, or failed to create, the climate within which the economy grew, wealth was created,
and people prospered. Clinton believed that Republicans under Reagan and George H. W. Bush had fostered an every-man-for-himself environment in which a few had done spectacularly well while most had
struggled just to stay even. Clinton declared, "We need a new covenant
to rebuild America. . . . Government's responsibility is to create more
opportunity. The people's responsibility is to make the most of it." In
accepting his party's nomination for president in 1992, Bill Clinton returned, as he would again and again during the general election contest
and through eight years as president, to the theme of the positive role
of government in people's lives. Clinton promised "a New Covenant—a
solemn agreement between the people and their government—based
. . . on old values. We offer opportunity. We demand responsibility. We
will build an American community again."[24]

Bill Clinton promised a "third-way" or "New Democrat" agenda that charged government to ensure that the benefits of economic growth were spread more evenly across all Americans. Clinton favored moderate Democratic positions, especially on social, fiscal, and military and defense policy where the Reagan Republican Party seemed to have gained decisive advantage. On controversial social issues Clinton put distance between himself and the liberal wing of his party by supporting tough criminal penalties, including the death penalty, and moderate positions on school prayer, gun control, and welfare reform.

The pivotal speech in Bill Clinton's 1992 campaign was delivered at his alma mater, Georgetown University. He sought to restore in the public mind the sense that government could be an effective and efficient servant and partner. Clinton declared, "Today we need to forge a New Covenant that will repair the damaged bond between the people and their government and restore our basic values—the notion that our country has a responsibility to help people get ahead. . . . People have lost faith in the ability of government to change their lives for the better."[25] But Clinton well understood that the American people were ambivalent about government; they wanted it to be both limited and good at what it did. He used his victory speech on election night to promise "a government that offers a hand up, not a handout."[26]

Throughout his first term as president, Clinton defined his purpose as the restoration of the American Dream. But unlike Reagan, for whom restoration meant returning to fixed principles, Clinton believed that restoration required adapting to new realities. Reagan spoke of continuity, Clinton of change. Like earlier presidents facing turbulent times, Clinton used his first inaugural address to place his administration and its program within the broader sweep of American history. Clinton reached back to the first Democratic president, Thomas Jefferson, to support his sense that change was necessary to growth and progress. Clinton declared, "Thomas Jefferson believed that to preserve the very foundations of our nation, we would need dramatic change from time to time. Well, my fellow citizens, this is our time. Let us embrace it."[27]

Clinton's goal was to link opportunity to responsibility so that Americans would be comfortable thinking about inclusion, community, and interdependence. In his 1994 State of the Union address, he asked Americans to return "again to the principle that if we simply give ordinary people equal opportunity, quality education, and a fair shot at the American dream, they will do extraordinary things."[28]

Clinton organized his 1996 reelection campaign as a referendum on the party's respective visions of the American Dream—at least as he wished to characterize them. In a book-length statement of his values and his intentions for a second term, *Between Hope and History*, he reminded voters that he had always been and remained committed to a reasonable and balanced view of America's traditional values. He said, "The promise embedded in our founding documents is clear: America promises liberty, but demands civic responsibility. America promises the opportunity to pursue happiness, but does not guarantee it . . . an America where the American Dream is alive and attainable for every single American willing to work for it."[29] Republicans offered a different view, Clinton warned. "Here, at the edge of a new century, we must decide between two visions of America. One vision," the Republican vision, "foresees an 'every man for himself,' 'you're on your own' America. . . . Our administration and the new Democratic party take a different view. We say the era of big government is over, but we must not go back to an era of 'every man for himself.'" The best summary of the difference that Clinton saw between his own vision and the one that had governed the Republican Party since Reagan, and in a sense for much longer, was his declaration that "America is not just about independence, but also about *interdependence*."[30]

However, Clinton was always careful to describe a role for government that helped people but did not dictate to them. Clinton learned from Reagan that the American people loathed big government and overweening bureaucracy. But Clinton knew far better than the Republicans of the 1990s that people also expected a great deal from government. Clinton framed his 1996 campaign by declaring, "America needs a government that is both smaller and more responsive. . . . One that shifts authority from the federal level to the states and localities as much as possible. One that relies upon entrepreneurs in the private sector when the private sector can do the job best. One that has fewer regulations and more incentives. One, in short, that has more common sense and seeks more common ground."[31] With a foot on every base, it was nearly impossible for Clinton to be called out. In fact, as Robert "Bob" Dole's challenge for the presidency stalled, Clinton reiterated his vision, saying, "the America I want in the year 2000—[is] an America in which all responsible citizens have a chance to live their dreams, an America growing together, an America leading the world to greater peace, freedom, and prosperity."[32] None of this, Clinton reminded his listeners, was likely to happen in an every-man-for-himself scramble for personal

advantage. Not surprisingly, the blunt message of Clinton's second inaugural address was "The preeminent mission of our new Government is
to give all Americans an opportunity, not a guarantee but a real opportunity, to build better lives."[33]

Philip Roth, *American Pastoral*

Presidents praise the American Dream to an eager public, but rarely
do they mention the vulnerability of the dream to the forces and vicissitudes of life. That is the job of the novelist, and none has taken it
up with more verve than Philip Roth. Roth has been a major figure on
the American literary scene for half a century. His first novel, *Goodbye,
Columbus* (1959), won the National Book Award. Almost forty years and
several dozen books later, *American Pastoral* won the Pulitzer Prize for
fiction. *American Pastoral* was the first of three books, along with *I Married a Communist* (1998) and *The Human Stain*, comprising *The American
Trilogy*. The trilogy charted changes in American life in the last two-
thirds of the twentieth century. As in most of Roth's fiction, the setting,
at least initially, was the Jewish section of Newark, New Jersey.

   The protagonist of *American Pastoral* was Seymour Irving "the Swede"
Levov. The chronicler and narrator of the story was Nathan Zuckerman, Roth's alter ego. Nathan was a few years younger than Seymour
and a friend of his younger brother, Jerry. The nickname "the Swede"
was the gift of a coach highlighting what made Seymour remarkable
among his peers. Nathan reported, "Of the few fair-complexioned Jewish students in our preponderantly Jewish public high school, none possessed anything remotely like the steep-jawed, insentient Viking mask of
this blue-eyed blond born into our tribe as Seymour Irving Levov. The
Swede starred as end in football, center in basketball, and first baseman
in baseball." The Swede, both for his looks and his athletic skills, was
the center of school and community attention. The "total, uncritical,
idolatrous adulation" of the Swede's high school years did not make
him arrogant, let alone cruel. Rather, it produced "his golden gift for
responsibility"; it made him gentle, solicitous, self-denying, and eager to
please.[34] Unlike Twain's "good little boy," who suffered evil immediately,
Seymour long seemed blessed.

   Upon graduation in June 1945, Seymour joined the U.S. Marines,
but the war ended before he saw action. Returning to Newark, he at-

tended nearby Upsala College, at his father's insistence, so he could also work in and learn the family business, manufacturing high-end gloves, and then married Dawn Dwyer, Miss New Jersey 1949. They soon had a daughter, Meredith, called "Merry." Seymour mastered the family business, took it over when his father retired, and eventually moved the family to upscale Rimrock, about 30 miles west of Newark. Seymour Levov, living the American Dream, said wonderingly to Dawn, "We own a piece of America, Dawn. I couldn't be happier if I tried. I did it, darling, I did it—I did what I set out to do."[35]

Seymour's strengths and weaknesses were one; he was a good man, committed to normality, to society's norms and expectations, and he assumed that others were as well. He came of age after World War II, "during the greatest moment of collective inebriation in American history. . . . There was a big belief in life and [Americans] were steered relentlessly in the direction of success." Seymour was dedicated to America and its dream and all they had meant in his life. He "lived in America the way he lived inside his own skin. All the pleasures of his younger years were American pleasures. . . . Yes, everything that gave meaning to his accomplishments had been American." Seymour worked hard, learned his trade thoroughly, and succeeded impressively through the late 1960s, and then the bottom fell out. The remainder of the novel explored the question, "Who is set up for tragedy and the incomprehensibility of suffering?," concluding, "Nobody, . . . that is every man's tragedy."[36]

Seymour's American pastoral, his American Dream, was reduced to rubble by his own daughter, Merry. The tiny crack through which chaos entered Seymour's wonderful life was a flaw in Merry: she had a serious stutter. Seymour and Dawn did everything they could, through personal understanding and professional assistance, to help her overcome it—to no avail. Merry's reaction, maybe to the frustration of stuttering, maybe to the Vietnam War and the social protests around it, was to withdraw and radicalize. While the Levovs saw it happening and tried to respond with understanding and reason, they were stupefied when, still in high school, she bombed the local post office, killed an innocent bystander, and disappeared into the protest underground. Dawn, who had thought herself so close to Merry, was hospitalized twice for suicidal depression and was heavily medicated for years. Seymour maintained a public presence and tried to restore some normality to life, but he was just as thoroughly pulverized as Dawn by Merry's crimes. His sense of self, nation, humanity, and life were destroyed. Jerry, Seymour's brother, declared,

"There was no way back for my brother from that bomb. . . . His perfect life was over. Just what she [Merry] had in mind. . . . He was so in love with his own good luck, and they hated him for it." Seymour argued with Rita Cohen, maybe an associate of Merry, maybe just an emanation of his own postbombing derangement, "You hate us not because we're reckless but because we're prudent and sane and industrious and agree to abide by the law. You hate us because we haven't failed. Because we've worked hard and honestly to become the best in the business and because of that we have prospered, so you envy us and you hate us and want to destroy us."[37]

Merry, the daughter upon whom he had doted, to whom he had given everything in his command, whom he had tried to understand and reason with and sympathize with, became the "daughter who transports him out of the longed-for American pastoral and into everything that is its antithesis and its enemy, into the fury, the violence, and the desperation of the counterpastoral—into the indigenous American berserk." Merry had taught him "the worst lesson that life can teach—that it makes no sense." This lesson, that the successful life, the admirable life, the life lived between the white lines and according to society's norms and rules, provided no protection, no defense, against the berserk, left him bereft. Only one conclusion remained: "Futile, every last thing he had ever done. The preparations, the practice, the obedience; the uncompromising dedication to the essential, to the things that matter most; . . . the systematization of futility is all it had ever been." Of life, "He had thought most of it was order and only a little of it was disorder. He'd had it backwards."[38]

Seymour was never the same after the berserk destroyed the pastoral in his life. Seymour and Dawn, unable to restore the equilibrium in their life, eventually divorced. Seymour married again, had three fine sons by the mid-1980s, and went through the motions of an upper-middle-class life. But the sense that he understood America, that he had won by her rules and had every right to enjoy in pastoral bliss the fruits of his victory, were gone. If preparation and effort were not rewarded, if the intrusion of the berserk could destroy it all, what was left of the dream? He died in 1995, saddened, maybe broken, but still trying to live well and do right for those closest to him.

Seymour Levov, a Jew, sought to immerse himself in the great American mainstream, to shed the uncertainty and fear, the separateness, of his ancestors to live the American Dream. When fate, the American berserk, laid waste to his dreams, Jerry asked, "What are you? Do you know?" These questions were again central to Roth's *The Human Stain.* Do people get to choose their identity, to make and remake themselves as opportunities and circumstances seem to suggest, or are they, either partially or wholly, born into an identity that both limits them and gives them substance and weight? The American Dream had long promised that one could define and even remake oneself, but within familiar limits.

Coleman Silk was born into a middle-class black family in East Orange, New Jersey, in 1926. His father, Clarence Silk, had been born, raised, and educated in Georgia before fleeing north for more security and choice. In Trenton, New Jersey, he studied optometry before being drafted to serve in World War I. After the war, he met and married Gladys, moved to East Orange, opened an optometry shop, and started a family. Though Clarence lost the shop during the Depression, he found work as a dining-car porter, and Gladys worked as a nurse. In this secure middle-class home, older brother Walt, sister Ernestine, and Coleman all thrived. Coleman, a star athlete and student, graduated valedictorian of his integrated high school class and moved toward his fateful choice of how to proceed in life.

The Silk family was indisputably black; no one inside or outside the family doubted it, though they were all, especially the children, light-skinned. Coleman was very light-skinned, and so on the way to a boxing tournament at West Point, his coach and mentor, the Jewish Doc Chizner, knowing that the boxing coach of the University of Pittsburgh would be there, advised Coleman not to mention race. The narrator, Nathan Zuckerman, explained, "Now, it wasn't that on the way up Doc told him to tell the Pitt coach that he was white. He just told Coleman not to mention that he was colored." When Coleman asked whether the coach wouldn't know, Doc responded, "You look like you look, you're with me, and so he's going to think that you're one of Doc's boys. He's going to think that you're Jewish."[39] He did. Pitt offered Coleman a boxing scholarship, but Coleman turned it down to follow his parents' dream that he attend Howard, find a profession and a light-skinned girl, and settle into the black professional class. But Coleman found the massive "we" of all-black Howard to be profoundly limiting—a denial of his freedom and individuality. So when his father died unexpectedly, Coleman jumped at the opportunity to leave Howard.

With World War II raging, Coleman, still a month shy of eighteen, lied about his age and race to enlist as a white man in the U.S. Navy. Passing for white was not uneventful, particularly at the social margins where identifying pretenders was a well-honed skill. One night, while on shore leave, Coleman presented himself at a white whorehouse. The madam looked him up and down, declared him black, and had him beaten and thrown into the street. Coleman's black background, even though middle class, had left some "tells" that the socially and culturally alert could pick up. Once out of the navy, Coleman enrolled at New York University and thrived academically. Again, racially and culturally, life was bumpier. After two wonderful years, Coleman's love affair with Steena Palsson, a beautiful white Minnesotan just moved to New York, collapsed. Coleman "didn't lie to Steena about anything. All he did was to follow the instructions that Doc Chizner had given him . . . : if nothing comes up, you don't bring it up." But when love turned to talk of marriage, without preparing Steena in any way, Coleman arranged a Sunday dinner with his mother and sister. The dinner, somewhat awkward at points, went as well as could be expected, but at the end of the train ride back to New York, Steena shrieked, "I can't do it!" and fled.[40]

Another girlfriend, almost equally beautiful, was "Ellie McGee, a petite, shapely, colored girl." On their first date, Ellie looked at Coleman and asked him the question that Jerry had asked Seymour:

> "What are you anyway? . . . "
> "What am I? Play it any way you like," Coleman says.
> "Is that the way *you* play it?" she asks.
> "Of course that's the way I play it," he says.
> "So white girls think you're white?"
> "Whatever they think," he says, "I let them think."[41]

Ellie was amused and, to Coleman's surprise, pointed out to him over the course of the evening several other young men, white to the world, who also were black and passing. Coleman liked Ellie, but though very light herself, she identified as black, and if he chose her, he would have to also.

After Ellie, Coleman met and married a white Jewish girl, Iris Gettelman. Still following Doc Chizner's advice, Coleman never told Iris that he was black and had grown up in a black family; in fact, having learned from the debacle with Steena, he never even admitted that he had a family. To Iris and to the world, Coleman claimed a Jewish identity, and as his studies proceeded toward a doctorate in classics, his chosen identity was never challenged. To ensure that it held, Coleman met with his doting mother, Gladys, who was aware that he had passed for white at points in his life, and informed her that she could not be part of his new life. She decried the ruthlessness and violence of this decision, denying all that he had been, denying her and his dead father, his brother and sister, but he was determined. In deep sadness, Gladys agreed, saying, "You're white as snow and you think like a slave. . . . Now, I could tell you that there is no escape, that all your attempts to escape will only lead you back to where you began." But she knew it would make no difference, so she concluded, "Little is going to turn out as you imagine it."[42] Coleman never spoke with his mother again; the separation had to be complete.

America offered Coleman a brutal choice, and he made it. In fact, he felt he really had no choice at all. The experience of being submerged in the great Negro "we" at Howard had repelled him: "He was Coleman, the greatest of the great *pioneers* of the I. . . . All he'd ever wanted, from earliest childhood on, was to be free: not black, not even white—just on his own and free. . . . Why accept a life on any other terms?" Why, indeed! Wasn't the great pioneer, Coleman Silk, "merely being another American and, in the great frontier tradition, accepting the democratic invitation to throw your origins overboard if to do so contributes to the pursuit of happiness?"[43] Yes, of course, on the white side of the racial divide, making a new life, striking out for parts unknown, was part of the dream. But as Coleman knew, jumping the color line, while possible, was always contested and was disallowed when discovered. Steena's reaction left him no choice but to deny mother and family.

For four decades after the cruel conversation with his mother, Coleman defied fate, he won the battle, and he not only pursued but thought he found happiness. Iris's Jewish heritage and bushy dark hair helped provide camouflage, which proved not to be needed as there was "not a sign of his secret on any of his kids. . . . How solid the earth felt beneath his feet after she had their beautiful twins. . . . The most frightening apprehension of them all had been eradicated from his life." Coleman's academic career at upstate New York's Athena College blossomed; eventually he became "the first and only Jew ever to serve at Athena as dean of faculty." "The brand of bulldozing vanity and autocratic ego" that helped him take Athena from a sleepy rural college to a modern intellectual vibrancy discomfited many, but when he retired as dean in the mid-1990s "in order to round out his career back in the classroom," he was not far past the height of his powers.[44] Coleman Silk had drawn to an inside straight; he had won, had made of himself the "I" that he had dreamed of being. The old black "we" was gone, submerged, no longer an impediment, but no longer available without making his life a lie, a joke.

More than a month into his second semester back in the classroom, he was calling the roll and came to the names of two students who had never appeared in class. The distinguished Professor Silk asked those present, "Does anyone know these people? Do they exist or are they spooks?"[45] It happened that the absent students were black, and one of them, hearing of Professor Silk's classroom banter, complained to the college administration that the professor had demeaned her with a racial epithet—calling her a spook. Coleman's enemies on the faculty feigned deep concern over this grave charge, and most of the faculty fell silent, not wanting to get involved in a nasty racial fight. Coleman disdained the charge of racism, stood on the obvious meaning of spooks— ghosts, apparitions, people not there—and sought no compromise. In late 1996, well into the disciplinary process, Iris died of a stroke, and the next day Coleman resigned, blaming his enemies and the college for his wife's death. Abandoned by everyone save his new friend Nathan Zuckerman, sad and angry, Coleman died in a car crash. Only when Coleman's sister, Ernestine, appeared at the funeral, intending to pay her respects incognito, did Zuckerman figure out who she was and, in conversation with her, begin to put Coleman's life story together.

Coleman and the Swede won, they lived the American Dream, but both severed ties to their people, to their historic communities, Coleman even more fundamentally than Seymour, so when the solid ground beneath their feet began to shift, there proved to be no foundation at all. The unexpected, whether the thoroughly berserk or simply the absurd, overwhelmed planning and careful construction, "because we don't know, do we? . . . What underlies the anarchy of the train of events, the uncertainties, the mishaps, the disunity, the shocking irregularities that define human affairs? . . . Intention? Motive? Consequence? Meaning? All that we don't know is astonishing."[46] Here, so distant from the smiling certainties of politicians, here, in uncertainty, disunity, anarchy, and the berserk, is the beating heart of fiction's challenge to the American Dream.

Jonathan Franzen, *Freedom*

Jonathan Franzen's *Freedom* explored the meaning of freedom in our highly individualized and fragmented urban society.[47] Franzen's early twenty-first-century America was governed by political and economic forces that individual citizens, isolated by the dominant individualist ethic, barely comprehend and cannot combat. *Freedom* was the story of Walter and Patty Berglund, their children, Jessica and Joey, and their friends, neighbors, and associates. The pressures of marriage and family, jobs, money and wealth, competition, and entrepreneurship in the mostly upper-middle-class affluence of modern America provided the context for the story. At another level, the nexus of great wealth and political power set tight limits on what average citizens, even comfortable, well-educated, upper-middle-class, white citizens could know, do, and accomplish.

Walter and Patty were born about 1960, Walter into a poor Minnesota family and Patty into a fairly wealthy suburban New York family. They met in college at the University of Minnesota, married and raised a family in St. Paul, Minnesota, in the 1990s, and moved to Washington, D.C., in the new century's first decade. In Washington, the tone, content, and character of national politics challenged and then crushed the tenuous goals and values of the Berglunds and those around them. They found, whether in time or too late remained unclear, that freedom was sad and debilitating unless noble purposes gave it direction and meaning.

Patty was born the first of four children to Ray and Joyce Emerson. Ray was a lawyer and Joyce was a Democratic activist and state assemblywoman. Neither was capable of much affection, though they encouraged the creative and artistic efforts of Patty's siblings while denigrating her prowess as a basketball player. The lack of early nurturing left her hollow, not so radically as Rabbit Angstrom, to whom she bore real similarities, but enough to compromise her emotionally. Like Rabbit, Patty set high school basketball records two years in a row and then starred as a second-team All-American guard at the University of Minnesota before blowing out a knee.

Patty sensed the hole at her core. As she was deciding whether to pursue the good and kind Walter or his bad-boy friend and roommate Richard Katz, she warned Walter, "There's something wrong with me. I love all my other friends, but I feel like there's always a wall between us. Like they're all one kind of person and I'm another kind of person. More competitive and selfish. Less good, basically." Walter assured her that she was a "genuinely nice person," and "the mistake she went on to make, the really big life mistake, was to go along with Walter's version of her." Patty's fairly modest life plan was to be a better parent than hers had been. She told Walter, "I want to live in a beautiful old house and have two children. . . . I want to be a really, really great mom." When Walter asked, "Do you want a career, too?," she responded, "Raising children would be my career." Walter suggested that she was selling herself short but soon signed on to the Patty-as-stay-at-home-mom plan because he wanted her to be happy. Patty proved a good mom, if somewhat overwhelming, while the children were young, but she did not evolve, mature, and grow. One heated exchange with Richard "illuminated in a flash what a self-absorbed little child she'd been able to remain by walling herself inside her lovely house. . . . She didn't have a job, her kids were more grown up than she was."[48]

Walter Berglund, a native Minnesotan, was defined by his "most salient quality, besides his love of Patty, . . . his niceness." Walter's niceness involved more than a bit of naivety. Walter graduated from law school and went to work for 3M in the counsel's office. He was soon "shunted into outreach and philanthropy, . . . where niceness was an asset."[49] Eventually, Walter left the corporate world to go to work for the Nature Conservancy. The public-interest sector fit him well, but he was not without ambition, so he took a chance to move up. Walter left the Nature Conservancy to head the Cerulean Mountain Trust in Washington, D.C. In doing so, he stepped into a world of money, power, and influence for which his "niceness" was no match.

The Cerulean Mountain Trust was presented as an initiative to preserve migratory bird habitats in the United States and Latin America. But there was more going on than Walter and his assistant, Lalitha, knew. They worked for a Houston-based oil-and-gas mogul named Vin Haven. Haven was close to George and Laura Bush and Dick and Lynne Cheney. The trust's first project, which Walter was hired to direct after several others had turned down the job, was "an opportunity to partner with coal companies to create a very large, permanent private reserve . . . as long as they were allowed to continue extracting coal . . . via mountaintop removal." Walter had convinced himself that while the mountaintop removal was unfortunate, a good reclamation plan could leave a 100-square-mile nature preserve. Soon, however, Walter and Lalitha discovered that the mountaintop removal was not the worst of it; "Vin . . . turned out to have some other motives." The Cerulean Mountain Trust had been hatched in 2001 when Vin attended Vice President Cheney's secret energy task force meetings, during which Cheney "mentioned to Vin Haven that the president intended to make certain regulatory and tax-code changes to render natural-gas extraction economically feasible in the Appalachians." "Long story short," Walter and Lalitha explained to Richard Katz, "he was using us for cover." "West Virginia's about to get the shit drilled out of it," Richard responded, "and meanwhile your boss's mineral rights are suddenly a lot more valuable. . . . In other words, you got played."[50] As Mr. Minty had told his son Jimmy in *Empire Falls*, the big boys, Vin Haven, Cheney, Bush, "got the whole thing figured out, believe me, and they've thought of everything." Now Walter had seen for himself that it was so.

Finding himself in the vortex of national political and policy forces that he was ill-prepared to combat left Walter as empty and bereft as Patty had ever been. He confessed to Richard, "He didn't know what to do, he didn't know how to live. . . . There was no controlling narrative: he seemed to himself a purely reactive pinball in a game."[51] Soon, Lalitha, in West Virginia to defend what was left of their vision, was mysteriously killed in a car crash, and Walter was back in Minnesota, living in a small, rural family cabin and working in a modest position again with the Nature Conservancy. Rising in the world was a rougher business than Walter had imagined, especially when one ran into the massed forces of power and wealth.

Walter's plaintive cry that he didn't know how to live was echoed throughout *Freedom*. Patty was a housewife and a mom, exactly the life she had wanted for herself: "She had all day every day to figure out some decent and satisfying way to live, and yet all she ever seemed to get for all her choices and all her freedom was more miserable. . . . She pitied herself for being so free." Walter's brother Mitch, at the other end of the economic spectrum, almost homeless, cleaning a fish that he had caught for dinner, with maybe fifty dollars in his tackle box, thrice married but alone, noted of his children, "They've got good mothers that know how to take care of them. I'm no help at that. I finally figured that out. I'm only good at taking care of me." Walter mused, "You're a free man," to which Mitch responded, "That I am."[52]

Finally, young people—especially those growing up in privilege, as Patty and her siblings had and as her children, Jessica and Joey, were—

seemed at sea. Patty tried to explain, "*It's a different world now, Walter. . . .* You don't understand how scared these kids are now. They're under so much pressure." Joey, the golden child from birth, demanded his freedom early and totally and was destined for success. Still in college, Joey became involved in a shady international arms transaction, part of the Bush-era freedom initiative in Afghanistan and Iraq, that promised big and easy money. Jenna, the beautiful sister of his University of Virginia roommate, urged him on, reminding him "that the world wasn't fair and was never going to be fair, that there would always be big winners and big losers, and that she personally, . . . preferred to be a winner and to surround herself with winners." Joey himself "couldn't stop imagining the excellence of being worth half a million dollars when he turned twenty-one" in a year. Joey did make a lot of money on the arms deal, but he found his balance and gave $100,000 to a population-control program that Walter started. Joey wished "there were some different world he could belong to, some simpler world in which a good life could be had at nobody else's expense." But since there wasn't, nobody expected Joey to do less than well in this world.[53]

Barack Obama and the Delicate Balancing of Doubts and Dreams

Barack Obama, like Reagan, Clinton, and so many before them, conjured the American Dream throughout his political career. But, not surprisingly, Obama always had a somewhat different perspective than his predecessors on America and its dream. Obama was of mixed race, with a black Kenyan father and a white Kansan mother; he struggled with his racial identity and made that struggle a major topic in his coming-of-age autobiography, *Dreams of My Father* (1995). American culture never afforded mixed-race persons the choice of whether they would be considered white or black. Mixed-race people were always considered black, unless like Cora Munro or Coleman Silk they were light enough to pass, and that passing was always contested. Obama knew that and owned being black, saying, "I ceased to advertise my mother's race at the age of twelve or thirteen, when I began to suspect that by doing so I was ingratiating myself to whites."[54] This too is curious, though perhaps at twelve or thirteen he imagined that claiming some white blood would ingratiate him with whites. Historically it had not been so.

In high school and college, first at the elite Punahou School in Honolulu and then at Occidental College in Los Angeles, which Obama attended from 1979 to 1981, racial identity was a major topic and concern. After long and sometimes intense conversations with a black high school friend named Ray, Obama concluded, more sadly than aggressively, "We were always playing on the white man's court, . . . by the white man's rules. . . . If he treated you like a man or came to your defense, it was because he knew that the words you spoke, the clothes you wore, the books you read, your ambitions and desires, were already his." Ray seemed more inclined to resist pervasive white cultural control and to pay the price for resistance, but Obama certainly knew the control was there and needed to be navigated. Nor did he take the course recommended by Joyce, a mixed-race friend at Occidental, or by Roth's Coleman Silk, though Coleman's instincts can be heard clearly in Obama's memory of Joyce. He recalled Joyce arguing, "Only white culture had individuals. And we, the half-breeds and the college-degreed, take a survey of the situation and think to ourselves, Why should we get lumped in with the losers if we don't have to? We become only so grateful to lose ourselves in the crowd, America's happy, faceless marketplace; . . . Don't you know who I am? I'm an *individual*!"[55] Being of mixed race in America always required a plan, a strategy.

Obama came to national political attention when he spoke compellingly about the American Dream at the 2004 Democratic National Convention.[56] From the opening words of that speech, he signaled that he had a distinctive relationship to the dream, that in fact he wrapped himself in it and made himself a test of it. He said, "Tonight is a particular honor for me because, let's face it, my presence on this stage is pretty unlikely." He knew that throughout American history, and not just in the "one drop" era, being of mixed race had been well-nigh disqualifying for America's top honors. But in a fascinating rhetorical move, both quick and smooth, he redirected attention from likely exclusion to the presumption of inclusion, saying, "I stand here knowing . . . that, in no other country on earth, is my story even possible."

Obama understood that America's self-image could be leveraged to his advantage. What made his story possible in America was that the American Dream rested on the foundation of Jefferson's declaration "that all men are created equal. That they are endowed by their Creator with certain inalienable rights. That among these are life, liberty and the pursuit of happiness." Obama declared, "This year, this election year, we are called to reaffirm our values and commitments, and to hold them up against a hard reality and see how we are measuring up, to the legacy of our forbearers, and the promise of future generations. And fellow Americans. . . . I say to you tonight: we have more work to do." Like Democrats back to FDR, Obama knew that calls for government action had to be balanced, immediately, with praise for individualism and hard work, so he said, "Don't get me wrong. The people . . . don't expect government to solve all their problems. They know they have to work hard to get ahead. . . . But they sense, deep in their bones, that with a change in priorities, we can make sure that every child in America has a decent shot at life, and that the doors of opportunity remain open for all." This speech, with its broad homage to the American Dream and to the values of Jefferson's declaration, made Obama a national figure and a Democratic Party hero.

Still, most Democrats were skeptical when the young senator from Illinois declared for the party's 2008 presidential nomination. Just forty-six, with seven years in the Illinois Senate and two in the U.S. Senate, few gave him much chance of defeating the favorite, New York senator and former first lady Hillary Clinton. One of the high points of the campaign was a speech Obama gave on the American Dream in Bettendorf, Iowa, on November 7, 2007.[57] Obama again made his disparate family and himself exemplars of a broad and inclusive American Dream. Traveling the country, he told the crowd, he had found that "in big cities and small towns; among men and women; young and old; black, white, and brown—Americans share a faith in simple dreams. A job with wages that can support a family. Health care we can count on and afford. A retirement that is dignified and secure. Education and opportunity for our kids. Common hopes. American dreams." Most aspirants to the presidency and most presidents praised the American Dream broadly; Obama always put more meat on the bones than most: good wages, affordable health care, education, and a secure retirement.

Obama claimed that the American Dream was beyond the reach of too many. "While some have prospered beyond imagination in this global economy, middle class Americans—as well as those working to become middle-class—are seeing the American dream slip further away." Obama blamed the George W. Bush administration's tax cuts for the wealthy and rising CEO pay for the hard times confronting most Americans. He promised instead "an American Dream agenda—to put some wind at the backs of working people, to lower the cost of getting ahead, and to protect and extend opportunity for the middle class." Obama won the Iowa caucuses in a come-from-behind victory, Clinton took New Hampshire less than a week later, and the campaigns battled on equal footing for months.

Deep into the 2008 Democratic nomination contest, with the fight still undecided, Obama was forced to respond to incendiary sermons by his Chicago minister, the Reverend Jeremiah Wright. Wright excoriated white Americans and America for denying blacks the rights and opportunities—the American Dream—open to others. Wright's offending comments threatened to drive white support from Obama. Critics asked, Did you know he held these views? Did you sit there while he spouted them? Why didn't you respond? Why didn't you stand up and leave? It was a critical and dangerous period for the campaign. Obama knew that he could not run for president as a "black" candidate, let alone as an "angry black man," but neither could he ignore race or deny the injury claims of American blacks.

Obama's rhetorical task was dangerously complex; he had to tell a plausible story of the historic denial and present limits on black rights and opportunities without seeming to impugn national motives and goals or alienating white voters. He delivered his remarks on March 18, 2008, in Philadelphia, "across the street" from where the Constitution was drafted in 1787.[58] Obama declared, "The document they produced was . . . ultimately unfinished. It was stained by this nation's original sin of slavery," leaving it to "successive generations . . . to narrow the gap between the promise of our ideals and the reality of their time." The Obama campaign, then, was just part of "the long march . . . for a more just, more equal, more free, more caring and more prosperous America." Obama worked to put the hurt and rage evident in Reverend Wright's comments into the context of American history. He said, "We do need to remind ourselves that so many of the disparities that exist in the African-American community today can be traced directly to inequalities passed on from an earlier generation that suffered under the brutal legacy of slavery and Jim Crow." But, as always, he was quick to add that whites also had legitimate grievances. Their grievances, however, flowed largely from recent flawed Republican policy. Most working- and middle-class whites, who "don't feel that they have been particularly privileged by their race, . . . are anxious about their futures, and feel their dreams slipping away; in an era of stagnant wages and global competition, opportunity comes to be seen as a zero-sum game, in which your dreams come at my expense." So Obama offered a positive-sum vision of the American Dream, restored for whites and expanded for blacks. Obama concluded with an observation that most whites could accept, that set a general direction rather than a specific destination: "This union may never be perfect, but generation after generation has shown that it can always be perfected."

Obama went on to narrowly defeat Hillary Clinton for the Democratic Party nomination and then to more comfortably defeat the Republican nominee, Arizona senator John McCain, for the presidency. The general election campaign was conducted against the backdrop of two extended wars and the worst economic collapse since the Great Depression. As these had occurred mainly on the Republican watch, Obama won going away, a seven-point victory and large Democratic majorities in both houses of Congress. Obama was exultant when he stepped to the microphones in Chicago's Grant Park on election night 2008.[59] He promised to restore the American Dream: "This is our time, to put our people back to work and open doors of opportunity for our kids; . . . to reclaim the American dream and reaffirm that fundamental truth, that, out of many, we are one; that while we breathe, we hope."

When Barack Obama was sworn in as the forty-fourth president of the United States on January 20, 2009, the economic recession that had been plain for a year and dangerously steep since the fall remained unchecked. Obama's first inaugural address, delivered in circumstances more troubling than any since Roosevelt's in 1932, was a hopeful but stern call to the nation to rise up and confront the threats of the day as other generations had before them. He began as Roosevelt had by saying, "That we are in the midst of crisis is now well understood," but he added that a more insidious danger threatened, "a sapping of confidence across our land, a nagging fear that America's decline is inevitable, that the next generation must lower its sights. Today I say to you that the challenges we face are real. . . . But know this, America: They will be met." Obama reminded the nation, "Our challenges may be new. The instruments with which we meet them may be new. But those values upon which our success depends—honesty and hard work, courage and fair play, tolerance and curiosity, loyalty and patriotism—these things are old. These things are true. . . . What is demanded then is a return to these truths."[60]

Though the broad economy, as measured by corporate profits, stock-market gains, and job creation, was in recovery by 2010, Obama was always careful to acknowledge that many were still hurting. In the 2010 State of the Union message, Obama said, "One in 10 Americans still cannot find work. Many businesses have shuttered. Home values have declined. Small towns and rural communities have been hit especially hard. And for those who'd already known poverty, life's become that much harder. This recession has also compounded the burdens that America's families have been dealing with for decades: the burden of working harder and longer for less." In the 2012 State of the Union address, Obama declared, "The basic American promise [was] that if you worked hard, you could do well enough to raise a family, own a home, send your kids to college, and put a little away for retirement. The defining issue of our time is how to keep that promise alive. No challenge is more urgent. No debate is more important."[61] No president since FDR in the early years of the Great Depression had been quite so clear that the historic American Dream was endangered for many.

Obama expanded on these themes in one of the most prominent speeches of the 2012 presidential campaign, delivered at Osawatomie, Kansas.[62] A little more than a century before, Theodore Roosevelt, plotting a comeback in the 1912 presidential election, delivered a famously populist speech in Osawatomie. With the Tea Party and Occupy Wall Street movements highlighting popular concerns about the state of the nation and its economy, Obama took a decidedly populist path as well. He again declared the decline of the American Dream as "the defining issue of our time. This is a make or break moment for the middle class, and all those who are fighting to get into the middle class. At stake is whether this will be a country where working people can earn enough to raise a family, build a modest savings, own a home, and secure their retirement."

Like Bill Clinton in the 1990s, Obama pointed to a conflict between two partisan ideologies. Of the right, he said, "Their philosophy is simple: we are better off when everyone is left to fend for themselves and play by their own rules. Well, I'm here to say they are wrong. I'm here to reaffirm my deep conviction that we are greater together than we are on our own." Like so many great presidential speeches of the past, Obama's described American history in a way that made his own policy prescriptions seem commonsensical and his opponents' prescriptions seem willfully perverse: "You see, this isn't the first time America has faced this choice. At the turn of the last century, . . . some people thought massive inequality and exploitation was just the price of progress. Theodore Roosevelt disagreed." The laissez-faire, minimalist, you're-on-your-own approach was tried again in the 1920s, Obama said. "Here's the problem: It doesn't work. It's never worked. . . . And it didn't work when we tried it during the last decade. . . . We simply can't return to this brand of you're-on-your-own economics." Fortunately, Obama argued, "there's another view about how we build a strong middle class in this country—a view that's truer to our history. . . . It's a view that says in America, we are greater together—when everyone engages in fair play, everyone gets a fair shot, everyone does their fair share."[63]

Obama won reelection comfortably, not by the seven-point margin of 2008 but by about half that, and carried the themes of Osawatomie into his second inaugural address. The second inaugural was built around the need, expressed by other presidents in difficult times, for the promises of life, liberty, equality, and the pursuit of happiness in the Declaration of Independence to be restored today and preserved for tomorrow. "Today we continue a never-ending journey to bridge the meaning of those words with the realities of our time. . . . For we, the people, understand that our country cannot succeed when a shrinking few do very well and a growing many barely make it. . . . This is our generation's task—to make these words, these rights, these values of life and liberty and the pursuit of happiness real for every American."[64] A year later, in his 2014 State of the Union message, Obama declared, "After four years of economic growth, . . . average wages have barely budged. Inequality has deepened. Upward mobility has stalled. The cold, hard fact is that even in the midst of recovery, too many Americans are working more than ever just to get by, let alone get ahead. And too many still aren't working at all."[65] Even after six years in office, Obama was keenly aware that many, especially the poor and minorities, remained outside the social and economic mainstream.

In the last years of the Obama presidency, police violence against young black men, urban unrest, and the fiftieth anniversary of the Selma, Alabama, civil rights march that culminated in the Bloody Sunday confrontation on the Edmund Pettus Bridge brought the issue of race back to the fore. Obama spoke boldly on race at several points in his presidency, but he was always aware that he was and was responsible to be the president of all Americans. Obama went to the Selma anniversary event and highlighted "the belief that America is not yet finished, that we are strong enough to be self-critical, that each successive generation can look upon our imperfections and decide that it is in our power to remake this nation to more closely align with our highest ideals."[66]

Obama's sense that America and its promise has been incomplete throughout its history, that successive generations have worked to complete it, and that it remains unfinished today contrasts strikingly with Reagan's sense of the nation and its promise as complete and perfect, only needing to be honored and, if backsliding has occurred, restored. Reagan's positive message made him the beau ideal of the modern Republican Party. Obama's more nuanced message, that more remained to be done to make the dream available to all, was met by sullen resistance in society's more comfortable quarters.

Conclusion

Though it was not immediately evident, middle-class incomes began to stagnate during the mid-1970s. For at least fifteen years the impact was masked because the ongoing movement of women into the paid workforce allowed family incomes to continue growing. Hence, Reagan's message that smaller government, lower taxes, and fewer regulations would rejuvenate and expand the economy resonated powerfully, especially with the white working class and the well-off. Reagan's blowout reelection victory in 1984 highlighted a resurgent national confidence. He left the presidency with an homage to the American Dream and with the hope that its benefits might be expanded globally.

John Updike's writings had long showed a small-town America where life and opportunity had a much narrower and darker feel. Janice's father built Springer Motors, first as a used-car lot and then as a new-car Toyota dealership, but neither Harry nor Nelson prepared themselves to build the business. Both felt entitled to its benefits. Harry assumed that he should run it, even though Janice and her mother owned it, and Nelson destroyed the business through drug dependency and greed. Richard Russo depicted Empire Falls in even bleaker terms. Empire Falls had been a Whiting company town when the factories and mills were open. Twenty years after they had closed, residents remained because it was home, they knew it, and they were comfortable there, even though jobs were scarce and poorly paid. Francine Whiting, the matriarch, presided over the town, owned much of it, and controlled everything that happened in it. A small factory town, whose time had passed, controlled by a single wealthy family—and all the towns like it in an economy evolving from industrial to postindustrial services—was a poor place to dream.

Former Arkansas governor Bill Clinton knew about poor, stagnant small towns. His 1992 presidential campaign offered a "New Covenant," focused on the working and middle classes, promising a hand up, not a handout. Clinton argued that the Republican promise of competition and property rights was actually an every-man-for-himself fight in which only the privileged would prosper. Instead, Clinton promised that government would foster a society and economy in which opportunity flourished and all who prepared well and tried hard could earn security. The New Covenant was at least partially fulfilled; job creation was robust during the Clinton years, but income gains continued to go predominantly to the wealthy.

Philip Roth drew attention to problems that still plagued the formerly excluded in the seemingly freer and more open decades of the late twentieth century. In Roth's *American Trilogy*, Coleman Silk, a very light-skinned black, sought to edge closer to the American mainstream by claiming, successfully for most of his adult life, a Jewish identity. To do so, he ruthlessly cut off his black family, including his doting mother, to seek the kind of successful professional life to which whites were entitled. Seymour Irving "the Swede" Levov, a Jew, sought, again, quite successfully for a time, an all-American life, through sports, the U.S. Marines, marriage, a successful business, and an exclusive address. Both Coleman and Seymour cut themselves off from their roots to claim a place in the great unhyphenated American mainstream. When tumult came and they most needed the strength and stability of deep roots, they had none, and they toppled. The formative choices they made, while sad, were by no means irrational in light of the mid-twentieth-century society they faced.

Jonathan Franzen's *Freedom* focused on the dilemmas facing white Americans. Walter Berglund was born into a poor, rural, Minnesota family, while Patty Emerson was born into a comfortable, upper-middle-class, artistic family in suburban New York. Though he was from a poor family, no obstacles stood between Walter, a law degree, marriage to Patty, and an upper-middle-class life. Yet comfort and security, without real goals and values, left the Berglunds adrift. Their move to Washington, D.C., and Walter's encounter with massed wealth and power demonstrated the vast distance between those who had chosen passive mediocrity and those who had chosen to ally with the devil. While Seymour and Coleman had struggled with the question Who are you?, the Berglund's struggled with the even more fundamental question How should we live? Their secure but empty lives loudly declared that without purpose and direction there was no freedom. Freedom was not being open, being at loose ends; it was making meaningful choices intended to bring about worthy goals. Franzen required us to ask whether America still had the moral and social cohesion to sustain freedom.

Finally, Barack Obama struggled with his racial and social identity before coming to feel that he had a distinctive relationship to the American Dream and its promises. By the time he addressed the Democratic National Convention in 2004, he understood that he could make his reception, his acceptance, a test of the American Dream. Always carefully, he suggested that only in America could a mixed-race person like himself, a member of a historically excluded group, stand before the nation with confidence; and, if he could not, the nation's fundamental values remained unfulfilled. In fact, much of the nation, though by no means all, thrilled to the prospect of a black president precisely because it suggested that historic barriers had been overcome. Obama's outsider status encouraged him to give the dream more specific content—a good job at a good wage, good schools, affordable health care, and a secure retirement—than any president since FDR. Especially after the Great Recession had run its destructive course and the recovery had made the comfortable classes whole again, Obama continued to focus on those left behind in rural areas, small towns, and the inner cities, where factories had closed, jobs had fled, and people struggled with unemployment and low pay. These large pockets of poverty, even in good times, remain a challenge to the nation and its dream.

9 | American Dreams and Doubts in the Twenty-First Century

Never mind the ridicule, never mind the defeat; up again, old heart!—
. . . there is victory yet for all justice.
—Ralph Waldo Emerson, "Experience," 1844

In this concluding chapter we assess the history, current status, and future of the American Dream. The epigraph, which was the closing sentence of Ralph Waldo Emerson's 1844 essay "Experience," seems particularly apt as it encourages us to see both the hope and the futility of the American Dream; yet in the end, it leaves our heart, if not our mind, turned toward hope. Emerson, a poet, essayist, and social critic, was one of the nation's leading intellectuals in the half century after 1835. This period encompassed the boisterous adolescence of America and its dream. There was a nation to build, a continent to subdue, and fortunes to make, but Emerson blows an uncertain trumpet. Many who write about the American Dream today blow the same uncertain trumpet; in fact, many seem unable to summon the energy and hope even for one more effort. The ridicule, the past disappointments and defeats, the rising inequality, the declining mobility, and the shrinking middle class have left many convinced that the American Dream is no more.

Before we shout "up again, old heart!," we must review closely what the American Dream has meant in our history, what reservations about the dream our great novelists have registered, and what the dream might mean in our future. As always, we must treat our politicians skeptically when they claim that the dream has characterized our history and that they can expand or restore it. Americans thrill to Jefferson's declaration that "all men are created equal" and "endowed by their Creator with certain unalienable rights, that among these are Life, Liberty, and the pursuit of Happiness." We might, if our collective feet were not held to the fire of the American novel, allow ourselves to believe that our country and its people always lived those noble principles. They did not. Our great novelists, from Nathaniel Hawthorne and Herman Melville to Philip Roth and Jonathan Franzen, have shown us the cultural constraints that have held the poor, minorities, and women outside the social, economic, and political mainstreams. Although great strides have been made over the course of our national history, a cursory survey of data on employment, income, and wealth shows stark differences between the privileged and the underprivileged. Moreover, the faces of the privileged and the underprivileged have changed little over the course of our history. So, like Emerson, we must ignore ridicule and past defeats if we are once again to call out, "up again, old heart!— . . . there is victory yet for all justice." Some will be able to muster the energy and hope; some will not.

The Promise and Meaning of the American Dream

The American Dream at its best has always involved a clear sense of the goals to be pursued and the means by which they might be achieved. For most of our history the American Dream had clear expectations both for the individual and the nation. At the individual level, as Penn, Franklin, Lincoln, and so many others knew, the dream demanded character, preparation in school and shop, honesty, hard work, frugality, and persistence. At the national level, the dream demanded that society provide an open, fair, competitive, entrepreneurial environment in which individual merit could find its place.

Americans have always had a sense that the world was watching, that God had a special role for them to play in the world, and that their insights and experiences should inform mankind. After narrower beginnings, a peculiarly attractive and balanced understanding of the American promise emerged over the course of the eighteenth century. Benjamin Franklin, Hector St. John de Crevecoeur, Benjamin Rush, Ezra Stiles, and others described America as a place in which a human flowering was about to occur. They foresaw a society characterized by peace and plenty, by political and economic freedom and opportunity, and by accomplishments in religion, morality, and art. They envisioned harmony between the outer plantation of the world and the inner plantation of the human heart and soul. Yet they knew from history and experience that such societies did not exist in nature. They had to be artfully created and carefully sustained against the ravages of time.[1]

The Founders had their blind spots and we have explored them, but they well understood that a free, stable, and prosperous society required carefully crafted constitutional rules of the game. Individuals were responsible for their own characters and preparation. They were expected to foster good habits and avoid bad habits; to be honest, fair, and truthful and to avoid lying, drinking, and gambling. They were also to prepare themselves, through education and preparation for a job or career, to be useful members of their societies. Then they were expected to work hard, save, invest, and persevere, and with a little luck, they were expected to succeed and perhaps to prosper. But no matter how well they prepared, how hard they were willing to work, society and the economy had to be well organized and vibrant enough to provide the opportunities over which they might compete. John Schwarz has correctly argued, "The founders believed that the federal government had a crucial role to play in fostering the level of economic opportunity necessary to enable Americans to attain independence and a decent livelihood."[2]

Through most of the nineteenth century, the American Dream of land in the woods or of independent craftsmanship remained open to each new generation and to a constantly increasing flow of immigrants. Yet over the course of the nineteenth century the balance of the Founders' dream eroded, the limits slipped away, and the American heart hardened. The push west and its steady annihilation of the Indians, the frantic scramble for wealth in the California goldfields, the seemingly endless horror of the Civil War, and breakneck industrialization stripped the American character of much of its sense of propriety, balance, and scale. Individualism and competition displaced community and cooperation as men fought to tame the continent, seize its wealth, and control the course of its development. Corporations grew beyond the ability of government to limit or discipline.

As the nineteenth century neared its close, thoughtful men were well aware that the dynamics of the old century would not be those of the new. The rough equality and competition allowed by a seemingly limitless western frontier had given way to a harsh competition in which the robber barons of the age threatened to deny hope and opportunity to everyone else. At this dangerous juncture, leading progressive intellectuals, including Herbert Croly and Walter Lippmann, struggled to describe the distinctive bases of American freedom, equality, and opportunity—of the American Dream—before they slipped away.

A debate arose among the nation's top political leaders about how to address the problems of the new century: with the traditional limited government model, or with a new regulatory model of expanded and empowered government? Citizens were worried and frightened, so they listened intently for an explanation of how the country was changing and what the implications would be for them. Every leading president of the twentieth century used his first inaugural address to answer two questions: How did we get to this place in our history? How do we ensure that the fundamental dynamics of the nation's early history live into the future? Theodore Roosevelt, Woodrow Wilson, Herbert Hoover, Franklin Roosevelt, Lyndon Johnson, Ronald Reagan, Bill Clinton, and Barack Obama all asked how to secure the American Dream in their time.

Three images—the city on a hill and its golden doors, the balance between the dollar and the man, and the fairly run footrace—were used through most of the nation's history, though less so in recent decades, to sharpen and clarify the fundamental meaning of the American Dream. First, from Winthrop to Reagan, America was described as a city on a hill. But this city was not a fortress, powerful, austere, and unapproachable; there were doors, golden doors, that gave access to the security and prosperity within. The shining city on a hill was both an example to the world and a destination for all who would be free. The city belonged not just to its defenders within but to kindred spirits without who wished to stand with them against the darkness of tyranny, poverty, and injustice in the world.

Second, within the city, care was taken, through culture, constitutions, law, and policy, to ensure that openness and opportunity continued to characterize the society through time. As Andrew Jackson, Theodore Roosevelt, and many others well knew and clearly said, freedom and opportunity demand that a balance be maintained between the dollar and the man, between wealth and opportunity, between property rights and human rights. If the dollar, wealth, and property become too powerful, too concentrated, they foreclose opportunity to the man on the make, the little man just starting out, and to the next generation.

Third, the image of the fairly run race was used by Abraham Lincoln, Herbert Hoover, Lyndon Johnson, and many others to humanize and soften thinking about the American Dream. It provided particular insight into the competition between the traditionally advantaged and the historically disadvantaged. A fairly run race does not demand that each runner be equally likely to win; some may be faster and stronger, and some may be better trained and prepared. But putting the demonstrably ill-prepared or the injured, sick, and crippled in a race against the strong and swift offends the common sense of justice. The strong must forebear while the weak are nourished and strengthened before the results of any race in which they are to compete can be given credence.

Many worry that the balance and limits of the traditional American Dream have been lost. One hears little about the balance between the outer plantation of work and accumulation and the inner plantation of heart, mind, and soul; little about balancing the interests of human rights and property rights, the man and the dollar; little about the fairly run race; and even less about the city on a hill, with its golden doors, before which the world's oppressed might appeal for entry. The sense of community that once framed and limited individualism has eroded. Post–World War II prosperity brought to the fore both a sense of entitlement and an unbounded individualism that have not been reconciled. Lyndon Johnson envisioned a Great Society, a society so secure in its wealth that all individuals might be encouraged to pursue their own goals, to develop their own talents, and make of themselves what they would. Ronald Reagan envisioned a society in which individuals were responsible for themselves and government was small, cheap, and unobtrusive. These conflicting visions have roiled our politics and public deliberations for decades.

As a result, analysts generally take a bleak view of the dream's current state and future prospects. In 2000 Kathryn Hume surveyed the health of the American Dream in fiction since 1960 and concluded, "The American Dream had promised an expansive future, and what we now find is a melancholy loss of faith in America's exceptionalism."[3] David Kamp, writing more recently in *Vanity Fair,* called for a more modest dream, saying, "The time has come to consider the idea of simple *continuity*: the perpetuation of a contented, sustainable middle-class way of life."[4] But it was not clear to the economist Thomas Piketty that a sustainable, middle-class way of life remained a live option. As we shall see more fully below, the middle class has been slowly shrinking since 1970, and Piketty recently concluded, "The New World may be on the verge of becoming the Old World of the twenty-first century's globalized economy."[5] More and more Americans have come to share these fears.

Fiction Has Long Told Us

The American Dream offered a linear counsel: prepare well, work hard, save and invest, and you will have a good chance to succeed and prosper in America. Our great literature, on the other hand, has always described a more complex, challenging, and indeterminate reality confronting Americans. We opened this chapter by examining the closing line of Emerson's "Experience," but the opening line of that essay, "Where do we find ourselves?," also commands our attention. Emerson was asking what kind of world man finds himself in and how he should try to live in that world. Emerson thought the world fluid, diffuse, and uninterpretable: "All things swim and glitter. . . . Dream delivers us to dream, and there is no end to illusion." Life for Emerson was a torrent of "Illusion, Temperament, Succession, Surface, Surprise, Reality, Subjectiveness,—these are threads on the loom of time, these are the lords of life."[6]

Men could exercise some, though limited and intermittent, control over "the lords of life"; at best, through custom and tradition, habit, and social institutions, men might dampen, limit, and channel the lords' otherwise torrential impact. Doing common things in common ways limited the flux and complexity of life. "So in this great society wide lying around us," Emerson observed, "a critical analysis would find very few spontaneous actions. It is almost all custom and gross sense." Emerson thought men were moved commonly by habit, custom, tradition, and necessity and rarely by reason, decision, choice, or volition. Social structures included "the largest and solemnest things, . . . commerce, government, church, marriage, and . . . the history of every man's bread, and the ways by which he is to come by it." Social structures, just or unjust, gave men a sense of place and a sense of how to act in that place. Cultural habits and social structures help men channel, even if they cannot control, the rush of events that is life.

Another seminal insight regarding how people understand and act in the world was articulated by the mid-twentieth-century black writer James Baldwin. Baldwin agreed that human action was, in Emerson's phrase, "all custom and gross sense," writing, "It is the peculiar triumph of society . . . that it is able to convince those people to whom it has given inferior status," the poor, minorities, and women, "of the reality"—he might better have said "propriety" or "necessity"—"of this decree." Society's power is such that the excluded find themselves "bound, first without, then within, by the nature of [their] categorization. . . . It must be remembered that the oppressed and the oppressor are bound together within the same society; they accept the same criteria, they share the same beliefs, they both alike depend on the same reality."[7]

The pressure that cultural norms place on individuals, limiting their options and choices, channeling them into favorable and unfavorable social and economic positions, has always been the raw material of fiction. Fiction provides a vehicle by which we see and, more important, hear characters—protagonists and antagonists, men and women, the privileged and the excluded—confront their world and the problems it presents. So constrained are most characters in our great fiction that they do not even imagine themselves pursuing great goals, pursuing the American Dream; rather, they think of themselves as struggling to survive, to find a small space, a modicum of peace and security, where they might make a life—often to no avail.

Culture, fate, class, race, and gender are the forces that fiction has most often described as governing life. Culture has offered white men the license to strive, but fate and class have checked the rise of most of them. Three-quarters of the American adult population—poor white men, nonwhite men, and women of any color—rarely even imagined that striving and achievement were open to them. Though we have seen culture, fate, class, race, and gender at work in fiction throughout the nation's history, limiting and often denying the American Dream of preparation, effort, and achievement to all but a fortunate and favored few, revisiting key examples will help remind us of their power.

Both Emerson and Baldwin taught that culture has always been the sea in which people, whether privileged or excluded, swam. Like the fish that does not know it is wet, having never been otherwise, only the rare individual can sustain opposition to the cultural assumptions that govern their society. The power of culture to define role, place, and options for individuals was on remarkable display in one of America's first great novels, Nathaniel Hawthorne's *Scarlet Letter*. Hester Prynne struggled against the cultural constraints defining the place of women in her day. For a time, and off and on for a long time, she felt justified in her struggle. Once her indiscretion—her sin—had been discovered, adjudicated, and punished with the scarlet *A* on her bosom, her social isolation left her free to think broadly. She imagined that men and women might be free to choose their courses in life, to choose their lovers and partners, and to find their happiness. But the Reverend Arthur Dimmesdale, the deeply cultured, well-educated, and trained minister, the man she loved and who loved her, briefly and fatefully her lover, could not follow, could not think, let alone live, beyond the bounds of his culture and religion.

Once Dimmesdale had chosen death over denial of the legal, religious, and cultural traditions by which he had tried to live and that had so tortured him once he violated them, Hester took Pearl, their daughter, away to Europe to give her a fresh start in a more cosmopolitan environment. But she herself eventually returned to Boston, to her isolated cottage where the city, the forest, and the sea met, and she placed the scarlet letter on her bosom once again and lived the rest of her life with her people and her culture. She knew and still felt that culture's limitations and counseled other women who ran afoul of them. She gave them no hope for change, let alone victory, in this or any foreseeable generation. But she tried to give them tools and strategies for surviving and even contributing, as she had, to a society that rejected them. And when eventually she died, she had herself buried near Dimmesdale, but not too near, because her culture forbade her close relationship to him in life and death.

We celebrate Hester Prynne and are saddened even to think about Arthur Dimmesdale because we imagine she struggled for the right to live as she chose and he did not. But in fact Dimmesdale struggled to lead the life that he had chosen and that his culture sanctioned, and ultimately Hester came round to him and their culture. She agreed that the culture of which they both were members rightly governed them in life and death. Among our great novelists, Hawthorne was rare but not alone in depicting cultural constraints on freedom as good, as the inner voice that worked to control the self-interest and evil in men and women. James Fenimore Cooper, the nation's first great novelist, very consciously sought to define a cultural consensus for white Americans and to place black and red cultures outside and beneath it.

Other novelists, certainly including Mark Twain, Sinclair Lewis, and Philip Roth, showed the power of culture over individuals only to laugh or cry over the absurdity of the results. Twain created Aunt Polly, Judge Thatcher, the widow Douglas, and others as representations of the mid-nineteenth-century cultural expectations of how best to live—working, attending school and church, saving, and investing. Tom resisted the consensus and Huck rejected it entirely in favor of the freedom of the river and the woods. Similarly, Sinclair Lewis's George F. Babbitt, a successful businessman in his forties with a wife, three kids, and a nice house and car, briefly sought freedom outside his well-sanctioned Chamber of Commerce routines, only to rush back to middle-class security when he found "freedom" to be lonely and uncertain. And Philip Roth's Seymour "the Swede" Levov and Coleman Silk gave up their ethnic and racial backgrounds to seek the comforts of white professional success. That the results of their efforts to conform to their culture's expectations were so catastrophic only testifies to the remarkable power of culture to mold and shape, and often misshape, its members.

Americans have been ambivalent about the constraints that culture and religion traditionally placed on freedom and autonomy. But if freedom unbounded by culture threatens anarchy, how are men to live? Jonathan Franzen's *Freedom* posed the question of how to live in modern America. Patty Berglund was determined not to make the mistakes her professional, distant, and unsupportive parents had made. Determined to be a "great mom," she constructed an upper-middle-class bubble for herself and her family and watched it come completely apart. Patty concluded that she "did not know how to live"—but neither did her husband Walter, her son Joey, or Walter's brother Earl. Without values to guide them, the "freedom" that was merely individualism could not sustain them in a world shaped by forces that, as Emerson had warned, were far greater than they could muster. Today, we are suspicious of culture because it may mask congealed injustice, but we feel the absence of consensus on the vital question of how to live.

Fate in human life, unlike chance and luck that strike in a moment, is an insistent pull over a long time in the direction of an inevitable outcome. In some of our greatest fiction, fate produced an obsession that drew forward and sped up pending doom. Others might reason, might search for options, might try to redirect the flow of events, but the person obsessed cannot turn aside, so the end comes on unbidden; fate has its way. Herman Melville's *Moby Dick* was the story of Captain Ahab's impending doom. Ahab knew that fate, not he, controlled events, but he could do no other than play his part. Those around him, especially the chief mate, Starbuck, but the crew more broadly as well, knew and came to, almost chose to, share in Ahab's fate. As frequently happens in the world, the power of one man's personality, of Ahab's monomaniacal focus and determination, buttressed by institutional position, the law, and the usages of the sea, left other men, normal men, average men, with no choice at all. Ahab had fought Moby Dick once before, losing a leg. Other whalers, especially Captain Boomer of the *Samuel Enderby* and Starbuck, advised and even implored Ahab to break off the chase and sail for safety, home, and family—but he could not. For crazed Ahab, Moby Dick, the great white whale, had become the singular personification of evil in the world and, if he were slain, so would evil be.

Singularly obsessed men, men who will do anything to get their way, who will not be moved, to whom law and usage mean nothing, leave no room for the good man, the law-abiding man, the average man, to pursue his modest goals. Melville's Billy Budd, a selfless, good, naturally beloved man, was brought down, unaccountably and unpredictably, by an unnaturally malevolent man. How could the good man prepare defenses against the shrewd and careful sociopath? He could not, so Billy was caught unawares, rendered speechless, unable to defend himself except by striking out. The sociopath fell dead, justly, but the good man hung, also justly, according to the law and custom of the sea. William Faulkner also made the role of fate a principal theme of his stories. Thomas Sutpen was Ahab's only fictional equal in obsession with a goal. Sutpen's obsession, to raise himself from rural southern poverty to command a plantation estate that he might hand forward to his heir, was lost early, though he did not know it until late, when he introduced black blood into his family line. Melville and Faulkner knew and taught that every towering obsession was built on a flaw, a weak spot, a fissure that would be exploited by fate to have its way.

Fiction has always seen class—the full spectrum that runs from upper to lower and from rich to poor—as drawing the dream back from some and holding it out to others. William Dean Howells, both in *The Rise of Silas Lapham* and in *A Hazard of New Fortunes*, and Frank Norris, in *The Octopus*, made the point that wealth challenged and reshaped character. Often, the good character that fueled steady but modest success early in life was compromised by the sharp practices required to build great wealth and the blinding pride that followed having won it. Silas Lapham, Jacob Dryfoos, and Magnus Derrick all achieved wealth that they subsequently lost by misplaced priorities and pride; only Lapham survived, recovered his early character, and lived decently without wealth. On the other end of the economic scale, Upton Sinclair showed in *The Jungle* how poverty systematically crushed Jurgis Rudkus and his immigrant family. In Richard Russo's *Empire Falls*, Francine Whiting's social and economic dominance of the town left others, most notably Miles Roby, fixed in the place she had chosen for them.

However, John Steinbeck's *Grapes of Wrath* remains the classic American novel on class and poverty. The Joad family, white Oklahoma farmers, were systematically ground down and destroyed by the Great Depression and the Dust Bowl. From landowners, hard times reduced them to sharecroppers, and the Depression and mechanization pushed them off the land entirely. Three generations of Joads concluded that California was the promised land, so they sold all the little they had left to finance the trip. The old people died on the way, the weaker members of the family drifted away, and when the survivors reached California they found fear, rejection, and public and private oppression. When finally they rose to defend themselves, Jim Casy was murdered and Tom Joad was forced into hiding. Ma Joad, Tom, and Casy carried Steinbeck's message that family unity and love are all that the poor and dispossessed have in hard times, but that they are no match for the selfish individualism of those determined to protect their advantages. The power of Steinbeck's novel, published near the end of the Depression, was in its destruction of a typical white American family by hard times that they could not understand and certainly could not control.

Race has been an ever-present motif in American fiction. Toni Morrison, the most prominent black novelist and one of the most prominent American novelists of the last several decades, chose to set her novels in slavery and the century following its formal end. Many white Americans take the view that slavery ended a century and a half ago and that therefore plenty of time has passed for blacks to enter the great American working and middle classes and pursue their benefits. Morrison's goal was not to educate whites but to inoculate blacks against the broader culture's self-serving understanding of black options and achievements. She understood, as Baldwin had, that the dominant culture shaped the understandings of both the privileged and the underprivileged of their places, high and low, in the society and the reasons for them.

Morrison's *Beloved* was a powerful novel depicting the soul-shattering impact of slavery and its aftermath on the individuals, families, and communities that experienced it. Understanding the depth and breadth of black oppression in slavery, particularly the impact that the inability to take care of loved ones had on black men and the inability to avoid sexual exploitation had on black women, explained the long and difficult road to wholeness and recovery. As Sethe, Paul D, and Stamp Paid all explained, the vulnerability of black life in slavery, but also in Reconstruction and segregation, taught blacks that their bodies could be soiled, their families scattered, and their lives forfeited at white whim. As Paul D related, blacks learned to love small because to love big, as one must with a child, a wife, a brother, hurt too much when the beloved was sold, stolen, broken, or stained. The emotional, familial, and community pulverization of slavery and its aftermath left blacks, at least in Morrison's novels, unable to love, unable to build and hold together families, for decades. Morrison's goal was to show how decimated blacks were by their American experience to help explain where they stand today. The point was not to blame blacks for their historical or contemporary place in American society, but to put the blame squarely on the whites that did the damage, that wreaked such havoc on nearly defenseless blacks. Richard Wright's *Native Son* and Ralph Ellison's *Invisible Man* depicted a Depression-era America in which blacks could find no foothold. For Bigger Thomas, murder provided the only moment of clarity and control in his young life. And Ellison's invisible man concluded that since the white world would not see him, he would locate himself in the fluidity of black Harlem.

Beyond race, race mixing has provided a related but distinct motif in American fiction. In several of our most prominent novels race was heritable; it bequeathed culture and fate from one generation to the next. Famously, though neither color nor culture was evident on Cooper's Cora, a tincture of black blood sealed her fate. She died so that the fair Alice might live and marry Major Heyward. Cora has often been described as the first example of the "tragic mulatto" in American fiction. In Twain's clever hands, Roxy was beautiful and fair-skinned, just one-sixteenth black, and her son, Chambers, was just one-thirty-second black. Twain made two points: one, that despite their limited black blood, they were slaves by American law and custom; and two, that they were culturally slaves, that they had internalized their status and could be no other. Harriet Beecher Stowe concluded *Uncle Tom's Cabin* by having George and Eliza Harris, escaped slaves light enough to pass in flight if not to live comfortably in pre–Civil War America, denounce the United States as deeply hostile to blacks and choose life in Africa rather than America.

Two more brief stories remind us of Baldwin's point about the ascendancy over all, high and low, of the dominant culture. Currer, the slave mother of the light-skinned octoroon daughters Clotel and Althesa, raised them in antebellum Virginia to attract wealthy white men, so that as "fancy girls," at least in their youth, they might be spared the horrors of the slave quarters and the fields. As slaves, though they were white to the eye, the best place the dominant culture made available to them was that of concubine, so Currer prepared them to take it as she had before them. A century later, another white-to-the-eye American black, Coleman Silk, in Philip Roth's *Human Stain*, concluded that living as an individual in America was only open to whites. When Coleman abandoned his race, his family, and his own past—abandoned the great Negro "we"—to live as a white man and pursue all the opportunities open to white men, his mother warned him that it would not work out as he hoped. And it did not: though he enjoyed nearly a lifetime of success and even acclaim, it all crumbled when he was accused of racism and could not respond, That's ridiculous, I'm black myself, without collapsing and rendering absurd the life story he had constructed.

For most of American history, gender was as powerful a bar to opportunity and accomplishment as race. Well into the twentieth century, the single great and fearsome choice that women could make, a choice that might bring an acknowledged social status and the prospect of economic security, was of a marriage partner. In Cooper's novels, the choice might be well and fortunately made, as when Mabel Dunham chose Jasper Western over Hawkeye, or it might be misplayed, as when Judith, the beauty of Lake Glimmerglass, was so eager that she rendered her virtue suspect. Similarly, in Stephen Crane's *Maggie*, the eponymous character, young and beautiful but subject to a bleak and abusive home life, bet on Pete and lost. Pete offered "a hell of a time." Maggie gave her best but could not hold him and fell quickly and finally to the streets.

The title character in Theodore Dreiser's *Sister Carrie* was one of the most fascinating women in American fiction. A pretty, small-town midwestern girl of eighteen, Carrie Meeber moved to Chicago to find her future. Initially, she stayed with her older sister and her taciturn and unwelcoming husband. Carrie had no plan other than finding a nice job and waiting for something good to happen. Finding no good, pleasant job, she took the same bleak industrial sewing work that so repelled Maggie. Soon her sense that other women had so much more, were loved and cared for by their families, their fathers and husbands, led Carrie into the care of two men, first the charming and good-hearted but complacent and carefree Charles Drouet, and then the infatuated, impetuous, but duplicitous George Hurstwood. Carrie took their help and support, paying the standard price, but always wishing for more, always seeing women who had so much more. Though without plan or drive, she had a talent for singing and the stage, like Helen Ford, and so achieved economic independence, even prosperity, but no rest, no satisfaction. We last see Carrie alone in her opulent New York hotel suite, sitting by her window, rocking and hoping for the satisfaction and completion that will never come.

Finally, even in our more recent novels, women struggle with the question of how to live, especially how to find a balance between family and the broader world. Janice Angstrom, Harry "Rabbit" Angstrom's wife in John Updike's four-volume Rabbit series, grew and matured over the four decades after World War II. She worked until she married, had her first child, and then disintegrated under a bad marriage, immaturity, alcohol, and family tragedy. In middle age, as Harry continued to drift, Janice found herself, her voice, and the motivation to go back to school and build a foundation under her life. Patty Berglund, on the other hand, chose to focus on home and family. She shined while the children were young, but as they outgrew the need for her constant guidance, she was lost. She realized that she had lived her American Dream, gotten exactly the upper-middle-class life she had wanted, but it left her empty, bereft, and asking how to live. Rounded pictures of female life and achievement are rare in our great fiction.

The Public on Its Dream

We turn now to polling on the American Dream and then to the best data available on how class, race, ethnicity, and gender structure access to opportunity in America. In the wake of the Great Recession, President Obama was as insistent as any president since Franklin Roosevelt that the American Dream was slipping away from too many. As we shall see, Americans still believe in the dream but have become increasingly wary and despondent. Their anxieties arise from both old and new concerns. The old concern is the long-standing fact that women and minorities have markedly less access to the American Dream than white men. The new concern is that even among white men, income inequality is increasing and social mobility is decreasing.

As we enter the twenty-first century, we are at one of those points in American history, not unlike the early years of the previous century, when many Americans feel ill at ease, vulnerable, and worried that the society provides fewer opportunities and less mobility than it once did.[8]

Recent surveys uniformly find Americans still committed to the belief that hard work remains the path to the American Dream, but they are increasingly doubtful that the dream will be available to future generations. Surveys suggest a continuing surface commitment to the American Dream but more doubt and fear beneath the surface.

The Gallup organization has for more than half a century asked Americans whether they were satisfied with "the future facing you and your family." Responses have risen and fallen within a fairly narrow range. When the question was first asked in 1963, 64 percent declared themselves satisfied, 25 percent said dissatisfied, and 11 percent had no opinion. The percent satisfied fell as low as 53 percent in 1973 and rose to as high as 80 percent in 1991, but by 2013 responses mirrored those of 1963. In 2013, 63 percent (compared to 64 percent in 1963) were satisfied, 34 percent (compared to 25 percent in 1963) were dissatisfied, and just 3 percent (compared to 11 percent in 1963) had no opinion. While satisfied respondents dropped just 1 percent in the half century between 1963 and 2013, "no opinion" responses dropped 8 percent, and all nine points went into the dissatisfied category.[9] Nonetheless, almost two-thirds of respondents were satisfied with their family's prospects.

Similarly, the highly regarded General Social Survey posed the following question two dozen times between 1973 and 2012: "Some people say that people get ahead by their own hard work, while others say that lucky breaks or help from other people are more important. Which do you think is most important?" By large and steady margins, respondents have said "hard work" was more important than "lucky breaks or help." In fact, hard work has been seen as more important in between 60 and 70 percent of responses; a mix of hard work and luck, in from 20 to 30 percent of responses; and luck and contacts alone, in just 10 to 15 percent of responses. Across four decades, an average of 66 percent have responded that hard work was more important, 22 percent have responded a mix of hard work and luck, and just 12 percent have said luck and help.[10] The Opportunity Agenda aggregated twenty polls done by Gallup, CBS/*New York Times*, the Henry J. Kaiser Family Foundation, and the Pew Research Center between 1965 and 2014 asking respondents, "In your opinion, which is generally more often to blame if a person is poor—lack of effort on their own part or circumstances beyond their control?" During the 1960s, more Americans blamed failure on lack of effort than on circumstances beyond a person's control.

But since 1980, it has been more common to blame circumstances, and since 2000, it has been increasingly common. In 2014, 50 percent blamed circumstances, while just 35 percent blamed lack of effort on the part of individuals.[11]

Like Harry and Janice Angstrom and Walter and Patty Berglund, parents worry that they have had it better than their children will. In 2013, Ronald Brownstein of *National Journal,* in a piece entitled "The American Dream under Threat," reported on an Allstate/*National Journal* Heartland Monitor Poll in which 79 percent of 1,000 adult respondents felt that it was better to be a child when they had been (meaning earlier) than today. Just 16 percent thought it would be better to be a child today.[12] In summer 2014, just 42 percent of respondents thought that their life chances were better than their parents' had been, while 32 percent thought that they were worse. Even more ominously, a May 2012 Gallup/*USA Today* poll reported that just 40 percent of respondents were satisfied that the opportunities available to the next generation would be better than theirs had been, while 58 percent thought that they would be worse."[13] Similarly, an Associated Press/NORC poll from January 2014 of 1,141 adults reported that 54 percent of respondents thought America had gotten worse since 1970, while just 29 percent thought it had gotten better. Looking forward to 2050, again, 54 percent thought the country would get worse, while just 23 percent thought that it would get better.[14] Finally, *New York Times* columnist Frank Bruni presented a *Wall Street Journal*/NBC News poll showing that 76 percent of American adults were skeptical that their children would do better than they had and that 60 percent thought America was a nation in decline.[15]

The General Social Survey has asked since 1978 whether Americans believe that government ought to reduce income inequality. In every survey more respondents have answered yes than no, but the proportions have barely budged over that time. In 1978, 48 percent responded yes and in 2014 46 percent did. In every survey from 1978 to 2014, between 40 and 50 percent said government should act to reduce inequality, while between 26 and 39 percent have said no. Not surprisingly though, Democrats are more favorable than Republicans to government action to reduce inequality, with independents between Democrats and Republicans but closer to Democrats. In 1978, 55 percent of Democrats, 48 percent of independents, and 37 percent of Republicans favored government action to reduce inequality. In 2014,

60 percent of Democrats, 51 percent of independents, and 24 percent of Republicans favored government action. As income inequality has increased, so has the partisan split on what, if anything, to do about it. Again, not surprisingly, Democrats, the young, and minorities favor government action, while Republicans, older people, and whites favor depending on market forces.[16]

Economic Inequality and Social Mobility in America

The American Dream has always been premised on the idea, really the promise and commitment, that anyone, by dint of developed abilities and hard work, could succeed and thrive. Some have always been wealthier than others, so obviously some children were born into more privileged families and thus had advantages that others did not have. But so long as one might start poor and through talent and effort rise to security and even prosperity—so long as there was social mobility—Americans have been and largely remain willing to accept and even at times celebrate income inequality. However, we have rarely experienced both rising income inequality and falling economic and social mobility at the same time. We have had this noxious combination now for some decades, but it has only recently begun to press on the public mind.

Social scientists and journalists have arrived at the place toward which novelists have long pointed. Harvard economist Joseph Stiglitz, the former chairman of President Obama's Council of Economic Advisers and winner of the Nobel Prize in Economics, wrote that in "the Horatio Alger stories . . . it was by dint of the individual's own effort that the hero . . . pulled himself out of poverty. They may contain a grain of truth, but it is only a grain."[17] Prominent University of North Carolina sociologist Arne Kalleberg noted, "People are now, more than ever, 'on their own.' . . . This situation is analogous to the ideology of Social Darwinism, popularized by Herbert Spencer and William Graham Sumner at the turn of the twentieth century, which applied Darwin's idea of the survival of the fittest to the economic and social realm."[18] When leading scholars feel the need to look back to the middle and late nineteenth century for analogies to the contemporary period, you can be pretty sure that big changes are afoot.

As the public's attention has turned to focus on rising inequality and falling mobility, the politician's promise—Elect me and I will restore the dream—has drawn increasing skepticism. Amy Traub and Heather C. McGee of *Demos*, in an article entitled "State of the American Dream," wrote, "Over recent decades, many political leaders have failed to reckon with a basic fact of the new economic era—for millions of Americans, no amount of individual effort or self-improvement or thrift can guarantee a secure middle-class life. The American social contract—a promise of opportunity and security for those who act responsibly—is fundamentally broken."[19] Moreover, Donald L. Bartlett and James B. Steele, in a series of books over several decades including *The Betrayal of the American Dream* (2013), have declared, "The dismal fact is that for tens of millions of middle-class Americans, as well as for the working poor who hope to achieve that status, the American dream is over."[20] These stark statements reflect the cumulative impact of four decades of economic change that have seen the related phenomena of rising economic inequality, declining social mobility, and a shrinking middle class.

Income inequality has risen and fallen in long waves over the course of American history. Very broadly, America was more egalitarian than Europe from early colonization through the end of the nineteenth century. French economist Thomas Piketty's prominent book *Capital in the Twenty-First Century* concluded, "The most striking fact is that the United States has become noticeably more inegalitarian than . . . Europe as a whole, . . . from the turn of the twentieth century until now, even though the United States was more egalitarian at the beginning of this period."[21] More important, Piketty and others have shown that the increase in American inequality from 1900 to today has not been smooth. Rather, inequality rose through the first two decades of the century, sharply in the 1920s, before falling in the 1930s and 1940s and moderating from the 1950s through the early 1970s. After the long moderation, income inequality began again to increase in the 1970s and has continued through the current day. Income inequality is as high today as it was in the 1920s, and that is the basis for the concern that we see in polls and academic studies.[22]

Moreover, as many have noted, the wage gains for a quarter century after World War II were widely shared—the old adage, A rising tide lifts all boats, was true. Income gains were spread across all classes; the rich got richer, but so did the poor, and the middle class expanded. Since the 1970s, the tide has continued to rise, though more slowly, but only the big boats have risen, and the yachts have risen the most.[23] As Traub and McGee summarized, productivity gains—the increase in the value produced by the average worker in a unit of time, such as an hour or a year—stopped going to workers in the 1970s. They wrote, "While productivity increased 80 percent in the three decades between 1979 and 2011, the inflation-adjusted wages of the median worker grew just 6 percent."[24] Worse, income inequality has continued to grow in recent years. Between 2010 and 2013, the incomes of the most affluent 10 percent grew by 10 percent, the middle ranges were stagnant, and the incomes of the bottom 20 percent of families fell by 8 percent.[25]

The well-respected Pew Research Center, using household income data from the U.S. Census Bureau, highlighted the rise of income inequality, the polarization of incomes, and the shrinking of the middle class since 1970. Between 1970 and 2015, households defined as upper income increased from 14 percent of all households to 21 percent, while households defined as lower income increased from 25 percent to 29 percent. Households defined as middle class shrunk from 61 percent of all households to 50 percent in 2015. One might be somewhat sanguine because though middle-income families have decreased, upper-income families have increased, but analyzing these numbers by race, as we will do more intensively below, is sobering. Only 7 percent of black and Hispanic families are upper income, with the remainder being divided equally between middle- and lower-income households.[26]

If the American Dream accepts income inequality so long as economic mobility is possible, what happens to the dream and to people's confidence in it when mobility declines? The claim that America is distinctively open to competitive gains, to moving from low income to higher and even to high income, has been the basis for decrying government action against rising inequality. Declining mobility undercuts the claim that market forces will limit income inequality. Without mobility, hard work and doing all the right things at the right time and in the right way are less sure to bring advancement. Reduced mobility means that more and more effort, greater and greater talent, well applied—eventually only extraordinary talent and herculean effort—will power upward mobility. Not surprisingly then, Stiglitz declared, "There's no use pretending. In spite of the enduring belief that Americans enjoy greater social mobility than their European counterparts, America is no longer the land of opportunity. . . . Today's reality is that for a large segment of the population that dream has now vanished."[27]

Economists have sought to measure what Timothy Noah has called "income heritability"—the relationship of parents' income to their children's income. Most income heritability studies have been based on the University of Michigan's Panel Study of Income Dynamics (PSID), U.S. Census Bureau and Social Security data, and Organization for Economic Co-operation and Development (OECD) data. Broadly, the PSID data cover from the early 1950s to recent years and so capture three or four generations. As data and analytical techniques have improved, it has become increasingly clear that parents' income strongly affects the income of the next generation. University of Michigan economist Gary Solon and his collaborators have been at the center of this inquiry. In 1992, Solon published an important paper, "Intergenerational Income Mobility in the United States," using PSID data. Previous research had purported to show that just 20 percent of the next generation's income was determined by or inherited from their parents. Solon's analysis showed income heritability to be at least 40 percent, and others have used U.S. Census Bureau and Social Security data to claim 60 percent. Clearly, the more income heritability, the less room for talent and hard work to fuel upward mobility in the next generation.

Finally, Timothy Noah described a 2007 OECD study showing that the United States did not have higher economic mobility than other wealthy nations—as the dream had always proclaimed. In fact, among a dozen advanced industrial nations—the United States, Canada, several European nations, and Australia—only two, Italy and the United Kingdom, allowed less intergenerational mobility than the United States. The rest—France, Spain, Germany, Sweden, Canada, Finland, Norway, Australia, and Denmark—offered more mobility, some two or three times as much. Noah summarized the findings of the OECD study and closed with an important, though rhetorical, question: "Clearly the U.S. lags the other industrialized democracies in offering opportunities for upward mobility. Why do Americans resist knowing that?"[28] Sociologist Mark Robert Rank and his colleagues, in a book entitled *Chasing the American Dream: Understanding What Shapes Our Fortunes* (2014), as if speaking directly to Noah, wrote, "And here may be the reason. As long as we believe that everyone has a fair shot at the American Dream, then if you do not succeed, it must be your fault, rather than the fault of society. . . . It provides a justification of the status quo. . . . It also provides a rationale for inaction among those . . . whose affluence may seem threatened if policies were enacted to truly make the Dream accessible to all."[29]

Half a dozen major studies in Europe and the United States have sought to describe what declining mobility means, who suffers from it, and what accounts for it. The Pew Charitable Trust's Economic Mobility Project has reported that almost two-thirds of children raised in families in the upper fifth of incomes stay in the upper two-fifths of income. Similarly, two-thirds of those raised in the bottom fifth of incomes remain in the bottom two-fifths. Only among the middle fifth of families does mobility remain fluid. Pew found that 23 percent of the middle fifth stay in the middle fifth, while about 36 percent move up and 41 percent move down. The sobering conclusion is that higher- and lower-income families are sticky, holding the next generation at their respective levels, while children of middle-income families are a bit more likely to drift down than up. Wealthy families transmit advantages—better nutrition, education, and health care—that promote the next generation's ability to remain in the upper-income categories. Poor families transmit their debilities, and as a result, children struggle to do much better than their parents.

Perhaps the most intriguing economic-mobility research program now under way is that of Harvard's, now Stanford's, Raj Chetty and his colleagues on the influence of place or context on opportunity and future income. Chetty and his colleagues used the earnings records of millions of families with children who moved from one city to another. Cities with better opportunity and higher mobility for poor children included San Diego, Salt Lake City, and Fairfax, Virginia. Cities with less opportunity and mobility for poor children included Atlanta, Los Angeles, Tampa, and Austin. Large urban centers with concentrated minority populations seemed to be particularly difficult environments in which to break out of poverty. More specifically, Chetty and his colleagues, in a piece entitled "Where Is the Land of Opportunity? The Geography of Intergenerational Mobility in the United States" found "High mobility areas have (1) less residential segregation, (2) less income inequality, (3) better primary schools, (4) greater social capital, and (5) greater family stability."[30] Reversing the polarity of the sentence just above will give an immediate and familiar sense of the cities and neighborhoods that are most difficult to escape. Chetty and his colleagues show that a child born in the bottom fifth of the income distribution has a 7.8 percent chance of reaching the top fifth in the United States as a whole. But "the probability that a child reaches the top quintile of the national income distribution starting from a family in the bottom quintile is 4.4% in Charlotte but 12.9% in San Jose."[31]

Race in the American Future

W. E. B. Du Bois, the prominent black sociologist and social activist, declared in 1900, when the yoke of Jim Crow segregation was still firmly fixed on the nation's neck, "The problem of the twentieth century is the problem of the color line, the question as to how far differences of race . . . will hereafter be made the basis of denying . . . to over half the world the right of sharing to utmost ability the opportunities and privileges of modern civilization."[32] Strikingly, James Truslow Adams, the noted historian who in 1931 popularized the phrase "the American Dream," wrote, "After a generation or two, these people [white ethnic immigrants] can be absorbed, whereas the negro cannot."[33] Differences of race and gender were and remain both obvious and permanent and, therefore, can be the basis for resistant and hardy forms of discrimination.

Americans of all races and ethnicities are aware of the nation's history of racial discrimination. While most minorities believe that racial and ethnic discrimination are real and present concerns, a majority of whites believe that they are historical vestiges and that little or no "white privilege" exists today. Unimpeachable data show that black concerns are well grounded. In an article entitled "The Black-White Economic Divide in 5 Charts," CNN mined U.S. Census Bureau, Federal Reserve, and Bureau of Labor Statistics (BLS) data to highlight economic disparities between blacks and whites.[34] CNN was interested only in the most recent data, but the Census Bureau, Federal Reserve, and BLS have collected employment, income, wealth, and poverty data for decades. For example, census data on median household income by race and ethnicity go back to the late 1960s. Soberingly, black and Hispanic median household income as a percent of white median household income has been glacially stable over the past half century. In 1970, black median household income was 58 percent of white median household income, and in 2014 it was 59 percent. Hispanic median household income in 1970 was 74 percent of white median household income, and by 2014 it had fallen to 71 percent.[35] Progress?

Median household wealth by race and ethnicity tells an even more striking story. According to the Federal Reserve's Survey of Consumer Finance, over the past three decades, the median net worth of white households has averaged about ten times that of black and Hispanic households. In 1983, the net worth of white households averaged about $100,000, while black and Hispanic households averaged about $10,000. In 1989, white households had seventeen times the wealth of black households and fourteen times the wealth of Hispanic households. The difference in net worth shrank through the 1990s and into the early part of the twenty-first century before it began to grow again during the Great Recession. In 2013, white median household wealth ($141,900) was thirteen times black household wealth ($11,000) and ten times Hispanic household wealth ($13,700).[36] Big differences, little movement.

Most Americans have the largest share of their net worth in home equity. About 72 percent of whites own their own home, while only about 45 percent of blacks and Hispanics do. Moreover, the collapse of the housing market during the Great Recession hit minorities hardest: "nearly 8 percent of blacks and Latinos who got home loans or refinanced between 2005 and 2008 ultimately lost their homes to foreclosure between 2007 and 2009, compared with only 4.5 percent of non-Hispanic whites."[37] Lower rates of home ownership and more vulnerability to economic downturns limit wealth accumulation among blacks and Hispanics.

Similar dynamics are evident in unemployment and poverty figures by race and ethnicity. BLS data going back three decades, from 1986 through 2015, report an average unemployment rate for whites of 5.4 percent, for blacks of 11.4 percent, and for Hispanics of 8.5 percent. Moreover, while the annual unemployment rate for whites never reached 9 percent during these decades, it has exceeded 10 percent for blacks in twenty-one of the thirty years between 1986 and 2015. So it is more than fair to say that black America has faced economic conditions worse than the Great Recession almost perpetually over the past thirty years. The 2015 unemployment rate, after more than six years of recovery from the Great Recession, was 4.6 percent for whites, 6.6 percent for Hispanics, and 9.7 percent for blacks.[38]

It should be no surprise at all that poverty rates vary dramatically by race and ethnicity. Excellent data on poverty by race and ethnicity go back to 1973. Over the forty-three years between 1973 and 2015, the average white poverty rate has been 8.7 percent, while it has been 28.9 percent for blacks and 25.4 percent for Hispanics. The poverty rate for whites reached 10 percent or more five times during this period, with 10.8 percent in 1983 being the highest. The lowest rate of black poverty was 22.5 percent in 2000, and the highest was 35.7 percent in 1983.

Among Hispanics, the lowest poverty rate was 20.6 percent in 2006, and the highest was 30.7 in 1994.

Poverty rates for children by race and ethnicity are even more adverse for minorities. Between 1974 and 2014, 11.4 percent of white children lived in poverty, while 39.7 percent of black children and 34.1 percent of Hispanic children did. The high for white children was 14.8 percent in 1983, while for black children was over 40 percent in every year from 1975 through 1995, with the highest being 47.6 percent in 1982. For Hispanic children, poverty rates ranged between a low of 36.2 percent and a high of 41.5 percent in every year between 1982 and 1997.[39] Clearly, poverty rates that would be thought well beyond catastrophic for white families and children have been the norm for minority families and children for as long as good records have been kept.

Finally, a study by the Institute for Assets and Social Policy (IASP) published in 2013 asked what caused the differences in wealth by race and ethnicity. The IASP study used the University of Michigan PSID data discussed earlier. The study found that two-thirds of the large and growing wealth gap between whites and blacks was explained by home ownership (more whites than blacks own homes and build equity), work and earnings (blacks make less and are unemployed more often and for longer than whites), college education (more whites go and graduate), and family financial support and inheritance (fewer blacks inherit, and they inherit less). The authors of the IASP study argue that policy initiatives addressing each of these areas might change the pattern of results, but the long stability of the income, wealth, unemployment, and poverty results suggest that change will be slow, if it occurs at all.[40]

Gender and the American Dream

Women now make up just over 47 percent of the U.S. labor force and earn about 80 percent of what men do. While single women have participated in the labor force at approximately the same rate as men for several decades, married women moved toward parity only in the late twentieth century. In 2013, 58.9 percent of the nation's married women were employed or actively seeking work. More women with children under age eighteen (74.8 percent) were in the labor force, and more than 80 percent of adult women with college degrees were employed in 2013.[41] These figures make clear that most women work, and given the stagnation in middle- and lower-income earnings, it seems safe to conclude that most families depend on women's wages, even when they are not the primary wage earner. Women's wages often provide the difference between working-class and middle- or upper-middle-class status for their families.

Women have made important income gains relative to men, and there are good reasons to believe that these gains will continue. The wage gap between women and men who work full-time year-round has been shrinking slowly for more than half a century. In 1960, women made 60.7 percent of what men made. These numbers remained essentially flat until 1980 and then began to rise. By 1990, women made 71.6 percent of what men made. Since 1990, a painfully slow rise of about one-third of 1 percent per year brought women's pay to 80 percent of men's pay. Women also made some progress, though not great progress, in breaking into the executive suites. Women now head twenty-five of the Fortune 500 companies, 5 percent, and hold 17 percent of corporate board seats.[42]

Increases in women's educational attainment have fueled the advance in earnings and promotion. Journalist David Leonhardt has reported, "The proportion of women earning a four-year college degree has jumped more than 75 percent over the last quarter-century. . . . Median adjusted female earnings are up almost 35 percent over the same span, census data show—while male earnings, incredibly, haven't risen at all."[43] Among young workers age twenty-five to thirty-two, 38 percent of women compared to 31 percent of men hold a bachelor's degree. Among young workers age eighteen to thirty-two, women made 93 percent of what men made, far better than the 80 percent made by all female workers, but the history even of recent decades suggests they will fall back as they marry, start families, and confront the dilemma of combining work and childcare and childrearing.[44] A 2014 study using 2012 BLS data reported that while never-married women made 96 percent of what never-married men made, married women with children made just 76 percent of what similarly positioned men made.[45]

Historically, the assumption was common that much of the pay gap was produced by women's choices, such as choosing teaching and social work over law and finance. But research by Harvard's Claudia Goldin found that less than one-sixth of the gap for all women and about one-third for college graduates was explained by professional choices. Most of the gap was attributable to hours worked, especially in highly paid, high-pressure occupations like law, medicine, finance, and accounting.

Men were more inclined and more free to work longer hours, while women often had greater household and childrearing responsibilities. Especially when children came, cultural assumptions about which career would be prioritized (the husband's) and who would do the bulk of the housework and childcare (the wife) asserted themselves, often against the wife's assumptions and hopes. Remarkably, data and experiments show that husbands get a pay bump when a child is born (6 percent), on the assumption it will make them more grounded and dedicated, while the wife takes a hit (4 percent) for each child, on the assumption that she will be more distracted. In one experiment, in which a job application included a line about membership in a parent-teacher association, women who indicated membership were called back half as often as women in a control group who did not provide that information, while men indicating membership were called back slightly more often.[46]

The pressure that marriage and children put on women's careers has generated a number of responses. In the past, well-educated women who wanted to prioritize their careers would often delay marriage and children into their forties and sometimes beyond. Over the past three decades, high-performing women have been more likely to marry, but the number delaying childbirth into their forties has doubled from 10 to 20 percent.[47] But the more common response to the pressures of work and home once children are born has been for mothers to leave the workforce. The proportion of women in the workforce rose throughout the second half of the twentieth century, reaching a high point of 60 percent in 1999 before slowly declining to 57 percent in 2013. While the decline was small, women's workforce participation in other advanced industrial nations, traditionally lower than in the United States, continued to rise and now has surpassed that of the United States. Most attribute the rising labor participation rates in other wealthy nations and falling rates in the United States to differences in public policy. The U.S. policy on parental leave requires large companies to give three months of unpaid leave at the birth of a child. Other wealthy nations require a year or more, most of it paid, and high-quality, subsidized childcare is available, so that women can confidently return to work. The United States does not, so female labor participation rates have fallen.

Finally, one of the most interesting comments on the roles of men and women in the workplace and at home has come from Brookings Institution researchers Richard V. Reeves and Isabel V. Sawhill. They contend that for decades women have been becoming more like men in terms of educational attainment and employment. Now, they argue, it is time for men to become more like women in assuming a more equal share—an equal share—in home and childcare.[48] The future, while still requiring some strong backs, will demand more and stronger minds, and women are excelling in education and their income is rising. Addressing women's ability to succeed comfortably at home and in the workplace over the course of their lifetimes will be a critical social and economic requirement of the twenty-first century.

Education as Preparation for Work and Life

Most Americans, from top political leaders to average citizens, believe that high-quality education, and particularly access to higher education, is the key to economic success and personal fulfillment in the modern world. Yet the rising cost of a college education, especially at the nation's top universities, and the debt burden that many graduates carry upon leaving college have raised deep concerns. In fact, of greater concern are high dropout rates, which leave too many students with debts but no degree.

Two of the most important books on education history and policy published in the past ten years were *The Race between Education and Technology* (2008), by Harvard economists Claudia Goldin and Lawrence Katz, and *Degrees of Inequality: How the Politics of Higher Education Sabotaged the American Dream* (2014), by Cornell political scientist Suzanne Mettler. Goldin and Katz explained how American education policy and results fueled economic growth over most of American history and why they do no longer. Mettler explained the elements of contemporary education policy and performance that produced a two-tier system of higher education that advantaged the children of the prosperous and burdened the children of the poor.

Goldin and Katz, as mentioned, are economists, so not surprisingly, they told a story of investment, public and private, and of supply and demand. Over the second half of the nineteenth century and the early decades of the twentieth century, education through high school increasingly became the norm, and after World War II college began to be the expectation of the middle class and up. The United States led the world both in educational attainment and in economic growth and prosperity over this long period. But Goldin and Katz report that during the last quarter of the twentieth century and the early years of the twenty-first century, educational attainment stalled, and "many other nations . . . have caught up to and some have even surpassed the high education levels that had once been set by the United States."[49]

Goldin and Katz contend that it was the high education levels of the first three-quarters of the twentieth century and the strong supply of well-educated workers to the labor force that produced the rising wages and increased economic equality of the mid-twentieth century. They argued, "The evolution of the wage structure reflects, at least in part, a race between the growth in the demand for skills driven by technological advances and the growth in the supply of skills driven by demographic change, educational investment choices, and immigration." The supply-and-demand argument stressed that so long as college was cheap and accessible, well-educated workers were in adequate supply. "During the great expansion of college-going from the 1950s to the 1970s, tuition at a public university was about 4 percent of the median family income. . . . Tuition at public universities increased to more than 10 percent of median family income by 2005." As costs increased, college attendance and graduation numbers plateaued, the supply of highly educated workers tightened, and the income differentials between those with and those without a bachelor's degree widened. As a result, "the last quarter of the twentieth-century and the early twenty-first century have been distinguished by exploding inequality, chiefly at the upper end of the income distribution."[50]

Moreover, too many scholars and analysts to count have made the argument and, more important, have shown with data that ours is a two-tiered educational system—from preschool through graduate school—that advantages the privileged and disadvantages the underprivileged. As *New York Times* columnist Nicholas Kristof wrote, "We have constructed an educational system, dependent on local property taxes, that provides great schools for the rich kids in the suburbs who need the least help, and broken, dangerous schools for inner-city children who desperately need a helping hand. Too often, America's educational system amplifies not opportunity but inequality."[51] Mettler made a similar point in *Degrees of Inequality*. Mettler pointed out that "students from high income backgrounds increasingly attend elite private universities and colleges and the flagship public universities—those with national and international reputations."[52] Another *New York Times* columnist, Frank Bruni, reported details that illustrate Mettler's point: "In 2011, . . . roughly 75 percent of the students at the 200 most highly rated colleges come from families in the top quartile of income. . . . Only 5 percent come from families in the bottom quartile." He concluded, "We're sorting students by class . . . becoming more and more stratified."[53]

An article by Paul Tough, "Who Gets to Graduate," highlighted the two-tiered opportunity structure of American higher education and the consequences of success and failure in navigating college. Tough wrote, "Rich kids graduate; poor and working class kids don't. . . . About a quarter of college freshmen born into the bottom half of the income distribution will manage to collect a bachelor's degree by age 24, while almost 90 percent . . . born into the top income quartile will . . . finish their degree."[54] Completing a four-year college degree more than triples the odds of students from low-income families moving into the top half of the income distribution. David Leonhardt of the *New York Times* reported that college degrees have become increasingly valuable. In the early 1980s college graduates made 64 percent more an hour than people without degrees; that had increased to 85 percent by the late 1990s, to 89 percent in 2008, and to 98 percent in 2013.[55] Wages for those without a college degree have been flat, while those for the college educated have been lifting off.

Fundamentally, one's experience in the educational system has a very great deal to do with how one enters and moves through the job market and occupational structure. The fortunate student, emerging from a secure and prosperous family into good schools and then good colleges, will enter the upper half of the occupational hierarchy and will, with some hard work and good fortune, advance from there. The unfortunate student, emerging from a broken, insecure, or impoverished family into poor schools and an unforgiving job market, will find it difficult to do more than just get by. The amount and quality of educational preparation determines how well Americans do economically, and class determines what educational opportunities are available. While the American Dream still beckons our well-educated elites, it mocks most others.

Looking Forward

Few nations have a dream, "the promise of American life" in Herbert Croly's wonderful phrase, as well worth protecting and nurturing as do we Americans. It may be that we were simply fortunate that our Founding occurred in a time and place where men could afford to be generous. With a continent stretching westward beyond the imagination and with too few men and women to take advantage of it, the poor could command good wages and a better future, and the newly arrived were valued even if not always welcomed. But in our haste to control and benefit from nature's bounty, breathtaking injustices were committed in the names of civilization and progress.

Today, America is the wealthiest and most powerful nation that the world has ever known. Yet other great nations, spectacularly wealthy and powerful in their day too, fell from their high places. Perhaps this is precisely the right time to ask how America can maintain and build upon its unprecedented wealth and strength. The answer, almost certainly, is by being ever truer to our initial values and aspirations—to make "life, liberty, and the pursuit of happiness" the right and real possession of every American. If all our children are well cared for and well educated, and every American adult—irrespective of gender or color—has the opportunity to compete for and enjoy the riches of this society, we would secure and extend our primacy among the nations of the world. No nation has ever harvested the full potential and creativity of all its citizens. If we were to do so, we would truly be "a shining city on a hill" and a light unto the nations.

Still, we know that our society as it is currently ordered does not meet these high standards. Even today, women and minorities make less than white men make. Glass ceilings keep all but a very few men of color and women of all colors out of the executive suite. Breaking these barriers, releasing these talents, is the great social and moral task of the twenty-first century. The special responsibility of social and political leaders is to work toward a future in which all can find an honorable place. This is asking a very great deal, but really it is simply asking that we continue to work toward Mr. Jefferson's self-evident truths "that all men are created equal, that they are endowed by their Creator with certain unalienable Rights, that among these are Life, Liberty, and the pursuit of Happiness." We will have redeemed Jefferson's promise when the American Dream of liberty, equality, and opportunity is the patrimony—the living inheritance—of every American.

Notes

Preface

1. Merriam-Webster's online dictionary defines a Greek chorus as "a chorus in a classical Greek play typically serving to formulate, express, and comment on the moral issue that is raised by the dramatic action or to express an emotion appropriate to each stage of the dramatic conflict" (http://www.merriam-web ster.com/dictionary/Greek%20chorus). In the fifth century BCE, Aeschylus, Sophocles, Euripides, and others used twelve to fifteen persons, usually dressed alike and wearing identical masks, to interpret the action on the stage and the often-hidden goals and motives of the actors. Similarly, while political and social elites often tout the promise of the American Dream, novelists just as often tell stories in which men and women seem to have no path to security and prosperity.

2. Kurt Vonnegut, *Slaughterhouse-Five* (London: Vintage Books, 2000; first published 1969), 134.

3. Lawrence Buell, *The Dream of the Great American Novel* (Cambridge, Mass.: Harvard University Press, 2014), 18, 111.

4. Azar Nafisi, *The Republic of Imagination* (New York: Viking Press, 2014), 31.

5. Mark Robert Rank, Thomas A. Hirschl, and Kirk A. Foster, *Chasing the American Dream: Understanding What Shapes Our Fortunes* (New York: Oxford University Press, 2014), 109.

Chapter 1: The Ambiguity of the Dream in American History

1. Barack Obama, "A More Perfect Union: The Race Speech," Philadelphia, Pennsylvania, March 18, 2008, http://obamaspeeches.com/E05-Barack-Obama -A-More-Perfect-Union-the-Race-Speech-Philadelphia-PA-March-18-2008.htm.

2. Louis Hartz, *The Founding of New Societies* (New York: Harcourt, Brace and World, 1964), 3.

3. G. K. Chesterton, *What I Saw in America* (New York: Dodd, Mead, 1922), 7.

4. Gunnar Myrdal, *An American Dilemma: The Negro Problem and Modern Democracy* (New York: Harper and Brothers, 1944), 1:4, 8.

5. Samuel P. Huntington, *American Politics: The Promise of Disharmony* (Cambridge, Mass.: Harvard University Press, 1981), 14–15.

6. Seymour Martin Lipset, *American Exceptionalism: A Double-Edged Sword* (New York: W. W. Norton, 1996), 19.

7. Rogers M. Smith, *Civic Ideals: Conflicting Visions of Citizenship in U.S. History* (New Haven: Yale University Press, 1997), 2.

8. All quoted in John E. Schwarz and Thomas J. Volgy, *The Forgotten Americans: Thirty Million Working Poor in the Land of Opportunity* (New York: W. W. Norton, 1992), 8.

9. Quoted in Jennifer Hochschild, *Facing Up to the American Dream: Race, Class, and the Soul of the Nation* (Princeton: Princeton University Press, 1995), 21.

10. J. Hector St. John de Crevecoeur, *Letters from an American Farmer* (New York: E. P. Dutton, 1957; first published 1782), 57, in letter 2, "What Is an American," 35–81; Henry Adams, *History of the United States during the Administration of Thomas Jefferson* (New York: Charles Schribner's Sons, 1889), 1:173–174.

11. Walter Lippmann, *Drift and Mastery* (Madison: University of Wisconsin Press, 1985; first published 1914), 103.

12. James Truslow Adams, *The Epic of America* (Boston: Little, Brown, 1931), 404.

13. Hochschild, *Facing Up to the American Dream*, 4.

14. John E. Schwarz, *Illusions of Opportunity: The American Dream in Question* (New York: W. W. Norton, 1997), 16–18.

15. Jane Flax, *The American Dream in Black and White: The Clarence Thomas Hearings* (Ithaca, N.Y.: Cornell University Press, 1998), 2.

16. Hochschild, *Facing Up to the American Dream*, 26.

17. Smith, *Civic Ideals*, 2.

18. Derrick Bell, *Faces at the Bottom of the Well: The Permanence of Racism* (New York: Basic Books, 1992), x.

19. Harriet Beecher Stowe, *Uncle Tom's Cabin; or, Life among the Lowly* (New York: Alfred A. Knopf, Everyman's Library, 1994; first published 1852), 25.

20. Ibid., 96.

21. Ibid., 126–127, 130.

22. Ibid., 216, 222, 425.

23. Ibid., 476.

24. Lori Merish, *Sentimental Materialism: Gender, Commodity Culture, and Nineteenth-Century American Literature* (Durham, N.C.: Duke University Press, 2000), 163.

25. Henry Adams, *Democracy: An American Novel* (New York: Modern Library, 2003), 8–9.

26. Ibid., 172.

27. Ibid., 185.

28. Ibid., 47, 79, 171.

29. Ibid., 186, 189.

30. Ibid., 205.

31. Vernon Parrington, *Main Currents of American Thought* (New York: Harcourt, Brace, Jovanovich, 1927), 3:285.

32. Paul Berman, *A Tale of Two Utopias: The Political Journey of the Generation of 1968* (New York: W. W. Norton, 1996), 186.

33. Pauline Maier, *American Scripture: Making of the Declaration of Independence* (New York: Alfred A. Knopf, 1998), 214.

34. Robert William Fogel, *The Fourth Great Awakening and the Future of Egalitarianism* (Chicago: University of Chicago Press, 2000), 8–9.

Chapter 2: The Promise and Peril of Life in the New World

1. Andrew Burstein, *Sentimental Democracy: The Evolution of America's Romantic Self-Image* (New York: Hill and Wang, 1999), 258; see also Joseph J. Ellis, *Founding Brothers: The Revolutionary Generation* (New York: Alfred A. Knopf, 2001), 109.

2. D. H. Lawrence, "Fenimore Cooper's Leatherstocking Novels," chap. 5 in *Studies in Classic American Literature* (first published 1923), 11, http://xroads.virginia.edu/~hyper/LAWRENCE/dhlcho5.htm.

3. Quoted in Edmund S. Morgan, ed., *Puritan Political Ideas: 1558–1794* (Indianapolis, Ind.: Bobbs-Merrill, 1965), 91–92.

4. Quoted in ibid., 168–169.

5. Zachary Karabell, *A Visionary Nation: Four Centuries of American Dreams and What Lies Ahead* (New York: HarperCollins, 2001), 19.

6. Perry Miller, *The New England Mind: The Seventeenth Century* (Cambridge, Mass.: Harvard University Press, 1939), 3–34.

7. Frederick B. Tolles, *Meeting House and Counting House: The Quaker Merchants of Colonial Philadelphia, 1682–1763* (New York: W. W. Norton, 1963), 56.

8. T. H. Breen, *Puritans and Adventurers: Change and Persistence in Early America* (New York: Oxford University Press, 1980), 109, 153, 126.

9. Alexis de Tocqueville, *Democracy in America* (New York: Vintage Books, 1954; first published 1835), 1:31–33.

10. Quoted in Morgan, *Puritan Political Ideas*, 90, 112, 169.

11. Perry Miller, *Errand into the Wilderness* (New York: Harper and Row, 1956), 142.

12. William Penn, *Frame of Government of Pennsylvania* (1682), Avalon Project: Documents in Law, History, and Diplomacy, preface, http://avalon.law.yale.edu/17th_century/pa04.asp.

13. Breen, *Puritans and Adventurers*, 114–115.

14. Calvin and Milton quoted in Sara M. Evans, *Born for Liberty: A History of Women in America* (New York: Free Press, 1997), 22.

15. Cotton quoted in Rogers M. Smith, *Civic Ideals: Conflicting Visions of Citizenship in U.S. History* (New Haven: Yale University Press, 1997), 67.

16. Nancy F. Cott, *Public Vows: A History of Marriage and the Nation* (Cambridge, Mass.: Harvard University Press, 2000), 11–12.

17. Winthrop and Peter quoted in Evans, *Born for Liberty*, 32.

18. Nathaniel Hawthorne, *The Scarlet Letter* (Garden City, N.Y.: International Collectors Library; first published 1850), 53.

19. Michael Dunne, "Hawthorne, the Reader, and Hester Prynne," *Interpretations* 10, no. 1 (1978): 34–40.

20. Hawthorne, *The Scarlet Letter*, 133, 136, 164–165.

21. Ibid., 137.

22. Ibid., 162–163.

23. Ibid., 203, 205–206.

24. Ibid., 144, 209.

25. Ibid., 213–214.

26. Tillam quoted in Karabell, *A Visionary Nation*, 18.

27. Miller, *Errand into the Wilderness*, 143.

28. Tolles, *Meeting House and Counting House*, 3, 54.

29. Ellis to Fox, June 13, 1685, quoted in ibid., 42; reprinted in *Journal of the Friends Historical Society* 6 (1909): 174.

30. Alan K. Simpson, *Puritanism in Old and New England* (Chicago: University of Chicago Press, 1955), 32.

31. Perry Miller, *The New England Mind: From Colony to Province* (Cambridge, Mass.: Harvard University Press, 1953), 49–51.

32. Tolles, *Meeting House and Counting House*, viii.

33. Ibid., 82.

34. Thomas Piketty, *Capital in the Twenty-First Century* (Cambridge, Mass.: Harvard University Press, 2014), 152.

35. *Advice of William Penn to His Children relating to Their Civil and Religious Conduct* (Philadelphia: Franklin Roberts, 1881), http://archive.org/details/adviceofwilliampoopenn.

36. Ibid.

37. Cotton Mather, *Bonifacius: An Essay . . . to Do Good* (Gainesville, Fla.: Scholars' Facsimiles and Reprints, 1967; first published 1710), 4, 41, 45, and see also 150–151, 164, http://archive.org/details/bonifaciusessayoomath.

38. Ibid., 67, 69, 145, 147.

39. Benjamin Franklin, *The Autobiography of Benjamin Franklin* (New York: Macmillan, 1962; first Touchstone edition 1997; first published 1791), 24; citations are to the Touchstone edition.

40. Peter Singer, *The Most Good You Can Do* (New Haven: Yale University Press, 2015).

41. Franklin, *Autobiography*, 37, 63.

42. Ibid., 86.

43. Ibid., 56, 82–85.

44. Benjamin Franklin, "The Way to Wealth," in *The Works of Benjamin Frank-*

lin, ed. Jared Sparks, 2:92–103 (Boston: Hillard Gray, 1836; essay first published 1758), http://www.swarthmore.edu/SocSci/bdorsey1/41docs/52-fra.html.

45. Franklin, *Autobiography,* 121.

46. Ibid., 91–92.

47. James Otis, "The Rights of the British Colonies Asserted and Proved," 1764 (Constitution Society), http://www.constitution.org/bcp/otis_rbcap.htm.

48. James Truslow Adams, *The Epic of America* (Boston: Little, Brown, 1931), 38.

49. Mayhew quoted in Burstein, *Sentimental Democracy,* 26.

50. Donald G. Darnell, *James Fenimore Cooper: Novelist of Manners* (Newark: University of Delaware Press, 1993).

51. James Fenimore Cooper, *The Last of the Mohicans* (New York: Barnes and Noble Classics, 2003; first published 1826), 117; Cooper, *The Deerslayer* (London: Wordsworth Classics, 1995; first published 1841), 325.

52. Cooper, *The Last of the Mohicans,* 48, 138, 308; see also Cooper, *The Pathfinder* (New York: Penguin Books, 1989; first published 1840), 25, 31, 59, 66, 70, 77–78, 92, 98, 307, 433.

53. Cooper, *The Deerslayer,* 28, 36; see also Tocqueville, *Democracy in America,* 1:344.

54. Cooper, *The Last of the Mohicans,* 28, 59, 75, 122, 187, 275; Cooper, *The Deerslayer,* 89, and see also 207, 235; and just as commonly in Cooper, *The Pathfinder,* 24, 27, 46, 59, 66, 70, 307, 433.

55. Cooper, *The Last of the Mohicans,* 11.

56. Ibid., 78, 104, 109.

57. Ibid., 161.

58. Ibid., 316.

59. Cooper, *The Pathfinder,* 189, 266–267, 270–271.

60. Ibid., 214–215, 419, 432–433.

61. Cooper, *The Deerslayer,* 9, 11.

62. Ibid., 67, 107, 119, 173, 116.

63. Ibid., 205, 421.

64. Hawthorne, *The Scarlet Letter,* 214.

65. Cooper, *The Pathfinder,* 468.

Chapter 3: The Founders' Dream and Its Limits

1. *The Works of John Adams,* ed. Charles Francis Adams, 10 vols. (Boston: Little, Brown, 1850–1856), 4:283–298.

2. *George Washington: Writings* (New York: Library of America, 1997), 517.

3. *The Works of John Adams,* 4:193–200; see also Russell L. Hanson, *The Democratic Imagination in America: Conversations with Our Past* (Princeton: Princeton University Press, 1985), 90.

4. David Hume, "Idea of a Perfect Commonwealth," in *Hume's Moral and Political Philosophy,* ed. Henry D. Aiken (Darien, Conn.: Hafner Publishing, 1970), 384–385.

5. Richard Hofstadter, *The American Political Tradition and the Men Who Made It* (New York: Vintage Books, 1989; first published 1948), 11.

6. Ezra Stiles, *The United States Elevated to Glory and Honour* (Worcester, Mass., 1785 [1783]), 9, 59, quoted in Andrew Burstein, *Sentimental Democracy: The Evolution of America's Romantic Self-Image* (New York: Hill and Wang, 1999), 130.

7. Rush to Charles Nisbet, December 5, 1783, in *Letters of Benjamin Rush,* ed. L. H. Butterfield (Princeton: Princeton University Press, 1951), 1:315–316, quoted in Burstein, *Sentimental Democracy,* 131.

8. Webster quoted in Burstein, *Sentimental Democracy,* 202.

9. Hofstadter, *The American Political Tradition,* 55.

10. Joseph J. Ellis, *American Sphinx: The Character of Thomas Jefferson* (New York: Vintage Books, 1998), 54.

11. Jefferson to William G. Munford, June 18, 1799, in *The Papers of Thomas Jefferson,* ed. Julian P. Boyd, 41 vols. (Princeton: Princeton University Press, 1950–2014), 31:127.

12. Pauline Maier, *American Scripture: Making of the Declaration of Independence* (New York: Alfred A. Knopf, 1998), 150.

13. Burstein, *Sentimental Democracy,* 110.

14. Jefferson quoted in ibid., 161–162.

15. Jefferson quoted in Hofstadter, *The American Political Tradition,* 36.

16. Alexander Hamilton, John Jay, and James Madison, *The Federalist,* ed. Edward Mead Earle (New York: Modern Library, 1937), 336–337.

17. *Letters and Other Writings of James Madison,* ed. William C. Rives and Philip R. Fendall (Philadelphia: J. B. Lippincott, 1867), 1:328.

18. Michael Lienesch, *New Order of the Ages: Time, the Constitution, and the Making of American Political Thought* (Princeton: Princeton University Press, 1988); see also David J. Siemers, *Ratifying the Republic: How Anti-Federalists Helped Found the American Regime* (Stanford: Stanford University Press, 2002).

19. J. Hector St. John de Crevecoeur, *Letters from an American Farmer* (New York: E. P. Dutton, 1957; first published 1782), 38–39.

20. Ibid., 20, 36.

21. Ibid., 53, 56.

22. Ibid., 55, 57.

23. Ibid., 63–64.

24. Abigail Adams, John Adams, and John Sullivan letters quoted in Alice Rossi, ed., *The Feminist Papers from Adams to de Beauvoir* (New York: Columbia University Press, 1973), 10–11, 13.

25. Murray quoted in Richard C. Sinopoli, ed., *From Many, One: Readings in*

American Political and Social Thought (Washington, D.C.: Georgetown University Press, 1997), 112–115.

26. James Baldwin, "Everybody's Protest Novel," in *Notes of a Native Son* (New York: Dial Press, 1963), 19–20.

27. William Wells Brown, *Clotel; or, The President's Daughter*, Documenting the American South (University Library, University of North Carolina at Chapel Hill, 2004; first published 1853), 60–61, http://docsouth.unc.edu/southlit/brown/brown.html.

28. Ibid., 62–63.

29. Ibid., 144.

30. Eric Foner, *Gateway to Freedom: The Hidden History of the Underground Railroad* (New York: W. W. Norton, 2015).

31. Brown, *Clotel*, 206.

32. Ibid., 218.

33. Herman Melville, *Benito Cereno* (1856), in *Billy Budd, and Other Stories* (New York: Penguin Books, 1986), 162, 169, 212–213.

34. Ibid., 219.

35. Ibid., 201.

36. Ibid., 257–258.

37. Bernard A. Weisberger, *America Afire: Jefferson, Adams, and the Revolutionary Election of 1800* (New York: William Morrow, 2000), 21.

38. Speech to the Federal Convention, June 22, 1787, in *The Papers of Alexander Hamilton*, ed. Harold C. Syrett, 27 vols. (New York: Columbia University Press, 1961–1987), 4:216.

39. Speech to the Federal Convention, June 18, 1787, in *The Papers of Alexander Hamilton*, 4:200.

40. Weisberger, *America Afire*, 58; see also Rogers M. Smith, *Civil Ideals: Conflicting Visions of Citizenship in U.S. History* (New Haven: Yale University Press, 1997), 140–141.

41. *The Reports of Alexander Hamilton*, ed. Jacob Cooke (New York: Harper Torchbook, 1964), 5.

42. Ibid., 48, 50–51.

43. Ibid., 121, 132.

44. In *The Papers of Alexander Hamilton*, 17:160.

45. Hamilton quoted in Richard Brookhiser, *Alexander Hamilton: American* (New York: Free Press, 1999), 172, and see also 8.

46. Hamilton quoted in ibid., 91.

47. James Fenimore Cooper, *The Pioneers* (New York: Signet Classics, 1964; first published 1823), 19–20.

48. Ibid., 88, 107.

49. Ibid., 152–153.

50. Ibid., 325, 328, 354.

51. Ibid., 432–433, 436.

52. James Fenimore Cooper, *The Prairie* (New York: Holt, Rinehart and Winston, 1950; first published 1827), 63, 377.

53. Ibid., 22, 437–438.

54. Herman Melville, *Billy Budd* (posthumously, 1924), in *Billy Budd, and Other Stories*, 298, 300.

55. Ibid., 293, 301–302.

56. Ibid., 314, 325–326.

57. Ibid., 323, 327–328.

58. Ibid., 350, 352.

59. Ibid., 358–359.

60. Ibid., 357, 354, 362.

Chapter 4: Democracy and Melancholy

1. Andrew Burstein, *America's Jubilee: How in 1826 a Generation Remembered Fifty Years of Independence* (New York: Alfred A. Knopf, 2001).

2. "Adams and Jefferson," August 2, 1826, in *The Papers of Daniel Webster: Speeches and Formal Writings*, ed. Charles M. Wiltse, 15 vols. (Hanover, N.H.: University Press of New England, 1974–1989), 1:269–271.

3. Jefferson to Francis Adrian Van De Kemp, January 11, 1825, in *Writings of Thomas Jefferson*, ed. Paul Leicester Ford, 12 vols. (New York: G. P. Putnam's Sons, 1904–1905), 10:377.

4. John C. Cawelti, *Apostles of the Self-Made Man* (Chicago: University of Chicago Press, 1965), 42; see also Richard Weiss, *The American Myth of Success* (New York: Basic Books, 1969), 7–8.

5. *New York Sun* quoted in James Truslow Adams, *The Epic of America* (Boston: Little, Brown, 1931), 186–187.

6. Richard Hofstadter, *The American Political Tradition and the Men Who Made It* (New York: Vintage Books, 1989; first published 1948), 73.

7. David Crockett, *A Narrative of the Life of David Crockett of the State of Tennessee* (Baltimore: E. L. Carey and A. Hart, 1834), 7, 101, 171.

8. Arthur M. Schlesinger Jr., *The Age of Jackson* (Boston: Little, Brown, 1953), 306.

9. Jackson quoted in Hofstadter, *The American Political Tradition*, 79.

10. Brownson quoted in Schlesinger, *The Age of Jackson*, 312.

11. Cawelti, *Apostles of the Self-Made Man*, 44.

12. Alexis de Tocqueville, *Democracy in America* (New York: Vintage Books, 1954; first published 1835), 2:100, 1:3.

13. Ibid., 2:104–105.

14. Ibid., 1:305, 2:78.

15. Ibid., 2:144, 147.

16. "The American Scholar," speech delivered August 31, 1837, before the Phi Beta Kappa Society at Harvard University, in *The Works of Ralph Waldo Emerson*, 14 vols. (Boston: Houghton, Mifflin, 1855–1893), 1:112.

17. "Self-Reliance" (1841), in *The Works of Ralph Waldo Emerson*, 2:77.

18. "The American Scholar," 1:100, 105.

19. "The Young American" (1844), in *The Works of Ralph Waldo Emerson*, 1:370.

20. *Emerson in His Journals,* ed. Joel Porte (Cambridge, Mass.: Harvard University Press, 1982), 197; see also Emerson, "Self–Reliance," 2:75.

21. "The Young American," 1:357.

22. "Wealth" (1860), in *The Works of Ralph Waldo Emerson*, 6:99.

23. "Experience" (1844), in *The Works of Ralph Waldo Emerson*, 3:47.

24. Ibid., 3:60–61, 62, 67, 83.

25. Henry David Thoreau, *Walden* (1854), in *Walden, and Other Writings* (New York: Barnes and Noble Books, 1993), 3, 45, 73, 265.

26. Ibid., 57, 58, 92, 93, 259, 269.

27. Ibid., 75, 14, 83, 88, 74, 267.

28. Andrew Delbanco, *Melville: His World and Work* (New York: Alfred A. Knopf, 2005), 123.

29. Frederic I. Carpenter, *American Literature and the Dream* (New York: Philosophical Library, 1955), 74–75.

30. Herman Melville, *Moby Dick* (Norwalk, Conn.: Easton Press, 1977; first published 1851), 85, 132.

31. Ibid., 214, 178, 472, 195.

32. Ibid., 228–229, 525, 582.

33. Ibid., 103, 155, 176, 197; see also Lawrence Buell, *The Dream of the Great American Novel* (Cambridge, Mass.: Harvard University Press, 2014), 359, 370–371.

34. Melville, *Moby Dick*, 180, 581.

35. Ibid., 194, 588, 612.

36. Ibid., 75, 79, 65.

37. Herman Melville, *Bartleby, the Scrivener* (1853), in *Billy Budd, and Other Stories* (New York: Penguin Books, 1986), 3–4.

38. Ibid., 24.

39. Ibid., 42, 46.

40. Gabor S. Boritt, *Lincoln and the Economics of the American Dream* (Urbana: University of Illinois Press, 1994), 22.

41. "The Perpetuation of Our Political Institutions," speech delivered before the Young Men's Lyceum of Springfield, Illinois, in January 1838, in *Collected Works of Abraham Lincoln*, ed. Roy P. Basler, 9 vols. (New Brunswick, N.J.: Rutgers University Press, 1953), 1:113–114.

42. Merrill D. Peterson, *The Jeffersonian Image in the American Mind* (New York: Oxford University Press, 1962), 220.

43. Lincoln, quoted in Hofstadter, *The American Political Tradition*, 135.

44. Lincoln, quoted in A. James Reichley, *The Life of the Parties: A History of American Political Parties* (New York: Rowman and Littlefield, 1992), 105.

45. "Letter to H. L. Pierce and Others," April 6, 1959, in *Abraham Lincoln: His Speeches and Writings*, ed. Roy P. Basler (New York: World Publishing, 1946), 488–489.

46. "Address before the Wisconsin Agricultural Society," September 30, 1859, in *Collected Works of Abraham Lincoln*, 3:482.

47. Michael J. Illuzzi, "Lincoln's 'Race of Life' Is Not the American Dream of Equal Opportunity," *American Political Thought* 3, no. 2 (Fall 2014): 228–253.

48. Tocqueville, *Democracy in America*, 1:344.

49. "The Repeal of the Missouri Compromise and the Propriety of Its Restoration," October 16, 1854, in *Abraham Lincoln: His Speeches and Writings*, 291–292.

50. Douglas quoted in Robert W. Johannsen, ed., *The Lincoln-Douglas Debates* (New York: Oxford University Press, 1965), 34.

51. *Collected Works of Abraham Lincoln*, 3:16, 4:24–25, 2:222, 266, 405, 3:145–146, 204, 222, 226.

52. "Speech at Springfield, Illinois," June 26, 1857, in *Collected Works of Abraham Lincoln*, 2:405, and see also 520.

53. Buell, *The Dream of the Great American Novel*, 292, 302.

54. William Faulkner, *Absalom, Absalom!* (New York: Modern Library College Editions, n.d.; first published 1936), 126, 220–221, 231.

55. Ibid., 222, 226, 238.

56. Ibid., 53.

57. Ibid., 276.

58. Ibid., 29–30.

59. Ibid., 341, 356.

60. Ibid., 177, and see also 180, 284.

61. Ibid., 53, 240, 165.

62. Mark Twain, *Tom Sawyer and Huckleberry Finn* (New York: Alfred A. Knopf, Everyman's Library, 1991; first published 1876 and 1885), 265–266.

63. Mark Twain, *Pudd'nhead Wilson* (New York: Book of the Month Club, 1992; first published 1894), 6.

64. Ibid., 14–17.

65. Ibid., 12.

66. Ibid., 10.

67. Ibid., 71–72.

68. Ibid., 123–124.

69. Ibid., 202.

70. "Message to Congress in Special Session," July 4, 1861, in *Collected Works of Abraham Lincoln*, 4:438.

71. John Patrick Diggins, *On Hallowed Ground: Abraham Lincoln and the Foundations of American History* (New Haven: Yale University Press, 2000), 23.

72. Gettysburg Address (1863), in *Abraham Lincoln: His Speeches and Writings*, 734.

73. The Dred Scott Decision: Speech at Springfield, Illinois, June 26, 1857, in *Abraham Lincoln: His Speeches and Writings*, 361.

74. Second Inaugural Address, March 4, 1865, in *Abraham Lincoln: His Speeches and Writings*, 793.

75. *The Works of James A. Garfield*, ed. Burke A. Hinsdale, 2 vols. (Boston: J. R. Osgood, 1882–1883), 1:86.

76. Stewart quoted in Eric Foner, *The Story of American Freedom* (New York: W. W. Norton, 1998), 104.

77. Wilson quoted in Alexander Keyssar, *The Right to Vote: The Contested History of Democracy in the United States* (New York: Basic Books, 2000), 96.

Chapter 5: Individualism and Combination in the Age of the Robber Barons

1. Charles Darwin, *On the Origin of Species by Means of Natural Selection; or, Preservation of Favoured Races in the Struggle for Life* (London: John Murray, 1859), 63, 95, 472, 468, 79.

2. E. L. Godkin, "Cooperation," *North American Review* 106 (January 1868): 173.

3. Sumner took this wonderful phrase from the famous frontiersman Davy Crockett. See David Crockett, *A Narrative of the Life of David Crockett of the State of Tennessee* (Baltimore: E. L. Carey and A. Hart, 1834), 118.

4. James Bryce, *The American Commonwealth*, 2 vols. (New York: Macmillan, 1891), 1:74.

5. P. T. Barnum, *Life of P. T. Barnum* (Buffalo, N.Y.: Courier, 1888; first published 1869), chap. 31, "The Art of Money Getting," 169, 175.

6. Ibid., 177.

7. Ibid., 188, 177, 182.

8. Ibid., 177–178, 188.

9. Andrew Carnegie, "Wealth," *North American Review* 148 (June 1889): 655.

10. Rockefeller quoted in Richard Weiss, *The American Myth of Success* (New York: Basic Books, 1969), 9.

11. Rockefeller and Hill quoted in Richard Hofstadter, *The American Political Tradition and the Men Who Made It* (New York: Vintage Books, 1989; first published 1948), 218.

12. Perkins quoted in Edward Chase Kirkland, *Dream and Thought in the Business Community, 1860–1900* (Chicago: Ivan R. Dee, 1990; first published 1956), 164.

13. Carnegie, "Wealth," 662–663.

14. "Speech to Wisconsin State Agricultural Society," 1858, in *Collected Works of Abraham Lincoln*, ed. Roy P. Basler, 9 vols. (New Brunswick, N.J.: Rutgers University Press, 1953), 3:479–480.

15. William T. Harris, "The Theory of American Education," in *Addresses and Proceedings, National Education Association of the United States* (Ann Arbor: University of Michigan Library, 2006; first published 1870), 191, http://quod.lib.umich.edu/g/genpub/0677752.1870.001?rgn=main;view+fulltext.

16. Carol Nackenoff, *The Fictional Republic: Horatio Alger and American Political Discourse* (New York: Oxford University Press, 1994), 3–7.

17. Horatio Alger Jr., *Ragged Dick; or, Street Life in New York with the Boot Blacks* (New York: Signet Classic, Penguin Group, 1990; first published 1868), 40.

18. Ibid., 42–43.

19. Ibid., 77.

20. Ibid, 78–79, 99.

21. Ibid., 137–138.

22. Michael Moon, "The Gentle Boy from the Dangerous Classes," *Representations* 19 (Summer 1987): 87–110.

23. Mark Twain, "The Story of the Good Little Boy," 1875, http://www.washburn.edu/sobu/broach/goodboy.html; Twain, "The Story of the Bad Little Boy," 1875, http://www.washburn.edu/sobu/broach/badboy.html.

24. Mark Twain, *Tom Sawyer and Huckleberry Finn* (New York: Alfred A. Knopf, Everyman's Library, 1991; first published 1876 and 1885), 7, 5, 35.

25. Ibid., 5, 11, 27, 37, 41.

26. Ibid., 45.

27. Ibid., 228–230; see also Sanford Pinsker, "Huckleberry Finn and the Problem of Freedom," in *The American Dream*, ed. Harold Bloom (New York: Infobase Publishing, 2009), 1–9.

28. Twain, *Tom Sawyer and Huckleberry Finn*, 337.

29. Ibid., 442, 398–399, 414.

30. Ibid., 559.

31. Lawrence Buell, *The Dream of the Great American Novel* (Cambridge, Mass.: Harvard University Press, 2014), 273.

32. William Dean Howells, *The Rise of Silas Lapham* (New York: W. W. Norton, 1982; first published 1885), 4–5, 15.

33. Ibid., 41–42.

34. Ibid., 114–116.

35. Ibid., 244, 262.

36. Ibid., 309.

37. William Dean Howells, *A Hazard of New Fortunes* (New York: Penguin Books, 2001; first published 1890), 77.

38. Ibid., 199.

39. Ibid., 202, and see also 204–210.

40. Ibid., 234–236.

41. Ibid., 396.

42. Edward Bellamy, *Looking Backward, 2000–1887* (Garden City, N.Y.: Dolphin Books, Doubleday; first published 1888), 12.

43. Ibid., 12–13.

44. Ibid., 43.

45. Ibid., 94–95.

46. Darwin, *On the Origin of Species*, 125–126.

47. "Politics an Evil to the Negro," in *Frederick Douglass: Life and Writings*, ed. Philip S. Foner, 4 vols. (New York: International Publishers, 1975), 4:272.

48. Toni Morrison, *Beloved* (New York: Alfred A. Knopf, 1988), 62, 251.

49. Ibid., 23, 66.

50. Ibid., 89, 104.

51. Ibid., 180, 235.

52. Ibid., 20, 38, 45–47.

53. Ibid., 162, 221.

54. Ibid., 244, 252, 266.

55. Phillips quoted in Alexander Keyssar, *The Right to Vote: The Contested History of Democracy in the United States* (New York: Basic Books, 2000), 177.

56. Declaration of Rights for Women quoted in Jean V. Matthews, *Women's Struggle for Equality: The First Phase, 1828–1876* (Chicago: Ivan R. Dee, 1997), 185.

57. Alger's Tattered Tom series featured a girl disguised as a boy to better survive on the streets who was rescued by kindly strangers before being reunited with her wealthy mother and pursuing a comfortable life as Jane Lindsay.

58. Horatio Alger Jr., *Helen Ford* (Philadelphia: John C. Winston, 1866), 59.

59. Ibid., 51, 44.

60. Ibid., 255–256; see also Nackenoff, *The Fictional Republic*, 85.

61. Alger Jr., *Helen Ford*, 50; see also Nackenoff, *The Fictional Republic*, 35; Moon, "The Gentle Boy," 95–96.

62. Alger, *Helen Ford*, 286–287.

63. Ibid., 285, 262, 265.

64. Ibid., 24, 30, 297.

65. Stephen Crane, *Maggie: A Girl of the Streets* (n.p.: Renaissance Classics, 2012; first published 1893), 5, 23.

66. Ibid., 23, 37.

67. Ibid., 24, 28, 37.

68. Ibid., 44, 59, 81.

69. Ibid., 83, 85, 93–95.

70. Theodore Dreiser, *Sister Carrie* (New York: Dover Publications, 2004; first published 1900), 1, 2, 10.

71. Ibid., 16, 37, 45, 49–50.

72. Ibid., 66–67, and see also 95, 87, 82.

73. Ibid., 78, 84.

74. Ibid., 191, 211, 215.

75. Ibid., 219.

76. Ibid., 319, 350–352.

Chapter 6: The Dream in Prosperity and Depression

1. Thomas Piketty, *Capital in the Twenty-First Century* (Cambridge, Mass.: Harvard University Press, 2014), 152.

2. Frank Norris, *The Octopus* (New York: Library of America, 1986; first published 1901), 627–630.

3. Ibid., 616–617, and see also 719.

4. Ibid., 797, 1096.

5. Ibid., 1090–1092.

6. Ibid., 659, 719, 1016–1017.

7. Ibid., 1036–1037.

8. Upton Sinclair, *The Jungle* (New York: Barnes and Noble Classics, 2003; first published 1906), 34, 23, 66, and see also 80.

9. Ibid., 71–72.

10. Ibid., 132.

11. Ibid., 171.

12. Ibid., 264, 330, 332.

13. Herbert Croly, *The Promise of American Life* (New York: E. P. Dutton, 1963; first published 1909), 116–117.

14. Ibid., 8–10.

15. Ibid., 206.

16. Ibid., 28.

17. Ibid., 181.

18. Theodore Roosevelt, *The New Nationalism* (New York: Outlook, 1910), 11–12, 119–121.

19. Ibid., 17, 241.

20. Ibid., 126, 178.

21. Ibid., 238–240, 18.

22. Ibid., 231, 240, 143.

23. Wilson quoted in Richard Hofstadter, *The American Political Tradition and the Men Who Made It* (New York: Vintage Books, 1989; first published 1948), 332.

24. First inaugural address, March 4, 1913, in *The Papers of Woodrow Wilson*, ed. Arthur S. Link, 69 vols. (Princeton: Princeton University Press, 1966–1994), 27:149–150.

25. Walter Lippmann, *Drift and Mastery* (Madison: University of Wisconsin Press, 1985; first published 1914), 112, 118, 103.

26. Ibid., 85, 172.

27. Ibid., 151.

28. Coolidge quoted in Lawrence B. Lindsey, *The Growth Experiment: How the New Tax Policy Is Transforming the U.S. Economy* (New York: Basic Books, 1990), 23.

29. Mellon quoted in Stanley Greenberg, *Middle Class Dreams*, rev. ed. (New Haven: Yale University Press, 1996), 77.

30. Michael Schudson, "American Dreams," *American Literary History* 16, no. 3 (Autumn 2004): 566–573.

31. F. Scott Fitzgerald, *The Great Gatsby* (New York: Charles Scribner's Sons, 1925), 2.

32. Ibid., 134, 172.

33. Ibid., 135, 148.

34. Ibid., 162.

35. Sinclair Lewis, *Babbitt* (New York: Penguin Group, Signet Classics, 1998; first published 1922), 174–175, 181.

36. Ibid., 57–58, and see also 260; see also Azar Nafisi, *The Republic of Imagination* (New York: Viking Press, 2014), 201.

37. Lewis, *Babbitt*, 7, 35, 268, 275.

38. Ibid., 342.

39. Ibid., 32–33, 63, 72, 284–285.

40. Ibid., 286, 378.

41. Ibid., 368.

42. Herbert Hoover, *American Individualism* (New York: Doubleday, Page, 1922), 9–10.

43. Hoover, untitled speech given August 21, 1928, quoted in Philip Abbott, *The Exemplary Presidency: Franklin D. Roosevelt and the American Political Tradition* (Amherst: University of Massachusetts Press, 1990), 40–42.

44. Reported in *New York Times*, November 13, 1932, quoted in James MacGregor Burns, *Roosevelt: The Lion and the Fox* (New York: Harcourt, Brace and World, 1956), 151.

45. Speech before the Commonwealth Club of San Francisco, September 23, 1932, in *The Public Papers and Addresses of Franklin Delano Roosevelt*, 13 vols. (New York: Random House, 1938), 1:742–756.

46. Franklin D. Roosevelt, Fireside Chat, September 30, 1934, http://miller center.org/president/speeches/speech-3303.

47. Democratic Party Platforms, "Democratic Party Platform of 1936," June 23, 1936, online by Gerhard Peters and John T. Woolley, *American Presidency Project*, http://www.presidency.ucsb.edu/ws/?pid=29596.

48. "We Are Fighting to Save a Great and Precious Form of Government for

Ourselves and the World," speech accepting the Democratic Party nomination for the presidency, Philadelphia, June 27, 1936, in *Public Papers and Addresses of Franklin D. Roosevelt,* 5:230–236.

49. John Steinbeck, *The Grapes of Wrath* (New York: Penguin Classics, 2006; first published 1939), 46, 109, 82–83, 188.

50. Ibid., 251.

51. Ibid., 21, 24, and see also 81.

52. Ibid., 77, 88, 238.

53. Ibid., 419.

54. Ibid., 3, 74.

55. Ibid., 422–423, 434–435.

56. Richard Wright, *Native Son* (New York: Harper Perennial Classics, 1998; first published 1940), 42, 105, 310.

57. Ibid., 44, 53, 174.

58. Ibid., 12, 19–20.

59. Ibid., 65.

60. Ibid., 350–356.

61. Ibid., 105, 189–190, 239.

62. Ibid., 399, 429.

63. Ibid., 451, 462.

64. Ralph Ellison, *Invisible Man* (New York: Vintage Books, 1972; first published 1952), 32, 97.

65. Ibid., 141, 346, and see also 372, 458–459, 3.

66. Ibid., 39, and see also 40, 37, 109.

67. Ibid., 152, 263–264.

68. Ibid., 16, 136–137, 151.

69. Ibid., 486–487, 499, 568.

Chapter 7: The Dream Unmoored

1. Johnson quoted in Doris Kearns Goodwin, *Lyndon Johnson and the American Dream* (New York: St. Martins Press, 1976), 96; see *Congressional Record,* June 4, 1946, A3170.

2. Lawrence R. Samuel, *The American Dream: A Cultural History* (Syracuse, N.Y.: Syracuse University Press, 2012), 57–58.

3. Eisenhower quoted in John Gerring, *Party Ideologies in America: 1828–1996* (New York: Cambridge University Press, 1998), 152.

4. First inaugural address, January 20, 1953, in *Public Papers of the Presidents of the United States: Dwight D. Eisenhower,* 8 vols. (Washington, D.C.: Government Printing Office, 1954–1960), *1953:* 1–7.

5. Second inaugural address, January 21, 1957, in *Public Papers: Eisenhower, 1957:* 61.

6. Untitled speech delivered in St. Louis, Missouri, September 27, 1956, in *The Papers of Adlai E. Stevenson*, ed. Walter Johnson, 8 vols. (Boston: Little, Brown, 1976), 6:244.

7. John Updike, *Rabbit, Run* (New York: Fawcett Books, 1960), 5–7.

8. Ibid., 58, 65, and see also 92.

9. Ibid., 11.

10. Ibid., 10.

11. Ibid., 39, 93.

12. Ibid., 83, 115.

13. Ibid., 79.

14. Ibid., 129, 213.

15. Ibid., 253, 259–260.

16. Sara Evans, *Born For Liberty* (New York: Free Press, 1997; first published 1989), 275.

17. Toni Morrison, *Sula* (New York: Plume, Penguin Books, 1973), 52.

18. Ibid., 41–44.

19. Ibid., 81–82, 102–103.

20. Ibid., 33, 67–69.

21. Ibid., 92, 142–144.

22. Baldwin quoted in Azar Nafisi, *The Republic of Imagination* (New York: Viking Press, 2014), 295.

23. John F. Kennedy, "City upon a Hill" speech, January 9, 1961, http://millercenter.org/president/speeches/speech-3364.

24. Inaugural address, in *Public Papers of the Presidents of the United States: John F. Kennedy*, 3 vols. (Washington, D.C.: Government Printing Office, 1962–1964), *1961*: 1–3.

25. Speech of September 30, 1962, in *Public Papers: Kennedy, 1962*: 728.

26. Speech of June 11, 1963, in *Public Papers: Kennedy, 1963*: 468–469.

27. Ibid., 469.

28. Martin Luther King Jr., "I Have a Dream" speech, August 28, 1963, http://www.americanrhetoric.com/speeches/mlkihaveadream.htm.

29. Norman Mailer, *An American Dream* (New York: Vintage Books, 1965), 6–7.

30. Kathryn Hume, *American Dream, American Nightmare: Fiction since 1960* (Urbana: University of Illinois Press, 2000), 133.

31. Mailer, *An American Dream*, 9, 36–37.

32. Ibid., 240–241.

33. Ibid., 31–32, 39, and see also 183–193.

34. Ibid., 246, 270.

35. Joseph A. Califano Jr., "What Was Really Great about the Great Society," *Washington Monthly*, October 1999, 13; Goodwin, *Lyndon Johnson and the American Dream*, 217, 287; Sidney M. Milkis, *The President and the Parties: The*

Transformation of the American Party System since the New Deal (New York: Oxford University Press, 1993), 184.

36. Address to Congress, November 27, 1963, in *Public Papers of the Presidents of the United States: Lyndon B. Johnson,* 10 vols. (Washington, D.C.: Government Printing Office, 1965–1970) vol. 1, entry 11, pp. 8–9.

37. Speech, May 22, 1964, in *Public Papers: Johnson, 1963–1964*: vol. 1, entry 357, pp. 704–707.

38. State of the Union address, January 4, 1965, in *Public Papers: Johnson, 1965*: vol. 1, entry 2, pp. 1–9.

39. Inaugural address, January 20, 1965, in *Public Papers: Johnson, 1965*: vol. 1, entry 27, pp. 71–74.

40. Commencement speech at Howard University, June 4, 1965, in *Public Papers: Johnson, 1965*: vol. 2, entry 301, pp. 635–640.

41. Wilkins quoted in Gareth Davies, *From Opportunity to Entitlement: The Transformation and Decline of Great Society Liberalism* (Lawrence: University Press of Kansas, 1996), 81.

42. John Updike, *Rabbit Redux* (New York: Fawcett Books, 1971), 16, 62–63, and see also 67–68.

43. Ibid., 55, 89–90.

44. Ibid., 210, 204.

45. Ibid., 145–146.

46. Ibid., 254.

47. Ibid., 337, 346.

48. McCarthy quoted in Davies, *From Opportunity to Entitlement,* 194. See *Congressional Record,* August 8, 1967, 21782.

49. Shelby Steele, *A Dream Deferred: The Second Betrayal of Black Freedom in America* (New York: HarperCollins, 1998), 13, 20.

50. Kurt Vonnegut, *Slaughterhouse-Five* (London: Vintage Books, 2000; first published 1969), 134.

51. Ibid., 51.

52. Ibid., 19, 50, 127.

53. Ibid., 105–106.

54. Ibid., 70.

55. Ibid., 95–96.

Chapter 8: The Dream in Doubt

1. U.S. Census Bureau, Historical Income Data, Current Population Survey Tables, Families, Table F-6, "Regions—Families (All Races) by Median and Mean Income," http://www.census.gov/hhes/www/income/data/historical/families/.

2. Thomas Piketty, *Capital in the Twenty-First Century* (Cambridge, Mass.: Harvard University Press, 2014), 294–299.

3. Saez reported in Cass Sunstein, "Top 1% Are the Big Winners in Recovery," *Dallas Morning News*, December 11, 2013.

4. Mark Robert Rank, Thomas A. Hirschl, and Kirk A. Foster, *Chasing the American Dream: Understanding What Shapes Our Fortunes* (New York: Oxford University Press, 2014), 70; see also Robert Putnam, *Our Kids: The American Dream in Crisis* (New York: Simon and Schuster, 2015).

5. Hugh Heclo, "Ronald Reagan and the American Public Philosophy," paper presented at the Conference on the Reagan Presidency, University of California, Santa Barbara, March 27–30, 2002, 6; see also H. W. Brands, *Reagan: The Life* (New York: Doubleday, 2015).

6. Ronald Reagan, "A Time for Choosing" (aka "The Speech"), October 27, 1964, http://odur.let.rug.nl/~usa/P/rr40/speeches/the_speech.htm.

7. First Inaugural Address, January 20, 1981, in *Public Papers of the Presidents of the United States: Ronald Reagan*, 15 vols. (Washington, D.C.: Government Printing Office, 1982–1991), *1981*: 1–2.

8. Quoted in Stanley Greenberg, *Middle Class Dreams*, rev. ed. (New Haven: Yale University Press, 1996), 135.

9. Speech, July 4, 1987, in *Public Papers: Reagan, 1987*: vol. 1, p. 744.

10. Farewell Address, January 11, 1989, in *Public Papers: Reagan, 1989*: vol. 2, p. 1722.

11. Heclo, "Ronald Reagan," 6–7.

12. John Updike, *Rabbit at Rest* (New York: Alfred A. Knopf, 1990), 295.

13. Kathryn Hume, *American Dream, American Nightmare: Fiction since 1960* (Urbana: University of Illinois Press, 2000), 120.

14. John Updike, *Rabbit Is Rich* (New York: Fawcett Books, 1981), 1, 4, 7, 19, 110.

15. Updike, *Rabbit at Rest*, 39–40, 58, 484–485.

16. Ibid., 328, 418, 476.

17. Ibid., 512.

18. Richard Russo, *Empire Falls* (New York: Random House, Vintage Books, 2001), 196, 317, 281.

19. Ibid., 317, 281.

20. Ibid., 394, 436, 118–119.

21. Ibid., 162, 168.

22. Ibid., 349, 434.

23. "A Campaign for the Future," announcement for president, Little Rock, Arkansas, October 3, 1991, in *Preface to the Presidency: Selected Speeches of Bill Clinton, 1974–1992*, ed. Stephen A. Smith (Fayetteville: University of Arkansas Press, 1996), 80, 85.

24. "A Vision for America: A New Covenant," acceptance speech, Democratic National Convention, July 16, 1992, in *Preface to the Presidency*, 219.

25. "A New Covenant: Responsibility and Rebuilding the American Community," speech at Georgetown University, October 23, 1991, in Clinton, *Preface to the Presidency*, 89.

26. Clinton's Old State House victory speech, Little Rock, November 3, 1992, in Clinton, *Preface to the Presidency*, 419.

27. First Inaugural Address, January 20, 1993, in *Public Papers of the Presidents of the United States: William J. Clinton*, 17 vols. (Washington, D.C.: Government Printing Office, 1994–2002), *1993*: vol. 1, pp. 1–3.

28. State of the Union Address 1994, in *Public Papers: Clinton, 1994:* vol. 1, p. 126.

29. William J. Clinton, *Between Hope and History: Meeting America's Challenges for the 21st Century* (New York: Random House, 1996), 6.

30. Ibid., 118.

31. Ibid., 91–92.

32. Ibid., 172.

33. Second Inaugural Address, January 20, 1997, in *Public Papers: Clinton, 1997*: vol. 1, p. 44.

34. Philip Roth, *The American Trilogy: American Pastoral* (New York: Library of America, 2011), 7, 9.

35. Ibid., 295.

36. Ibid., 41, 199, 82.

37. Ibid., 66–67, 200.

38. Ibid., 82, 77, 239, 390.

39. Philip Roth, *The American Trilogy: The Human Stain* (New York: Library of America, 2011), 795–796.

40. Ibid., 813, 820.

41. Ibid., 827.

42. Ibid., 834.

43. Ibid., 804, 816, 1013.

44. Ibid., 868–869, 709, 713.

45. Ibid., 710.

46. Ibid., 715, 897.

47. Lawrence Buell, *The Dream of the Great American Novel* (Cambridge, Mass.: Harvard University Press, 2014), 3–4.

48. Jonathan Franzen, *Freedom* (New York: Farrar, Straus and Giroux, 2010), 76, and see also 101, 104–107, 95, 119, and 155.

49. Ibid., 21.

50. Ibid., 210, 215–216.

51. Ibid., 318.

52. Ibid., 181, 503.

53. Ibid., 327, 404–405, 411, 438.

54. Barack Obama, *Dreams of My Father,* large print ed. (New York: Random House, 1995), xx.

55. Ibid., 129, 151–152.

56. Barack Obama, Keynote Address at the 2004 Democratic National Convention, July 27, 2004, Boston, Massachusetts, Best Speeches of Barack Obama through His 2009 Inauguration, http://obamaspeeches.com/002-Keynote-Address-at-the-2004-Democratic-National-Convention-Obama-Speech.htm.

57. Barack Obama, "American Dream" speech, November 7, 2007, Bettendorf, Iowa, CNN transcript, http://www.cnn.com/2007/POLITICS/12/21/obama.trans.americandream/.

58. Barack Obama, "A More Perfect Union," the Race Speech, March 18, 2008, Philadelphia, Pennsylvania, Best Speeches of Barack Obama through His 2009 Inauguration, http://obamaspeeches.com/E05-Barack-Obama-A-More-Perfect-Union-the-Race-Speech-Philadelphia-PA-March-18-2008.htm.

59. Barack Obama, Grant Park Speech, November 4, 2008, Chicago, Illinois, CNN transcript, http://edition.cnn.com/2008/POLITICS/11/04/obama.transcript/.

60. First Inaugural Address, January 20, 2009, in *Public Papers of the Presidents: Barack Obama, 2009* (Washington, D.C.: Government Printing Office, 2010), 1:1–4.

61. Barack Obama, State of the Union Address, January 27, 2010, *American Presidency Project,* http://www.presidency.ucsb.edu/ws/index.php?pid=87433, State of the Union Address, January 24, 2012, *American Presidency Project,* http://www.presidency.ucsb.edu/ws/index.php?pid=99000.

62. Barack Obama, Economic Speech, December 6, 2011, Osawatomie, Kansas, https://www.washingtonpost.com/politics/president-obamas-economic-speech-in-osawatomie-kans/2011/12/06/gIQAVhe6ZO_story.html.

63. See also A. G. Salzberger, "Obama Sounds a Populist Call on G.O.P. Turf," *New York Times,* December 7, 2011; David Nakamura, "Obama Invokes Teddy Roosevelt in Speech Attacking GOP Policies," *Washington Post,* December 7, 2011.

64. Barack Obama, Second Inaugural Address, January 21, 2013, *American Presidency Project,* http://www.presidency.ucsb.edu/ws/index.php?pid=102827.

65. Barack Obama, State of the Union Address, January 28, 2014, *American Presidency Project,* http://www.presidency.ucsb.edu/ws/index.php?pid=104596.

66. Obama quoted in Julie Hirschfeld Davis and Michael D. Shear, "Unrest over Race Is Testing Obama's Legacy," *New York Times,* December 9, 2014; see also Kevin Sack and Gardiner Harris, "Obama Scorns Racism in Soaring, Singing Eulogy," *New York Times,* June 27, 2015.

Chapter 9: American Dreams and Doubts in the Twenty-First Century

1. J. G. A. Pocock, *Politics, Language, and Time: Essays on Political Thought and History* (New York: Atheneum, 1973), 233–272.

2. John E. Schwarz, *Illusions of Opportunity: The American Dream in Question* (New York: W. W. Norton, 1997), 124.

3. Kathryn Hume, *American Dream, American Nightmare: Fiction since 1960* (Urbana: University of Illinois Press, 2000), 288.

4. David Kamp, "Rethinking the American Dream," *Vanity Fair*, April 2009, http://www.vanityfair.com/culture/features/2009/04/american-dream 200904.

5. Thomas Piketty, *Capital in the Twenty-First Century* (Cambridge, Mass.: Harvard University Press, 2014), 514.

6. "Experience," in *The Works of Ralph Waldo Emerson*, 14 vols. (Boston: Houghton, Mifflin, 1855–1893), 3:49, 51, 53, 60–61, 83; see also E. Thomas Finan, "The 'Lords of Life': Fractals, Recursivity, and 'Experience,'" *Philosophy and Rhetoric* 45, no. 1 (2012): 65–88.

7. James Baldwin, *Notes of a Native Son* (New York: Dial Press, 1963), 19–20.

8. Kevin Phillips, *Wealth and Poverty: The Political History of the American Rich* (New York: Broadway Books, 2002).

9. Art Swift, "Americans' Satisfaction with Life Similar to Levels in 1998," Gallup News Service, November 1, 2013, http://gallup.com/poll/165683 /americans-satisfaction-life-similar-levels-1998.aspx.

10. Sandra L. Hanson and John Zogby, "The Polls—Trends: Attitudes about the American Dream," *Public Opinion Quarterly* 74, no. 3 (Fall 2010): 573.

11. Opportunity Agenda, "Public Opinion on Opportunity and the American Dream, Homeownership, and Housing," memorandum, November 2011, https://opportunityagenda.org/files/field_file/memo_public_opinion_0.pdf; see also Opportunity Agenda, "A Window of Opportunity: A Meta-Analysis of Public Opinion on Poverty," June 2014, https://opportunityagenda.org/files /field_file/2.publicopinion-metaanalysis.pdf.

12. Ronald Brownstein, "The American Dream—Under Threat," *National Journal*, September 19, 2013, https://www.nationaljournal.com/s/70247/american -dream-under-threat.

13. Reported in American Enterprise Institute for Public Policy Research, "What Does the American Dream Mean?," *AEI Political Report* 10, no. 11 (December 2014): 5.

14. Cited in Connie Cass, "Most Americans Have a Gloomy Outlook for Life in 2050." Associated Press, January 3, 2014. http://pbs.org/newshour/rundown /most-americans-have-a-gloomy-outlook-for-life-in-2050/.

15. Frank Bruni, "Lost in America," *New York Times*, August 25, 2014.

16. Associated Press and NORC, "Inequality: Trends in Americans' Attitudes," issue brief, March 2015, http://www.apnorc.org/PDFs/Inequality/InequalityFinaltoDTP-Final.pdf.

17. Joseph E. Stiglitz, *The Price of Inequality: How Today's Divided Society Endangers Our Future* (New York: W. W. Norton, 2013), 102.

18. Arne L. Kalleberg, *Good Jobs, Bad Jobs* (New York: Russell Sage Foundation, 2011), 78.

19. Amy Traub and Heather C. McGee, "State of the American Dream: Economic Policy and the Future of the Middle Class," *Demos,* June 2013, http://www.demos.org/publication/state-american-dream-economic-policy-and-future-middle-class.

20. Donald L. Bartlett and James B. Steele, *The Betrayal of the American Dream* (New York: Public Affairs, 2013), xx.

21. Piketty, *Capital in the Twenty-First Century,* 292.

22. Timothy Noah, *The Great Divergence* (New York: Bloomsbury Press, 2012), 24.

23. Kalleberg, *Good Jobs, Bad Jobs,* 107–108.

24. Traub and McGee, "State of the American Dream," 2.

25. Binyamin Appelbaum, "Least Affluent Families' Incomes Are Declining, Fed Survey Shows," *New York Times,* September 15, 2014.

26. Pew Research Center, "The American Middle Class Is Losing Ground," December 9, 2015, www.pewsocialtrends.org/2015/12/09/the-american-middle-class/; see also Patricia Cohen, "Middle Class, or So They Think," *New York Times,* April 11, 2015; Stiglitz, *The Price of Inequality,* 9.

27. Stiglitz, *The Price of Inequality,* 332, 344.

28. Noah, *The Great Divergence,* 32–37.

29. Mark Robert Rank, Thomas A. Hirschl, and Kirk A. Foster, *Chasing the American Dream: Understanding What Shapes Our Fortunes* (New York: Oxford University Press, 2014), 161.

30. Raj Chetty et al., "Where Is the Land of Opportunity? The Geography of Intergenerational Mobility in the United States," working paper no. 19843, National Bureau of Economic Research, January 2014, abstract; www.nber.org/papers/w19843.pdf. See also David Leonhardt, Amanda Cox, and Claire Cain Miller, "Change of Address Offers a Pathway out of Poverty," *New York Times,* May 4, 2015.

31. Chetty et al., "Where Is the Land of Opportunity?," abstract.

32. W. E. B. Du Bois, "To the Nations of the World," Westminster Hall, London, July 25, 1900; see also Du Bois, *The Souls of Black Folk* (New York: Oxford University Press, 2007; first published 1903), 15.

33. James Truslow Adams, *The Epic of America* (Boston: Little, Brown, 1931), 315.

34. CNN, "The Black-White Economic Divide in 5 Charts," November 25, 2015, http://money.cnn.com/2015/11/24/news/economy/blacks-whites-in equality/.

35. U.S. Census Bureau, Historical Income Tables: Households, Table H-5, "Race and Hispanic Origin of Householder—Households by Median and Mean Income, 1967–2014." https://www.census.gov/hhes/www/income/data/his torical/household/index.html.

36. Rakesh Kochhar and Richard Fry, "Wealth Inequality Has Widened along Racial, Ethnic Lines since End of Great Recession," Pew Research Center, December 12, 2014, 1, http://www.pewresearch.org/fact-tank/2014/12/12 /racial-wealth-gaps-great-recession/; see also Roy Boshara, William R. Emmons, and Bryan J. Noeth, "Race, Ethnicity, and Wealth," Demographics of Wealth, no. 1 (St. Louis, Mo.: Federal Reserve Bank of St. Louis, February 2015), Table 1, page 6, https://www.stlouisfed.org/~/media/Files/PDFs/HFS/essays/HFS -Essay-1-2015-Race-Ethnicity-and-Wealth.pdf.

37. Tom Pugh, "Minorities Hurt More by Foreclosure Crisis, Study Says," McClatchy Newspapers, June 18, 2010. www.mcclatchydc.com/news/nation -world/national/economy/article24585790.html.

38. Bureau of Labor Statistics, Databases, Tables, and Calculators by Subject, unemployment rates, for whites, Series ID LNS14000003, http://data.bls.gov /timeseries/LNS14000003; for blacks, Series ID LNS14000006, http://data.bls .gov/timeseries/LNS14000006; and for Hispanics, Series ID LNS14000009, http://data.bls.gov/timeseries/LNS14000009.

39. U.S. Census Bureau, Historical Poverty Tables—People, Table 2, "Poverty Status, by Family Relationship, Race, and Hispanic Origin," and Table 3, "Poverty Status, by Age, Race and Hispanic Origin," http://www.census.gov /hhes/www/poverty/data/historical/people.html.

40. Thomas Shapiro, Tatjana Meschede, and Sam Osoro, "The Roots of the Widening Racial Wealth Gap: Explaining the Black-White Economic Divide," research and policy brief, Institute on Assets and Social Policy, February 2013, http://iasp.brandeis.edu/pdfs/Author/shapiro-thomas-m/racialwealthgap brief.pdf.

41. U.S. Bureau of Labor Statistics, "Women in the Labor Force: A Databook," report 1052, December 2014, 1–2, www.bls.gov/opub/reports/womens -databook/archive/women-in-the-labor-force-a-databook-2014.pdf.

42. Ariane Hegewisch and Heidi Hartmann, "The Gender Wage Gap: 2014," report from the Institute for Women's Policy Research, September 2015, 1, http://www.iwpr.org/publications/pubs/the-gender-wage-gap-2014; see also Catalyst, *Pyramid: Women in S&P 500 Companies* (New York: Catalyst, February 3, 2016), http://www.catalyst.org/knowledge/women-sp-500-companies.

43. David Leonhardt, "A Link between Fidgety Boys and a Sputtering Economy," *New York Times*, April 29, 2014.

44. Pew Research, "On Pay Gap, Millennial Women Near Parity—For Now," Social and Demographic Trends, http://www.pewsocialtrends.org/2013/12/11/on-pay-gap.

45. Lydia DePillis, "The Real Gender Gap," *Washington Post*, February 23, 2014.

46. Claire Cain Miller, "Why a Gender Gap?," *New York Times*, April 28, 2014; see also Claire Cain Miller, "The Motherhood Penalty vs. the Fatherhood Bonus: A Child Helps Your Career, if You're a Man," *New York Times*, September 6, 2014, http://www.nytimes.com/2014/09/07/upshot/a-child-helps-your-career-if-youre-a-man.html.

47. Paul Taylor, *The Next America* (New York: Public Affairs, 2014), 14; see also Tamar Lewin, "More Highly Educated Women Are Also Having Children," *New York Times*, May 8, 2015.

48. Richard V. Reeves and Isabel V. Sawhill, "Men, Step into Women's Shoes," *Dallas Morning News*, December 6, 2015.

49. Claudia Goldin and Lawrence F. Katz, *The Race between Education and Technology* (Cambridge, Mass.: Harvard University Press, 2008), 23.

50. Ibid., 91, 278, 87; see also Stiglitz, *The Price of Inequality*, 69.

51. Nicholas Kristof, "The American Dream Is Leaving America," *New York Times*, October 26, 2014.

52. Suzanne Mettler, *Degrees of Inequality: How the Politics of Higher Education Sabotaged the American Dream* (New York: Basic Books, 2014), 30.

53. Frank Bruni, "Class, Cost and College," *New York Times*, May 18, 2014.

54. Paul Tough, "Who Gets to Graduate," *New York Times Magazine*, May 18, 2014, 28.

55. David Leonhardt, "Is College Worth It?" *New York Times*, May 27, 2014.

Bibliography

Abbott, Philip. *The Exemplary Presidency: Franklin D. Roosevelt and the American Political Tradition.* Amherst: University of Massachusetts Press, 1990.

Adams, Henry. *Democracy: An American Novel.* New York: Modern Library, 2003. Initially published 1880.

———. *History of the United States during the Administration of Thomas Jefferson.* 4 vols. New York: Charles Scribner's Sons, 1889.

Adams, James Truslow. *The Epic of America.* Boston: Little, Brown, 1931.

Adams, John. *The Works of John Adams.* Edited by Charles Francis Adams. 10 vols. Boston: Little, Brown, 1850–1856.

Alger, Horatio, Jr. *Helen Ford.* Philadelphia: John C. Winston, 1866.

———. *Ragged Dick; or, Street Life in New York with the Boot Blacks.* New York: Signet Classic, Penguin Group, 1990. Initially published 1868.

American Enterprise Institute for Public Policy Research. "What Does the American Dream Mean?" *AEI Political Report* 10, no. 11 (December 2014).

Appelbaum, Binyamin. "Least Affluent Families' Incomes Are Declining, Fed Survey Shows." *New York Times,* September 15, 2014.

Arieli, Yehoshua. *Individualism and Nationalism in American Ideology.* Cambridge, Mass.: Harvard University Press, 1964.

Associated Press and NORC. "Inequality: Trends in Americans' Attitudes." Issue brief, March 2015. http://www.apnorc.org/PDFs/Inequality/InequalityFinaltoDTP-Final.pdf.

Baldwin, James. *Notes of a Native Son.* New York: Dial Press, 1963.

Barnum, P. T. *Life of P. T. Barnum.* Buffalo, N.Y.: Courier, 1888. Initially published 1869.

Bartlett, Donald L., and James B. Steele. *The Betrayal of the American Dream.* New York: Public Affairs, 2013.

Bell, Derrick. *Faces at the Bottom of the Well: The Permanence of Racism.* New York: Basic Books, 1992.

Bellamy, Edward. *Looking Backward, 2000–1887.* Garden City, N.Y.: Dolphin Books, Doubleday. Initially published 1888.

Berman, Paul. *A Tale of Two Utopias: The Political Journey of the Generation of 1968.* New York: W. W. Norton, 1996.

Boritt, Gabor S. *Lincoln and the Economics of the American Dream.* Urbana: University of Illinois Press, 1994.

Boshara, Roy, William R. Emmons, and Bryan J. Noeth. "Race, Ethnicity, and Wealth." Demographics of Wealth, no. 1. St. Louis, Mo.: Federal Reserve

Bank of St. Louis, February 2015. https://www.stlouisfed.org/~/media /Files/PDFs/HFS/essays/HFS-Essay-1-2015-Race-Ethnicity-and-Wealth.pdf.

Brands, H. W. *Reagan: The Life.* New York: Doubleday, 2015.

Breen, T. H. *Puritans and Adventurers: Change and Persistence in Early America.* New York: Oxford University Press, 1980.

Brookhiser, Richard. *Alexander Hamilton: American.* New York: Free Press, 1999.

Brown, William Wells. *Clotel; or, The President's Daughter.* Documenting the American South. University Library, University of North Carolina at Chapel Hill, 2004. Initially published 1853. http://docsouth.unc.edu/southlit/brown /brown.html.

Brownstein, Ronald. "The American Dream—Under Threat." *National Journal,* September 19, 2013. https://www.nationaljournal.com/s/70247/american -dream-under-threat.

Bruni, Frank. "Class, Cost and College." *New York Times,* May 18, 2014.

———. "Lost in America." *New York Times,* August 25, 2014.

Bryce, James. *The American Commonwealth.* 2 vols. New York: Macmillan, 1891.

Buell, Lawrence. *The Dream of the Great American Novel.* Cambridge, Mass.: Harvard University Press, 2014.

Burns, James MacGregor. *Roosevelt: The Lion and the Fox.* New York: Harcourt, Brace and World, 1956.

Burstein, Andrew. *America's Jubilee: How in 1826 a Generation Remembered Fifty Years of Independence.* New York: Alfred A. Knopf, 2001.

———. *Sentimental Democracy: The Evolution of America's Romantic Self-Image.* New York: Hill and Wang, 1999.

Califano, Joseph A., Jr. "What Was Really Great about the Great Society." *Washington Monthly,* October 1999.

Carnegie, Andrew. "Wealth." *North American Review* 148 (June 1889): 653–664.

Carpenter, Frederic I. *American Literature and the Dream.* New York: Philosophical Library, 1955.

Cass, Connie. "Most Americans Have a Gloomy Outlook for Life in 2050." Associated Press, January 3, 2014. http://pbs.org/newshour/rundown/most -americans-have-a-gloomy-outlook-for-life-in-2050/.

Catalyst. *Pyramid: Women in S&P 500 Companies.* New York: Catalyst, February 3, 2016. http://www.catalyst.org/knowledge/women-sp-500-companies.

Cawelti, John C. *Apostles of the Self-Made Man.* Chicago: University of Chicago Press, 1965.

Chesterton, G. K. *What I Saw in America.* New York: Dodd, Mead, 1927.

Chetty, Raj, Nathaniel Hendren, Patrick Kline, and Emmanuel Saez. "Where Is the Land of Opportunity? The Geography of Intergenerational Mobility in the United States." Working paper no. 19843, National Bureau of Economic Research, January 2014, abstract. www.nber.org/papers/w19843.pdf.

Clinton, William J. *Between Hope and History: Meeting America's Challenges for the 21st Century.* New York: Random House, 1996.

———. *Preface to the Presidency: Selected Speeches of Bill Clinton, 1974–1992.* Edited by Stephen A. Smith. Fayetteville: University of Arkansas Press, 1996.

———. *Public Papers of the Presidents of the United States: William J. Clinton.* 17 vols. Washington, D.C.: Government Printing Office, 1994–2002.

CNN. "The Black-White Economic Divide in 5 Charts," November 25, 2015. http://money.cnn.com/2015/11/24/news/economy/blacks-whites-in equality/.

Cohen, Patricia. "Middle Class, or So They Think." *New York Times*, April 11, 2015.

Cooper, James Fenimore. *The Deerslayer.* London: Wordsworth Classics, 1995. Initially published 1841.

———. *The Last of the Mohicans.* New York: Barnes and Noble Classics, 2003. Initially published 1826.

———. *The Pathfinder.* New York: Penguin Books, 1989. Initially published 1840.

———. *The Pioneers.* New York: Signet Classics, 1964. Initially published 1823.

———. *The Prairie.* New York: Holt, Rinehart and Winston, 1950. Initially published 1827.

Cott, Nancy F. *Public Vows: A History of Marriage and the Nation.* Cambridge, Mass.: Harvard University Press, 2000.

Crane, Stephen. *Maggie: A Girl of the Streets.* N.p.: Renaissance Classics, 2012. Initially published 1893.

Crevecoeur, J. Hector St. John de. *Letters from an American Farmer.* New York: E. P. Dutton, 1957. Initially published 1782.

Crockett, David. *Narrative of the Life of David Crockett of the State of Tennessee.* Baltimore: E. L. Carey and A. Hart, 1834.

Croly, Herbert. *The Promise of American Life.* New York: E. P. Dutton, 1963. Initially published 1909.

Darnell, Donald G. *James Fenimore Cooper: Novelist of Manners.* Newark: University of Delaware Press, 1993.

Darwin, Charles. *On the Origin of Species by Means of Natural Selection; or, Preservation of Favoured Races in the Struggle for Life.* London: John Murray, 1859.

Davies, Gareth. *From Opportunity to Entitlement: The Transformation and Decline of Great Society Liberalism.* Lawrence: University Press of Kansas, 1996.

Davis, Julie Hirschfeld, and Michael D. Shear. "Unrest over Race Is Testing Obama's Legacy." *New York Times*, December 9, 2014.

Delbanco, Andrew. *Melville: His World and Work.* New York: Alfred A. Knopf, 2005.

Democratic Party Platforms. "Democratic Party Platform of 1936," June 23,

1936. Online by Gerhard Peters and John T. Woolley, *American Presidency Project.* http://www.presidency.ucsb.edu/ws/?pid=29596.

DePillis, Lydia. "The Real Gender Gap." *Washington Post,* February 23, 2014.

Diggins, John Patrick. *On Hallowed Ground: Abraham Lincoln and the Foundations of American History.* New Haven: Yale University Press, 2000.

Douglass, Frederick. *Frederick Douglass: Life and Writings.* Edited by Philip S. Foner. 4 vols. New York: International Publishers, 1975.

Dreiser, Theodore. *Sister Carrie.* New York: Dover Publications, 2004. Initially published 1900.

Du Bois, W. E. B. *The Souls of Black Folk.* New York: Oxford University Press, 2007. Initially published 1903.

Dunne, Michael. "Hawthorne, the Reader, and Hester Prynne." *Interpretations* 10, no. 1 (1978): 34–40.

Eisenhower, Dwight David. *Public Papers of the Presidents of the United States: Dwight D. Eisenhower.* 8 vols. Washington, D.C.: Government Printing Office, 1954–1960.

Ellis, Joseph J. *American Sphinx: The Character of Thomas Jefferson.* New York: Vintage Books, 1998.

———. *Founding Brothers: The Revolutionary Generation.* New York: Alfred A. Knopf, 2001.

Ellison, Ralph. *Invisible Man.* New York: Vintage Books, 1972. Initially published 1952.

Emerson, Ralph Waldo. *Emerson and His Journals.* Edited by Joel Porte. Cambridge, Mass.: Harvard University Press, 1982.

———. *The Works of Ralph Waldo Emerson.* 14 vols. Boston: Houghton, Mifflin, 1855–1893.

Evans, Sara M. *Born for Liberty: A History of Women in America.* New York: Free Press, 1997. Initially published 1989.

Faulkner, William. *Absalom, Absalom!* New York: Modern Library College Editions, n.d. Initially published 1936.

Finan, E. Thomas. "The 'Lords of Life': Fractals, Recursivity, and 'Experience.'" *Philosophy and Rhetoric* 45, no. 1 (2012): 65–88.

Fitzgerald, F. Scott. *The Great Gatsby.* New York: Charles Scribner's Sons, 1925.

Flax, Jane. *The American Dream in Black and White: The Clarence Thomas Hearings.* Ithaca, N.Y.: Cornell University Press, 1998.

Fogel, Robert William. *The Fourth Great Awakening and the Future of Egalitarianism.* Chicago: University of Chicago Press, 2000.

Foner, Eric. *Gateway to Freedom: The Hidden History of the Underground Railroad.* New York: W. W. Norton, 2015.

———. *The Story of American Freedom.* New York: W. W. Norton, 1998.

Franklin, Benjamin. *The Autobiography of Benjamin Franklin.* New York: Macmillan, 1962. First Touchstone edition 1997. Initially published 1791.

———. *The Papers of Benjamin Franklin.* Edited by Leonard W. Larabee. New Haven: Yale University Press, 1959–1999.

———. "The Way to Wealth." In *The Works of Benjamin Franklin,* ed. Jared Sparks, 2:92–103 (Boston, 1836; essay initially published 1758). http://www.swarth more.edu/SocSci/bdorsey1/41docs/52-fra.html.

Franzen, Jonathan. *Freedom.* New York: Farrar, Straus and Giroux, 2010.

Garfield, James A. *The Works of James A. Garfield.* Edited by Burke Hinsdale. 2 vols. Boston: J. R. Osgood, 1882–1883.

Gerring, John. *Party Ideologies in America: 1828–1996.* New York: Cambridge University Press, 1998.

Godkin, E. L. "Cooperation." *North American Review* 106 (January 1868): 150–176.

Goldin, Claudia, and Lawrence F. Katz. *The Race between Education and Technology.* Cambridge, Mass.: Harvard University Press, 2008.

Goodwin, Doris Kearns. *Lyndon Johnson and the American Dream.* New York: St. Martin's Press, 1991.

Greenberg, Stanley. *Middle Class Dreams.* Rev. ed. New Haven: Yale University Press, 1996.

Hamilton, Alexander. *The Papers of Alexander Hamilton.* Edited by Harold C. Syrett. 27 vols. New York: Columbia University Press, 1961–1987.

———. *The Reports of Alexander Hamilton.* Edited by Jacob Cooke. New York: Harper Torchbook, 1964.

Hamilton, Alexander, John Jay, and James Madison. *The Federalist.* Edited by Edward Mead Earle. New York: Modern Library, 1937.

Hanson, Russell L. *The Democratic Imagination in America: Conversations with Our Past.* Princeton: Princeton University Press, 1985.

Hanson, Sandra L., and John Zogby. "The Polls—Trends: Attitudes about the American Dream." *Public Opinion Quarterly* 74, no. 3 (Fall 2010): 570–584.

Harris, William T. "The Theory of American Education." In *Addresses and Proceedings, National Education Association of the United States.* Ann Arbor: University of Michigan Library, 2006. Initially published 1870. http://quod.lib .umich.edu/g/genpub/0677752.1870.001?rgn=main;view+fulltext.

Hartz, Louis. *The Founding of New Societies.* New York: Harcourt, Brace and World, 1964.

Hawthorne, Nathaniel. *The Scarlet Letter.* Garden City, N.Y.: International Collectors Library. Initially published 1850.

Heclo, Hugh. "Ronald Reagan and the American Public Philosophy." Paper presented at the Conference on the Reagan Presidency, University of California, Santa Barbara, March 27–30, 2002.

Hegewisch, Ariane, and Heidi Hartmann. "The Gender Wage Gap: 2014." Report from the Institute for Women's Policy Research, September 2015. http://www.iwpr.org/publications/pubs/the-gender-wage-gap-2014.

Hochschild, Jennifer L. *Facing Up to the American Dream: Race, Class, and the Soul of the Nation*. Princeton: Princeton University Press, 1995.

Hofstadter, Richard. *The American Political Tradition and the Men Who Made It*. New York: Vintage Books, 1989. Initially published 1948.

Hoover, Herbert. *American Individualism*. New York: Doubleday, Page, 1922.

Howells, William Dean. *A Hazard of New Fortunes*. New York: Penguin Books, 2001. Initially published 1890.

———. *The Rise of Silas Lapham*. New York: W. W. Norton, 1982. Initially published 1885.

Hughes, Langston. *The Collected Works of Langston Hughes*. Edited by Arnold Rampersad. 15 vols. Columbia: University of Missouri Press, 2001–2003.

Hume, David. "Idea of a Perfect Commonwealth." In *Hume's Moral and Political Philosophy*, 373–385. Darien, Conn.: Hafner Publishing, 1970.

Hume, Kathryn. *American Dream, American Nightmare: Fiction since 1960*. Urbana: University of Illinois Press, 2000.

Huntington, Samuel P. *American Politics: The Promise of Disharmony*. Cambridge: Mass.: Harvard University Press, 1981.

Illuzzi, Michael J. "Lincoln's 'Race of Life' Is Not the American Dream of Equal Opportunity." *American Political Thought* 3, no. 2 (Fall 2014): 228–253.

Jefferson, Thomas. *The Papers of Thomas Jefferson*. Edited by Julian P. Boyd. 41 vols. Princeton: Princeton University Press, 1950–2014.

———. *Writings of Thomas Jefferson*. Edited by Paul Leicester Ford. 12 vols. New York: G. P. Putnam's Sons, 1904–1905.

Johannsen, Robert W., ed. *The Lincoln-Douglas Debates*. New York: Oxford University Press, 1965.

Johnson, Lyndon B. *Public Papers of the Presidents of the United States: Lyndon B. Johnson*. 10 vols. Washington, D.C.: Government Printing Office, 1965–1970.

Kalleberg, Arne L. *Good Jobs, Bad Jobs*. New York: Russell Sage Foundation, 2011.

Kamp, David. "Rethinking the American Dream." *Vanity Fair*, April 2009. http://www.vanityfair.com/culture/features/2009/04/american-dream200904.

Karabell, Zachary. *A Visionary Nation: Four Centuries of American Dreams and What Lies Ahead*. New York: HarperCollins, 2001.

Kennedy, John F. *Public Papers of the Presidents of the United States: John F. Kennedy*. 3 vols. Washington D.C.: Government Printing Office, 1962–1964.

Keyssar, Alexander. *The Right to Vote: The Contested History of Democracy in the United States*. New York: Basic Books, 2000.

Kirkland, Edward Chase. *Dream and Thought in the Business Community, 1860–1900*. Chicago: Ivan R. Dee, 1990. Initially published 1956.

Kochhar, Rakesh, and Richard Fry. "Wealth Inequality Has Widened along Racial, Ethnic Lines since End of Great Recession." Pew Research Center, December 12, 2014. http://www.pewresearch.org/fact-tank/2014/12/12/racial-wealth-gaps-great-recession/.

Kristof, Nicholas. "The American Dream Is Leaving America." *New York Times*, October 26, 2014.

Lawrence, D. H. "Fenimore Cooper's Leatherstocking Novels." Chapter 5 in *Studies in Classic American Literature*. Initially published 1923. http://xroads .virginia.edu/~hyper/LAWRENCE/dhlch05.htm.

Leonhardt, David. "Is College Worth It?" *New York Times*, May 27, 2014.

———. "A Link between Fidgety Boys and a Sputtering Economy." *New York Times*, April 29, 2014.

Leonhardt, David, Amanda Cox, and Claire Cain Miller. "Change of Address Offers a Pathway out of Poverty." *New York Times*, May 4, 2015.

Levy, Frank. *The New Dollars and Dreams: American Incomes and Economic Change.* New York: Russell Sage Foundation, 1998.

Lewin, Tamar. "More Highly Educated Women Are Also Having Children." *New York Times*, May 8, 2015.

Lewis, Sinclair. *Babbitt.* New York: Penguin Group, Signet Classics Edition, 1998. Initially published 1922.

Lienesch, Michael. *New Order of the Ages: Time, the Constitution, and the Making of American Political Thought.* Princeton: Princeton University Press, 1988.

Lincoln, Abraham. *Abraham Lincoln: His Speeches and Writings.* Edited by Roy P. Basler. New York: World Publishing, 1946.

———. *Collected Works of Abraham Lincoln.* Edited by Roy P. Basler. 9 vols. New Brunswick, N.J.: Rutgers University Press, 1953.

Lindsey, Lawrence B. *The Growth Experiment: How the New Tax Policy Is Transforming the U.S. Economy.* New York: Basic Books, 1990.

Lippmann, Walter. *Drift and Mastery.* Madison: University of Wisconsin Press, 1985. Initially published 1914.

Lipset, Seymour Martin. *American Exceptionalism: A Double-Edged Sword.* New York: W. W. Norton, 1996.

Madison, James. *Letters and Other Writings of James Madison.* Edited by William C. Rives and Philip R. Fendall. Philadelphia: J. B. Lippincott, 1867.

Maier, Pauline. *American Scripture: Making of the Declaration of Independence.* New York: Alfred A. Knopf, 1998.

Mailer, Norman. *An American Dream.* New York: Vintage Books, 1965.

Mather, Cotton. *Bonifacius: An Essay . . . to Do Good.* Gainesville, Fla.: Scholars' Facsimiles and Reprints, 1967. Initially published 1710. http://archive.org /details/bonifaciusessayoomath.

Matthews, Jean V. *Women's Struggle for Equality: The First Phase, 1828–1876.* Chicago: Ivan R. Dee, 1997.

Melville, Herman. *Billy Budd, and Other Stories.* New York: Penguin Books, 1986.

———. *Moby Dick.* Norwalk, Conn.: Eaton Press, 1977. Initially published 1851.

Merish, Lori. *Sentimental Materialism: Gender, Commodity Culture, and Nineteenth-Century American Literature.* Durham, N.C.: Duke University Press, 2000.

Mettler, Suzanne. *Degrees of Inequality: How the Politics of Higher Education Sabotaged the American Dream.* New York: Basic Books, 2014.

Milkis, Sidney M. *The President and the Parties: The Transformation of the American Party System since the New Deal.* New York: Oxford University Press, 1993.

Miller, Claire Cain. "The Motherhood Penalty vs. the Fatherhood Bonus: A Child Helps Your Career, if You're a Man." *New York Times,* September 6, 2014. http://www.nytimes.com/2014/09/07/upshot/a-child-helps-your-career-if-youre-a-man.html.

———. "Why a Gender Gap? *New York Times,* April 28, 2014.

Miller, Perry. *Errand into the Wilderness.* New York: Harper and Row, 1956.

———. *The New England Mind: From Colony to Province.* Cambridge, Mass.: Harvard University Press, 1953.

———. *The New England Mind: The Seventeenth Century.* Cambridge, Mass.: Harvard University Press, 1939.

Moon, Michael. "The Gentle Boy from the Dangerous Classes." *Representation* 19 (Summer 1987); 87–110.

Morgan, Edmund S., ed. *Puritan Political Ideas: 1558–1794.* Indianapolis, Ind.: Bobbs-Merrill, 1965.

Morrison, Toni. *Beloved.* New York: Alfred A. Knopf, 1988.

———. *Sula.* New York: Plume, Penguin Books, 1973.

Myrdal, Gunnar. *An American Dilemma: The Negro Problem and Modern Democracy.* 2 vols. New York: Harper and Brothers, 1944.

Nackenoff, Carol. *The Fictional Republic: Horatio Alger and American Political Discourse.* New York: Oxford University Press, 1994.

Nafisi, Azar. *The Republic of Imagination.* New York: Viking Press, 2014.

Nakamura, David. "Obama Invokes Teddy Roosevelt in Speech Attacking GOP Policies." *Washington Post,* December 7, 2011.

Noah, Timothy. *The Great Divergence.* New York: Bloomsbury Press, 2012.

Norris, Frank. *The Octopus.* New York: Library of America, 1986. Initially published 1901.

Obama, Barack. "American Dream" speech. November 7, 2007. Bettendorf, Iowa. CNN transcript. http://www.cnn.com/2007/POLITICS/12/21/obama.trans.americandream/.

———. *Dreams of My Father.* Large print ed. New York: Random House, 1995.

———. Economic Speech. December 6, 2011. Osawatomie, Kansas. https://www.washingtonpost.com/politics/president-obamas-economic-speech-in-osawatomie-kans/2011/12/06/gIQAVhe6ZO_story.html.

———. Grant Park Speech. November 4, 2008. Chicago, Illinois. CNN transcript. http://edition.cnn.com/2008/POLITICS/11/04/obama.transcript/.

———. Keynote Address at the 2004 Democratic National Convention. July 27, 2004. Boston, Massachusetts. Best Speeches of Barack Obama through

His 2009 Inauguration. http://obamaspeeches.com/002-Keynote-Address
-at-the-2004-Democratic-National-Convention-Obama-Speech.htm.

———. "A More Perfect Union: The Race Speech." March 18, 2008. Philadelphia, Pennsylvania. Best Speeches of Barack Obama through His 2009 Inauguration. http://obamaspeeches.com/E05-Barack-Obama-A-More-Perfect
-Union-the-Race-Speech-Philadelphia-PA-March-18-2008.htm.

———. Public Papers of the Presidents of the United States: Barack Obama, 2009.
Washington, D.C.: Government Printing Office, 2010.

———. Second Inaugural Address. January 21, 2013. American Presidency Project. http://www.presidency.ucsb.edu/ws/index.php?pid=102827.

———. State of the Union Address. January 27, 2010. American Presidency Project. http://www.presidency.ucsb.edu/ws/index.php?pid=87433.

———. State of the Union Address. January 24, 2012. American Presidency Project. http://www.presidency.ucsb.edu/ws/index.php?pid=99000.

———. State of the Union Address. January 28, 2014. American Presidency Project. http://www.presidency.ucsb.edu/ws/index.php?pid=104596.

Opportunity Agenda. "Public Opinion on Opportunity and the American Dream,
Homeownership, and Housing." Memorandum, November 2011. https://op
portunityagenda.org/files/field_file/memo_public_opinion_0.pdf.

———. "A Window of Opportunity: A Meta-Analysis of Public Opinion on Poverty." June 2014. https://opportunityagenda.org/files/field_file/2.public
opinion-metaanalysis.pdf.

Otis, James. "The Rights of the British Colonies Asserted and Proved." 1764.
Constitution Society. http://www.constitution.org/bcp/otis_rbcap.htm.

Parrington, Vernon. Main Currents of American Thought. 3 vols. New York: Harcourt, Brace, Jovanovich, 1927.

Penn, William. Advice of William Penn to His Children relating to Their Civil and
Religious Conduct. Philadelphia: Franklin Roberts, 1881. http://archive.org
/details/adviceofwilliampoopenn.

———. Frame of Government of Pennsylvania (1682). Avalon Project: Documents
in Law, History, and Diplomacy. http://avalon.law.yale.edu/17th_century
/pa04.asp.

Peterson, Merrill D. The Jeffersonian Image in the American Mind. New York: Oxford University Press, 1962.

Pew Research Center. "The American Middle Class Is Losing Ground." Social
and Demographic Trends, December 9, 2015. http://www.pewsocialtrends.org
/2015/12/09/the-american-middle-class/.

———. "On Pay Gap, Millennial Women Near Parity—for Now." Social and
Demographic Trends, December 11, 2013. http://www.pewsocialtrends.org
/2013/12/11/on-pay-gap.

Phillips, Kevin. Wealth and Poverty: The Political History of the American Rich. New
York: Broadway Books, 2002.

Piketty, Thomas. *Capital in the Twenty-First Century*. Cambridge, Mass.: Harvard University Press, 2014.

Pinsker, Sanford. "Huckleberry Finn and the Problem of Freedom." In *The American Dream*, edited by Harold Bloom, 1–9. New York: Infobase Publishing, 2009.

Pocock, J. G. A. *Politics, Language, and Time: Essays on Political Thought and History*. New York: Atheneum, 1973.

Pugh, Tom. "Minorities Hurt More by Foreclosure Crisis, Study Says." McClatchy Newspapers, June 18, 2010. www.mcclatchydc.com/news/nation-world/national/economy/article24585790.html.

Putnam, Robert. *Our Kids: The American Dream in Crisis*. New York: Simon and Schuster, 2015.

Rank, Mark Robert, Thomas A. Hirschl, and Kirk A. Foster. *Chasing the American Dream: Understanding What Shapes Our Fortunes*. New York: Oxford University Press, 2014.

Reagan, Ronald. *Public Papers of the Presidents of the United States: Ronald Reagan.* 15 vols. Washington, D.C.: Government Printing Office, 1982–1991.

———. "The Speech: A Time for Choosing." October 27, 1964. http://odur.let.rug.nl/~usa/P/rr40/speeches/the_speech.htm.

Reeves, Richard V., and Isabel V. Sawhill. "Men, Step into Women's Shoes." *Dallas Morning News*, December 6, 2015.

Reichley, A. James. *The Life of the Parties: A History of American Political Parties.* New York: Rowman and Littlefield, 1992.

Roosevelt, Franklin D. Fireside Chat, September 30, 1934. http://millercenter.org/president/speeches/speech-3303.

———. *The Public Papers and Addresses of Franklin Delano Roosevelt.* 13 vols. New York: Random House, 1938.

Roosevelt, Theodore. *The New Nationalism*. New York: Outlook, 1910.

Rossi, Alice, ed. *The Feminist Papers from Adams to de Beauvoir*. New York: Columbia University Press, 1973.

Roth, Philip. *The American Trilogy: American Pastoral.* New York: Library of America, 2011.

———. *The American Trilogy: The Human Stain.* New York: Library of America, 2011.

Russo, Richard. *Empire Falls*. New York: Random House, Vintage Books, 2001.

Sack, Kevin, and Gardiner Harris. "Obama Scorns Racism in Soaring, Singing Eulogy." *New York Times,* June 27, 2015.

Salzberger, A. G. "Obama Sounds a Populist Call on G.O.P. Turf." *New York Times*, December 7, 2011.

Samuel, Lawrence R. *The American Dream: A Cultural History*. Syracuse, N.Y.: Syracuse University Press, 2012.

Schlesinger, Arthur M., Jr. *The Age of Jackson*. Boston: Little, Brown, 1953.

Schudson, Michael. "American Dreams." *American Literary History* 16, no. 3 (Autumn 2004): 566–573.

Schwarz, John E. *Illusions of Opportunity: The American Dream in Question.* New York: W. W. Norton, 1997.

Schwarz, John E., and Thomas J. Volgy. *The Forgotten Americans: Thirty Million Working Poor in the Land of Opportunity.* New York: W. W. Norton, 1992.

Shapiro, Thomas, Tatjana Meschede, and Sam Osoro. "The Roots of the Widening Racial Wealth Gap: Explaining the Black-White Economic Divide." Research and policy brief, Institute on Assets and Social Policy, February 2013. http://iasp.brandeis.edu/pdfs/Author/shapiro-thomas-m/racialwealthgap brief.pdf.

Siemers, David J. *Ratifying the Republic: How Anti-Federalists Helped Found the American Regime.* Stanford: Stanford University Press, 2002.

Simpson, Alan K. *Puritanism in Old and New England.* Chicago: University of Chicago Press, 1955.

Sinclair, Upton. *The Jungle.* New York: Barnes and Noble Classics, 2003. Initially published 1906.

Singer, Peter. *The Most Good You Can Do.* New Haven: Yale University Press, 2015.

Sinopoli, Richard C. *From Many, One: Readings in American Political and Social Thought.* Washington, D.C.: Georgetown University Press, 1997.

Smith, Rogers M. *Civic Ideals: Conflicting Visions of Citizenship in U.S. History.* New Haven: Yale University Press, 1997.

Steele, Shelby. *A Dream Deferred: The Second Betrayal of Black Freedom in America.* New York: HarperCollins, 1998.

Steinbeck, John. *The Grapes of Wrath.* New York: Penguin Classics, 2006. Initially published 1939.

Stevenson, Adlai E. *The Papers of Adlai E. Stevenson.* Edited by Walter Johnson. 8 vols. Boston: Little, Brown, 1976.

Stiglitz, Joseph E. *The Price of Inequality: How Today's Divided Society Endangers Our Future.* New York: W. W. Norton, 2013.

Stowe, Harriet Beecher. *Uncle Tom's Cabin; or, Life among the Lowly.* New York: Alfred A. Knopf, Everyman's Library, 1994. Initially published 1852.

Sunstein, Cass. "Top 1% Are the Big Winners in Recovery." *Dallas Morning News,* December 11, 2013.

Swift, Art. "Americans' Satisfaction with Life Similar to Levels in 1998." Gallup News Service, November 1, 2013. http://gallup.com/poll/165683/ameri cans-satisfaction-life-similar-levels-1998.aspx.

Taylor, Paul. *The Next America.* New York: Public Affairs, 2014.

Thoreau, Henry David. *Walden* (1854). In *Walden, and Other Writings.* New York: Barnes and Noble Books, 1993.

Tocqueville, Alexis de. *Democracy in America.* 2 vols. New York: Vintage Books, 1954. Initially published 1835.

Tolles, Frederick B. *Meeting House and Counting House: The Quaker Merchants of Colonial Philadelphia, 1682–1763.* New York: W. W. Norton, 1963.

Tough, Paul, "Who Gets to Graduate." *New York Times Magazine,* May 18, 2014.

Traub, Amy, and Heather C. McGee. "State of the American Dream: Economic Policy and the Future of the Middle Class." *Demos,* June 2013. http://www .demos.org/publication/state-american-dream-economic-policy-and-fu ture-middle-class.

Twain, Mark. *Pudd'nhead Wilson.* New York: Book of the Month Club, 1992. Initially published 1894.

———. "The Story of the Bad Little Boy." 1875. http://www.washburn.edu /sobu/broach/badboy.html.

———. "The Story of the Good Little Boy." 1875. http://www.washburn.edu /sobu/broach/goodboy.html.

———. *Tom Sawyer and Huckleberry Finn.* New York: Alfred A. Knopf, Everyman's Library, 1991. Initially published 1876 and 1885.

Updike, John. *Rabbit at Rest.* New York: Alfred A. Knopf, 1990.

———. *Rabbit Is Rich.* New York: Fawcett Books, 1981.

———. *Rabbit Redux.* New York: Fawcett Books, 1971.

———. *Rabbit, Run.* New York: Fawcett Books, 1960.

U.S. Bureau of Labor Statistics. "Databases, Tables, and Calculators by Subject." Unemployment Rates: for whites, Series ID LNS14000003, http:// data.bls.gov/timeseries/LNS14000003; for blacks, Series ID LNS14000006, http://data.bls.gov/timeseries/LNS14000006; for Hispanics, Series ID LNS14000009, http://data.bls.gov/timeseries/LNS14000009.

———. "Women in the Labor Force: A Databook." Report 1052. December 2014. www.bls.gov/opub/reports/womens-databook/archive/women-in-the -labor-force-a-databook-2014.pdf.

U.S. Census Bureau. Historical Income Data. Current Population Survey Tables. Families, Table F-6, "Regions—Families (All Races) by Median and Mean Income." http://www.census.gov/hhes/www/income/data/historical /families/.

———. Historical Income Tables: Households. Table H-5, "Race and Hispanic Origin of Householder—Households by Median and Mean Income, 1967– 2014." https://www.census.gov/hhes/www/income/data/historical/house hold/index.html.

———. Historical Poverty Tables—People. http://www.census.gov/hhes /www/poverty/data/historical/people.html.

Vonnegut, Kurt. *Slaughterhouse-Five.* London: Vintage Books, 2000. Initially published 1969.

Washington, George. *George Washington: Writings*. New York: Library of America, 1997.

Webster, Daniel. *The Papers of Daniel Webster: Speeches and Formal Writings*. Edited by Charles M. Wiltse. 15 vols. Hanover, N.H.: University Press of New England, 1974–1989.

Weisberger, Bernard A. *America Afire: Jefferson, Adams, and the Revolutionary Election of 1800*. New York: William Morrow, 2000.

Weiss, Richard. *The American Myth of Success*. New York: Basic Books, 1969.

Wilson, Woodrow. *The Papers of Woodrow Wilson*. Edited by Arthur S. Link. 69 vols. Princeton: Princeton University Press, 1966–1994.

Wright, Richard. *Native Son*. New York: Harper Perennial Classics, 1998. Initially published 1940.

Index